**SAGE** was founded in 1965 by Sara Miller McCune to support the dissemination of usable knowledge by publishing innovative and high-quality research and teaching content. Today, we publish over 900 journals, including those of more than 400 learned societies, more than 800 new books per year, and a growing range of library products including archives, data, case studies, reports, and video. SAGE remains majority-owned by our founder, and after Sara's lifetime will become owned by a charitable trust that secures our continued independence.

Los Angeles | London | New Delhi | Singapore | Washington DC | Melbourne

# EMINENT INDIAN
# PSYCHOLOGISTS

# EMINENT INDIAN
# PSYCHOLOGISTS

## 100 YEARS OF PSYCHOLOGY IN INDIA

Edited by
# BRAJ BHUSHAN

Los Angeles | London | New Delhi
Singapore | Washington DC | Melbourne

*First published in 2017 by*

**SAGE Publications India Pvt Ltd**
B1/I-1 Mohan Cooperative Industrial Area
Mathura Road, New Delhi 110 044, India
*www.sagepub.in*

**SAGE Publications Inc**
2455 Teller Road
Thousand Oaks, California 91320, USA

**SAGE Publications Ltd**
1 Oliver's Yard, 55 City Road
London EC1Y 1SP, United Kingdom

**SAGE Publications Asia-Pacific Pte Ltd**
3 Church Street
#10-04 Samsung Hub
Singapore 049483

Published by Vivek Mehra for SAGE Publications India Pvt Ltd, typeset in Minion 10.5/12.5 pts by Zaza Eunice, Hosur, Tamil Nadu and printed at Saurabh Printers Pvt Ltd, Greater Noida.

**Library of Congress Cataloging-in-Publication Data**

Name: Bhushan, Braj, editor.
Title: Eminent Indian psychologists : 100 years of psychology in India / edited by Braj Bhushan.
Description: Thousand Oaks, California : SAGE Publications Inc, 2017. | Includes bibliographical references and index.
Identifiers: LCCN 2017017772 (print) | LCCN 2017029751 (ebook) | ISBN 9789386446435 (E pub 2.0) | ISBN 9789386446428 (E Book) | ISBN 9789386446411 (print pdf : alk. paper)
Subjects: LCSH: Psychology—India—History. | Psychologists—India.
Classification: LCC BF108.I6 (ebook) | LCC BF108.I6 E45 2017 (print) | DDC 150.92/254—dc23
LC record available at https://lccn.loc.gov/2017017772

**ISBN:** 978-93-864-4641-1 (HB)

**SAGE Team:** Rajesh Dey, Sandhya Gola, and Ritu Chopra

# Contents

# Foreword

Like life itself, India's history of psychology is diverse. Nevertheless, some major trends can be detected; not all readers may agree with the following that I have observed.

## Emergence from Philosophy

Since the biographies give us a sense of history, the lives of early pioneers naturally tell us how they stumbled into psychology while studying philosophy. Many of them had read psychology abroad in Europe, particularly in Britain, and a few in the USA, usually at famous universities under the supervision of famous psychologists. They broke the philosophical tradition of scholarly debates and stopped asking unanswerable questions:

Is there a soul? What does your psychology tell you?

How do you know? Since you say all knowledge must come through perception and the experience of our sense-organs, you know these are obviously unreliable. So how do we know for sure?

Is the 'red' I see in blood the same 'red' that you see?

The early pioneers, as their biographies reveal, avoided focusing on such problems, and persuaded the authorities in their colleges and the bureaucrats in their provinces to believe that psychology was a science, a science like physics and biology. Such questions are not asked in science.

In fact, to assert that psychology is a science, some educational institutions such as the University of Calcutta offered a Master in Science degree in psychology. In any case, they pointed out, the students had to do lab experiments using psychophysical methods on the estimation of size and weight, application of Weber's law to discriminate increments in weight, study of the intensity of sounds and hues, investigation of the two-point threshold measures, or demonstration of how our minds may be tricked to believe in illusions. However, these were hardly used for 'research' that required specialized equipment.

## Absence of Empirical Studies That Need Instrumentation

It was a hard task for the pioneers who had flown away from their philosophical nests to establish new centres of experimental psychology, especially because of lack of instruments to establish labs in psychological science. Only some of them could pursue experimental psychology, even though their doctoral training in the West had given them the skills to do so. I had studied eyelid conditioning for my PhD dissertation, for instance, but on return to Odisha, how could I expect to establish a conditioning lab? So I switched to verbal conditioning instead, having prepared myself to pursue the closest alternative to conditioning. Even then, it was hard to find time to do experiments, burdened as I was with a heavy load of teaching undergraduates as a lecturer in the premier college of my province. This was a common experience with many of my cohorts.

## Help from Biological Sciences

Some of my cohorts did experiments on animals, if their dissertation research trained them to work with animals—mice and monkeys—in collaboration with medical schools and physiological labs. This was true, for example, with some of Eysenck's students who had worked in the animal lab.

The latter research trend has flourished in contemporary Indian psychology, opening opportunities for collaborative research in diverse fields including genetics and brain-imaging.

## Low Grade Research: Adaptation of Questionnaires and Assessment Tests

The easier path to follow was the translation and adaptation of questionnaires borrowed from British and American publications. The other path was to make assessment tests for intelligence and measurement of motivation, which need not be original. The worst were surveys of attitudes and practices that lacked generalizability. There were of course exceptions, such as in the Bhatia test of intelligence.

As the need for publication grew, so did the number of journals. Most of these were thankfully short-lived, and the few that survived could attain a reasonable status. Until the mid-1980s, most Indian journals and their articles presented low-grade research. Only a few research studies were accepted for publication in standard international journals. Given the depressing environment provided by universities and colleges that made it nearly impossible to do research, it was a miracle to see a good internationally published paper. Miracles do happen, as you will read in some biographies in this book.

Some exceptional pioneers like S.M. Mohsin and one of his former students, Biswanath Mukherjee facilitated the use of statistical methods. Mohsin studied for his PhD with Sir Godfrey Thomson, an early architect of factor analysis and intelligence testing. He pursued the development of both experimental and applied psychology in India. Biswanath Mukherjee did his doctoral research at the University of North Carolina, a prominent centre for mathematical statistics. I think, he was the best-trained psychologist for the application of statistics in psychology. By the way, he and I were classmates during our MA course at Patna University. Both of us studied under S.M. Mohsin and were much influenced by him.

Psychometrics and applied statistical research could be pursued in India at that time, as it did not require much instrumentation. In fact, many of us could do a factor analysis without using even a calculator. Later, the Indian Statistical Institute (where Mukherjee worked during the last part of his career; he passed away at a relatively young age), other organizations such as IITs and IIMs, and defence laboratories promoted the growth of psychometrics. Contemporary use of psychometric tests for personnel selection is a mixed bag of transparent copies of American and British tests and a few genuinely indigenous ones that are culturally sensitive.

The exceptions are neuropsychological tests and assessments, some of which have been developed in India. Biographies of a few such people are included in this book. How could some of the pioneers nevertheless escape the constraints that inhibit good research?

## Exploiting Unique Social-cultural Materials in India

An early pioneer whose work on how rumour travels was Jamuna Prasad. The research (Prasad, 1950) used rumours that floated around following a devastating earthquake in Bihar. What he found was quite surprising— the number of rumours circulating afterwards was much greater among people who were inhabitants of surrounding regions that were *not hit by the earthquake*. Stories of impending doom and gloom were going around, spreading fear and anxiety. A subsequent study published by Durganand Sinha (1952) focused on the aftermath of a different disaster—it confirmed that rumours were remarkably few among the people of the region that was directly affected. Both studies gained prominence, expanding the famous work of F.C. Bartlett. How does one explain this unexpected result? Among several explanations of the surprising findings is the following: Because the inhabitants of unaffected adjacent regions were naturally fearful of what might happen and anticipated the worst, the rumours were used for self-justification.

Perhaps, by exploiting indigenous conditions, social psychology has continued to gain prominence among researchers. For instance, Durganand Sinha and others have focused on cultural disadvantage. Subsequently, younger psychologists have made significant contributions to social psychology and management issues in leadership and motivation, and have suggested theoretical models.

Cross-cultural research has taken advantage of the diversity of ethnic and caste groups. Mostly social, but sometimes cognitive, issues are addressed by a number of psychologists in differentiating the behaviour of groups under study. Thus, over and above social and economic class variations, ethnicity, and caste are powerful determinants that may override the known effects of socioeconomic status (SES).

## Social Psychology in Organizations

Kamla Chowdhury (different spellings of her name are found) seized the opportunity for a serious study of motivation in a large industrial organization in 1950 when she began working in Ahmedabad Textile Industries' Research Association (ATIRA). Perhaps, her large-scale survey (Chowdhry, 1953) was the beginning of the introduction of social psychology to industrial organization. It attracted several prominent American scholars, McClelland and Erikson among them, to the organization. She was herself recognized as a promising social psychologist by T. Newcomb in his 1950 book on social psychology that I read in my MA course at Patna University. Just like Jamuna Prasad, whose work was included in Woodworth's text on experimental psychology.

The point of discussion is how some exemplary pioneers in Indian psychology had taken advantage of opportunities suddenly provided to them, in spite of the poor support system for psychological research (Chowdhry & Kakar, 1971). Dalal (2010) has written an important review of the early beginnings, a journey back to the roots of Indian psychology.

## Turning the Tide—Back to Indigenous Roots

If you ask professors of psychology in the West what image of Indian psychology comes to their mind, they will most probably say something about Yoga and meditation. Those are the topics that were rejected by modern Indian psychology emerging out of philosophy in order to have an identity of its own. The first book with the term Indian Psychology I I read was *Indian Psychology of Perception* (Sinha, 1934). Its contents, however, turned out to be perception as in classical systems of philosophy in India. I promptly closed the book. For me, psychology, as in the West, was true psychology of human behaviour after all.

As psychology was a young science in India, topics such as Yoga and meditation, and even consciousness, were shunned. In any case, the topics could not be found in Western textbooks that we read in college.

However, early research into Yoga was fuelled by a scientific curiosity in regard to strange yogic accomplishments; the early researchers in this field were experimental physiologists and medical doctors who were curious to understand extreme yogic fits such as an apparent absence of breathing for days when a Yogi was buried in an almost airless pit. Anand and Bagchi, working with Wenger, an American psychologist, recorded the electroencephalography (EEG) and heart rate functions of yogis (Anand, Chhina, & Singh, 1961; Wenger, Bagchi, & Anand, 1961).

As psychology matured, scientific aspects of Yoga and consciousness appeared in journals of consciousness and psychological science. A respectable APA journal, *Psychological Bulletin*, published an article titled 'Meditation States and Trait' (Cahn & Polich, 2006). Among psychologists in India, K.R. Rao (1998) should be regarded as the best exponent (see his biography). Since then, when my book *Consciousness Quest Where East Meets West* was published (Das, 2014), Rao commented,

> I find this book remarkable and fascinating in at least two important respects. First it indicates the maturity of psychology itself.… Second it reveals the relevance of classical Indian thought to psychological discourse at this time beyond the borders of India. (excerpt from his Foreword)

Several psychologists have now written on Indian contemplative traditions (Cornelissen, Misra & Varma, 2010) and its integration with contemporary psychological science (see biographies of A. Paranjpe and others in the Allahabad group who have argued in favour of research on indigenous psychology).

Psychology as a science has come of age in the world. Active research on consciousness and its neurological correlates are now frequently reported in journals of psychological science. The use of brain imaging techniques has advanced making much of this research explain consciousness and effects of meditation (Das, 2014). It will no longer be necessary to consider such research as indigenous Indian psychology.

## What's Left for the New Generation of Psychologists in the Next Book of Biographies?

As psychologists have access to brain-imaging techniques and genetic analyses, the next group of biographies will find several researchers who have international standing in interdisciplinary sciences. This new generation of psychologists often shy away from the label 'Indian psychology' as a descriptor of their research—they are pursuing 'psychology' per se. Taking advantage of what is indigenous to India will spawn research relating to, for instance, language and reading, particularly multilingualism, and therapeutic procedures for atypical groups such as autism, dyslexia, and mathematics disability. The integration of drugs and cognitive behaviour therapy using mindfulness for a variety of mental health conditions including depression, stress, and mood disorders will mark the new era. The emerging need for treatment of dementia as Indians live longer will encourage applied research in cognition and rehabilitation.

I can also see biographies to include those who use sophisticated math and computer modelling for explaining behaviour, based as they are on the pre-eminence of Indian scientists in those fields.

Finally, one fervently hopes that the next generation of psychologists will focus on redressing the woeful condition of education in our public schools, especially at the primary level. Let us hope knowledge gained from cognitive science will be increasingly applied to improve education.

For hopes are the wings of the future.

# References

Anand, B.K., Chhina, G.S., & Singh, B. (1961). Some aspects of electroencephalographic studies in yogis. *Electroencephalography and Clinical Neurophysiology, 13*(3), 452–456.

Cahn, B.R., & Polich, J. (2006). Meditation states and traits: EEG, ERP, and neuroimaging studies. *Psychological Bulletin, 132*(2),180–211.

Chowdhry, K. (1953). An analysis of the attitudes of textile workers and the effect of those attitudes on work efficiency. Atira Research Note. Ahmedabad.

Chowdhry, K., & Kakar, S. (Eds). (1971). *Understanding organisational behaviour: Cases and concepts.* Bombay: McGraw-Hill.

Cornelissen, M., Misra, G., & Varma, S. (2010). *Foundations of Indian psychology: Theories and concepts, Vol. 1.* New Delhi: Longman, Pearson Education.

Dalal, A.K. (2010). A journey back to the roots: Psychology in India. In M. Cornelissen, G. Misra, & S. Varma (Eds), *Foundations of Indian psychology: Theories and concepts, Vol. 1, 27–56.* New Delhi: Longman, Pearson Education.

Das, J.P. (2014). *Consciousness quest where East meets West: On mind, meditation and neural correlates.* New Delhi: SAGE Publications.

Editorial. (1979). *The Journal of Social Psychology, 108*(2). doi: 10.1080/00224545.1979.9711623

Newcomb, T.M. (1950). *Social psychology.* New York, NY: Holt, Rinehart & Winston.

Prasad, J. (1950). A comparative study of rumours and reports in earthquakes. *British Journal of Psychology, 41*(3–4), 129–144.

Sinha, D. (1952). Behavior in a catastrophic situation: A psychological study of reposts and rumours. *British Journal of Psychology, 43*(3), 200–209.

Sinha, J. (1934). *Indian psychology: Perception.* London: Kegan Paul, Trench, Trubner & Co. Ltd.

Wenger, M.A., & Bagchi, B.K. (1961). Studies of autonomic functions in practitioners of yoga in India. *Behavioral Science, 6*(4), 312–323.

Wenger, M.A., Bagchi, B.K., & Anand, B.K. (1961). Experiments in India on 'voluntary' control of the heart and pulse. *Circulation, 24*, 1319–1325.

**J.P. Das**
Emeritus Director
J.P. Das Centre on Developmental Disabilities and Learning
University of Alberta, Canada

# Preface

Like all other humans, I did not have the option of choosing my birth time and place. Historically, I came into being much later than many stalwarts in psychology. I found a few of them in books and heard about many others from those who came into being much earlier than me and had the privilege of interacting with these stalwarts. I do feel that I should have known many names early in my career but came to know about them much later. This was primarily because of the absence of these names and their work in books and classroom discussions. This made me think of compiling the life and work of the psychologists from India who contributed to the field in one way or the other, making it achieve the place it enjoys right now. By collating the life and work of these stalwarts who paved the way for many Indians like me, I am, perhaps, doing a little service to the discipline. Through this, coming generations would get a chance to know them because, perhaps, they would not have anyone to narrate about these stalwarts later. During the course of this work, I realized that many colleagues of various departments, both the seniors and the new ones, had not even heard some of the names from their own department. This effort is only to recollect some of the facts before they fade out. I know my limitations, but I am grateful to all those who decided to join me in this venture. It is a well-known fact that documents and other relevant sources are not preserved in our country, thus, making the writing of history extremely difficult. The same happened even this time. I must admit that many names could not be included in this book, either due to lack of information or because I could not find someone to contribute a write-up on them.

Psychology has completed 100 years of its existence in India in 2016. At this juncture, it is important to create a compendium highlighting the major milestones and the work of imminent psychologists who have significantly contributed to the development of this discipline in the country. Some authors have systematically presented the historical antecedents pertaining to psychology in India, and the five surveys of research in psychology under the auspice of the Indian Council of Social Sciences Research have brought forth the collective contribution of the discipline. However, the individual contribution of the eminent scholars and their bio-sketches are still missing. This book is a small effort to document the history of psychology in India to commemorate its centennial celebration. The motivation behind coming forward with this edited book is to present a coherent chronology of events in the growth of psychology as a discipline in India; more so to bring forth the contribution of eminent psychologists who contributed to the growth and development of this discipline of study.

16 April 2013 was the auspicious day when three eminent scholars of psychology in India—Girishwar Misra, Professor of psychology at University of Delhi, Ajit Dalal, Professor of psychology at University of Allahabad, and Ramadhar Singh, Distinguished Professor at IIM Bangalore—assembled at IIT Kanpur for recording their talks which are now available as video lectures in the *Selected Topics in Psychology* series. The idea of coming forward with this book was conceived during this interaction. Later, two methods were adopted to evolve the selection criteria for choosing eminent

Indian psychologists to be included in this book. At the first step, three professors were asked to nominate psychologists whose biographies should be included based on their contribution to the growth and development of psychology in India. They were Girishwar Misra, editor of *Psychological Studies*; Ajit Dalal, editor of *Psychology and Developing Societies*; and Ramadhar Singh, former editor of *Asian Journal of Psychology* and current editor of *IIMB Management Review*. The idea of seeking nomination from them was that they were editors of three different respected journals published in India. Further, two of them had written independent chapters on the history of psychology in India. In the second step, this list was shared with some other imminent psychologists such as Rama Charan Tripathi, Department of Psychology, University of Allahabad; Arvind Sinha, Department of Humanities and Social Sciences, IIT Kanpur; and Satishchandra Kumar, University Department of Applied Psychology and Counselling Center, University of Mumbai, and few more names were included. This list was further enriched by inputs from legendary Indian psychologists H.S. Asthana, former professor of psychology at University of Lucknow; J.P. Das, emeritus director of J.P. Das Centre on Developmental Disabilities and Learning, Canada; and G.G. Prabhu, former professor of psychology at NIMHANS, Bangalore. The nomination criteria included scientific contributions (research, test development, publications, etc.), academic leadership (establishment of department/ institute, laboratory, etc.), and leadership in professional organizations (association with national level bodies, publication/editorship of journals, etc.).

The final move towards searching contributors began in November 2013. With the first few disappointments, I received immense support from large number of former professors who very kindly agreed to contribute write-ups on one or other eminent Indian psychologist. The collective effort of digging out the facts was herculean, as history was not systematically preserved by academic departments across universities. Fortunately, life gave me few opportunities to come close to some of the stalwarts and seek their blessings. I personally felt enthralled to have got the opportunity to talk to some of the eminent psychologists of the country whom I either read about or heard of but could not get a chance to academically interact with. The first in this series was a call on 18 November 2013 that I received from Velusami Kaliappan, former professor of psychology at the University of Madras. He was more than willing to contribute to this book, and along with Vadakkupet Swaminathan, professor of psychology at the University of Madras, he wrote on T.E. Shanmugam. He had also agreed to write on G.D. Boaz, but destiny had something else to offer. He left to rest in peace on 15 March 2015. It was an unbelievable moment for me when he received an international call in the evening of 20 April 2014. On the other side was none other than the man whom I had heard and read so much about, H.S. Asthana, former professor of psychology at University of Lucknow. I must admit, I consider the day I had the opportunity to talk to him over phone as a very special day in my life. His help in knowing facts about Indian scholars was exemplary. He was more than generous to accept to contribute to this book. I express my indebtedness to M.S. Thimmappa, former professor of psychology and vice-chancellor of Bangalore University, for connecting me to many contributors. I also express my profound gratitude to Anand Paranjpe, Emeritus Professor of Psychology and Humanities at Simon Fraser University, Canada, for his advice. My indebtedness is owed to Satishchandra Kumar, University of Mumbai, for his continuous help throughout this journey.

The biggest challenge of this project was identifying the contributors and making them agree to contribute to this project. I would like to express my special gratitude to each one of them. This book has been possible because people like them decided to help me and the forthcoming generation by writing this small piece of history. Many contributors traced and contacted family members of the psychologist whom they were supposed to write for; all this without any external support.

Their support in completing this project has been phenomenal and I thank them again from the core of my heart.

Lastly, I would like to reiterate that many eminent scholars could not be included in this book, despite being in the list, because either contributors could not be found for them or the contributor(s) who agreed did not submit their write-ups till the book went to the press. Unlike the typical Indian style, this book does not have honorific terms such as 'Professor' and 'Doctor' before the names of the scholars. This is to align with the international practice. Before I complete, let me confess that this book could not highlight the contribution of many other psychologists due to limitations mentioned previously, and this phase of recollecting pieces of history must continue. The nature and framework of each chapter is by and large uniform, encompassing a brief biography of the eminent psychologist, their professional affiliations, and, most prominently, their contribution to the field of psychology. A few write-ups are very brief because, despite their best effort, the authors could not find details about them from authentic sources.

# 1

# Centenary Year of Psychology in India: A Brief Review

Braj Bhushan

Psychology can be dated as old as human civilization. Owing to the rich cultural heritage, many scholars have traced the roots of psychology in India through ancient texts and scriptures. Some trace it back to two millennia BCE, connecting it to ancient Indian texts such as the Vedas and Upanishads (1500–600 BCE). Misra and Paranjpe (2012) have presented a systematic summary of psychology in ancient as well as modern India. They have referred to the contributions of eminent philosophers such as Krishna Chandra Bhattacharyya (1875–1949), S. Radhakrishnan (1888–1975), B.G. Tilak (1856–1920), and Aurobindo Ghose (1872–1950), highlighting the significance of their work in understanding psychology in the Indian tradition. Paranjpe (2008) has drawn attention to Sri Ramana Maharshi's *Advaitic* method of meditation and *karma yoga* (path of action) by Tilak. Hymns of the Vedas have been interpreted signifying the psychological significance of the parables. The Gita has been considered as one of the ancient books on counselling (Dalal, 2011).

## Establishment of Departments and Beginning of Teaching of Psychology

The teaching of psychology in modern India began in 1905 with the introduction of experimental psychology as an independent subject. This was followed by the establishment of the Department of Experimental Psychology at the University of Calcutta in 1916. Girindrasekhar Bose established the first psychological clinic in 1933. Later, in 1938, this became a section of applied psychology with a goal to develop psychological tests and offer vocational counselling to the students. In 1945, the university offered a certificate course in applied and abnormal psychology. In 1965, this section was made the Department of Applied Psychology. This new department started offering courses from 1967. The department played a significant role in the development of psychology as a discipline of study and practice in India (Kundu & Chakrabati, 1979). Western experimental and clinical approaches were visible in the formative years at the University. However, the 'experimental model flourished, while psychoanalysis lagged far behind' (Misra & Paranjpe, 2012, p. 882). Later, the Indian Psychoanalytical Institute was established. This institute offered training programmes in clinical psychology. Girindrasekhar Bose also established the Lumbini Park Mental Hospital in Calcutta in 1940. Girindrasekhar Bose was the first recipient of a doctoral degree in psychology from the University of Calcutta. This was the first doctoral degree in psychology conferred by an Indian university. S.C. Mitra of the University of Calcutta is the first and only Indian to earn a DPhil from Leipzig (Asthana, 2015, personal communication). The Asiatic Society (formerly the Royal Society) instituted a plaque in his honour to award psychologists.

Till 1947, only three universities had psychology departments—Calcutta, Mysore, and Patna. According to Ganguli (1971), the establishment of a psychology department at the University of Calcutta (1916) was followed by the establishment of university departments at Mysore (1924), Dacca (1921, now in Bangladesh), Lucknow (1929), Aligarh (1932), Madras (1943), and Patna (1946). The Department of Psychology at the University of Mysore was established in 1924, with M.V. Gopalaswamy as its head. The two other renowned scholars who joined the department were B. Kuppuswamy and B. Krishnan. Kuppuswamy established himself as a celebrated social psychologist, whereas B. Krishnan is famous for his work on Indian psychology. B. Krishnan started a journal, *Psychological Studies*. Upon his retirement, M.A. Farooqui of Calicut University took up the responsibility of editing this journal. In 2000, the National Academy of Psychology (NAOP) took over the charge of this journal, and since 2009, Springer is publishing this journal. N.S. Narayana Shastry (1902–1955) was the student of the first batch of the University of Mysore PG programme. He obtained his doctorate from there itself under the guidance of M.V. Gopalaswamy. Subsequently, he was a demonstrator in the Department of Psychology of the Maharaja's College. He left the department in the late 1940s to join the newly established Department of Humanities at the Indian Institute of Science (then Tata Institute). There he worked in the area of industrial and social psychology. On 4 September 1955, he was in Delhi on the invitation of UNESCO for the discussion and finalization process of a job offered to him as a consultant psychologist which he accepted. By an unfortunate coincidence, he suffered a massive heart attack to which he succumbed the very same evening. Patna University was established in 1917, and the department was established in 1946. The departments at Calcutta and Mysore had common ancestry in Leipzig tradition. The first head of Calcutta department, N.N. Sen Gupta, had worked with Hugo Munsterberg, whereas M.V. Gopalaswamy, the first head of Mysore department, was a student of Charles Spearman. Both Munsterberg and Spearman were, in turn, students of Wilhelm Wundt at Leipzig. As most of the people serving other departments in the country had either graduated from or done short-term orientation from this department, other university departments also had the 'Wundtian influence' (Sinha, 1990). There is yet another link between the Calcutta and Mysore universities. Brajendranath Seal was the one who first advised and then developed the first PG programme in psychology and got it introduced at the University of Calcutta in 1916. He went over to Mysore University in 1920 as its second vice-chancellor (VC) and remained so till 1929, when poor health forced him to step down on his own. As the VC, he was instrumental in getting psychology introduced during his tenure, but he was not solely responsible for it. S. Radhakrishnan, who was at the university earlier, and the Mysore royal family (patrons of the university) too were equally involved.

*Students (with the teachers) of the first three batches (1951, 1952, and 1953) of the University of Madras admitted to the newly opened (1951) PG programme in psychology*

Some of them have made an impact on the discipline of psychology in India. They are (seated from left): (2) Veeraraghavan (then Assistant Professor at Presidency College, Madras; later pioneering psychologist at South Indian Textile Research Association (SITRA), (4) T.E. Shanmugam (then lecturer; later Professor and Head at the University of Madras), (5) G.D. Boaz (Founder Professor and Head of the University of Madras Department), (6) S. Parthasarathy (then Professor and Head at the Presidency College, Madras; later Professor at S.V. University, Tirupati), (7) P. Rama Rao (then Asst Professor at Presidency College, Madras; later Professor at S.V. University, Tirupati). Standing (first row, from left): (2) Rajalakshmi Verma (then PG student; later Professor at NCERT); standing (second row, from left): (1) E.G. Parameswaran (then PG student; later Professor at Osmania University), (2) P.V. Ramamoorthy (then PG student; later Professor at S.V. University, Tirupati), (9) T.V.A. Raghavan (then PG student; later Professor at Annamalai University Distance Education); standing (third row, from left): (5) G.G. Prabhu (then PG Student; later Professor and Dean at NIMHANS, Bangalore).

*Photo courtesy and copyright*: G.G. Prabhu.

The post-Independence era saw massive expansion in the number of universities and departments. Following the old legacy, psychology was initially part of the course curriculum of philosophy and education departments in most of the universities. For instance, Banaras Hindu University was founded in 1916. As part of the Department of Philosophy and Religion a small experimental laboratory of psychology was established in 1934 which could not achieve full potential. The department offered psychology as an independent subject for masters' level examination in 1948. The formal Department of Psychology began in 1949. In 1949–1950, PG courses in psychology were offered with experimental psychology, parapsychology, and industrial psychology as optional subjects. The department introduced a 1-year diploma course in clinical psychology in 1951.

*The six students (along with their examiners) who did their postgraduate diploma in clinical psychology from the Banaras Hindu University in 1951*

Seating (from left to right): L.B. Shukla, Padma Agrawal, K.N. Chakrabarti, B.L. Atreya, and D.P. Mitra. Standing (from left to right): B.N. Chaube, L.J. Arora, J.P. Atreya, M.S.L. Saxena, and J.K. Srivastava.

*Photo courtesy and copyright:* This photograph was presented to G.G. Prabhu by Padma Agarwal. The photograph is released to the editor for publication in the forthcoming book commemorating the 100 years of psychology in India but the copyright remains with the original copyright holders.

The expansion of higher education was further strengthened by bilateral academic exchange programmes of the University Grants Commission and the Ministry of Education. This facilitated a large number of Indian scholars to get trained in US and European universities. This resulted in a better trained faculty who made significant contributions to teaching as well as research. The Indian Council of Social Science Research (ICSSR) was established on 12 December 1968 as an autonomous organization to encourage development in the areas of social sciences, including psychology. Besides supporting funded projects in psychology, it also supported critical review of the work done in the country. This resulted in five surveys reflecting a wide area of topics covered under psychological research in India.

The first survey was edited by S.K. Mitra, and it covered trend reports of the work done up to 1969 in nine different fields of psychology—clinical, developmental, educational, experimental, industrial, military, personality, physiology, and comparative and social psychology. The second survey, *A Survey of Research in Psychology, 1971–76* was edited by Udai Pareek and was published in two volumes in 1980 and 1981 by Popular, Bombay. It focused on psychological theory and research method, culture and personality, developmental processes, deviance and pathology, counselling and therapy, communication and influence processes, organizational dynamics, psychology of work, political processes and behaviour, environmental psychology, and social issues such as poverty, inequality, population, and so forth. The third and fourth surveys were edited by Janak Pandey.

The third survey, *Psychology in India*, was published in three volumes by SAGE, New Delhi, in 1988. The first volume focused on personality and mental processes, with specific focus on psychological assessment, developmental psychology, personality, stress and anxiety, perceptual and cognitive processes, and higher mental processes. The second volume focused on basic and applied psychology with chapters on attitude and social tension, dynamics of rural development, and social psychology of education. The third volume focused on organizational behaviour and mental health, talking about job attitude, organizational effectiveness, mental health, and mental illness and treatment. The fourth survey covered contemporary developments in the discipline between 1983 and 1992. It was published as a three-volume book entitled *Psychology in India Revisited: Developments in the Discipline* by SAGE, New Delhi. The first volume focused on physiological foundation and human cognition, the second on personality and health psychology, and the third on applied social and organizational psychology. The topics covered in the first volume were animal behaviour, physiological foundation of behaviour, perceptual, learning and memory processes, intelligence and cognitive processes, and language. The second volume focused on consciousness studies, child and adolescent development, personality, self and life events, psychology of gender, health psychology, mental health, and illness and therapy, whereas the third volume had chapters on attitude, social cognition, justice, social values, poverty and deprivation, environment and behaviour, motivation, and leadership and human performance. The fifth survey, *Psychology in India*, covered developments in the discipline between 1993 and 2003 and was edited by Giriswar Misra. It was published by Pearson in four volumes. The first volume focused on basic psychological processes and human development, with specific chapters on biological and ecological bases of behaviour, human development, language and communication, cognitive processes, affective and motivational processes, and trends in personality research. The second volume focused on social and organizational processes with emphasis on social world, self and identity, and individual and group-level processes in organizations in India. It also had chapters on culture, institutions and organizations, dynamics of schooling, and societal development. The third volume focused on clinical and health psychology emphasizing research trends in the study of disorders, disabled, geropsychology, health psychology, psychological interventions, and psychological interventions for community development. The fourth volume focused on theoretical and methodological developments. Besides talking about qualitative and quantitative methods, this volume highlighted the psychoanalytic vista in India and the Indian indigenous concepts. It also talked about gender issues.

Psychology started expanding from university system to the Indian Institutes of Technology (IITs) and Indian Institutes of Management (IIMs). The Department of Humanities and Social Sciences at IIT Kharagpur started with the very inception of the institute in 1951. The department at IIT Madras was established in 1959. IIT Bombay started in 1958 and the humanities department started in 1964–1965. The department at IIT Kanpur started offering courses in 1963. Unlike IITs, which offered undergraduate and PG courses in different areas of psychology, IIMs largely focused on organizational behaviour. The expansion of psychology to the medical setting was possible a little after Independence. Mental illness remained the focus during the pre-Independence era. This is substantiated by the establishment of lunatic asylums. The Bangalore Lunatic Asylum was founded in 1847. In 1918, European Lunatic Asylum was established at Ranchi. It was renamed as European Mental Hospital in 1922. This was further changed to Inter-provincial Mental Hospital in 1948 and Hospital for Mental Diseases in 1952. In 1977, it was renamed as the Central Institute of Psychiatry. The All Indian Institute of Mental Health, now known as the National Institute of Mental Health and Neurosciences (NIMHANS), Bangalore, was established in 1954. In 1955, the institute began a 2-year PG-level professional training programme in clinical psychology. This was followed by the establishment of the Postgraduate Training Center at the Central Institute of Psychiatry, Ranchi, in 1962 and the B.M. Institute, Ahmedabad, in 1973. Looking back at these three centres, G.G. Prabhu said,

> To a large extent (but not completely) the Ranchi Centre was a replication of the AIIMH programme. On the other hand, the B.M. Institute programme was quite different from these two. The first two were Mental hospital based while BM programme was based in an exclusive mental health outpatient setting. Admission to it was open to psychologists, child development (home science) students, sociologists as well as social work students. The Bangalore/Ranchi (BR) programmes were open only to Psychology MAs with experimental psychology (!!!) as one of the subjects. The BM programme had heavy therapeutic emphasis (Dynamic model: Eric Erikson) while the BR programmes, till 1968, were on the British model (diagnosis oriented). However, the nomenclature of the diploma and the duration of the programme was the same in all the three. (personal communication)

H.N. Murthy is given the credit of introducing behaviour therapy (BT) in India which is also shared by N.N. Sen.

> H.N. Murthy is the one who introduced learning-theory-based behaviour therapy techniques in AIIMH in 1968 and is given the credit of introducing BT in the Indian setting. It brought about a change in the professional proficiency profile, the professional role and the self-esteem of the clinical psychology trainees in India. N.N. Sen had interest in BT but he left AIIMH and the clinical setting in 1963 to join the educational setting at CIE (DU) which later merged with NCERT. In the refresher training programmes of the NCERT he introduced theoretical modules on learning theories and their applications in the educational setting. (G.G. Prabhu, 2016, personal communication)

Presently, 402 universities, including technical, agricultural, and health sciences (Association of Indian Universities, 2014), offer courses in various streams, and psychology is one of the important courses besides other social sciences disciplines. Psychology modules have started making an entry into legal education programmes as well as media studies programmes.

## Birth of the Nation and Early Recognition of Importance of Psychology

The achievement of independence from the colonial rule witnessed extreme tension and bloodbath during the partition of the country. Partition resulted in the division of two provinces that existed in British India—Bengal province was divided into East Pakistan (now Bangladesh) and West Bengal (one of the states of India) and Punjab province into Punjab (part of West Pakistan) and Punjab (one of the states of India). According to UNCHR, approximately 14 million Hindus, Sikhs and Muslims were displaced and around 200,000 to 500,000 people were killed (Brass, 2003). Understanding the importance of social scientists, especially psychologists, in understanding and mitigating this issue, the Government of India planned a study of religious, provincial, linguistic, and racial tensions with the help of UNESCO in 1948. UNESCO appointed Gardner Murphy, City College, New York, as a consultant to the Government of India for a period of 6 months. Six teams were constituted for this along with five other projects. The first team worked on 'a study of the attitudes of (a) Hindu residents (b) Hindu refugees (c) Muslims, towards present Government policies regarding communal matters' with C.N. Vakil, School of Economics and Sociology, the

University of Mumbai, as leader of the research team. Kali Prasad, Department of Philosophy and Psychology, University of Lucknow, was the leader of the second team and it worked on 'A study of sources of insecurity among members of a minority community'. The third team was led by H.P. Maiti, Patna University and it worked on 'A study of villages in Bihar exemplifying (a) high (b) low general level of social tension utilizing psychological techniques'. The fourth team was headed by B.S. Guha, Department of Anthropology, Government of India, and they worked on the 'study of Hindu-Muslim and inter-caste tensions in West Bengal and their bearing on the integration of communities, by means of anthropological and psychological techniques'. Kamala Chowdhry, Ahmedabad Textile Industry Research Association, was the leader of the fifth team and it worked on the '[s]tudy of attitudes of textile workers to their supervisors and their work'. The sixth team was led by Pars Ram, East Punjab University (Muslim University), and it worked on '[a] study of techniques of reducing Hindu-Muslim tension through the establishment of Groups Goals towards which both communities may work'.

Besides these six teams, five other projects were also initiated. V.K. Kothurkar, University of Poona, worked on the project entitled 'An experiment in the reduction of inter-caste tension among secondary school students'. Radhakamal Mukerjee, University of Lucknow, worked on 'A sociological and psychological study of inter-caste hostilities (a) in the villages of U.P. (b) among textile operatives in Kanpur'. Hilda Raj (from anthropology) and L.C. Bhandari (from psychology), University of Delhi, took up 'A study of characteristic differences between Hindus, Sikhs and Muslims in the manner of handling aggressive impulses arising from frustration'. G.D. Boaz, University of Madras, conducted 'A study of the part played by textbooks in the development of tensions', whereas B. Kuppuswamy, Presidency College, Madras, undertook the 'Study of sources and forms of language tensions with special reference to Telugu and Tamil'. It is heartening to see how much the Government of India relied on the psychologists of the country for contemporary social problems. It is equally interesting to see that psychologists collaborated with experts from other domains of knowledge right at the beginning of the academic work in independent India.

Along with commissioning these studies, realizing that the early twentieth century had witnessed multiple wars and political strife, the Joseph Bhore Committee was constituted by the government to examine the facilities for the mentally ill. The committee submitted its report in 1946, highlighting the need to strengthen existing facilities and reformulate policies for mental illness.

## Academic Contribution of Indian Psychologists

Several scholars have written on Indian psychology. Their contributions are available in the form of books, book chapters, and journal articles. Some of the prominent books include *Indian Psychology: Perception* (Sinha, 1934), *Indian Psychology: Cognition* (Sinha, 1958), *Development of Psychological Thought in India* (Rao, 1962), *Indian Psychology* (Safaya, 1975), *Theoretical Psychology: The Meeting of East and West* (Paranjpe, 1984), *Self and Identity in Modern Psychology and Indian Thought* (Paranjpe, 1998), *Elements of Ancient Indian Psychology* (Kuppuswami, 1985), *Ethics in Management: Vedantic Perspectives* (Chakraborty, 1995), *Culture, Socialisation and Human Development: Theory, Research and Applications in India* (Saraswathi, 1999), *Perspectives on Indigenous Psychology* (Misra & Mohanty, 2002), *Consciousness, Indian Psychology and Yoga* (Joshi & Cornelissen, 2004), *Towards a Spiritual Psychology* (Rao & Marwaha, 2006), and *Handbook of Indian Psychology* (Rao, Paranjpe, & Dalal, 2008), and *Foundations of Indian Psychology* (Cornelissen, 2011a, 2011b).

Historically, many Indian scholars have brought forth Indian notions that have found equal importance from scholars from other parts of world as well. Several others have connected ideas originating from the West to Indian roots or elaborated indigenous concepts and practices. Some of the significant notions described in books by Indian authors include the Indian science of affect (Das, 1908), nurturant task leadership (Sinha, 1980), selfhood and inter-group relations (Nandy, 1983, 2004), self and identity (Paranjpe, 1984, 1998), the integral psychology of Sri Aurobindo (Sen, 1986), values in managerial transformation (Chakraborty, 1995), violence (Kakar, 1995), indigenous healing practices (Kakar 1996), bhakti (devotion to God; Paranjpe, 1998), consciousness (Cornelissen, 2001), the outlook of cognitive processes from Sāṁkhya Yoga perspective (Rao, 2002a, 2011) and integral intelligence (Srivastava & Misra, 2007).

The scholarly contributions on Indian ideas and concepts in the form of book chapters includes the description of achievement value (Mukherjee, 1974), Indian typology of personality (Krishnan, 2002[1976]), *lajja* (shame; Menon & Shweder, 1994), basic cognitive processes in diverse eco-cultural settings (Mishra, 1997), Hindu parents' ethno theories (Saraswathi & Ganapathy, 2002), scope and substance of India psychology (Rao, 2005), implications of *ahaṁkāra* (ego; Salagame, 2011), native cognition in Himalayas (Pirta, 2011), and so forth.

Noteworthy among the journal articles referring to Indian ideas and concepts include work on extension motivation (Pareek, 1968), dependency proneness (Sinha, 1968), concept of self in the Sufi tradition (Beg, 1970), dissatisfaction-based achievement motivation (Mehta, 1972), Guru-*chela* therapy for promoting mental health (Neki, 1973), significance of *anasakti* (non-attachment) for health (Pande & Naidu 1992), cognitive, experiential analytical, and reflective bases of oriental thought systems (Gupta, 1999), conception of health and well-being (Dalal & Misra, 2005), notion of *dana* (charity; Krishnan, 2005), and so forth.

Sudhir Kumar Bose, formerly at the University of Calcutta, helped organize the first psychology laboratory at the University of Dhaka, now in Bangladesh (Asthana, 2015, personal communication). Comparative psychology too had a glorious presence in the country. Kothurkar gets the credit of introducing animal and neurophysiological experiments way back in 1962 in the University of Mumbai. M.M. Sinha and Sheo Dhan Singh get the credit of establishing comparative psychology laboratories at Banaras Hindu University, Varanasi, and Meerut University, Meerut, respectively. S.K. Misra also established a comparative psychology laboratory at Utkal University, Bhubaneswar.

Although Indian scholars recorded their contributions in their research articles, monographs, book chapters, and books, only a handful made their impact on the Western psychologists. Taylor (1988) has highlighted the deep impact of Swami Vivekananda's talks in 1883 at the world conference on religions in Chicago on William James and how it influenced his ideas about the higher states of consciousness. Prasad (1935) examined the responses to an earthquake in Bihar, and published a comparative analysis of earthquake rumours which provided basis for Leon Festinger's (1957) cognitive dissonance theory. Jamuna Prasad's work was published even before Cantril (1940), Allport and Lepkin (1945), and Allport and Postman (1947), but came into limelight later, when it was rediscovered by Festinger in connection with cognitive dissonance theory. Today, when students of psychology read this theory, Prasad's contribution appears neither in the textbooks nor in the classrooms. Incorporating Lewin's field theory, Asthana (1960) described the process of perceptual distortion in the light of gestalt and learning theories. Kothurkar (1968) challenged the Stimulus-Response (S-R) theory of learning. Sheo Dhan Singh's initiatives on primate behaviour research in India and his own research at the Primate Research Laboratory, Meerut University, are worth mentioning. He had worked with Harlow in the USA. His seminal work on the urban monkey (Singh, 1969) published in *Scientific American* influenced other Western researchers (Zuckerman, 1981). The work of B.S. Gupta (Gupta, 1976, 1977, 1990; Gupta & Kaur, 1978; Gupta

& Nagpal, 1978; Gupta & Shukla, 1989; Nagpal & Gupta, 1979) of Banaras Hindu University has been cited by many Western scholars including Eysenck (1981). Suresh Kanekar's (of the University of Mumbai) work on Fritz Heider' attribution theory was also well received. Extending the earlier work on PASS (Planning, Attention, Successive, and Simultaneous Processes) theory, Das, Kar, and Parrila (2000) have brought out its significance in various cognitive functions.

## Associations

A close look at the foundation of professional associations indicates that the then psychologists had started forming associations just a few years after the first academic department was established. The Indian Psychoanalytic Society, Calcutta, was founded in 1922 by Bose. The Indian Science Congress Association first initiated the participation of foreign scientists in its Silver Jubilee Session. Jung, Meyers, and Spearman were invited for this session. The Indian Science Congress Association added a new section—anthropological and behavioural sciences (including archaeology, and psychology and educational sciences)—in 1923, thus inducting psychology. The Indian Psychological Association was founded in 1924.

Since the 1960s, more and more of professional associations came into the picture, including the Indian Academy of Applied Psychology (IAAP, 1962), the Indian Association of Clinical Psychologists (IACP, 1968), the Indian Society for Applied Behavioral Science (1972), the Community Psychology Association of India (CPAI, 1987), the National Academy of Psychology (NAOP, 1989) and the Indian Association of Human Behaviour (1992). Other associations are Bharat Psychological Association, Punjab; Bihar Psychological Association, Bombay; Psychological Association; Indian Academy of Health Psychology; Indian Association of Human Behaviour; Indian Association of Mental Health, Indian Association of Positive Psychology; Indian Psychological Association; Indian Psychometric and Educational Research Association, Madras; Psychological Society, Chennai; Marathi Manasshastra Parishad; National Association of Psychological Science; Psycho-lingua Council of Behavior Scientists; and the Indian Academy of Psychologists. However, this is not a complete list.

A close look at the number of members of these professional organizations reflects many concerns. If you look at the list of office bearers, some names are common across organizations. The number of members also varies across the years. The lack of consistency in the list of members, common names as office bearers across organizations in different years and similar observations suggest that these organizations did not conduct themselves as professionally as one would ideally expect them to. However, most of them have published or continue to publish journals.

## Journals

A year after the first association was founded, the first journal of psychology was published; The *Indian Journal of Psychology* was published in 1925. Since then, many journals have come up. The journals published in India includes *Andhra Pradesh Journal of Psychological Medicine, Behavioural Scientist, Disabilities and Impairments, Indian Journal of Applied Psychology, Indian Journal of Clinical Psychology, Indian Journal of Community Psychology*, Indian Journal of Experimental Psychology, *Indian Journal of Positive Psychology, Indian Journal of Psychological Science, Indian Journal of Psychology, Indian Journal of Psychology and Education, Indian Journal of Psychology and*

*Mental Health, Indian Journal of Psychometry & Education, Indian Psychological Review, Indian Psychometric and Educational Research, Journal of Contemporary Psychological Research, Journal of Indian Psychology, Journal of Parapsychology, Journal of Personality and Clinical Studies, Journal of Positive Psychology, Journal of Projective Psychology & Mental Health, Journal of Psychological Researches, Journal of the Indian Academy of Applied Psychology, Journal of Vocational and Educational Guidance, Personality Study and Group Behavior, Prachi Journal of Psycho-Cultural Dimensions, PSYBER NEWS: International Psychology Research Publication, Psychological Studies, Psychology and Developing Societies, The Bombay Civic Journal,* and *United Journal of Awadh Scholars* (UJAS). While some of these journals are official journals of the state- or national-level professional organizations some are outcome of individual passion and enthusiasm. Few of them still do not have ISSN which makes them lag behind other journals with respect to rules and regulations governing journal publications.

## R&D Activities

Research and development is the backbone of scientific progress of any discipline. Besides sponsored research and consultancies, psychology has contributed to the Indian society through three important establishments—Research Designs and Standards Organisation (RDSO), Lucknow; Defence Institute of Psychological Research (DIPR), Delhi; and Institute of Banking Personnel Selection (IBPS), Mumbai.

In an order to implement standardization in the Indian Railways, the Indian Railway Conference Association (IRCA) and the Central Standards Office (CSO) were established in 1903 and 1930, respectively. After Independence, the government established the Railway Testing and Research Centre (RTRC) at Lucknow in 1952 with the objective of testing and conducting applied research related to the railways. In 1957, the CSO and the RTRC were merged and named as Research Designs and Standards Organisation (RDSO). Owing to the recommendations of the Railway Accident Committee 1962, the Railway Board inducted a unit for 'psycho-technology and psycho-technological analysis' in its office. This unit was later transferred to RDSO in 1970. Although RDSO had different directorates, the psycho-technical unit was given the status of a full-fledged directorate in 1990. Their mandate is to enhance safety, prevent accidents due to human failures, and maximize 'functional efficiency through matching of job requirements with workers aptitude'. The unit has been instrumental in the development and standardization of appropriate assessment tools, personnel testing programmes, on-job training and other cognitive behavioural aspects, thus addressing safety issues of the Indian Railways. Currently, this directorate has professionals working at RDSO and nine zonal railways.

For the purpose of selection of officers of the Armed Forces, an experimental board was set up in 1943 at Dehradun, which was later converted into the Psychological Research Wing (PRW) in 1949. This was renamed as Directorate of Psychological Research (DPR) in 1962 with expansion in its scope of work. Finally, it was designated as a full-fledged institute as Defence Institute of Psychological Research (DIPR) in 1982, with a mandate to deal with emerging, new operational challenges. It has been involved in the design, development and evaluation of a whole gamut of psychological tools. DIPR has significantly contributed to research in personnel selection and has developed customized tests of personality, intelligence, aptitude, motivation, attitude, morale, leadership, and so forth. It has the credit of developing the behavioural training modules and psycho-biosocial assessment, as well as successfully running the human factor laboratory. The most celebrated products developed by DIPR that are currently in use include the Air Traffic Controller Cognitive Assessment System (ATC-CAS), aptitude and psychomotor ability tests for the selection of sharpshooters, screening test battery for the territorial army, and computer-based personality test for recruitment of personnel below officer rank in the Indian Army (PBOR). On 13 July 2012, ATC-CAS was handed over to the Indian Air Force. It measures 22 cognitive aptitudes pertaining to air traffic controlling. The aptitude and psychomotor ability test battery comprises of eight sub-tests measuring perceptual and psychomotor abilities necessary for the selection of sharpshooters. To fulfil the requirements of selection of personnel for the Territorial Army, a test battery comprising of personality and intelligence tests has been developed and handed over to the territorial army in 2012. Another tool devised by DIPR is the computer-based personality test for the screening of PBORs.

IBPS plays a pivotal role in testing, selection, assessment, and management of human resources. It was established in 1975 as Personnel Selection Services (PSS) as a unit of the National Institute of Bank Management (NIBM). It became an independent entity with the name IBPS in 1984. The Department of Scientific and Industrial Research, Ministry of Science and Technology, of the Government of India recognized IBPS as a scientific and industrial research organization (SIRO) in the same year. It has been involved in developing ability and aptitude test batteries. It serves all public sector banks, regional rural banks, State Bank of India (SBI), the Reserve Bank of India (RBI), National Bank for Agriculture and Rural Development (NABARD), and Small Industries Development Bank of India (SIDBI). It also serves government departments, state-owned companies and corporations in selection of suitable employee. It designs and develops assessment tools for highly specialized jobs. Besides engaging in research in the area of testing, it serves the country by evolving and applying psychometric tools for personnel selection.

## Virtual Network of Psychologists

On 21 November 2006, L.S.S. Manickam, then professor of psychology at University of Mysore, took a major initiative as a moderator and started the e-group of Indian psychologists. Besides psychologists studying/working in India, this group includes Indian psychologists working/living in Austria, Australia, Belgium, Canada, Denmark, Ethiopia, Hong Kong, Malaysia, New Zealand, Singapore, South Africa, Sweden, Thailand, the UK, the USA, and some Middle East countries. Few psychologists from Bangladesh, Nepal, Maldives, Iran, Pakistan, and Sri Lanka have also become members of the group. As of now (1 July 2017), the group has 7,666 members (Manickam, 2017, personal communication). This development has given impetus to knowledge dissemination, especially allowing academic discussions on specific issues on a virtual network. Several activities pertaining to professional growth, such as workshop and conference announcements, research findings, etc., are being carried out in this group.

## The Story of Rise and Fall

Critically examining the past, G.G. Prabhu has shared:

> It is not that Psychology in India did not come to the limelight. Between 1920–55/60, it was centre stage. At that juncture psychology got 'assassinated' instead of being nurtured…. Psychology in India, was at its peak around 50/55. Many were quick to perceive the promise the subject provided. There was a mad

rush to introduce the subject at PG level in many Universities. Around '55 there were just about 10/12 Universities imparting PG programmes. By about 65/67, the programmes had gone up to 51 (Prabha Ramalingaswami). This rapid growth (cancerous?) brought about a series of problems…. Unlike the first generation wherein the faculty was from among trained psychologists, the rush provided an opportunity for 'semi baked psychologists' to masquerade as psychologists…. Training programmes got adulterated to include soft branches and areas like experimental, physiological, psychometrics, statistics and research methodology were put on the back burner. The programmes started becoming more theoretical with declined emphasis on soft skills…. At this juncture because of the availability of PL-480 funds a large number of American Text books in Psychology became available at throw away prices. This became a damper on the possibility of indigenous book writing. Original thinking by few of the Psychologists from India could not get disseminated…. In '72, I termed this as 'Transplantology' and a little later K.G. Agarwal named it 'Adaptology'. Just like 'Indian Made Foreign Liquor' (IMFL) we were getting busy creating 'Indian Made Western Psychologists' (IMWP)…those because of their training were finding it difficult to resonate with the outer reality of the Indian setting. The applied aspect was getting into difficulties because of the psychology of irrelevance. A paralysed psychologist was in a web of incapability to act. Nothing new….

He further added:

There was a collapse in the Leadership too. The passing away of Prof G. Bose left a void at CU. The 'first' Department could not guide and provide leadership as it did in the earlier 3/4 decades. Local satraps emerged and psychologists were found talking in different tongues…the Tower of Babel? Let us face the truth despite it is bitter. Groupism emerged with power orientation at the cost of commitment to the interests of the discipline…. The last straw was the collapse of the Indian Psychological Association. A profession always speaks as one by a collective voice which is evolved on the basis of the contributions of individuals. To influence any societal system what is required is the mutually agreed contributions arrived at by debate/discussion by the members of a profession. IPA was an effective functioning body till the early sixties. Then the infighting started ultimately leading to its collapse…. J.P. Nayak, the internationally renowned educationist and the founder Member-Secretary of the ICSSR, over a period of one decade continuously tried to revive the Indian Psychological Association and make it functional. First he [J.P. Nayak, JPN] tried to get a constitution for the IPA on the lines of the APA (with federal character). This was done by Harper of Allahabad (I was his Junior team mate) but psychologists did not see reason to come together under that umbrella. The constitution developed is in print and still exists. Second, JPN created a nominated EC for IPA under the Presidentship of S.K. Mitra (NCERT). I was a Member of it. Of that 22 Member EC H.S. Asthana and myself are, to the best of my knowledge, the two who are still around. Psychologists showed very little interest to function as a Group. JPN made yet another effort in 1979 (Centenary of the Leipzig lab) and failed…. IPA became a memory. (Prabhu, 2016, personal communication)

Learning from the past, it is important for us to rethink the role of psychology in India.

## Rethinking the Role of Psychology in India

As summarized by Dalal (2011, p. 32), 'Indian psychology has developed around the existential quest to overcome human suffering and in the process to raise the person to higher levels of awareness and mental state'. He and many other scholars have raised the need for distinguishing 'native psychological viewpoints (culturally-rooted) from the 20th century Western psychology in India'. However, historically, psychology in India seems to have lost the support that it initially received after Independence. A large number of them confined to 'testing of Western theories on Indian samples' (Sinha, 1997). The readers may also see the article by Asthana (2008) to get acquainted with the growth of the subject in the country.

Although the country invested its confidence in psychologists for contemporary social issues, the academic community as a whole could not satisfy it. As a result, the involvement of psychologists in policy, planning, and other relevant areas was replaced by other social science disciplines. Based on the Indian experience, Murphy (1953, p. 44) stated that

> over long periods and throughout large regions caste and religion have been relatively free of the phenomena to which we would apply the word 'tension'. There must always have been some jealousies of those who enjoyed a more favourable station, but this is an entirely different thing from the seething unrest and bitterness which often characterise the relationships of caste and of religious groups in recent years.

While some other disciplines of social sciences continue to address these issues, psychologists have largely shifted their focus to Western concepts with corroborative research findings. Neither the academic departments nor the research institutes have extended help in making the country achieve its set goals. Although, as one of the signatories of Alma Ata Declaration (1978), India was supposed to strive for 'health for all by the year 2000', we seem to have failed on many counts. The academic and practicing psychologists do not seem to have worked towards attaining this goal.

The Gita has been the choice of many scholars who have connected it to psychological counselling (Dalal, 2011), assessment of attitude (Pande & Naidu, 1992), and so forth. Working on the propositions of *anasakti*, Pande and Naidu (1992) developed a tool to measure attitude towards non-attachment, correlating it with mental health. As a consequence of following Western concepts and tools, a large number of tools developed in the USA and Europe have been adapted for the Indian population. Most of these tools have been adapted in dominant Indian languages. However, India has 1,652 spoken languages (Ministry of Information and Broadcasting, 1994) and any adaptation that would cater to larger Indian population is doubtful. Citing Misra (1990), Bhatia and Sethi (2007, p. 185) have reiterated the concern that 'the rural and urban constitute two largely independent sub-systems that require separate tools for data collection and separate parameters for analysis and understanding in their own right. One cannot understand the rural by applying the parameters and principles derived from urban samples'.

One of the major challenges before the academic community is to publish in reputed journals. A closer look at the journals published by internationally acclaimed publishers show that, compared to yesteryears, the number of articles by Indian authors (with Indian affiliation) has reduced. Another challenge relates to citation. While articles from Indian authors are largely dominated by citations of foreign authors, the reverse is not true. Some of the Indian journals are accessible online (limited volumes), but many are not. Hence, finding relevant Indian studies online is difficult compared to studies with foreign origins.

Formulation and adherence to ethical guidelines in research and publication is one of the major requirements of the current time. Although data is not available and, hence, one cannot state with conviction, but many universities/institutions still do not have the Institutional Ethics Committee (IEC). There has also been demand for a regulating and licensing body. The academic community and publication houses need to work on this. One of the recent developments is offering that the authors make their articles available through open access against payment. Fund deprivation does not allow this to happen in many cases. Recently, Dutch universities joined hands together to negotiate with scientific publishers about open access policy and have managed agreements with some publishers. This is done with the intention to make all publications by Dutch scientists available through open access by 2024. In India, the professional organizations/ bodies are not even talking about it. It is evident that there are challenges and the fraternity need to work on them to compete with contemporary changes/challenges.

Having briefly examining the existence of psychology in India in the last 100 years, let us now look at the life and work of some of the eminent Indian psychologists.

# References

Allport, F.H., & Leplin, M. (1945). Wartime rumors of waste and special privilege: Why some people believe them. *Journal of Abnormal and Social Psychology, 40*(1), 3–36.

Allport, G.W., & Postman, L. (1947). *The psychology of rumor.* New York, NY: Holt, Rinehart & Winston.

Association of Indian Universities. (2014). *Universities handbook* (33rd ed.). New Delhi: Association of Indian Universities.

Asthana, H.S. (1960). Perceptual distortion as a function of the valence of perceived object. *Journal of Social Psychology, 52*(1), 119–125.

———. (2008). Modern psychology in India: Reminiscences and reflections. *Psychological Studies, 53*(1), 1–6.

Beg, M. A. (1970). A note on the concept of self, and the theory and practice of psychological help in the Sufi tradition. *Interpersonal Development, 1*, 58–64.

Bhatia, S., & Sethi, N. (2007). History and theory of community psychology in India: An international perspective. In S. Reich, M. Riemer, I. Prilleltensky, & M. Montero (Eds) *International community psychology: History and theories* (pp. 180–199). New York, NY: Springer.

Brass, P.R. (2003). The partition of India and retributive genocide in the Punjab, 1946–47: Means, methods, and purposes. *Journal of Genocide Research, 5*(1), 71–101.

Cantril, H. (1940). The invasion from Mars: A study in the psychology of panic. Princeton, NJ: Princeton University Press.

Chakraborty, S.K. (1995). *Ethics in management: Vedantic perspectives.* New Delhi: Oxford University Press.

Cornelissen, R.M.M. (Ed.). (2001). *Consciousness and its transformation.* Pondicherry: SAICE.

Cornelissen, R.M.M., Misra, G., & Varma, S. (Eds). (2011a). *Foundations of Indian psychology: Theories and concepts* (Vol. 1). New Delhi: Pearson Education.

———. (Eds). (2011b). *Foundations of Indian psychology: Practical applications* (Vol. 2). New Delhi: Pearson Education.

Dalal, A.K. (2011). Indigenisation of psychology in India. *Psychology Teaching Review, 17*(2), 29–37.

Dalal, A.K., & Misra, G. (2005). Psychology of health and well-being: Some emerging perspectives. *Psychological Studies, 51*(2–3), 91–104.

Das, B. (1908). *The science of the emotions.* London and Benares: Theosophical Publishing Society.

Das, J.P., Kar, B.C., & Parrila, R.K. (2000). *Cognitive planning: The psychological basis of intelligent behaviour.* New Delhi: SAGE Publications.

Eysenck, H.J. (1981). General features of the model. In H.J. Eysenck (Ed.), *A model for personality* (pp. 1–87). Heidelberg: Springer-Verlag.

Festinger, L. (1957). *A theory of cognitive dissonance.* California: Stanford University Press.

Ganguli, H.C. (1971). Industrial psychology research in India, 1920–1969. *Indian Journal of Industrial Relations, 6*(3), 223–276.

Gupta, B.S. (1976). Extraversion and reinforcement in verbal operant conditioning. *British Journal of Psychology, 67*(1), 47–52.

———. (1977). Dextroamphetamine and measures of intelligence. *Intelligence, 1*(3), 274–280.

———. (1990). Impulsivity/sociability and reinforcement in verbal operant conditioning: A replication. *Personality and Individual Differences, 11*, 585–589.

Gupta, B.S., & Kaur, S. (1978). The effects of dextroamphetamine on kinaesthetic figural after effects. *Psychopharmacology*, *56*(2), 199–204.

Gupta, B.S., & Nagpal, M. (1978). Impulsivity/sociability and reinforcement in verbal operant conditioning. *British Journal of Psychology*, *69*(2), 203–206.

Gupta, B.S., & Shukla, A.P. (1989). Verbal operant conditioning as a function of extraversion and reinforcement. *British Journal of Psychology*, *80*(1), 39–44.

Gupta, G.C. (1999). Cognitive, experiential analytical and reflective bases of oriental thought systems: Making of a paradigm for psychology. *Journal of Indian Psychology*, *17*(2), 1–8.

Joshi, K., & Cornelissen, M. (Eds). (2004). *Consciousness, Indian psychology and yoga* (Vol. 11, Part 3). New Delhi: Centre for Studies in Civilizations.

Kakar, S. (1995). *The colors of violence*. New Delhi: Oxford University Press.

———. (1996). *The Indian psyche*. New Delhi: Oxford University Press.

Kothurkar, V.K. (1968). More about transfer in probability learning. *Psychological Studies*, *13*, 73–83.

Krishnan, B. (2002[1976]). Typological conceptions in ancient Indian thought. In G. Misra & A. K. Mohanty (Eds), *Perspectives on indigenous psychology* (pp. 292–304). New Delhi: Concept Publishing Company.

Krishnan, L. (2005). Concepts of social behaviour in India: *Daan* and distributive justice. *Psychological Studies*, *50*(1), 21–31.

Kundu, R., & Chakrabati, P.H. (1979). *From Leipzig to Calcutta*. Calcutta: Department of Psychology, Calcutta University.

Kuppuswami, B. (1985). *Elements of ancient Indian psychology*. New Delhi: Vikas Publishing House.

Mehta, P. (1972). A validation of the theory of achievement motivation. *Manas*, *19*, 91–102.

Menon, U., & Shweder, R.A. (1994). Kali's tongue: Cultural psychology, cultural consensus and the meaning of 'Shame' in Orissa, India. In S. Kitayama & H. Markus (Eds), *Culture and the emotions* (pp. 241–284). Washington, DC: American Psychological Association.

Ministry of Information and Broadcasting. (1994). *India 1993: A reference annual*. New Delhi: Author.

Misra, G. (Ed.). (1990). *Applied social psychology in India*. New Delhi: SAGE Publications.

———. (Ed.). (2011). *Handbook of psychology in India*. New Delhi: Oxford University Press.

Misra, G., & Mohanty, A. (2002). *Perspectives on indigenous psychology*. New Delhi: Concept Publishers.

Misra, G., & Paranjpe, A.C. (2012). Psychology in Modern India. In R.W. Rieber (Ed.) *Encyclopedia of the history of psychological theories* (pp. 881–892). New York: Springer.

Mishra, R.C. (1997). Cognition and cognitive development. In J.W. Berry, P.R. Dasen, & T.S. Saraswathi (Eds), *Handbook of cross-cultural psychology* (Vol. 2, pp. 147–179). Boston, MA: Allyn & Bacon.

Mukherjee, B.N. (1974). Towards a conceptualization of the achievement value construct. In S.K. Roy & A.S.K. Menon (Eds), *Motivation and organizational effectiveness* (pp. 43–74). New Delhi: Shri Ram Centre for Industrial Relations.

Murphy, G. (1953). *In the minds of men*. New York, NY: Basic Books.

Nagpal, M., & Gupta, B.S. (1979). Personality, reinforcement and verbal operant conditioning. *British Journal of Psychology*, *70*(4), 471–476.

Nandy, A. (1983). *Intimate enemy: Loss and recovery of self under colonialism*. New Delhi: Oxford University Press.

———. (2004). *Return from exile*. New Delhi: Oxford University Press.

Neki, J.S. (1973). Guru-chela relationship: The possibility of a therapeutic paradigm. *The American Journal of Orthopsychiatry*, *43*(5), 755–766.

Pande, N., & Naidu, R.K. (1992). Anasakti and health: A study of non-attachment. *Psychology and Developing Societies*, *4*, 89–104.

Paranjpe, A.C. (1984). *Theoretical psychology: The meeting of East and West*. New York, NY: Plenum Press.

———. (1998). *Self and identity in modern psychology and Indian thought*. New York, NY: Plenum Press.

———. (2008). Sri Rama a Maharshi: A case study in self-realization. In K. Ramakrishna Rao, A.C. Paranjpe, & A.K. Dalal (Eds), *Handbook of Indian psychology* (pp. 564–576). New Delhi: Cambridge University Press.

Pareek, U. (1968). A motivational paradigm of development. *Journal of Social Issues*, *24*(1), 115–124.

Pirta, R.S. (2011). Biological and ecological bases of behaviour. In G. Misra (Ed.), *Psychology in India: Basic psychological processes and human development* (Vol. 1, pp. 1–67). New Delhi: Pearson.

Prasad, J. (1935). The psychology of rumor: A study relating to the great Indian earthquake of 1934. *British Journal of Psychology, 26*(1), 1–15.

Rao, K.R. (1962). *Development of psychological thought in India.* Mysore: Kavyalaya.

———. (2002a). *Consciousness studies: Cross-cultural perspectives.* Jefferson, NC: McFarland Publishing.

———. (2002b). Consciousness studies: A survey of perspectives and research. In J. Pandey (Ed.), *Psychology in India revisited* (Vol. 2, pp. 19–162). New Delhi: SAGE Publications.

———. (2005). Scope and substance of India psychology. In K.R. Rao & S.B. Marwaha (Eds), *Towards a spiritual psychology: Essays on Indian psychology.* New Delhi: Samvad Indian Foundation.

———. (2011). *Cognitive anomalies, consciousness and yoga.* New Delhi: Centre for Studies in Civilizations.

Rao, K.R., & Marwaha, S.B. (Eds). (2006). *Towards a spiritual psychology: Essays on Indian psychology.* New Delhi: Samvad Indian Foundation.

Rao, K.R., Paranjpe, A.C., & Dalal, A.K. (Eds). (2008). *Handbook of Indian psychology.* New Delhi: Cambridge University Press.

Safaya, R. (1975). *Indian psychology: A critical and historical analysis of psychological speculation in India philosophical literature.* New Delhi: Munshiram Manoharlal.

Salagame, K.K.K. (2011). Indian indigenous concepts and perspectives: Developments and future possibilities. In G. Misra (Ed.), *Psychology in India: Theoretical and methodological developments* (Vol. 4, pp. 97–171). New Delhi: Pearson Education.

Saraswathi, T.S. (1999). *Culture, socialisation and human development: Theory, research and applications in India.* New Delhi: SAGE Publications.

Saraswathi, T.S., & Ganapathy, H. (2002). Indian parents' ethnotheories as reflections of the Hindu scheme of child and human development. In H. Keller, Y.H. Poortinga, & A. Scholmerich (Eds), *Between culture and biology: Perspectives on ontogenetic development* (pp. 79–88). New York, NY: Cambridge University Press.

Sen, I. (1986). *Integral psychology: The psychological system of Sri Aurobindo.* Pondicherry: The Aurobindo International Centre of Education.

Sinha, D. (1990). Wundtian tradition and the development of scientific psychology in India. *The Creative Psychologist, 2,* 1–6.

Sinha, J. (1934). *Indian psychology: Perception.* London: Kegan Paul, Trench, Trubner & Co. Ltd.

———. (1958). *Indian psychology: Cognition* (Vol. 1). Calcutta: Sinha Publishing House.

Sinha, J.B.P. (1968). The nAch/cooperation under limited/unlimited resource conditions. *Journal of Experimental Social Psychology, 4,* 233–248.

———. (1980). *The nurturant task leader: A model of effective execution.* New Delhi: Concept Publishing Company.

Singh, S.D. (1969). Urban monkeys. *Scientific American, 221*(1), 108–115.

Srivastava, A.K., & Misra, G. (2007). *Rethinking intelligence: Culture and conceptualization of competence.* New Delhi: Concept.

Taylor, E.I. (1988). Contemporary interest in classical eastern psychology. In A.C. Paranjpe, D.Y.F. Ho, & R.W. Rieber (Eds), *Asian contributions to psychology* (pp. 79–122). New York, NY: Praeger.

Zuckerman, S. (1981). *The social life of monkeys and apes* (2nd ed.). Boston, MA and London: Routledge and K. Paul.

# SECTION 1

# Life and Work

# 2

# Brajendranath Seal

(1864–1938)

## Amitranjan Basu

*Pilgrim, the highest peaks of knowledge, hard to climb, you've scaled,*
*Where rise before your eyes summits of man's endeavour's ranges;*
*Whence from caverns deep flow vocal streams through arid lands*
*Down towards the ocean, giving birth the pilgrim-cities;*
*Where, piercing illusion's mists, rise lofty peaks of vision clear*
*That read the morning's gloom-dispelling script; where the Time Eternal*
*Appears in rosaries of fire, wheeling in stellar heavens*
*Incandescent; where One 'whose hue is as the rising sun's'*
*Uncovers in mortal earth's far sunrise-gilded eastern horizon*
*The awakening of deathless realm that rings in throats of seekers*
*Of Eternity; 'Listen immortality's children all!*
*That Person vast I've known 'whose hue is as the rising sun's'*
*Effulgent beyond the darkness'; where man hears the tongue of gods,*
*And suddenly a luminous vision he attends, and thus*
*Discovers anew the Infinite beyond earth's finite frontiers.*
*In the universe's hermitage where seekers congregate*
*An honoured guest you are, a seer of Truth; there in the skies*
*Of meditation, from age to age stars and planets greet*
*Each other, flashing into view from the deep unknown.*
*There, on imagination's canvas, in diverse tints and colours,*
*Is painted the invitation of Eternal Beauty;*
*The radiance white from there, garland of glory that is*
*The Goddess of Wisdom's caressing hand, plays round your noble brow.*
*Because you deem my friend, this poet has brought this verse's gift*
*Of my country's benediction, and my parting offering,*
*This thread, token of regard and love, I twine around your arm.*

—Tagore (1964)

This is how Rabindranath Tagore described Brajendranath Seal on his 72nd birthday! It is known that Brajendranath Seal took the initiative to start the study of psychology as an independent discipline in India way back in the early twentieth century. He started the initiative at vice-chancellor Ashutosh Mukherjee's insistence in 1905, and in 1911, after becoming the George V Professor of

Mental and Moral Philosophy, took specific charge of starting a psychology department. He consulted several courses offered in America and Europe to develop a curriculum in experimental psychology for the University of Calcutta. However, it took a decade to start the first batch (Bose, 1938). Brajendranath Seal was a distinguished scholar, philosopher, and a historian of science—a polymath of his time. His doctoral work in 1910 titled, 'Mechanical, Physical and Chemical Theories of Ancient India' that came out as the book *The Positive Sciences of the Ancient Hindus* in 1915 was well acclaimed, and is still consulted by scholars. Though it has been mentioned that Brajendranath studied animal psychology, child psychology, and abnormal psychology and researched in experimental psychology (S. Gupta, P.K. Gupta, & S.G. Gupta, 2014), he hardly wrote anything on psychology, though he was crucial in facilitating the study of a new science. Also one should not forget that in those times, much of the scholarly studies on the mind were done in philosophy.

In the journey of 100 years of disciplinary psychology in India, it dissociated itself from philosophy to establish its credibility as an objective, experimental science, and the speculative and critical power of philosophy disappeared from the new-found discipline. Even in its early phase, the first department of psychology established in the University of Calcutta, teachers simultaneously wrote articles from philosophical and critical perspective on received modern knowledge (Basu, 2013). It is interesting to note that at the turn of the century, studies in psychology in India are trying to rediscover its early critical tradition in the last three decades.[1] At this juncture, remembering Brajendranath, his time, and his work can be productive, particularly for the younger scholars, to treat this narrative as a piece of critical thinking, more importantly when Brajendranath Seal has just completed his 150th birth anniversary. I will first give an idea about the context of nineteenth-century Calcutta in which Seal grew up to make my reader understand how this context made him what he was known for. Then I would like to explore the available biographical details and, finally, I will engage with some of his works to find out its relevance for our contemporary thinking.

## Nineteenth-century Calcutta

Most of the scholars who have worked on colonial Bengal have described nineteenth-century Calcutta as crucial in establishing modernity by bringing its various institutional forms. It has been observed that

[I]n the first half of the nineteenth century, of early modernity in Calcutta when new urban institutions, practices and arts were beginning to emerge that were not yet shaped by the forms of colonial modernity. The latter, powerfully produced by the institutions of colonial education and government, would dominate the second half of the nineteenth century. (Chatterjee, 2008)

---

[1] These critical and new approaches started emerging with scholars like Ashis Nandy, who has used psychology as a social critic. I am only mentioning two of his most read works (Nandy, 1983, 1995). Sudhir Kakar's (1982) study on indigenous psychotherapeutic healing is seminal to understand the healing processes and its relation to culture. Recently, Anand Paranjpe (2010, pp. 5–48, 2014, pp. 107–109) has been exploring ancient Indian philosophy through modern psychological categories. A group of scholars working with Indian thought and psychology have recently brought out a volume that conceptualises Indian psychology (Cornelissen, Mishra, & Varma, 2014). This is only a small, exemplary list from an impressive bibliography of critical work that is being done in India.

In early nineteenth-century Calcutta, the elites or *Bhadraloks*[2] were much active in public affairs when Bombay was decades behind them! From 1815, Raja Ram Mohan Roy started *Atmiya Sabha* with an intention to reform Hindu religion and society. The Hindu College was set up in 1817, which soon became an intellectual hub, creating a far reaching impact on the social history of Calcutta and Bengal. It was followed by the formation of the School Book Society, which printed new textbooks and opened new type of schools, ushering a new educational system. The emphasis of teaching in both the primary and higher levels was on English, mathematics, geography, natural sciences, and English history (Mukherjee, 1977, pp. 87–88). The medical college would start by 1835 and the University of Calcutta was established in 1858.

By the second half of the nineteenth century, the publishing industry, comprising the writing, printing, and distribution of books and periodicals, was perhaps the largest indigenous enterprise in Calcutta. In 1911, when the six jute mills located in Calcutta employed 15,111 people, there were 99 printing presses with 11,880 people working in them, making printing the second largest industry in the city (Roy, 1995). Roughly estimated, a total of 212,000 copies of books were published in 40 languages between 1801 and 1832 from the Srirampur Mission (K. Chaudhuri & P. Chaudhuri, 1978).

Calcutta, by virtue of being at the centre of this 'informal empire', saw the fruits of industrialization by getting her first printing press, her first steamer, and her first motorcar, which were important cultural markers of the age. Nineteenth-century Calcutta was also marked to a large extent by the industrialization of cultural expressions. Books, handwritten and illustrated on palm leaves, now gave way to print ones. *Pālkis* and horse-drawn carriages were no longer in use; bicycles, trams, and steam engines changed the face of transportation. The shift in taste that followed the introduction of some of these mechanical innovations in the middle ranks of the populace and the market opportunities that opened up is a fascinating history of how the colonized mastered some of these 'alien technologies' and how often imitation gave way to invention, to foster a new sense of national identity. New media such as printed books, newspapers, and the theatre were marked by multi-applicability and accessibility for all; theoretically, anyone could buy a book or a newspaper. But at the same time, only a handful of the urban elite could access them (Sengupta, 2002).

The colonial discourse was a two-way process and the exchange of ideas started when both the cultures had to interact—from the everyday running of city life to the higher intellectual discourses. One can say, taking the risk of sounding somewhat simplistic, that from Ram Mohan an intellectual tradition grew where Western knowledge was accepted, but with a critique. Indian intellectuals, no less erudite in modern philosophical and scientific discourse, tried to prove their points as the desire for nationalism was also taking shape as an effect of the liberal knowledge that arrived in the colony. From 1829 to 1900, 157 scientific articles were published by Bengalis in various journals (Roy & Sen, 2010). The history of education in colonial Bengal though talks about active collaboration by the Indian intellectuals in framing colonial education policy (Acharya, 1995), this was the space where critical knowledge also developed that challenged the master's narrative.

---

[2] Bhadralok is Bengali for the new class of 'gentlefolk' who arose during the colonial times approximately from 1757 to 1947 in Bengal. Most, though not all, members of the bhadralok class are upper caste. There is no precise translation of bhadralok in English, since it attributes economic and class privilege on to caste ascendancy. However, anybody who could show considerable amount of wealth and standing in society was a member of the bhadralok community. The bhadralok community includes all gentlefolk belonging to the rich as well as middle class segments of the Bengali society.

## Biographical Discourse of Brajendranath

I will now attempt to read Seal's life in the context of nineteenth-century Bengal, of high modernity. Though there is no full-length biographical book on Brajendranath, writings on his life are many.[3] Brajendranath was born on 3 September, 1864, in a well to do family, where his father Mahendranath Seal was a distinguished lawyer of the Calcutta High Court, a polyglot, a mathematician, and a philosopher. Mahendranath died young, at 32, when Brajendranath was only 7. His mother, Radha Rani, had passed away several years before, leaving two sons and two daughters. At the crisis of this family, Kishori Mohan Nun, his maternal grandfather provided shelter to the children and took care of them with his humble means. Brajendranath's brother Rajendranath, who was only 2 years older than him, left his studies and took up a job to support the family.

Brajendranath's academic career was exceptional. After his primary education, he took admission into General Assembly's Institution (now known as Scottish Church College) and in 1878 he passed his entrance examination in first division. In the college, he earned reputation in mathematics of such a quality that sometimes teachers approached him for solving difficult problems! Brajendranath got a new erudite friend from his junior class in 1881, who was also then a member of Sadharan Bramho Samaj and spent a lot of time with him discussing philosophical issues and the question of truth. He was Narendranath Datta (later Swami Vivekananda). Brajendranath visited Ramakrishna Paramahnsa with him for the first time. In an article on Vivekananda, Brajendranath wrote:

> Undeniably a gifted youth, sociable, free and unconventional in manners, a sweet singer, the soul of social circles, a brilliant conversationalist, somewhat bitter and caustic, piercing with the shafts of a keen wit[h] the shows and mummeries of the world, sitting in the scorner's chair but hiding the tenderest of hearts under that garb of cynicism; altogether an inspired Bohemian but possessing what Bohemians lack, an iron will; somewhat peremptory and absolute, speaking with accents of authority and withal possessing a strange power of the eye which could hold his listeners in thrall… This was the beginning of a critical period in his mental history, during which he awoke to self-consciousness and laid the foundations of his future personality. (Sarcar, 1964)

Brajendranath got his first job as a teacher after passing his BA at the General Assembly's Institution itself and was also elected fellow of the college. During his MA, one of his teachers wanted him to study mathematics and another philosophy, but he finally took up philosophy. There is an interesting anecdote on his MA exam!

> It so happened that he was not able to answer the required number of questions for want of time, although he knew the answers of all the questions very well. He spent the whole time in answering only one question in each paper. He used four answer books for only one answer in each paper. Brajendranath did not expect that he would even get pass marks in the examination. But when the results came out, it was found that Brajendranath stood First in First Class and that no other student was able to get a first class. It was indeed a great surprise for Brajendranath who thought that the examiner must have committed a serious mistake

---

[3] This is not an exhaustive search and I speculate there could be more: Indian Statistical Institute (1964); Pramathanath Pal (1984); Ranjan Kumar Pal and Sunil Bandyopadhyay (1984); Amal Chattopadhyay (1999); Haripada Mandal (1999); Tapan Kumar Ghosh (2013, pp. 9–30); Sumit Mukherjee (2014); Sujata Gupta, Prabir K. Gupta, and Supratim Gupta (2014); and *Brajendra Nath Seal (1864–1938)*. Retrieved 12 September 2014, fromhttp://people.stfx.ca/wsweet/seal.html

in assessing his answer papers. It was known later that Brajendranath wrote the answer of only one question in each paper in such a masterly way, showing his deep knowledge and profound scholarship that the examiner gave him very high marks. The matter was referred to the Senate and the members of the Senate agreed to place Brajendranath First in First Class as a very special case. (Sarcar, 1964)

Brajendranath's professional career shows a frequent change of jobs. He joined City College, Calcutta, as a professor of English in 1884, but by 1885 he joined Morris College, Nagpur, and later became the principal. By 1887, he left Nagpur and joined as the principal of Krishnanath College, Baharampur, in Bengal, where he served till 1896. In 1897, he was approached by the Maharaja of Coochbehar Nripendranarayan to be the principal of Victoria College. Here, Seal spent about 15 years of his life and now this college is named after him. While teaching there, he was invited to participate at the International Congress of Orientalists at Rome in 1899 and presented several papers. After his second visit to Europe in 1905, where he stayed for about four months to discuss Indian philosophy among Western scholars, he made another visit in 1911. This time he was invited to inaugurate the First Universal Races Congress in London and proposed,

[A] scientific study of race characteristics does not in the least establish the superiority or inferiority of any race, since each has its share of inferior characteristics conditioned by environment, and consequently social theory should recognize the possibility of progress on the part of all races. Not only are all derived from a common prototype, but all have had a common social history running through the stages of family, clan, tribe, people, nation. The nation is not final, but is only the predecessor of universal humanity. (Weatherly, 1911)

When Brajendranath joined as the King George V Professor of Mental and Moral Philosophy in the University of Calcutta in 1913, he had already started contemplating on a book. *The Positive Sciences of Ancient Hindus* came out in 1915 and was well received among the scholars. He served the University of Calcutta, actively supporting Asutosh Mukherjee's reorganisation drive. In 1921, he was offered the post of vice-chancellor of the University of Mysore. He initially declined but later agreed after being persuaded by Sir Michael Sadler (who considered Seal as his 'guru') and Radhakumud Mukherjee. Brajendranath stayed there for a decade bringing in many reforms. On framing the constitution of Mysore state, the Maharaja honoured him with the 'Rajtantra Prabin', and he was elected as a member of the legislative council. During this period, he was awarded knighthood in 1926. He came back to Calcutta after retirement in the 1930s; his health was also compromised as he suffered from a stroke. His last public lecture was during the International Parliament of Religions organised by the Ramakrishna Centenary Committee at Calcutta on 1 March 1937, as the general president of the conference (The Ramakrishna Mission Institute of Culture, 1938). He passed away on 3 December 1938.

Brajendranath got married when he was 20. He married Indumati, the eldest daughter of Joygopal Rakshit of Assam. Indumati was educated and read poetries by Wordsworth, Byron, Keats, and others. Besides her domestic chores and raising children, she managed time to discuss the poetries she read with Brajendranath. Unfortunately, she died at only 28 leaving behind three sons and one daughter, the youngest son having died at infancy.

What kind of a person was Brajendranath? Krishna Chandra Bhattacharya, the famous philosopher, who was junior to Brajendranath and also became the King George V. Professor later, said:

I had occasions to see him in connexion with the Calcutta Philosophical Society of which I was then the Secretary. He received me very kindly, spoke appreciatively of some of my writings and made me feel at once as though we had long been working together on the same plane of philosophical thought. (Bhattacharya, 1964)

A student from Victoria College, Coochbehar, where Brajendranath was the principal, wrote:

In our B. A. Test Examination, a fellow student was detained for very poor marks in English. When, however, Dr. Seal noticed that this student has secured very high marks in Mathematics, he was visibly moved and pleaded with Professors of English to waive their objection, himself undertaking to polish up his English. (Chakraborti, 1964)

Another known intellectual of the time wrote:

About 1921, when he was Vice-Chancellor of the Mysore University, I went to spend some time with him at Mysore…I remember our going to a picnic, to which Dr. Seal had invited us, on the bank of a small rivulet. He seemed to enjoy the outing greatly, happy and relaxed as a child. (Sen, 1964)

Edward Thompson remarked: 'Throughout his life, Brajendranath Seal, was without fear; and he was incapable of intellectual dishonesty. He was an Aryan indeed, in the original meaning of the word, which is *noble*' (Thompson, 1964). The famous historian Ramesh Chandra Majumdar recalled:

So I went to Dr. Seal's house, somewhere near the Hedua tank, not without some trepidation of heart at the prospect of coming face to face with such a profound scholar. But when I met him, all my fears were over. He was so simple and generous, and talked with a young man like me in such a genial and courteous manner, that I was overwhelmed by his wonderful personality…I have a shrewd suspicion that he was incapable of bringing himself down to the level of ordinary man when he wrote on a subject. But he was quite different with his conversation which was charming and erudite, but not difficult of comprehension. (Majumdar, 1964)

These anecdotes clearly indicate that he was a kind person who treated everyone as equal and was fearless in expressing his views. Let us now have a look at him as a thinker of his time and how contemporary scholars have responded to his thinking.

## Brajendranath as a Thinker

As mentioned earlier, it is impossible to categorize Seal only as a philosopher. The definition of a polymath itself resists it. At a mature age of seventy, he said to an interviewer on his *jibanbodh* (perception of life):

An internal unity has to be achieved between philosophy, science, literature and creation of art. Otherwise, achieving extraordinary domination over nature man may become a love-less, conscience-less, and aesthetics-less fearful monster. A new philosophy of life has to be created by incorporating everything. (Sengupta, 1984 as cited in Sarkar, 2014)

What we see today in the field of humanities and liberal arts, and surely in history of science, is that an interdisciplinary approach has become a standard scholarly practice. However, the universalizing claims he made (or even others) has been looked at critically by the continental philosophers. He thought:

> A holistic human unity is needed removing all geographical and religious differences, for that we need a capital of the world, and we also need the aspiration for a universal consciousness and thinking by churning the knowledge form all religion, civilisation and culture. (Sengupta, 1984 as cited in Sarkar, 2014)

Seal was interested in Hegel in his early years for its philosophy of unilinearity in history as was the domination of Hegel studies in those days. But he was soon to become critical, and for a younger scholar to do that was considered courageous. Seal's critique of the Hegelian thesis was that historical progress in a linear flow from East to West is limited in scope and narrow. The consequences of the Hegelian idea saw all human races as being subordinate to the dominant Greco-Roman-Gothic type, which is another example of orientalism. Seal criticised this discourse as being Eurocentric and denied any equitable cultural dialogue. Seal rejected the Hegelian worldview that Western civilization is the centre where civilizations of the world culminated. He argued in detail about the rich and diverse cultural heritages of Hindu, Islamic, and Chinese civilizations that equally contribute to human civilization. As more time passed, Brajendranath developed his idea of universal humanism and universal religion, and he used the term 'synthetic philosophy' in distilling the truth derived from various philosophical thoughts. Much of his critique on Hegel can be found in his *New Essays on Criticism* (1903). His book of poetry *Quest Eternal* (*Saswata Sandhan* in Bengali) published in 1936 presented the evolution of cultural history in human society and bears the reflection of the quest of a scholar on his philosophic mind.

His *Positive Sciences of the Ancient Hindus* (1915) brought out a strong argument in the favour of Indian epistemology with extensive research about scientific practices in various disciplines to establish our traditions of objectivity, experimentation, and search of truth. In the foreword, he claimed it to be a comparative philosophical work that would make the Indian scientific knowledge emerge as an equal:

> The Hindus no less than Greeks have shared in the work of constructing scientific concepts and methods in the investigation of physical phenomena, as well as of building up a body of positive knowledge which has been applied to industrial technique; and Hindu scientific ideas and methodology (e.g. the inductive method or methods of algebraic analysis) have deeply influenced the course of natural philosophy in Asia—in the East as well as the West—in China and Japan, as well as the Saracen Empire. A comparative estimate of Greek and Hindu science may now be undertaken with some measure of success—and finality. (Seal, 1915, p. iv)

He also asserted that he has not written a single line without the support of 'clearest texts', and the 'ground trodden in, for the most part, is absolutely new'. He organized his thoughts that attempted to include all the basic tenets of a scientific discourse: The mechanical, physical, and chemical theories of the ancient Hindus; Hindu ideas on mechanics (kinetics); Hindu ideas on acoustics; Hindu ideas about plants and plant life; Hindu physiology and biology; and Hindu doctrine of scientific method. Each of these ideas is elaborated in detail with explanations and interpretations from Sanskrit texts. A contemporary and noted philosopher from India, Jitendra Nath Mohanty, while writing an entry on 'Indian Philosophy' in the *Encyclopaedia Britannica* recently, mentioned this as one of the major works by Seal, 'which, besides being a work on the history of science, shows interrelations among the ancient Hindu philosophical concepts and their scientific theories' (Mohanty, 2014). It is interesting to note that two very well-known Indian scholars of the time were influenced by this work and both of them used his method in interpreting ancient Indian knowledge reflecting that in their titles.[4]

Brajendranath Seal was also a key figure on the development of sociology and social anthropology in India. During his birth centenary, the famous anthropologist Nirmal Kumar Bose[5] focused on his presentation at the First Universal Races Congress in 1911 and was surprised to find out that Seal said things which were advanced from the contemporary anthropological perspective:

> It is surprising that Seal thus suggested in 1911 that the multiple bonds of utility led to the formation of a complex whole entitled social structure, and which was distinctive of a particular community in a given age. These were, moreover, not static; but evolved like organisms in a biological series. It is also surprising that such a view should have been stated twenty years before Malinowski laid the foundations of, the Functional School in social anthropology. (Bose, 2016)

Writing on the development of sociology and social anthropology in India, M.N. Srinivas and M.N. Panini said:

> It was during the 1900–1920 that the first steps were taken to introduce sociology and social anthropology as academic disciplines in Indian universities. The efforts of Brajendranath Seal deserve special mention in this context. Seal, who was for many years Professor of Philosophy at Calcutta, wrote, lectured and initiated studies on what he called 'comparative sociology.'…. He contended that social development was multilinear and ramifying, and that judgements regarding the superiority of social customs and institutions were irrelevant. (Srinivas & Panini, 1973)

Another stalwart of Indian sociology, Radhakamal Mukerjee, who was a student of Brajendranath Seal at the University of Calcutta, saw Seal as a 'legend in intellectual Bengal', respected for his 'encyclopaedic knowledge' and acknowledged that it was from Seal that Mukerjee learned to appreciate the 'comparative method in the study of civilization', and in the 'study of economic and political institutions', bringing out 'the multilinear character of human social evolution in different regions and cultures' (Mukerjee, 1997).

Another major area where Seal's creative mind was engaged is aesthetics. Here too, his work *New Essays in Criticism* (1903) differed from the Hegelian view on art. Nandi's article gives a detail analysis of this, who, however, commented at the end:

> Whenever he wrote on aesthetics, classical art examples from the West were cited again and again, and the influence of classical aesthetics of the West was too pronounced. This one factor was responsible for the fact that many of his judgments have been rejected as unsound and lopsided. (Nandi, 1965)

Another commentator worked on Seal's aesthetics related to Keats and closely read his *New Essays in Criticism* and judged it to be 'a brilliant sketch of the Neo-Romantic movement in literature, a

---

[4] Acharya P. C. Ray's book *History of Hindu Chemistry* was published in two volumes in 1902 and 1909, respectively, and in the second volume, Professor Seal wrote a preface and an appendix. For a contemporary review of this book, see Harsha and Nagaraja (2010). Benoy Kumar Sarkar, in his seminal book *The Positive Background of Hindu Sociology* (1937) also mentions Seal's work appreciatively.

[5] This is a Bengali translation of Nirmal Kumar Bose's original lecture in English titled 'Brajendranath Seal as a Social Thinker' at the Symposium on the Birth Centenary of Acharya Brajendranath Seal at the Bose Institute Lecture Hall, Calcutta, 1965. Translated to Bengali by Debarshi Talukdar.

historical survey of literary art since the French Revolution, and the Neo-Romantic movement in Bengali literature' (Mukherjee, 1965).

## Brajendranath Seal Continues to Provoke Contemporary Scholars

So far we have travelled through discourses that characterized Seal as more than a historical phenomenon. This exploratory review brought out many issues that continue to provoke our critical thinking. Nineteenth-century Bengali intellectuals and reformers still attract scholarly attention for how, in a modernity ushered by colonialism, they provoked critical thinking with a notion of self-assertion. The challenge Seal faced in reconciling two different worldviews through modern methods still remains, though with more complexities of a post-colonial world. The dominating historical viewpoint still looks through the 'developed/underdeveloped' categories, and the advancement flows from the Euro-American culture to the non-Western world. So the fight for equality of knowledge is renewed in a new context. The hegemonic knowledge is being challenged more from the post-colonial condition today and carries the critical thinking culture that our early modern thinkers practiced. So it is not surprising that Seal (and other thinkers from his time) still provides a resource when one analyses a present problem of history and philosophy of science and traces the genealogically to thinkers like him. A recent article read Seal's essay on Ram Mohan Roy closely to explore his early Hegelian influence and relates it to the conceptualization of civil society that would remain problematic in the post-colonial situation (Chatterjee, 2010). Eric Dorman's article thoroughly reviews literature on South Asian science and religion discourse critically to show how the scientific discourses from this region has been doubted to be 'speculative' and of lesser value by the Western scholars. This only echoes what Seal said about the Eurocentric bias of Western scholars (Dorman, 2011). In a recent chapter of a book, a philosopher studying Seal's 'disenchantment' with Hegel commented:

> Having imbibed the wisdom of the East and the West, he developed his own philosophy characterized by syncretism, internationalism and interdisciplinarity. He drew the attention of the Western world to the scientific temper of the Indian mind garnering evidence from the ancient Indian philosophical treatises. He was the architect of the subject 'Indian philosophy' as we study it today. His philosophy of education and academic administration are still relevant. (Chatterjee, 2015)

When we now have more critical studies engaging with texts from our cultural past, Seal's teachings and influence is a living thing and not a dead object of history.

## References

Acharya, P. (1986, April 26). Development of modem language text-books and the social context in 19th century Bengal. *Economic and Political Weekly*, Vol. *21*(17), 745–751.

———. (1995, April 1). Bengali 'bhadralok' and educational development in 19th century Bengal. *Economic and Political Weekly*, *30*(13), 670–673.

Basu, A.R. (2013). The birth of psychology in India. In G. Mishra (Ed.), *Psychology and psychoanalysis. A series on history of science, philosophy and culture in Indian civilization* (Vol. XI, Part 3, pp. 91–116). New Delhi:

Centre for Studies in Civilizations (CSC) for the Project of History of Indian Science, Philosophy and Culture (PHISPC).

Bhattacharya, K.C. (1964). Reminiscences. In Saroj Kumar Das (Ed.). *Acharya Brajendranath Seal birth centenary souvenir* (p. 52). Calcutta: Indian Statistical Institute (ISI).

Bose, G. (1938). *Progress of science in India during the past twenty-five years* (p. 336). Calcutta: Indian Science Congress, Baptist Mission Press.

Bose, N.K. (2016). Samājcintak Brajendranath Seal. In N.N. Chakrabarty (Ed.), *Smarane Manane Brajendranath Seal* (pp. 35–38). Kolkata: Alochonachakra.

Chakraborti, K.B. (1964). Reminiscences. In Saroj Kumar Das (Ed.). *Acharya Brajendranath Seal birth centenary souvenir* (p. 56). Calcutta: ISI.

Chatterjee, A. (2010). Welfare, personalism and Hegel in the colonial night: The forgotten readings of Brajendranath Seal. *Indian Journal of Social Work*, *71*(2), 145–166.

———. (2015). Brajendra Nath Seal: A disenchanted Hegelian. In S. Deshpande (Ed.), *Philosophy in Colonial India* (p. 81). New Delhi: Springer India.

Chatterjee, P. (2008). Foreword (S. Roy, Trans.). In *The observant owl: Kaliprasanna Sinha's Hootum Pyanchar Naksha* (p. xi). Ranikhet: Permanent Black.

Chattopadhyay, A. (1999). *Ananta eshanā, Brajendranāth Sīl, Jīban O Cintā*. Calcutta: Dipa Prakashana.

Chaudhuri, K., & Chaudhuri, P. (Eds). (1978). *Kalkātā Chāpākhānā* (p. 16). Calcutta: Naba-yuvak Sangha.

Cornelissen, R.J.M., Mishra, M., & Varma, S. (Eds). (2014). *Foundations and applications of Indian psychology*. Delhi: Pearson.

Dorman, E.R. (2011). Hinduism and science: The state of the South Asian Science and religion discourse. *Zygon*, *46*(3), 593–619.

Ghosh, T.K. (Ed.). (2013). *Bānglā Racanā: Brajendranāth Seal*. Calcutta: Patralekha.

Gupta, S., Gupta, P.K., & Gupta, S. (2014). Brajendra Nath Seal: A sesquicentenary birth anniversary tribute. *Current Science*, *106*(5), 760–762.

Harsha, N.M., & Nagaraja, T.N. (2010). The history of Hindu chemistry: A critical review. *Ancient Science of Life*, *30*(2), 58–61.

Indian Statistical Institute. (1964). *Acharya Brajendranath Seal birth centenary souvenir*. Calcutta: Author.

Kakar, S. (1982). *Shamans, mystics and doctors*. Delhi: OUP.

Majumdar, R.C. (1964). Reminiscences. In *Acharya Brajendranath Seal birth centenary souvenir* (p. 64). Calcutta: ISI.

Mandal, H. (1999). *Acharya Brajendra Nath Seal (1864–1938): A tribute*. Midnapore.

Mohanty, J.N. (2014). Indian philosophy. In *Encyclopædia Britannica*. Retrieved 21 August 2014, from Encyclopædia Britannica Online http://www.britannica.com/EBchecked/topic/285905/Indian-philosophy

Mukherjee, K. (1965). *Keats in India*. Retrieved 15 June 2016, from http://www.yabaluri.org/triveni/cdweb/keatsinindiajan67.htm

Mukerjee, R. (1997). *India: The dawn of a new era: An autobiography*. New Delhi: Radha Publications.

Mukherjee, S. (2014). *Swārdha Shato Barshe Āchāryya Brajendra Nāth Seal. Nāgarik*, *7*, 34–48.

Mukherjee, S.N. (1977). *Calcutta: Myths and history* (p. 3). Calcutta: Subarnarekha.

Nandy, A. (1983). *The intimate enemy: Loss and recovery under colonialism*. Delhi: OUP.

———. (1995). *The savage freud*. Delhi: OUP.

Nandi, S.K. (1965). Studies in the aesthetics of Acharya Brojendra Nath Seal. *The Journal of Aesthetics and Art Criticism*, *24*(1, Oriental Aesthetics, Autumn), 53–58.

n.d. (Preface authors: B. C. Chatterjee, Swami Madhavananda and Benoy Kumar Sarkar). (1938). *The religions of the world* (Vol. I, pp. 107–115). Calcutta: The Ramakrishna Mission Institute of Culture.

Pal, P. (1984). *Mahāmanishā Brajendranāth: Bisvabikhyāta Bidyābāridhi Brajendranāth Sīl Mahāsayer Jībaner Kichu Kathā*. Calcutta: ISI.

Pal, R.K., & Bandyopadhyay, S. (1984). *Brajendranāth Sīl Ebam Anyānya*. Calcutta: Riddhi-India.

Paranjpe, A. (2010). Theories of self and cognition: Indian psychological perspectives. *Psychology and Developing Societies*, *22*(1), 5–48.

Paranjpe, A. (2014). On getting best of both the worlds. *Psychological Studies*, *59*(2), 107–109.

Roy, S.B., & Sen, S.K. (2010, December 25). Scientific research papers by native Bengali authors during the 19th century. *Current Science*, *99*(12), 1849–1857.

Roy, T. (1995). Disciplining the printed text: Colonial and nationalist surveillance of Bengali literature. In P. Chatterjee (Ed.). *Texts of power: Emerging disciplines in colonial Bengal* (p. 30). Calcutta: Samya.

Sarcar, B.B. (1964). Acharya Brajendranath Seal: A life sketch. In Saroj Kumar Das (Ed.). *Acharya Brajendranath Seal birth centenary souvenir* (p. 13). Calcutta: ISI.

Sarkar, I. (2014, January–December). Philosophy of life of Acharya Brajendranath Seal: Exposition and beyond. *Philosophy and Progress, LV–LVI* (Jan-Dec), 11.

Seal, B. (1915). *The positive sciences of the ancient Hindus*. London, New York, Bombay, Calcutta and Madras: Longmans, Green and Co.

Sen, K.C. (1964). Reminiscences. In Saroj Kumar Das (Ed.). *Acharya Brajendranath Seal birth centenary souvenir* (p. 58). Calcutta: ISI.

Sengupta, D. (2002). Mechanicalcutta: Industrialisation, new media in the 19th century. In Ravi S. Vasudevan, Jeebesh Bagchi, Ravi Sundaram, Monica Narula, Geert Lovink & Shuddhabrata Sengupta (Eds). *Sarai reader 2002: The cities of everyday life* (pp. 149–150). Delhi: CSDS.

Srinivas, M.N., & Panini, M.N. (1973). Development of sociology and social anthropology in India. *Sociological Bulletin*, *22*(2), 186.

Tagore, R. (1964). To Brajendranath Seal: A tribute (K.C. Sen, Trans.) In *Acharya Brajendranath Seal birth centenary 1864–1964 souvenir* (p. 2). Calcutta: ISI.

Thompson, E. (1964). Reminiscences. In *Acharya Brajendranath Seal birth centenary souvenir* (p. 59). Calcutta: ISI. (Originally a broadcast talk from Empire Transmission III, 26 January 1939 at 4:20–4:35 pm, London).

Weatherly, U.G. (1911, November). The first universal races congress. *American Journal of Sociology*, *17*(3), 319.

# 3

# Girindrasekhar Bose

(1886–1953)

## Divya G. Mukherjee

Girindrasekhar Bose, DSc, MB, FNI, one of the illuminaries and founder of the Indian Psychological Association, was born in Darbhanga (Bihar) on 30 January 1886. Being the youngest of nine siblings, his parentage consisted of his father Chandrasekhar Bose, well-known for his exhaustive learning on Indian Philosophy and heritage, who worked as the Dewan of the Darbhanga Raj Estate and mother, Laxmimani Devi. However, the ancestral home of the Bose family was at Birnagar, in the district of Nadia in West Bengal (Sinha, 1953).

Following early years of schooling at Darbhanga, Girindrasekhar came over to Calcutta with his father and family members. Though he was not studious in his early life, his intelligence earned him good marks in the examination. In 1903, at the age of 17, he got married to Indumati, who was then a 10-year-old girl. Later, Girindrasekhar completed graduation in science in 1905 from Presidency College, Calcutta, and secured record marks in chemistry honours, which possibly still remains unsurpassed. Following graduation, he entered Calcutta Medical College and began his career as a medical practitioner after obtaining his medical degree in 1910.

## Girindrasekhar Bose: Interest in Magic

From an early period of his life, Girindrasekhar was much interested in magic and hypnotism, which later transformed into interest in the deeper workings of the mind. Due to this inclination, he gradually moved towards psychiatric practice and to the study of the science of psychology. In 1917, Bose took his master's degree (MSc) in experimental psychology from the University of Calcutta in its first batch and stood first in the final examination. In 1921, the University of Calcutta conferred on him the doctor of science (DSc) degree on his thesis titled 'The Concept of Repression' (Mitra, 1953).

As a medical practitioner, he had to struggle in his early days. Despite that, he used to treat many patients absolutely free of cost. He also used to make home visits to care for his patients. His clientele ranged from the poor destitute to the aristocratic Bengali families on the one hand and the European, Burmese, and Chinese community patients on the other (Sinha, 1953).

## The Background

Girindrasekhar's medical career started gradually moving towards psychiatric practice, and he renewed his interest in the field of psychology in an era when the British had gained ascendancy over all other European powers in India. The colonial history of psychiatry needs to be re-examined in a wider perspective to evaluate its achievements and pitfalls. Concepts of health, mind, and body in the Western colonial medicine system evolved different meanings as compared to traditional Eastern concepts. Moreover, scientific achievements, reforms of services, and legal establishments of the colonial era had conflicting and derogatory effects on the Eastern traditional medical practices. Indigenous practices and local healing methods were discarded as 'unscientific' and 'superstitious' by the predators of Western colonial medicine. The treatment practices by the East India Company doctors were clinical approaches similar to those practised in the nineteenth century in England, with emphasis on physiological and organic causes of insanity. There was reluctance to explore psychological models of therapy and the emphasis was on moral therapy. However, in the early twentieth-century, knowledge of Indian languages was made mandatory for the East India Company doctors. Acquiring local language facilitated the recognition of indigenous knowledge. In 1918, the hospital for the European insane was instituted in Ranchi (Bihar) with Colonel Berkeley Hill as its first superintendent. Berkeley Hill used psychoanalysis, occupational therapy, amusements, and hypnosis for the treatment of the patients. He also attempted to formulate classification of mental disorders. Girindrasekhar Bose had exchanged letters with him and wrote a touching obituary in the *Indian Journal of Psychology* when he died in 1944 (Bose & Berkeley-Hill, 1944).

*Girindrasekhar Bose*

Under these circumstances, he founded the Indian Psychoanalytic Society in 1922 which was immediately accepted as a constituent member of the International Psychoanalytical Association. Bose by then had mastered the technique of hypnosis as he was already experimenting on psychological methods of treating psychiatric patients. The development of psychoanalysis in India, thus, took a distinctive course which was unique of its kind.

During this period, the government in Bengal was running a few hospitals under the Indian Lunacy Act with its routine administration. There was neither any mental health programme nor any positive attitude towards the unfortunate victims of the various kinds of mental disorders. Calcutta, the second largest city of the British Empire, had no state mental hospital or even a lunatic asylum. The government had only a small mental observation ward at Bhowanipore for the purpose of certification of 'lunatics' in a court of law (Lumbini, 1966).

*Medical case record of the psychological clinic, Carmichael Medical College, written by Girindrasekhar Bose*

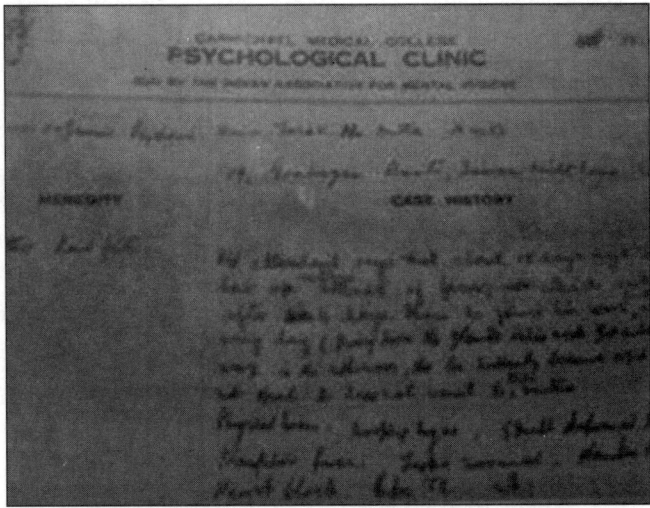

Following the census conducted by the British Government in 1921, it was observed that the community lunatics received little sympathy and most mentally ill were confined to jails with a small percentage admitted in hospitals. On 23 August 1928, in a meeting held in Shimla, the Indian Association for Mental Hygiene was formed, with Colonel Berkeley Hill being its first president. This association was modelled in parity with the USA and the UK where the Mental Hygiene Council was formed primarily for de-institutionalisation and community care of the mentally ill. Towards the end of 1929, the Calcutta branch of the Indian Association for Mental Hygiene was formed with five members, with Girindrasekhar Bose heading the association.

The Indian Mental Hygiene Association started an outdoor mental clinic at the Carmichael Medical College (now R.G. Kar Medical College) under the guidance of Girindrasekhar Bose on 1 May 1933. He served this institution from 1933 to 1949. The authorities of this private institution provided space, electricity, and furniture and the outpatient clinic started functioning on every Tuesdays and Thursday with two honorary medical officers assisting Bose. The only paid staff was a male attendant who was paid a monthly salary of two rupees. Again on 5 February 1940, the Indian Psychoanalytic Society established a mental hospital, namely, Lumbini Park Mental Hospital at Natore Park, Tiljala, in Calcutta. Girindrasekhar Bose played a significant role in instituting and running the hospital with no financial help from the government. The institution had to rest entirely on its own resources. In addition, grave problems arose due to the fact that the hospital started functioning in the wake of the Second World War with all its inevitable eventualities and difficulties with regard to transportation, food, and medicine supplies. The depiction of these hard times and circumstances is distinctly visible from an article in the Lumbini Park Silver Jubilee Souvenir (1966) which describes,

> Soon after starting the hospital, Japan joined the World War. Following Pearl Harbour disaster, Singapore fell to Japanese forces. Burma was in danger. Evacuees from Burma started flowing up India through hazardous dense forests and hilly terrain. Some of them lost their mental balance and became mentally sick on their way to India. In Bengal famine broke out. People rushed from village to Calcutta for food and lived on streets and footpaths. Thousands died; many fell victims to mental disorders. There were no arrangements to house them or to treat them with any care and medicines. On the top of that Japanese bombs fell in Calcutta and the city was largely evacuated. Food supply became extremely uncertain, quality of food deteriorated; many among the hospital staff left their jobs and ran to their village homes for their safety. (Lumbini, 1966)

> Towards the end of the War and while the country was yet trying to take its breath, came a terrific communal riot followed by the partition of the country into India and Pakistan. Refugees started swarming in and around Calcutta, and many became mentally sick. There was an acute economic crisis in the society. And with still no assistance from the government, the condition of the hospital became precarious, hardly being able to balance its income and expenditure. Notwithstanding the array of problems, the workers of Lumbini Park to a man stood up and faced ordeals one after another with unflinching faith in the future of their institution. (Lumbini, 1966)

## Affiliations

Girindrasekhar Bose has the unique distinction of being the first physician in India to treat mental patients with the help of psychoanalysis. He was not only the founder of psychoanalysis in India but truly the founder of the Indian Psychoanalytical Society in India in 1922. After graduation from Calcutta Medical School, initially he worked as a lecturer of physiology in the same institution from 1911–1915. From the medical school, he shifted his interest to psychology, joining the MSc course in 1916. He also was the in-charge of the first psychiatric clinic of India opened by him in 1933 at Carmichael Medical College (now R.G. Kar Medical College), Calcutta, and served till 1949. He was the university professor and head of the Department of Psychology and served the department from the 1929 to March 1940. He was the founder of Lumbini Park Mental Hospital in Calcutta in 1940 and started a city clinic at 14 Parsibagan Lane, Calcutta, for the benefit of outdoor patients. He was also a founder of 'Bodhyana', a day school for mentally handicapped children in 1949 at Calcutta.

Bose was the founder fellow of the National Institute of Sciences of India (FNI) in 1935. He was the president of the psychology section of the India Science Congress Association twice—in 1933 and 1938. He was also a Fellow of the Royal Asiatic Society of Bengal. He was the founder editor of *Samiksa*, an English journal of the Indian Psychoanalytical Society, from 1947 till his death and the associate editor of *International Journal of Psycho-analysis* from 1922 till his death.

## Awards and Recognition

Girindrasekhar Bose passed with double honours in BSc from the University of Calcutta in 1905 securing high marks in both chemistry and physiology. He also passed with flying colours in the MB examination in 1910. He was first-class first in MSc (experimental psychology) securing the highest marks in the science group of the year 1917 and winning the H.C. Gossain gold medal and cash prize money of ₹500 only. He was the first DSc (doctor of science) in psychology in India from the University of Calcutta in 1921. He received the Sir J.C. Bose Scholarship from Bangiya Sahitya Parishad awarded for coining technical terms of psychology and psychoanalysis in Bengali. His books and research papers were highly acclaimed by eminent researchers in India and abroad.

## Contribution to Indian Psychology

Girindrasekhar Bose's contribution to Indian psychology is immense, wide, diverse, and need intense in-depth exploration. He was a man of outstanding ability and an acknowledged authority on mental abnormalities. He made original contributions in the study of the origin and treatment of mental disorders and threw new light on the nature of the unconscious.

Though, he initially experimented with psychological methods of treating mental patients which was closely akin to psychoanalysis, he did not have any access to the original works or English translations published in the realm of psychoanalysis. Being acquainted with this method through only a few journal articles, Bose went ahead to submit his famous thesis titled 'The Concept of Repression' for which he was conferred the doctor of science degree in 1921. Bose put forward the theory of 'opposite wishes' where he explained that for every wish in our mind there exists an opposite wish. Exemplifying, a wish to torture simultaneously exists with a wish to be tortured, the wish to kill couples with the wish to get killed, and the wish to donate exists with refusal to divulge with one's belongings. These opposite wishes, according to Bose, repress one another if they have the same intensity, but if one is more intense than the other, then the former gets expressed while the other delves into the unconscious to find its way and expression in same form or the other.

In those days, not many people in India, even among the men of medicine or psychology, had heard of Sigmund Freud's and neither were any of Freud's work available in the country. Yet, following receipt of a copy of Bose's thesis 'Concept of Repression', Sigmund Freud wrote

> It was a great and pleasant surprise that the first book on a Psychoanalytic subject which came to us from the part of the World (India) should display so good a knowledge of Psychoanalysis, so deep an insight into its difficulties and so much of deep-going original thought.

Though Sigmund Freud acknowledged Bose's contribution, he however disagreed with his theory of opposite wishes, as he wrote, 'Your theory of the opposite wish appear to me to stress rather a formal element than a dynamic factor' (Bose & Freud, 1964). But simultaneously, he later admitted about this theory,

> I see that we did neglect the fact of the existence of opposite wishes from the three sources of bisexuality (male and female), ambivalence (love–hate) and the opposition of active-passive. These phenomenon have to be worked into our system to make us see what modification or corrections are necessary and how far we can acquiesce to your ideas. (Bose & Freud, 1964)

The debate about the differences was explored much later by an Austrian researcher, faculty in 'cultural studies' in Danube University in the late twentieth century. Christiane Hartnack in her publication *Psychoanalysis in Colonial India* (2001) argues for Bose that he had propounded an original theory which did not flourish due to the overpowering dominance of the British Empire in colonial India. The alternative path of delving into the unconscious, the 'opposite wishes', required more attention from analysts and further ramification of the innovative idea.

Apart from 'Concept of Repression', Bose published several papers on 'free association method' (1926), 'dream' (1930a), 'ambivalence' (1938), 'sex in psychoanalysis' (1927b), and 'nature and genesis of love' (1947) in various journals, which are still regarded as the groundwork of psychoanalytical studies in India. His article published in the *British Journal of Psychology* on 'the reliability of psychoanalytical findings' (1923) is considered to be significantly viable even today. But his in-depth studies on the 'psychological outlook in Hindu Philosophy', the *Patanjali's* 'Yoga sutra', reflects the Eastern thoughts and the confluence the Western methods and Indian philosophical doctrines.

Girindrasekhar Bose not only dealt with psychoanalysis but also emphasised on quantification methods in psychology. During his tenure in the Department of Psychology, University of Calcutta, several psychological tests/apparatuses were devised by him and his associates. A few among these tests were 'Word Association Tests' (with M.N. Banerjee and N.N. Chatterjee, 1953), 'Group Matching Tests' (with M. Deb, 1940), 'Sand Motor Test' (1927a), 'Group Pass Along' (1933), 'Big Muscle Ergograph' (1949a), 'Dotting Test' (1949b), and 'Neurotic Questionnaire' (1950). Not only were these tests devised, standardization and norms of usage were also constructed. Bose significantly contributed to the development of the first psychological laboratory in India and stressed the necessity for objective quantification of psychological constructs. He also dealt with the realm of psycholinguistics and its significance in understanding psychopathology. In his publications, he tried to find the inner psychological meaning of language (1950, 1951) and its usage. Studying languages such as Sanskrit and German at a much later age, he was interested in understanding mental concepts described in various languages. Bose's contribution ranged from the formulation of classification of mental disorders (1951) to the study of individual categories of mental disorders (e.g., periodic depression or unipolar depression).

Girindrasekhar Bose was a versatile genius. Apart from contributing on psychoanalysis and psychology he published his interpretation of the *Puranas*, annotations of the Bhagavad Gita, and many other treatises on ancient Indian history, philosophy, and mythology.

He had also contributed significantly in the organisational aspect of developing the Department of Psychology, University of Calcutta. During his tenure in the Department of Psychology, gradual expansion in terms of infrastructure and manpower development occurred with increase in faculty positions The applied psychology department was opened in 1938. A certificate course in applied psychology was started to train personnel who were interested in social work in 1945. During his tenure in the Department of Psychology, all-round development was distinctly visible. Not only the advancement of abnormal psychology, but the same was also true for experimental psychology, general psychology, tests, and application of psychology in different fields such as industrial psychology and organizational psychology. During his period, the department also started working jointly with different industries, helped in the selection of appropriate personnel, which in turn increased the production and thereby social commitments.

While continuing to work in early 1949, he met with a stroke, following which he gradually took retirement. He had to bear with prolonged physical sufferings of his illness, though his mental alertness was unaffected till his death on 3 June 1953.

# References

Bose, G. (1923). The reliability of psycho-analytical findings. *British Journal of Psychology*, *3*(2), 105–115.

———. (1926). The free-association method in psychoanalysis. *Indian Journal of Psychology*, *1*, 187–199.

———. (1927a). Sand motor test. *Indian Journal of Psychology*, *2*, 80–83.

———. (1927b). Sex in psychoanalysis. *Indian Journal of Psychology*, *2*, 107–126.

———. (1930a). Dream. *Indian Journal of Psychology*, *5*, 38–87.

———. (1930b). The psychological outlook in Hindu philosophy. *Indian Journal of Psychology*, *5*, 119–146.

———. (1933). Group pass long. *Indian Journal of Psychology*, *8*, 77–79.

———. (1938). Ambivalence. *Indian Journal of Psychology*, *13*, 1–19.

———. (1944). Owen Berkeley-Hill: In memoriam. *Indian Journal of Psychology*, *19*, 145–146.

———. (1947). The nature and genesis of love. *Samiksa*, *1*, 118–136.

———. (1949a). Big muscle ergograph. In S.K. Bose (Ed.), *Psychological testing and survey*. Calcutta: Applied Psychology Section, Department of Psychology, Calcutta University.

———. (1949b). *Dotting test*. In S.K. Bose (Ed.), *Psychological testing and survey*. Calcutta: Applied Psychology Section, Department of Psychology, Calcutta University.

———. (1950). Neurotic questionnaire. *Indian Journal of Psychology*, *25*, 95–97.

———. (1951). Classification of mental disorder. *Samiksa*, *5*, 149–152.

———. (1957). The yoga sutras, *Samiksa*, *11*, 44–63, 73–138, 157–185, 217–237.

Bose, S.K., & Deb, M. (1997). Experimental psychology: Its debut in India. *Psychological Research Journal*, *3*, 79–101.

Ganguli, M., Bose, G., Banerjee, M.N., & Chatterjee, N.N. (1953). *Word–association test.* Report on the working of the section 1942–1943. Calcutta: Applied Psychology Section, Department of Psychology, University College of Science.

Hartnack, C. (2001). *Psychoanalysis in colonial India.* New Delhi: Oxford University Press.

Indian Psychoanalytical Society. (1964). *Bose–Freud correspondence: The beginnings of psychoanalysis in India.* Calcutta: Indian Psychoanalytical Society.

Law, S., Ganguli, D., & Bose, G. (1950). Psychological study of language-1. *Samiksa*, *4*, 26–29.

Lumbini Park. (1966). *A brief outline.* Lumbini Park Silver jubilee souvenir, 25–30.

Mitra, S.C. (1953). Professor Girindrasekhar Bose. *Samiksa* (Special number), *8*, 57–61.

Sinha, T.C. (1953). A short life sketch of Girindrasekhar Bose. *Samiksa* (Special number), *8*, 62–74.

# 4

# Narendranath Sengupta

(1889–1944)

## Hari Shanker Asthana

Narendranath Sengupta was born on 23 December 1889, at Faridpur in Bengal, India, to Muktakashi and Turuni Charan. He married Kamala in 1916 and had two daughters and a son.

*Narendranath Sengupta*

Sengupta's early education took place in his hometown. When the family moved to Calcutta (now Kolkata), he studied there. During that period, the elite in Bengal were involved in the freedom struggle and the younger generation was drawn into it. At school, Sengupta was attracted by it. He hoisted the national flag in his school for which he was rusticated by the colonial rulers. The highly educated nationalist leaders founded the National College of Bengal where German- and American-educated professors were employed. Sengupta was admitted for his schooling there. There he had the privilege of studying English under the great revolutionary and highly educated philosopher Sri Aurobindo (founder of the ashram in Pondicherry) and studied Pali under Sri Goswami, the great scholar of the language.

Seven students from the college were selected for study abroad in different countries. Sengupta was to go to Harvard University. He spent 3 years there (from 1910 to 1913) earning his PhD in philosophy with distinction, with a dissertation on anti-intellectualism in Western philosophy. He was honoured with the membership of Phi Beta Kappa. He had earned the degree from the Department of Philosophy, then chaired by the famous philosopher-psychologist William James, and he had Floyd Allport, brother of Gordon Allport, the personality psychologist, as his classmate. Toward the end of his stay at Harvard in 1913, Sir Ashutosh Mukerjee, the great attorney who was also the vice-chancellor of the University of Calcutta, advised him to study psychology before returning to initiate study of modern psychology at the university.

Accordingly, Sengupta studied with Hugo Munsterberg, chairman of the psychology department at Harvard. As is well known, William James had moved over from psychology to philosophy department to put Munsterberg in his stead. He had got Wundt's student Hugo Munsterberg from Leipzig. Munterberg had disagreed with his teacher Wundt for he advocated what he called 'action psychology'. His utilitarian approach was closer to the American ethos. Sengupta also had the opportunity to learn from Holt and Yerkes. Later, he went to E.B. Titchener's famous Cornell laboratory before returning to India in 1914.

Sengupta joined as lecturer in philosophy at the University of Calcutta where he was required to teach philosophy from 1915. A year later, he was required to organize courses in psychology and, as the head of the newly created psychology department, in 1916, he set up the first laboratory of experimental psychology in the country. There he trained the early teachers of modern psychology, many of whom distinguished themselves later. One of them was S.K. Bose who was lent out to the Department of Philosophy, then chaired by the well-known philosophy scholar Haridas Bhattacharya at the University of Dacca (now Dhaka in Bangladesh) to set up a psychology programme including a laboratory in 1921. In 1913, Rabindranath Tagore had gone to lecture in the USA. Sengupta met him; thereafter he talked and wrote on Tagore's national educational programme which was consonant with the Indian ethos.

The Calcutta Psychology Department was strengthened gradually, with the addition of M.N. Bannerji, who initiated studies in industrial psychology and S. Sinha, trained in Europe, as well as Suhrit Chandra Mitra, the most influential Wundtian student in India who had gone to study at Leipzig and earned his doctorate working under Felix Krueger, Wundt's successor at Leipzig. Sengupta had met Krueger earlier in Boston when he was in the country.

> The wave of Indian nationalist psychology in Calcutta soon began transmitting its pressure to other institutions in the subcontinent…. M.V. Gopalaswamy established the University of Mysore Laboratory in 1924 (*author's addition*: after working under Charles Spearman in the UK). Psychology Departments soon arose at Lahore (before Partition) under Paras Ram, Mohd. Aslam and Mohan Ganguli, and at Patna, Lucknow, and in Aligarh respectively, in 1930s. (Manjopra, 2014)

Having served at the University of Calcutta till 1928, Sengupta was invited to the University of Lucknow as professor and chairman of the Department of Philosophy. The department then consisted of N.N. Sengupta, PhD (Harvard) as professor; Mr Edward Ahmed Shah, BLitt (Oxford) as Reader; and Kali Prasad, MA, LLB (Allahabad) as lecturer. Raj Narain, MA (Lucknow), who was working as a research assistant, joined as temporary lecturer in 1942. A year later, Hari Shanker Asthana, MA (Lucknow), then a research fellow under Sengupta, was appointed as temporary lecturer in 1943.

*April 1943. In front of the first Psychology Laboratory (enclosed veranda at the end of north-west wing of the main university building, housing Faculty of Arts). Standing (left to right) Mr Kali Prasad, Lecturer (going for a game of tennis); N.N. Sengupta, Head, Department of Philosophy; Haridas Bhattacharya, Head, Department of Philosophy, University of Dacca (presently Dhaka in Bangladesh), visiting viva-voce examiner in philosophy); and Mr Raj Narain, Temporary Lecturer in philosophy.*

Sengupta had acquired proficiency in a number of languages in addition to his mother tongue Bengali. These were Pali, Sanskrit, English, German, and French. He was also a very jovial person; when something humorous occurred, his laughter would resonate in the whole corridor adjoining his room.

Sengupta was Fellow of the National Institute of Sciences of India and the Indian National Science Academy. Sengupta proposed and got psychology accepted as one of the sections of the Indian Science Congress Association in 1923. A year later, in 1924, he founded the Indian Psychological Association, the first organization of psychologists in the country. In 1925, he started the first psychology journal in the country—the Indian *Journal of Psychology,* acting as its first editor.

The psychology laboratory then (around 1939, when the author joined as a student) comprised a couple of kymographs, Hipp's chronoscope, a few stop watches, a time marker with a stylus to mark on (then smoked) kymograph paper for recording, a few aesthesiometers, telegraphic keys, etc., all imported earlier from Palmers in the UK. Owing to the Second World War, all import was later suspended. Sengupta started improvising to teach and train research scholars. He devised a lip key, hooked to the chronoscope to record 'free associative' reaction time to Jung's list, an assembled pneumograph, a time marker made out of steel strips scratching on smoked kymograph paper, a Mosso's ergograph, a 'sand-motor kymograph' (based on 'the old sand-clock' model), a weight pulling the string (as sand trickled down from the upper to lower vessel through the narrow opening) attached to the recording device, and a makeshift Vernier chronoscope, fall-type tachistoscope with adjustable exposure intervals, and he advised the author to fabricate a device for demonstrating the Phi-phenomenon (He read Wertheimer's article in German, translating for the author). He was happy when he saw a makeshift device made using a reduction screen, an epistecotister mounted on a small electric motor whose speed could be varied with a rheostat to expose the vertical and horizontal lines). Sengupta's ingenuity was very important as no entrepreneur had yet ventured to make psychological instruments in the country. He instructed the local technicians to fabricate psychological instruments.

Sengupta was held in very high esteem by his colleagues. He was fond of tea, and the common philosophy teachers' sitting room was frequented by some very senior professors around afternoon teatime. S.N. Dasgupta of botany, B.N. Dasgupta of commerce, A.V. Rao of English, who later became vice-chancellor and used to contribute humorous weekly articles to the *Pioneer*, an English daily, were frequent visitors at tea. The jokes provoked laughter and Sengupta's laughter would resonate in the entire corridor of the building.

He published three books. In 1928, *Introduction to Social Psychology* was published from London, Heath (co-authored by Radhakamal Mukerji). This had a foreword by Jerome Davis, and an introduction by Robert M. Yerkes. In 1941, *Heredity in Mental Traits* was published by Macmillan & Co. and *Mental Growth and Decline* was published in 1942.

Owing to his broad interests and language proficiency he published in various areas such as anthropology, sociology, philosophy, psychology, religion, etc. He had deep knowledge, not only of Western thought but also a very good understanding of *Shaivism*, *Vaishnavism*, and of Sufism. Some of the papers published by him are (Sengupta, 1921, 1926a, 1926b, 1928, 1940, 1943, n.d.).

Sengupta passed away on 13 June 1944 at Lucknow in Uttar Pradesh. It was unfortunate that Sengupta's magnum opus 'Mechanism of Ecstasy' got lost in the confusion following the stroke and his demise. His son Arun donated his father's library of books to the Central Tagore Library of the University of Lucknow. A fairly detailed paper by Raj Narain (1935) sums up Sengupta's major contributions to the profession.

## Notes

Material for this chapter was collected from the following:

Dr Sengupta's architect grandson Arindam and various records, some of which were excavated by the engineer son of the author. Arindam also retrieved some records of his grandfather's correspondence from old records of his grandfather; the paper was old and brittle. He laboriously scanned them and communicated to the author. The author had the privilege of being (perhaps the only surviving) student, a research fellow, and, for a brief period of 6 months, a lecturer in the then Department of Philosophy till the professor's demise in summer 1944 at Lucknow. During that period, the author had the opportunity of learning many facts from the professor himself.

Interested readers may like to see the author's paper 'Modern Psychology in India: Reminiscences and Reflections', including the notes at the end in (Asthana, 2008).

# References

Asthana, H.S. (2008). Modern psychology in India: Reminiscences and reflections. *Psychological Studies, 53*(1), 1–6.

Manjopra, K. (2014). *Age of entanglement: German and Indian intellectuals across empire.* Cambridge, Massachusettes: Harvard University Press.

Narain, Raj. (1935). Biographical Memoirs of Fellows of the Indian National Science Academy, Volume 8. Retrieved 5 July 2017, from https://insaindia.res.in/bm.php.

Sengupta, N. (1921). On the nature of immediate experience in the light of contemporary epistemological discussions. *Sir Ausotosh Mukerjee Silver Jubilee Volumes* (Vol. 1: Arts & letters). Calcutta: Calcutta University and Baptist Mission Press.

———. (1926a). Mental work in isolation and in group (Jt. with C.P.N. Sinha). *Indian Journal of Psychological Medicine, 1*, 106–110.

———. (1926b). Psychology, its present development and outlook. *Indian Journal of Psychological Medicine, I*(1), 9.

———. (1928). The field of race psychology. *Indian Journal of Psychological Medicine, 3*, 59–68.

———. (1940). *Doctrine of sudden ecstasy in Shaivism and Vaishsnavism.* Sengupta Collection, Tagore Library, University of Lucknow, India.

———. (1943). *A study in spiritual 'leftism': An aspect of Vamamarga or the Sahaja cult.* Sengupta Collection, Tagore Library, University of Lucknow, India.

———. (1946). Attention and mystical discipline: A psychological approach: In *Bharata-Kaumudi II. : Studies in Indology in honour of Dr. Radha Kumud Mukerji* (pp. 779–816). Allahabad: The Indian Press Ltd.

# 5

## Suhridchandra Mitra

(1895–1962)

### Nrisingha Kumar Bhattacharyya and Dipes Chandra Nath

The great psychologist Suhridchandra Mitra was born on 28 October 1895, in North Kolkata, West Bengal. His family originally belonged to Pani Shaola village of Haripal in Hooghly district, West Bengal. But everything of his family revolved around Kolkata only. His father, Bhubanmohan Mitra, was a lawyer who practiced in Ranaghat Court. His mother, Upendra Mohini Devi, was a pious housewife. Suhridchandra was the youngest offspring of his parents. He had six brothers and three sisters. His father also kept himself absorbed in literary and other cultural activities besides practicing as a lawyer in the Ranaghat Court. Suhridchandra grew up in a highly educated, joint family of middle socio-economic status of that period.

*Suhridchandra Mitra*

Suhridchandra's educational life began in the Metropolitan Institution in Kolkata. Because of his poor health, he had to get himself admitted in the school a bit late, at the age of 8 years. He lost his father when he had just started his school education. He could continue his studies only because he was a member of a joint family. He was very bright and this brightness was manifested from his very boyhood. He crossed every barrier in his life. He got himself well prepared for appearing at the entrance examination in 1911. But at that time, Beriberi disease assumed an epidemic form in Kolkata, and as ill luck would have it, Suhridchandra Mitra fell prey to this disease. He had to stop his studies. He even faced the danger of losing his eyesight. As per the advice of the doctor, he had to keep himself confined in a dark room. During this period, his guardians observed in him an aptitude for music. They gave him the opportunity to play on the violin and within a considerable period he became a good violinist. The violin was his companion throughout his life.

Because of his illness, Suhridchandra Mitra had to sit for entrance examinations as a private candidate. He passed the examinations with credit in 1913, and from then on no obstacle could thwart his progress in his academic career. He passed BA with first-class honours in philosophy in 1917 from Scottish Church College under the University of Calcutta and stood first in order of merit. At this time, the University of Calcutta started running a course in experimental psychology. Suhridchandra was interested in this course as this would allow him the opportunity to test in a laboratory what he had learned in philosophy. He got himself admitted in MA in this course, and in 1919 he passed MA in experimental psychology with first class honours, class being first in order of merit.

After passing his MA he got a job in the finance department of the Central Government of India. But he did not like this job. It was quite natural as his mind was roaming in the research laboratory of the academic world. Within a short period, an opportunity came to him through a call from Sir Ashutosh Mukherjee, the then vice-chancellor of the University of Calcutta. He responded to the call of Sir Aushutosh Mukherjee, resigned from the high-salaried job of the central government, and joined the low salaried temporary post of lecturer in the Department of Psychology, University of Calcutta, in 1920. In 1921 he was married to Uma Bhanja of a zamindar family of South 24 Parganas, West Bengal. This couple had only one child, a daughter named Alaka Mitra (Chandra).

After joining the University of Calcutta, he became engrossed in conducting experiments in the laboratory. He conducted so many experiments and became a reputed experimental psychologist, and fortune also smiled on him. He got an opportunity to conduct research work in the first laboratory of experimental psychology at Leipzig University. He started for Leipzig in 1923. He conducted his research work on perceptual brightness of monocular and binocular vision under the supervision of Chrisman and obtained his doctorate degree in psychology in 1926. He was the first Indian psychologist who got the chance of conducting research work at the Leipzig University laboratory of experimental psychology.

On his return from Leipzig, he joined the post of lecturer in the Department of Psychology, University of Calcutta. He started experiments on different topics of psychology such as attention, perception, thinking, memory, etc., but within a short span of time his interest in experimental psychology started lessening and he became interested in psychoanalysis. Not only this, he also gave a good number of radio talks on psychoanalysis to popularize the science of psychoanalysis. He was a psychoanalyst but he never practiced it. His mission was to attract students towards this science. He did his best to do this. He also sent a paper to Sigmund Freud on psychoanalysis which was appreciated by Freud. He authored a book on psychoanalysis which made the students and general public aware of this science.

Besides, we got the evidence of his talent through a paper on 'instincts' which resembles the ideas expressed in a book by Gardner Murphy. Murphy's book was published later than the paper written by Suhridchandra. He was honoured with the post of president in the Indian Philosophy Congress in 1932. In that congress, he presented a new theory of 'emotion', which earned him fame in our country as well as abroad. In 1935, he delivered a lecture on the utility of psychology in everyday life and work in the National Science Congress, which revolutionized the thought of the science fraternity. In this way, he spread the knowledge of different aspects of psychology to the specialists, and through radio talks and articles in newspapers to the ordinary people. He never desired to keep psychology confined within the boundary of the psychology laboratory. Rather, he wanted to deliver the fruits of psychology to the common mass. With this mental set-up, he was devoted to his long professional career.

In 1950 he became the professor of psychology in the University of Calcutta. After attaining this post, he became engrossed in how to spread psychology to the public in general. He could realize that the psychology department would not be able to attain a good status without the advancement of knowledge in different fields of psychology. So, as a first step, he introduced new subjects such as history of psychology and criminal psychology. As the second step, he started conducting research in the department conducive to the need of the hour. And as the third step, he thought of spreading activities of psychology in different corners of India. He did not stop here and introduced a certificate course in applied psychology in the department. This was the golden age of the department when it shined in every respect.

He was associated with different national and international organizations. He was president of the Psychological Association and the Indian Psychoanalytical Society. He was editor of the *Indian Journal of Psychology* and also of the *Indian Journal of Education*. He was a member of the Bangiya Bigyan Parisad and Sahitya Parisad. He was the second person to become Fellow of National Academy (FNA) from the Department of Psychology, University of Calcutta.

Suhridchandra was an ideal teacher. He was absorbed in studies throughout his whole life. His main thought of life was psychology and students of psychology. Let us here quote his own words:

> I had never been able to consider my teaching work as a money earning profession, but I have always taken it as a mission of my life. There is so much talk of establishing rapport before starting a psychological experiment or beginning a counselling interview; my feeling is that even an academic subject cannot be well taught to a student by anyone who has no personal ties with him.

He tendered his resignation from the Department of Psychology, University of Calcutta, at the fag end of his career and served as professor of psychology in Indian Institute of Social Welfare between 1959 and the first quarter of 1962. He died of cancer on 4 May 1962. Though he is no more with us, yet we remember him with reverence and gratitude.

# 6

# M.V. Gopalaswamy

(1896–1957)

## H.S. Eswara

At the beginning of twentieth century, during the days that higher education was making inroads in India, the Maharaja's College in Mysore was at the forefront of academic programmes in literature, philosophy, humanities, and social sciences. People thought of it as the Oxford of India and the college was privileged to have a celebrated faculty. The college included such distinguished persons on its faculty as S. Radhakrishnan (philosopher and later President of India), C.R. Reddy, K.T. Shaw, M. Hiriyanna, A.R. Wadia, K.V. Puttappa (the Poet Laureate and Jnanpith Award winner), and others. M.V. Gopalaswamy, the founder of the psychology department in the University of Mysore, was in this galaxy of academic luminaries.

*M.V. Gopalaswamy*

The details of Gopalaswamy's life and contributions are almost lost in the fogs of history. The mighty scholar published very little, and what little he published is presently untraceable. Much of what we know of him is in the form of anecdotes about his personality and achievements that his students fondly passed on to their juniors. Nevertheless, some recorded information is available in the tributes that his students paid to him in commemorative volumes and souvenirs published here and there. The references to Gopalaswamy and his work in books published outside this country (Barnes, 2004; Brock, 2006; Irvine & Berry, 1988) provide ample testimony to his role as maker of psychology in India.

Gopalaswamy was born in the present day Tamil Nadu on 31 December 1896. He hailed from a respectable family. His father, Viswanath Iyer was in the judicial service of the then Madras Presidency. His father died when Gopalaswamy was still young and he was left to the care of his mother, along with his brothers. At school, Gopalaswamy was brilliant and was interested in sports such as cricket and tennis. Later, he graduated from the prestigious Pacchiappa's College in Madras, majoring in philosophy at the Bachelors level. His next destination was the University College of London from where he obtained his BSc degree. His interest in psychology attracted him to Charles Spearman at the University of London and, working under Spearman, Gopalaswamy obtained his PhD in psychology in the year 1923. The influence of Spearman on Gopalaswamy's academic interests remained solid in his future academic career.

At the time when Gopalaswamy came back to India in 1923, the study of psychology was still a part of the curriculum of the philosophy departments in Indian universities, and the only exception was the University of Calcutta, where an independent department of psychology was established in 1916. It goes to the credit of Gopalaswamy that he started the second department of psychology in India in Maharaja's College in 1924 at the invitation of Sir Brijendranath Seal, the then vice-chancellor of the University of Mysore. It is perhaps interesting to note here that the first two departments of psychology in this country had common roots in Leipzig tradition, but this tradition was inherited through different routes. While Sengupta, the first head of Calcutta Department, had worked with Hugo Munsterberg, Gopalaswamy was a student of Charles Spearman. Both Munsterberg and Spearman were, in turn, students of Wilhelm Wundt in Leipzig. Gopalaswamy achieved the distinction of being the first professor of psychology in India at the young age of 27 years. He continued as professor and head of the Department of Psychology from 1924 to 1949, and held the position of Principal of Maharaja's college during the years 1949–1952. The efforts of Gopalaswamy in psychology gaining a status of an independent discipline of study is well acknowledged (Irvine & Berry, 1988).After his retirement from the University of Mysore, he was invited to head the Department of Psychology at All India Institute of Mental Health (now National Institute of Mental Health and Neurosciences, NIMHANS). Accepting this assignment, he served in this position from 1 April 1955 until his death on 29 June 1957. During the short stint that he had at that institute, he laid a solid foundation for psychological training as part of postgraduate programmes in mental health. Recalling the course curriculum during his days as student in the Institute of Mental Health, M.S. Thimmappa (2014) says that even anthropology formed a part of this mental health education programme, and he attributes the inclusion of such a subject in the programme to the vision of Gopalaswamy.

Gopalaswamy is regarded as a first-rate scholar, great teacher, and researcher par excellence. Writing about him, one of his students makes these glorious remarks,

> Dr. Gopalaswamy was an erudite scholar with a passion for reading, research, and teaching. He was an immensely popular professor who was able to enlighten his hearers with ease and grace. He loved the student population and they adored him. He was precise, clear and to the point and this was keenly appreciated by his students. (Vasudeva Rao, 1974)

The generations of students trained under him occupied important teaching and research positions in various universities and institutions. Included in this list of his illustrious students are B. Kuppuswamy, B. Krishnan, P. Krishnamurthy—these three succeeded him in the University of Mysore as professors and chairpersons of the department that he founded—Govindaswamy, who became the Director of All India Institute of Mental Health at Bangalore, S.K. Ramachandra Rao and H.N. Murthy, who held the position of professorship in NIMHANS. Although his main focus in psychology remained with cognitive processes a' la Spearman, it was not limited to this area. He showed interest in other areas too and encouraged and guided his students to work in such diverse fields as personality, psychological measurement, animal behaviour, psychokinesis, and Indian psychology. By the present day standards, his own research output was rather lean. Nevertheless, he promoted research by motivating and guiding his students to undertake research, both fundamental and applied. A sample of research areas that his students pursued provides ample evidence to his multifaceted interests. Kuppuswamy got his DLitt degree working on Lamarckian thesis of inheritance of acquired traits, conducting his experiments in the animal laboratory; Krishnan developed personality inventories and made studies in Indian psychology; Govindaswamy researched in the area of psychogalvanic reflex; Ramachandra Rao made in depth research in Indian Psychology; and Narayana Rao Pawar showed interest in areas of parapsychology.

Gopalaswamy never identified himself with any school of psychology, nor did he focus on any particular branch of psychology. He was interested in all aspects of human behaviour. Prabhu (1997, p. 167), in his Centenary Tribute to Gopalaswamy, rightly points out 'Dr. Gopalaswamy refused to get involved in the division of psychology into various branches as social, comparative, abnormal and so on and insisted on viewing a human being as an integrated bio-psycho-social organism. His interest was bio- and psycho-synthesis'.

The psychological laboratory in Maharaja's college that Gopalaswamy founded and developed was considered first-rate. It included a variety of tests and instruments to measure different psychological processes, and W. Leslie Barnette (1955), a Fulbright visiting scholar, after surveying the departments in Indian universities during 1952–1953 remarks, 'At Mysore was possibly the best equipped laboratory which I was privileged to see in India; furthermore, it seemed to be extensively used'.

Gopalaswamy was not just an ivory tower theorist. He was keenly interested in the application of psychology for the welfare of the society. Being a psychologist, he showed keen interest to bring about reforms in education and examination systems. He initiated the nursery school movement in Mysore in the 1930s and was instrumental in starting '*Sishu Vihars*' (child care centres). The underlying objective and philosophy behind the nursery school movement was to cater to the all-round development of preschool children.

Outside the field of psychology, Gopalaswamy is best remembered for his contribution to public broadcasting in India, particularly in the erstwhile state of Mysore. He set up the first private radio in the nation in his residence '*Vittal Vihar*', very close to the present day All India Radio station in Mysore. It was managed single-handedly by him, using his own personal resources. The first programme was broadcast on 10 September 1935, and incidentally this was a rendering of the poems of well-known Kannada writer and later Jnanapith Award winner Kuvempu, who happened to be a colleague of Gopalaswamy in the college (Kamat, 2012). His interest in setting up a broadcasting station suggests that he strongly believed in using mass media for promoting education among the masses and furthering cultural activities. Further, it is attributed to Gopalaswamy that he, together with his colleague N. Kasturi, coined the term *Akashavani* for radio broadcasting, the term which is presently used for All India Radio. Although it is generally acknowledged that Gopalaswamay is responsible for naming Akashavani for radio broadcast, lately, some dissenting voices have been made contesting this claim. Nevertheless, these dissentions do not in any way undermine the unique contributions of Gopalaswamy for the cause of public broadcasting.

He presided over the section of psychology and educational sciences of the Indian Science Congress held in 1928. Later, it is recorded that he attended the International Congress of Psychologists at Vienna, where he presented his notions on laughter and humour. Further, Gopalaswamy never restricted his activities to the academic confines. The records indicate that he was president of Rotary Mysore during 1946–1947, and this is indicative of his participation in social and cultural activities.

Gopalaswamy's contribution to the growth of psychological science in India can be identified and succinctly stated in the following terms—first, he founded the department and nurtured it to become an important centre for the study of psychology in India. This paved way for establishing psychology as an independent discipline of study, which was till then part of the philosophy programmes in Indian universities. Second, he built a first-rate psychology laboratory, equipped with sophisticated tests and instruments to measure various psychological processes, thus, enabling valuable research in many basic and applied areas of psychology. Third, Gopalaswamy trained a large number of students and guided their research projects, and these students went on to occupy important positions in various universities and organizations. Finally, his contribution lies in the application of psychology to the fields of education, study of criminal behaviour, industry, and other social problems.

# References

Barnes, B. (2004). *Psychology in India*. In Michael J. Stevens (Ed.) *The handbook of international psychology*. Brunner & Rutledge.

Barnette, W.L. (1955). Survey of research with psychological tests in India. *Psychological Bulletin, 52*(2), 105–121.

Brock, A. C. (2006). *Internationalizing the history of psychology*. New York: New York University Press.

Irvine, S.H., & Berry, J.W. (1988). *Human abilities in cultural context*. Cambridge: Cambridge University Press.

Kamat, J. (2012). *My days in All India Radio*. Amma's Column, Kamat's Potpurri.

Prabhu, G.G. (1997). Prof. M. V. Gopalaswamy: A centenary tribute. *Indian Journal of Clinical Psychology, 24* (2), 186–188.

Thimmappa, M.S. (2014). Interview. *Hosathu, 15*(6), 88.

Vasudeva Rao, C.K. (1974). *A tribute to the memory of Dr M.V. Gopalaswamy*. In P. Krishnamurthy (Ed.). *Golden jubilee souvenir: Department of psychology* (pp. 6–12). University of Mysore.

# 7

# B.L. Atreya

(1897–1967)

## Ram R. Tripathi

Born in 1897 in Saharanpur district of Uttar Pradesh, B.L. Atreya pursued his higher studies at Banaras Hindu University, Varanasi. His academic achievements are filled with many firsts. He was the first recipient of a DLitt degree in philosophy on his thesis 'The Philosophy of Yog-Vashisth' in 1931. He joined the Department of Philosophy, Banaras Hindu University, as an assistant professor in 1923 and became the head of the department in 1947. He was the first one in the university to receive the Padma Bhushan in 1957 while in service. He was instrumental in starting graduate and postgraduate classes in psychology. He also established a small laboratory of psychology in 1934. It was in 1948 that psychology emerged as an independent subject in the university. Under his stewardship, the teaching of courses in psychology started in the year 1949–1950 with experimental psychology, industrial psychology, and parapsychology as optional papers. He also started a diploma course in clinical psychology in 1951. His forte was parapsychology for which he had arranged an experimental device to study extrasensory perception. This was further developed by S.S. Jalota who joined the department as a reader in psychology. Thus, the induction of psychology at Banaras Hindu University was the singular contribution of B.L. Atreya.

He published many books and papers in philosophy. His paper entitled 'Supernormal Factors in Human Personality', published in the *Indian Journal of Psychology* (1943, pp. 1–10), was much appreciated by the academic community. He delivered invited lectures at Duke University and the University of Cambridge in the area of his expertise—parapsychology and *yoga-vashistha*. Because of his varied academic contributions, especially his research on yoga-vashistha and comparison of Indian and Western philosophy, the Department of Philosophy and Psychology of Banaras Hindu University received international recognition followed by visits of a large number of foreign scholars and students for their PhD degrees. He also kept the link between psychology and philosophy alive. Its impact is clearly discernible in *Textbook of Psychology* (Jalota, 1952).

He breathed his last in 1967.

## Reference

Jalota, S. (1952). *A textbook of psychology*. Banaras: Hindu University Press.

# 8

## Kali Prasad*

(1901–1963)

### Hari Shanker Asthana

Kali Prasad was born in 1901 in Ahiyapur (Allahabad) to Mr Sitab Rai, a postmaster. He lost his parents in childhood and as the only surviving boy was brought up by his elder stepsister. Extreme poverty forced him to give tuition even at school. He opted for subjects where he could borrow books, but passed matriculation with distinction. To supplement his meagre earnings, he prepared the *akharas* (wrestling ground) and this physical labour was the secret of his good health. His college education was supported by an attorney, Roop Narain, part time work, and scholarships which enabled him to earn his MA in philosophy in the first division and a Law degree, both from the University of Allahabad. He married in 1928 and had two sons and three daughters.

*Kali Prasad*

---

* Photograph, biographical details, and some other information was provided by the professor's family. Some material was retrieved by the son of the author from published records.

He joined the University of Lucknow as a lecturer in Philosophy in 1924. During his service career, he rose to Readership in 1944 and to full professorship in 1948. He served as vice-chancellor of the university from 1960 for about 3 years before relinquishing his office and taking over as an honorary member and a director in the Board of India International Centre, New Delhi, till his demise.

Prasad's work and research interests included psychological theory, social and political psychology, criminology, and industrial psychology. This is glaringly visible in the published papers and technical reports as well as memos that he submitted to various institutions and organizations. Most of his publications are in the form of reports, conference addresses, and memos to government/organizations on criminology, industry, morale, political behaviour and international relations, criminal tribes, delinquency, and even parapsychology. In 1949, he published a book titled *The Psychology of Meaning* from Maxwell Press.

He went to Harvard and MIT as a Rockefeller Fellow. Under the Fulbright programme, he visited Oxford, UK, lecturing and participating in research activities. He visited the South-eastern Asian countries for on-the-spot studies in international relations under a UNESCO programme. At home, he presided over sessions of the Indian Philosophical Congress, the Section of Psychology and Educational Sciences of the Indian Science Congress Association and the Indian Sociological Congress, and was co-chairman at the International Conference of Diplomats in Asia at Colombo in Ceylon (now Sri Lanka).

Apart from professional activities, he was chairman/member of various statutory, professional and central and state government bodies. He was on the editorial boards of professional journals including the *Journal of Social Psychology* and the *Journal of Conflict Resolution*.

## Organizational Work

By far the greatest contribution Prasad made was in organizing and developing the activities of an institution of higher learning which made the department he presided over an enviable centre of academic activities in the country. As the chairman of the department of philosophy, he enlarged its activities in the fields of psychology and education. To strengthen teaching of philosophy, he was able to avail of the services of Athar Rasheed, PhD (Gottingen, Germany), a student of the famous philosopher Windelband, to join as Reader to specially teach Western philosophy. But a few years later, Rasheed moved over to Pakistan. To fill the vacancy, he was able to attract Surima DasGupta, a scholar in her own right and also the wife of the famous Indian philosopher S.N. DasGupta, with the temptation to have the famous ailing philosopher on the campus to advice teachers and research scholars. Thus, he was able to strengthen teaching and research in Indian philosophy. When he moved over as vice-chancellor, he got S.K. Saksena, a good scholar of both Indian and Western philosophy, then teaching in Hawaii, to take his chair in philosophy.

*1950 group photo (Murphy's visit). Teachers with postgraduate students of psychology after the inauguration of the laboratory of experimental psychology by Gardner Murphy. Sitting in chairs: (left to right) Lecturers: Sri Chandra; R.M. Loomba; Off. Reader: Rajnarain (in Indian dress); Kali Prasad, Professor and Head, Philosophy-Psychology Department; Gardner Murphy, Columbia University; Radhakamal Mukerji, Head, Economics and Sociology; Kanchanlata Sabberwal, Principal; Mahila Vidyalaya, Professor and Dean, Iyer, Dean Arts Faculty; R.B. Mathur, Reader in Education.*

The other thing he accomplished was to organize teaching in education as a graduate course, then called BEdSc (bachelor of educational science). Since most teachers at schools were required to have a licentiate in teaching diploma to enter the teaching profession, he decided to offer the graduate BEdSc course. He got a Readership instituted in the department for the purpose and got R.B. Mathur, who had returned from the UK with a doctorate, to start instruction with two new lecturers and support from the faculty of philosophy and psychology to teach philosophy of education, educational psychology and vocational counselling psychology and laboratory work in mental testing. Slowly, it was possible to have an independent department of education.

Inheriting the initiative of N.N. Sengupta, the founder of modern psychology in the country since his return to Calcutta from Harvard, Prasad began developing teaching of psychology and research in a big way. He managed to get a new double-storied building constructed as a laboratory of experimental psychology. Once Sengupta asked Hari Shanker Asthana to fabricate a device to demonstrate Michote's 'perception of causality' phenomena in connection with Fritz Heider's work. Michote's book had not been translated from French yet. Employing angular velocity and using a reduction screen, it became possible to demonstrate 'entrailment', 'pushing', and other phenomena. Besides the experimental psychology laboratory, the building housed a mental test library, a small animal experimental laboratory with guinea pigs, and a clinical and counselling laboratory with a one-way screen and audio system to teach and train teachers and students in testing and counselling. Prasad managed to arrange visits of two clinical psychologists, Hubert S. Coffey from Berkeley Campus of the University of California and Delton C. Beier from the Urbana Campus of the University of Illinois, to spend one year each under the Fulbright programme. A small workshop was also added to repair and fabricate minor apparatus for teaching and research. Owing to the Second World War, both instruments and equipment could not be imported and industry in the county was yet to take interest in constructing psychological equipment. A small departmental library also came into existence with some books bought, donated, and borrowed. As honorary librarian (since 1945) of the main university library (Tagore Library), he managed to subscribe many psychology journals of the American Psychological Association such as *Psychological Abstract, Psychological Review, Psychological Bulletin, Annual Review of Psychology, etc.*

He was resourceful to be able to invite visiting professors to come over to Lucknow in the department and deliver lectures. He invited Gardner Murphy of Columbia University, who had come as an advisor to the Government of India for the study of social tension in the country (following the partition of the country into India and Pakistan, resulting in communal divide), and migration (people of two religious groups, Hindus and Muslims and the subsequent violence) to Lucknow and had him inaugurate in 1950 the newly built laboratory of experimental psychology. Murphy delivered a lecture (reproduced in MANSASI: Bulletin of Department of Psychology, Vol. 1, University of Lucknow, 1951).

Prasad was able to attract other noted psychologists to visit the department and lecture to faculty and students. Among them were Hadley Cantril from Princeton, Clyde Kluckhohn from Harvard, Ithiel de Sola Pool from MIT, and Medard Boss, the famous existential psychiatrist from Switzerland who had challenged Sigmund Freud. Boss spent a few days in the city. One other distinguished visitor came in the absence of Prasad and was shown around by the author. He was Kirpal Singh Sodhi (b. 1911), the son of a doctor who had studied with one of SenGupta's students at Panjab University before proceeding for higher studies abroad and was the then chairman of psychology department at the Free University of Berlin. Dagmer Norell, the director of (the only at that time) psychiatric facility 'Noor Manzil', a Swiss psychiatrist and her assistant Mr Rajan were frequent visitors who interacted with the teachers and students.

Yet another landmark was the study of a 'wolf boy' named Ramu, perhaps the only one found in India. He was fished out by the railway police underneath a sleeping berth in a carriage at the local railway station in February 1954. Delivered to the care of the local state Balrampur Hospital in the city, the doctors thought him to be a 'wolf boy' and invited Prasad for a psychological study of the child. The present author was taken along and involved in psychological testing (he has photographs which he took). Prasad was contacted by *Illustrated London News,* London, and an article *solicited* on Ramu appeared in its 27 February 1954 issue. In Prasad's opinion, Ramu was an imbecile freak who was abandoned by his parents after efforts to restore him may have failed. The present author, the only survivor who had seen him, was interviewed by the chief of bureau of the Japanese daily *Ashai Shimbaum*, Tokyo, with the aid of interpreter; the report appeared 2 days later.

*Ramu, the wolf-boy. Ramu made to sit in his hospital bed. Being fed by attending nurse holding the dish. The doctor attending is with the wrist watch. The boy licks food from the dish; he cannot use his hands which are twisted awkwardly. Psychological testing by Prasad and the author revealed the boy to be an imbecile freak who, sadly, was abandoned by his parents after efforts to restore him may have failed.*

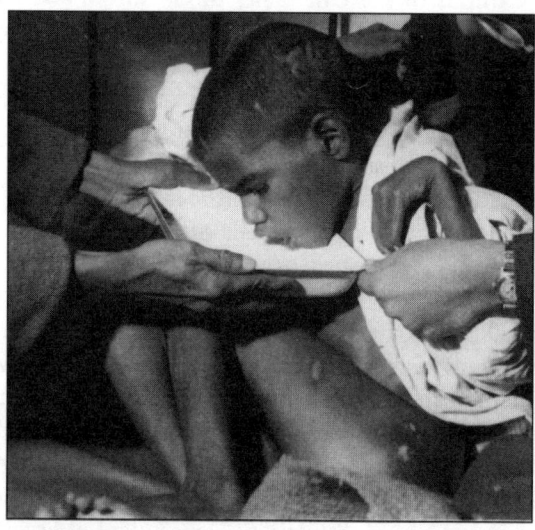

# Champion of University Autonomy

Prasad was a strong champion of university autonomy. He believed that the institutions of higher learning should be free from external control in the interest of creative thinking, innovations, and growth. But for those who subscribe to a different ideology and believe in the exercise of 'power' and 'control', such freedom is repugnant. A clash of ideologies is thus inevitable. The old philosophical distinction between 'ends' and 'means' is blurred. Politicians seek 'power and control', business 'profit', and management 'goals'. 'Ends' matter, 'means' are irrelevant; the only restriction is to avoid offending the laws or circumvent them. Prasad faced the onslaughts but did not yield. To get rid of him, the University Act, common to all state universities, had to be changed by the state legislature. This led to a ridiculous situation. Vice-chancellors of all state universities had to be relieved unceremoniously lest the government be guilty of discriminating! The politician won, but it was a pyrrhic victory; the politician assumed control and academia became subservient to both him and the bureaucracy. Quest for knowledge was sacrificed at the altar of power! Relieved in 1962, Prasad was immediately invited to the India International Centre at New Delhi as member of the board of directors and provided facilities to pursue his research interests. He died suddenly of heart attack in 1963 while he was working at the India International Centre at New Delhi. Looking in retrospect, Prasad made the department of philosophy-psychology at the University of Lucknow a vibrant and envious institution to which students and teachers from all over the country flocked.

# 9

# Sudhir Kumar Bose

(1901–1995)

## Amal Kumar Mallick

Way back in 1923, an ordinary science graduate of Calcutta University having no extraordinary examination results aspired to become an entrepreneur in small-scale industry (as known today) dealing with manufacture of soap, glue, etc. for the purpose of dyeing cloths. His unusual aspiration was inspired by Acharya Profulla Chandra Roy as part of the ongoing Swadeshi Movement. For this purpose, he met P.N. Ghosh, the then head of the applied physics department at the University College of Science, Calcutta University. He then came to know that a person having a PhD degree from Harvard University had started a department to teach experimental psychology, a new subject in India. He met the in-charge of the department, Narendranath Sengupta, who was in search of a student of physics, chemistry, and mathematics at BSc level so that he could subsequently initiate experiments in Calcutta University's Laboratory of Experimental Psychology, the first of its kind in India and the second in Asia after Japan. At that very moment, Bose decided to take admission in the postgraduate course. That person was none other than Sudhir Kumar Bose or S.K. Bose, as he was widely known throughout India in later years during the third to sixth decades of the twentieth century. Since 1962, S.K. Bose was an unforgettable name among the contemporary psychologists as well as other social scientists not only in India but also abroad.

The glimpse of S.K. Bose, his academic achievement, professional attainment, and personality characteristics in the context of self as well as beyond it is described in his own words which were written during the last few years of his life and also expressed during many hours of almost weekly evening conversations with the present author in those years till the very last day.

Born towards the end of 1901 in a well-to-do family owning a small estate or *Mouja* in the vast zamindari of the Maharaja of Burdwan of the then Bengal (now West Bengal) and brought up in the years when the social environment of the country was charged with the freedom movement, primarily propagated as non-violent notwithstanding the recurrence of the opposite characteristics, Sudhir Kumar's personality was developed in the expectedly inevitable direction of Swadeshi spirit. His reminiscences vouch the same in his sole autobiographical account written at the age of 90 (Bose, 1991, p. 22). He wrote, 'I was a little ahead of the overage, to speak in language of Statistics, not more than one standard deviation above the normal'. What an excellent sample of introspection. He further wrote, 'I am content with what I attained in my career. Without affluence, influence and outstanding ability what more could I expect?….I am primarily a teacher. The best reward for a teacher is lasting cordial relations with his students. I have been amply rewarded' (Bose, 1991, p. 30). This is how he sums up his life achievements. No word is sufficient to represent a true teacher's level of contentment towards the end of his life.

Having passed the matriculation, ISc, and BSc examinations from Calcutta University in 1919, 1921, and 1923, respectively, he took his MSc degree in experimental psychology in 1925 and MA degree in philosophy in 1930. Bose joined his alma mater as a laboratory assistant in December 1925 and thereafter joined as assistant lecturer in July 1926 in the Department of Philosophy, Dacca University. He then came back to the parent department in 1928 and stayed there for over 28 years, upto 1955. In between he went on lien during 1943–1945 to work as a senior psychologist (Grade I) with the Army Selection Board, Section of Personnel Directorate, General Headquarters during the Second World War. He then joined the Indian Institute of Science, Bangalore, as head of the social science section, where he stayed during January 1956 to June 1959. In July that year, Bose joined as senior research officer at the UNESCO Research Centre for Social and Economic Development in Southern Asia and later became its acting director. A remarkable event of positive consequences took place. The chair of psychology of his parent department, which remained vacant for 3 years since November 1959, had to be filled in by 1962. Bose was appointed as the third university professor of Psychology in December 1962, after Girindrasekhar Bose and Suhridchandra Mitra who were Sudhir Kumar Bose's mentors and colleagues too. After retirement in October 1966, he remained associated with the department under University Grants Commission's Research Scheme for the Retired Professors till 31 March 1971, nine months before the expiry of the term.

He has several laurels to his credit. He was recipient of Sri Asutosh Mookerjee Gold Medal in Science (Psychology) in 1936 and Sir Asutosh Mookerjee Gold Medal in Letters (Philosophy) in 1939, both from Calcutta University. He also received the Honorary UNESCO Fellowship for 1950–1951. He was invited for the Professor Jamuna Prasad Memorial Lectureship of the Indian Psychological Association in 1977 and was conferred the Professor S.C. Mitra Memorial Plaque of the Asiatic Society in 1985 for his contributions in the field of psychology. In addition to these, mention must be made about his classical essay, 'Language and Meaning' submitted for the Griffith Memorial Prize in 1997 which was adjudged the second best and was recommended to be published in the Calcutta University's prestigious *Journal of the Department of Letters*. Bose was also one of the recipients of Swamy Vivekananda Birth Centenary Felicitation by Narendrapur Ramakrishna Mission Ashrama.

Bose was not simply an ordinary academic psychologist, but much more than that. As an erudite scholar, a voracious reader, a prolific writer, a patient listener, and above all an introspectionist, he was unparalleled in the world of Indian psychologists. He was the pioneer of tension study in India in the field of industrial psychology. His presidential address at the psychology and educational sciences section of the Indian Science Congress Association (1951) entitled 'Man and his Work' brought him great recognition. He had to shift from his most favourite field of introspection to industrial psychology at the advice of Shyama Prasad Mookerjee in 1945 (Bose, 1991; Mallick, 1995). Thus, he became the pioneer Indian industrial psychologist. Interestingly, Bose reverted to his favourite 'introspection' during the last few years of his life.

Bose loved to be an introspectionist, so to say, primarily because of his personality pattern and secondarily because of his being involved for about 10 years in the psychophysical experiment on differential limen (DL) and Ritz limen (RL) conducted by his teacher Gopeswar Pal who later became the second Indian DSc degree holder in psychology awarded by Calcutta University after Girindrasekhar Bose. That was a classic case of 'N = 1', that is, single-subject research design in the domain of psychology—the rarest of the rare example indeed.

Bose traversed many paths far away from introspection while conducting many psychological studies with the industrial workers of Adamji Jute Mill, Bata Shoe, Calcutta TramWays Company, National Carbon Company, entrants to the College of Engineering at Jadavpur, Medical College, Calcutta, and aspirants for joining the army. He was also associated with many social surveys in India and South Asian countries. Yet he returned to the original field of interest close to his heart, mind, and soul: Introspection. Possibly, this homecoming was the triumph of the Indian Philosophy of 'Atmanam Viddhi', the last word to say silently before one's departure from this world. He died on 17 March 1995.

# Bibliography

Bose, S.K. (1991). In retrospect: Career of an old student of psychology department. Calcutta University. *Psychological Research Journal*, *15*, 21–30.

Deb, M. (1995). Professor S.K. Bose. *Psychological Research Journal*, *19*, 13–17.

Mallick, A.K. (1995). Professor S.K. Bose: A closer view. *Psychological Research Journal*, *19*, 81–87.

———. (2012). Preface, In S.K. Bose (Ed.), *Language and meaning & other works*. Kolkata: Levant Books.

# 10

# B. Kuppuswamy

(1907–1981)

## Jyoti S. Madgaonkar

*B. Kuppuswamy*

B. Kuppuswamy has significantly contributed to the field of psychology in India. Born on 25 February 1907, B. Kuppuswamy belonged to a respectable family of Ulsoor, Bangalore. He was not the only son of his father, Venkataswamy Naidu. Apart from his mother, his family comprised of two elder brothers and one younger brother who were equally successful in their respective careers. In 1931, B. Kuppuswamy married Smt Kameshwaramma in Mysore, who was one of the few women graduates in the 1920s, having passed out from Presidency College. The marriage lasted till 1979, when Kameshwaramma died after 47 years of companionship. The couple was blessed with two daughters and both of them were trained to be professionally and economically independent. B. Kuppuswamy was greatly venerated and adored by his students, not so much for his achievements in research and publications but more so as a teacher. As researchers, students always found in him a willing listener and an inspiring teacher who taught them to deal with problems patiently rather than look for ready-made or easy solutions. A person with high academic and towering achievements, he was friendly, warm, and charming to everyone, and his convivial smile had been a perennial source of encouragement to his juniors. His guidance was persuasive and democratic at the same time. In academic discussions, he respected the opinions of his critics and his demeanour was never inappropriate. In spite of being an atheist who was sceptical about God and rituals, he was an ardent student of the 'Vedas', 'Bhagwat Gita', Upanishads', 'Yogavashshita', and many other treatises on Indian philosophy.

## Affiliations

B. Kuppuswamy received his college education at St. Joseph's College, Bangalore, and later went to the University of Mysore to attain his masters in psychology in 1929. He was a brilliant student, and in the same year, he was appointed as a lecturer in the Department of Psychology, University of Mysore. There he was bestowed with the responsibility of setting up the experimental psychology section and preparing a manual for the students. He was later awarded the DLitt in psychology in 1944. After his retirement as the professor of psychology in 1962, he joined the India International Centre, New Delhi, as its joint director. From 1964 to 1967, B. Kuppuswamy was appointed as research consultant for the Research Council for Cultural Studies, Associated Institute of UNESCO for South and South East Asia, an autonomous body under the India International Centre. Besides, he also served as the chairman of The Review Committee for Psychology of the University Grants Commission. He further held the position of the president at the Delhi branch of the Indian Psychological Association and All India Association on Mental Retardation. As the director of Social and Psychology Research Institute, he had conducted regular study circle meetings on various topics concerning social issues which were attended by eminent scholars.

## Awards and Recognition

In 1945, B. Kuppuswamy was elected president of the education and the psychology section of the Indian Science Congress. Following this, in 1949, he was invited by the Madras government to establish the Department of Psychology at the Presidency College from which later several students were to pass out with their qualifying degree in psychology. In 1952, he returned to the University of Mysore as a professor of psychology. In 1984, his son-in-law, Mr B.V. Kumar, IRS, former member of Central Board of Excise and Customs, instituted a prize money in his memory for the best outgoing master's degree student of psychology at the University of Mysore. The University of Madras awarded him with the 'Dravidian Language Prize' for the content and style of his book on psychology, written in Telugu. To celebrate his 60th birthday in 1968 a seminar was held and a commemoration volume entitled *Contributions to Psychology* was published and released in which eminent psychologists such as Professor Gardner Murphy, Dr Charles E. Osgood, Leon A. Jakobovits,

Harry C.Triandis, H.M.M. Fortman, E.A.J. Johnson, and many others contributed on several subjects related to Psychology. As the chairman of the section on social change at the International Conference on Human Relations (the Netherlands, 1956), leader of the Third Education team (the USA, 1958) and in many other assignments, he travelled widely to many parts of the world including the USA, Egypt, Sri Lanka, Greece, Malaysia, the Philippines, and Denmark.

## Contributions

B. Kuppuswamy strongly believed in the ethical and moral values of life and tried to instil these values in his family members, students, and colleagues. He had a holistic approach towards life, and his interests were varied extending beyond the boundaries of his own discipline. He was interested in social problems, Hindu philosophy, and literature and wrote several articles on these topics for many journals and newspapers. In October 1981, just before his death, he edited a collection of articles on philosophy, written between the years 1885 and 1914 and reprinted from *Brahmavadin*. He further wrote an 'Introduction' for the same book, which in itself was a brief treatise on Hindu philosophy. He authored several books which have relevance to Indian life even today. These books have stood the test of time and till date they are referred to by students of psychology and sociology, aspirants appearing for the civil services, and others in almost all universities. Some of his books have been translated into Hindi and are widely used by the students of North India.

Some of his well-known and outstanding books are entitled, Introduction to *Social Psychology*, *Social Change in* India, *Child Behavior and Development*, *Psychology and Life*, and *Communication and Social Development in India*. Having an extensive knowledge on ancient Indian thought, he published some excellent articles on it. In these books he was able to indulge in a comparative study between the ancient Indian thoughts and the modern theories of psychology starting from Carl Gustav Jung to the contemporary ones. Some of his notable contributions are books such as *Elements of Indian Psychology*, *Source Book of Ancient Indian Psychology*, *Dharma and Psychology*, and *Quintessence of Yogavashshita*. Before his death in 1981, he completed his manuscript *Substance of Yogavashshita*, which is still to be published.

In the early 1940s, while in Mysore, B. Kuppuswamy was very actively involved with the adult education council, Mysore. The primary aim of the council was to promote adult literacy. One of his main concerns was to help the illiterate adults to learn Kannada. In this regard, he wrote towards the end of 1944:

> I was asked to go through the primers of adult education council to make suggestions and revision. I was struck by the way in which lessons had been written purely for the purpose of introducing the adult to letter forms. Since then I have been thinking about the problem of reducing the task of the adult and the child by modifying the script.

With this in mind, he prepared a proposal for easy learning of vowels, vowel combinations, and the consonants. In 1947, he prepared a list of Kannada words that could be used to compile simple readable books for adults and also wrote a number of simple Kannada books on child psychology, child development, child education, child growth, and child behaviour. In the same year, he also prepared a Kannada primer without '*Mahaprana*'. These books were published under the aegis of the University of Mysore from 1942 to 1949, in order to promote an understanding of these issues for the benefit of the common people.

Under his guidance, from 1930 to 1962, several students completed their doctoral studies and many of them later went on to work as professors of psychology at universities in India and aboard. Some of the topics on which he provided guidance were 'level of aspiration among workers', 'measurement of attitude towards some social and economic problems', 'a study of certain personality characteristics of leaders among high school studies', 'A study of difference in value patterns between service men and civilians', and 'A diagnostic study of reading difficulties of students in high school'. In fact, in 1981, just before his death, while he was in Ahmadabad, he was asked to examine the PhD thesis of a student of Gujarat University and this was the last thesis he had approved.

B. Kuppuswamy, even after his retirement, continued to be active in his field. One of his outstanding achievements was the development of the socio-economic scale. The scale was standardized and primarily used in socio-economic investigations in urban areas of India. The scale which was a simple instrument that could be used to obtain a correct measure of the socio-economic status of a person without spending much time and effort. The scale has been widely used by social research scientists all over India. He also had future plans to upgrade the socio-economic scale but this was left unfulfilled due to his demise on 21 November 1981, at Ahmedabad.

Being compassionate by nature, he often arranged for the fees, meals, and accommodation of poor but deserving students, so that they could continue with their studies without any expense and problems. Just after the demise of his wife, B. Kuppuswamy decided to set up a trust in her memory. Each year, on 29 July, the trust organizes a lecture on women's issues, where a lady speaker addresses the audience at NMKRV Women's College. Similarly, a lecture is also held at the Institute of World Culture, Basavanagudi, Bangalore, where several eminent women speak about several burning women's issues. The trust also provides food on the same day, each year to four residential institutions which take care of destitute women and children. Although this was Kuppuswamy's way of paying tribute to his dear wife, his own concern for women is amply depicted in his book, *Social Change in India*, wherein he deals with the 'status of women and education'.

# 11

# Trivikram Ramchandra Kulkarni

(1912–1983)

## Satishchandra Kumar and Anjali Majumdar*

Trivikram Ramchandra Kulkarni was a prominent educationist as well as a licensed medical practitioner (LMP). Even though he had a license to practise medicine, he pursued his interest in Indian philosophy and psychology. He played an important role in the establishment of psychology as a university subject in Mumbai. He was a part of the committee that worked out the courses to be taught at the BA and MA levels in 1957. The other members of the committee included Jaindani, Mrs Pratap (Jaihind College), V.V. Kamath (Institute of Education), Fr. Filella and T.A. D'Souza (St. Xavier's College), and P.H. Prabhu (Tata Institute of Social Sciences; Ghorpade, 1984). He was the first head of the Department of Psychology of D.G. Ruparel College, Mumbai, when the department started on 20 June 1958. During the second session of 1959, he joined the Department of Applied Psychology, Bombay University (the then University of Mumbai) as a Reader (Annual Report, 1960–61). During his tenure at the University of Mumbai, he wrote many phenomenal papers.

He published 'Psycho-Pharmacological Trends in Indian Psychology' (1961), 'Comparison of Judgments of Short Intervals of Time' (1962), 'Personality Correlates of 'Doubtful' Judgments in Weight Lifting' (Annual Report, 1962–63), 'Empirical Basis of Yoga'(Annual Report, 1967–68), 'Psychosynthesis and Psycholysis' (Annual Report, 1968–69), and so forth. His seminal paper 'Pranayama and Perception' was an experimental attempt to test *Patanjali's* theory of the relationship between pranayama and perception.

In 'Empirical Basis of Yoga' (1968), he attempted to shed some light on 'whether Yoga permits consideration and logical manipulation conforming to standard methods of empirical analysis' (Kulkarni, 1968). In simpler words, Kulkarni attempted to understand Yoga through empirical analysis. He discussed the concept or principle of '*samapatti*', which implies a reduction in general mental functioning, allowing a person to focus on an object chosen for attention. He further spoke about '*nirodh*', which means inhibiting all mental functions except one, rather than a general

* We wish to thank Nandini Diwan, Professor and Head, Department of Psychology, D.G. Ruparel College, Mumbai and Anagha Barve, Former Head of the Department, D.G. Ruparel College, Mumbai. Our thanks are also due to a colleague of T.R. Kulkarni and former Vice Principal of D.G. Ruparel College, C.T. Yeolekar, who is 90 years old now and whom we telephonically interviewed for getting the details.

inhibition of all mental functions. This is the 'necessary precondition' (Kulkarni, 1968) for the basic purpose of any *yogic* task of 'maintaining any one particular attentive state to the exclusion of all others' (Kulkarni, 1968). He also spoke about the perceptual learning theory which emerged from *Patanjali*. This theory has three main propositions:

> [P]erceptual learning is an acquisition of identity of form with the object of perception; the acquisition of such an identity is a function of general inhibition directed to a specific arousal corresponding to the object of perception; the general inhibition in turn is the function, among others, of such factors as postural fixation (*Asana*), breath regulation (*Pranayama*), and a factor called withdrawal of 'organs' (*Pratyahara*). (Kulkarni, 1968)

In 'Psychosynthesis and Psycholysis' (1969), Kulkarni drew a parallel between the mystical and philosophical interpretations of the *Rigveda*, and its empirical implications. He discussed how *Rigveda* can be used as evidence for the fact that,

> [L]ong before pharmacology discovered these drugs (which have effects like clearer perceptions, finer discriminations, revival of memories, euphoric states and greater insights among many others) they had actually been in use, apparently, with some knowledge of their properties, in some or other primitive races at all the stages in history. (Kulkarni, 1969)

He also described the internal world of man being made of 'goings' (*rta*). These flow and consequences of these goings, both in upward direction (white path) and downward direction (black path) are determined by the 'propellant' (*agni*), which has the 'peculiar tendency to dissipate and rebuild itself quickly' (Kulkarni, 1969). The rebuilding and dissipating phases of the propellant characterize the wakefulness and sleep cycles respectively of a person, as well as being linked to cognitions and actions of a person respectively. Therefore, 'according to Rigveda the 'blocking' or arresting of actions is an important factor in the determination of cognitions' (Kulkarni, 1969). He described how Rigveda provided a chemical theory of behaviour. While distinguishing between psychosynthesis and psycholysis, he says that the psychical energy, at any given moment, may appear either in a state of dissipation (psycholysis) or reintegration (psychosynthesis).

In 1973, Kulkarni wrote a paper 'Western Psychotherapy and Hindu Sadhna'. This paper was published in a souvenir titled 'Geeta Gyana Yagna' (Annual Report, 1972–73). In the same year, he gave a talk on 'Yoga and Mental Health' at the Yoga Health Center, Kaivalyadhama, Bombay. In August 1974, he presented a paper entitled 'Psychology—the Indian Point of View' (Annual Report, 1974–75) at the International Conference of Humanistic Psychology at Waltair. Later, this was published in the first volume of the *Journal of Indian Psychology* in 1978.

In 1984, his paper 'A Blueprint for Developing an Indian School of Psychology' was published in the combined volume of *Bombay Psychologist* (Vol. V, No. 2, Vol. VI No.1). In this paper, he drew out a roadmap of how the ancient Indian texts or the Upanishads, in their purest forms, guide the Indian school of psychology. He mentioned that ancient Indians describe mind as 'a metabolic energy that has the tendency to stabilize itself in the uppermost part of the body, presumably the head' (Kulkarni, 1984). This is in direct contrast of the Western view of the mind being of immaterial nature. He also drew attention to how some basic concepts are misinterpreted in the process of translation. For example, the Sanskrit terms '*adhatmika*' and '*adhyatma*' are generally translated as spiritual and spiritualism, whereas they actually mean subjective and subjectivity (Kulkarni, 1984). He described that the central theme of the Upanishads is 'the person (*Purusa*), self (*Atman*) or Brahman which, among other ways they also describe as "real of the real" (*satyasya satyam*)'

(Kulkarni, 1984). He goes on to describe the nature of *atman* and Brahman of *purusa* and concludes that these synonymous terms, used in the Upanishadic texts, 'seem primarily to bear a psychological significance' (Kulkarni, 1984). After bringing out some generalizations about the psychological features of the Upanishad, the article ends with the observation that 'systematic studies in Indian psychology can hardly make headway unless its source books such as Rigveda, Upanishads, Yoga Sutra, Bhagvadgita and the like are retranslated, preferably by psychologists' (Kulkarni, 1984). He passed away on 7 April 1983, at the age of 71 (Ghorpade, 1984). This article was published after he passed away, with the permission of his wife.

One of his projects where he collaborated with Dr Nirodh Mukerji and Shri Jog was funded by National Council of Educational Research and Training (NCERT) (Annual Report, 1964–65). He was part of the University Grant Commission funded project on delinquency along with Nirodh Mukerji (Annual Report, 1965–66). He was involved in a project titled 'Systematic and Empirical Studies in Indian Psychology' in 1977. This project was funded by the Indian Council for Social Science Research (ICSSR), New Delhi (Annual Report, 1977–78). This project was completed the following year (Annual Report, 1978–79). He was also a consulting editor for Volume 2, Number 2 of the *Journal of Indian Psychology* in 1979. The *Journal of Indian Psychology*, published from Vishakhapatnam, Andhra Pradesh, is a peer-reviewed journal of ideas as well as facts, which invites papers from authors in topics of Indian psychology including Yoga, meditation and spirituality. It publishes both theoretical papers and empirical papers. One of his articles, 'Psychology: An Indian Point of View' was published in the first volume of this journal (Kulkarni, 1978).

Pursuing his scientific temper he conducted a study entitled 'Psychological evaluation of Sri Sathya Sai Bal Vikas Centres, Bombay: A Scientific Investigation of Spiritual Training Centres'. For this study, he took up 20 Bal Vikas children of Bombay and studied them with the help of IQ tests, two scales of parent evaluation, Upbringing Scale, Youth Adjustment Analyzer Inventory, Allport-Vernon Lindzey Study of Values and Moral Development Scale. The interim report of this study was published in 1975 (Ruhela, 1996).

The first doctoral degree in psychology from the Department of Applied Psychology, University of Mumbai, was conferred to Mehroo Bengalee in 1965 (Ghorpade, 1984). This thesis entitled 'A Multiphasic Personality Inventory Suitable to Indian Conditions of Youth Adjustment Analyzer' was guided by Kulkarni (Kale, 1984). Mehroo Bengalee went on to become the first woman vice-chancellor of the University of Mumbai from 1986 to 1992. In 1970, Dr Kulkarni also guided the thesis submission of Smt. Vimala Sarma, titled 'Some Behavioural and Personality Correlates of Functional Dysmenorrhoea in Married and Unmarried Women' (Annual Report, 1969–70).

In 1972, his book *Upanishads and Yoga* was published. The book contained seven chapters that discussed the Upanishads, the Upanishads and Yoga, Yoga, neurophysiological considerations, some implications of Yoga for psychopathology, and Yoga and personal efficiency. The publishers' note on the book mentioned that the author made the point that ancient texts should first be studied purely as 'linguistic facts'. Only such facts can provide any philosophical or religious meaning, or generalizations of the contents and forms of the ancient texts, like the Upanishads. In the preface, Kulkarni pointed out that objective studies of ancient Indian texts 'appeared smothered from adventitious pressures to prove or disprove something insistently held by the varying traditions belonging to different ages of history'. At the end, he candidly mentions that everything stated in the book has only 'tentative value' and was meant only to 'stress the need for organized research' (Kulkarni, 1972).

He was the consulting editor of Volume 2 (Number 2) of the *Journal of Indian Psychology* published in 1979 from Vishakhapatnam, Andhra Pradesh.

# References

Ghorpade, M.B. (1984). A chronicle of psychology in Bombay 1914–1984. *Bombay Psychologist. A Journal of Bombay Psychological Association, 6*(1), 9–17.

Kale, S.V. (1984). A brief historical note on the development of the department of applied psychology and a look into future. *Bombay Psychologist: A Journal of the Bombay Psychological Association, 6*(1), 9–17.

Kulkarni, T.R. (1968). Empirical basis of yoga. *Yoga-Mimamsa, 10*(3), 1–10.

———. (1969). Psychosynthesis and psycholysis: A broad outline of an important psychological aspect of ancient Indian thought. *Yoga-Mimamsa, 11*(4), 1–14.

———. (1972). *Upanishads and yoga.* Bombay: Bharatiya Vidya Bhavan.

———. (1978). Psychology: An Indian point of view. *Journal of Indian Psychology, 1*(1), 22–39.

———. (1984). A blueprint for developing an Indian school of psychology. *Bombay Psychologist: A Journal of the Bombay Psychological Association, 5*(2) & 6(1), 18–34.

Ruhela, S.P. (1996). *In search of Sai divine.* New Delhi: MD Publications Pvt. Ltd.

University of Bombay. (1960, 1 April–1961, 31 March). *Annual report for the year 1960–61* (pp. 59–61). Bombay: Author.

———. (1962, 1 April–1963, 31 March). *Annual report for the year 1962–63* (pp. LIX–LX). Bombay: Author.

———. (1964, 1 April–1965, 31 March). *Annual report for the year 1964–65* (pp. LIX–LX). Bombay: Author.

———. (1965, 1 April–1966, 31 March). *Annual report for the year 1965–66* (pp. 65–66). Bombay: Author.

———. (1967, 1 April–1968, 31 March). *Annual report for the year 1967–68* (pp. 103–104). Bombay: Author.

———. (1968, 1 April–1969, 31 March). *Annual report for the year 1968–69* (pp. 154–157). Bombay: Author.

———. (1969, 1 April–1970, 31 March). *Annual report for the year 1969–70* (pp. 151–154). Bombay: Author.

———. (1972, 1 April–1973, 31 March). *Annual report for the year 1972–73* (pp. 121–124). Bombay: Author.

———. (1974, 1 April–1975, 31 March). *Annual report for the year 1974–75* (pp. 83–85). Bombay: Author.

———. (1977, 1 April–1978, 31 March). *Annual report for the year 1977–78* (pp. 80–81). Bombay: Author.

———. (1978, 1 April–1979, 31 March). *Annual report for the year 1978–79* (pp. 73–74). Bombay: Author.

# Website Reference

http://www.exoticindiaart.com/book/details/upanishad-and-yoga-empirical-approach-to-understanding-IDE894/

# 12

# Vasudeo Krishna Kothurkar

(1912–2008)

## Chandrashekhar Gangadhar Deshpande

*Vasudeo Krishna Kothurkar*

Vasudeo Krishna Kothurkar was born at 'Kothure', a small village in Nashik District, on 2 March 1912. He had his education at Nashik, Pune, and Cambridge. After completing his matriculation at Nashik, he migrated to Poona and joined the renowned Fergusson College. He had his first degree, BA (honours) in 1934 from this college, which was then affiliated to the University of Bombay. He was a scholar even in his school and college career. He achieved first rank in logic among candidates from Karachi to Dharwar and was awarded the prestigious F.G. Selby Memorial Scholarship. He was also a Tutor in Fergusson College during 1935–1936. Nonetheless, it was recognition to his scholarship in Logic. Besides, he was a recipient of Senior Dakshina Fellowship from Fergusson College. He had his MA Philosophy (including psychology) in 1936 from the University of Bombay. He had a first rank in the whole of the Bombay Presidency. He started his academic career in Fergusson College, where he served as a lecturer in Logic and Philosophy (including psychology) during 1936–1938. He had another master's degree from St. Catherine College, University of Cambridge, UK, in 1940. While at Cambridge, he helped in 'War Research' at the Cambridge Psychological Laboratory during 1939–1940.

On his return from the UK, he taught at Tilak College of Education, Pune. He setup the first Experimental Psychology Laboratory in this College in 1941. Till then Experimental Psychology Laboratory was unknown in Maharashtra. After serving at Tilak College of Education for 2 years, he moved over to Elphistone College, Bombay, as a Gazetted Officer, Class II, and taught philosophy and psychology at undergraduate and postgraduate levels from 1943 to 1947. Further he was transferred to Karnataka College, Dharwar, where he taught philosophy and psychology at postgraduate level till 1950.

His real career in psychology started in 1950 when he was appointed as Reader and Head of the Department of Experimental Psychology, University of Poona. He set up the department here from scratch. Prior to the establishment of this department there were no independent teaching and research facilities in psychology available in the University of Poona area or any of its contiguous regions. He pioneered and managed the department almost single-handed under personal direction and supervision from the minutest details of office routine to the wider considerations of policy, planning and strategy in regard to teaching of and research in psychology and the organization, and administration and the public relations attendant thereon, 1950 onwards.

He developed the strength of the postgraduate department, which grew from one postgraduate student in 1953 through 20, 25, and 35 over the next 5 years to 38 in 1962. He also took initiative and active interest in the preparation, institution, and implementation of a full eight-paper MA course in psychology. Besides, he took initiative in framing and implementing BA psychology special course (1958) and BSc psychology subsidiary Experimental Psychology course in colleges affiliated to the University of Poona.

## Building-up Experimental Psychology Laboratory

He built-up the Experimental Psychology Laboratory in the Department of Psychology, University of Poona, from scratch. K.P. Bhagwat was a great help to him in this regard. Gradually this laboratory became one of the best in the whole country and Far and Middle East. Late Maiti, member of the Triennial Inspection Committee in 1956, commented that 'This laboratory is one of the best in India'. Charles E. Osgood had visited the department in 1960. His concluding remarks on his visit were,

> I do want to tell you how much I enjoyed the opportunity to tour your laboratory in Experimental Psychology. When I said that it was, without question, the best laboratory in Experimental Psychology we saw during our travels in the Far and Middle East. I mean just that.

Fisher of Rutgers University had visited the department in 1962. On her visit she said, 'Your department and equipment is something to be proud of not only in India but anywhere. It really shows the work and thought that you have put into it'.

Kothurkar took interest in comparative psychology also. He introduced animal and neurophysiological experiments in the university department for the first time in 1962.

## Achieving Independent Status for Psychology

There was a peculiar problem in early 1970s about the status of psychology as an independent subject. The tricky situation was that though psychology was recognized as an independent subject at the post-graduate level in the university, it continued to be a part of philosophy at the under graduation level in colleges. In most of the colleges it had no independent status. Kothurkar, along with S.B. Gogte and P.A. Bhagwatwar, took the initiative to separate psychology from philosophy and urged upon the university authorities to constitute the independent Board of Studies for these two subjects. The heartening and encouraging fact in this regard was that Barlinge, then head of the Department of Philosophy, University of Poona, supported the bifurcation move of these two subjects wholeheartedly. He realized the fact that courses in psychology, like abnormal psychology, educational psychology, experimental and industrial psychology, etc. were least related to philosophy. Around 1972, psychology got its independent status and it paved the way for its research and development. After that many colleges affiliated to the University of Poona started the department of psychology at special level.

## Kothurkar as a Scholar

Kothurkar was a thorough scholar in psychology, especially experimental psychology. Both Indian as well as foreign experts had unequivocally conceded his expertise in the subject. During the post-Partition period he collaborated with well-known American Psychologist Gardner Murphy in social tensions research. He had visited the Department of Experimental Psychology, University of Poona, in 1950, 1955, and 1960. He wrote about Kothurkar after his last visit as,

> I hope it will not be inappropriate to say a few words about your unusual qualifications. I found you to be one of the best trained, best informed, most creative, and most effective in both teaching and research among all the psychologists in India whom I met. Starting from scratch, you have developed almost single-handedly one of the finest departments of psychology in India.

A research article by Kothurkar was accepted for publication in the *Journal of Experimental Psychology* in 1962. After reading and processing the article, the Associate Editor of the Journal remarked in his letter,

> [Y]our manuscript was slightly revised to make it conform more closely to usual practices in the Journal and to make it a little more like colloquial American writing. Very little had to be done; you write more clearly than do most American and English Investigators. He was a student of F.C. Bartlett, who was a fellow of St. John's College in the University of Cambridge. He was also Editor of the British Journal of Psychology. He commented on research papers sent by Kothurkar 'it seems to me that what you did in the preparation of two papers was admirably planned and carried out and that your reports were clear and convincing'.

When Kothurkar was in service at the University of Poona he was offered the post of professorship by UP government. He declined the offer. On learning this, M.R. Jayakar, the first vice-chancellor of the university, wrote to him,

> The offer which came to you from the UP government is exactly what is your due and in that sense, it does not surprise me. A qualified professor attracts attention from long distances and I am very glad that,

in your case, this has happened. Personally, I am conscious of the good work that you are doing and I am glad that you have declined the offer. While it lies in my power to recognize your good work, I shall not fail to remember what you have done in connection with the offer of the UP government. You will always find me completely appreciative of your work and so far it lies in my power to give you help in maintaining your Department at the highest level, you will not find me wanting.

The opinion and remarks of experts mentioned above about the work and research of Kothurkar clearly reveal his erudite academic activities. He was a known psychologist in his own right. He had published about 56 research articles in reputed national and international journals as well as conferences. The journals from abroad which published his papers were like *The Annals of the American Academy of Political Sciences, Journal of Experimental Psychology, American Journal of Psychology, British Journal of Psychology, The Quarterly Journal of Experimental Psychology, and Psychological Abstracts.* The prestigious Indian journals in which his articles were published were *Philosophical Quarterly, Indian Journal of Psychology, Poona University Journal, Journal of Education and Psychology, Oriental Thought, Psychological studies, Journal of Psychological Researches, Kannad Encyclopedia* and the *Proceedings of Indian Science Congress.* His work entitled, 'An experimental study of modification of social attitudes' found a place in the form of summary in Murphy's famous book *In the Minds of Men.*

He was more devoted to experimental psychology and that too, in learning and memory. He conducted basic experimental studies about memory processes. This work included research in general learning, perception, and other cognitive and motivational processes. He was also interested in verbal behaviour and verbal learning, short-term memory, long-term memory, etc. He was equally interested in examination research. He advocated various valuable suggestions and modified the examination process. He had undertaken many 'rural studies'. They were in the natural tradition of the sociologists and anthropologists. His survey entitled, 'Psychological survey of the Kolhapur community project' was funded by the Planning Commission, Government of India. He had also done research in 'Village leadership in the *grampanchayats*' in collaboration with the University Department of Politics. His research priorities were social relevance and practical application. He intensively studied many social problems in the context of 'group relations' such as attitude towards minority communities, Hindu–Harijan relations, caste feelings, the problems of navabuddhas, provincial stereotypes, etc. He constructed and standardized the 'Group Test of Scholastic Ability'.

Sixteen students obtained PhD degree under his guidance. He guided wide range of topics for PhD degrees, namely, perception, learning, leadership, creativity, intelligence, achievement motivation, marriage, community development, and educational and social psychology. Some of his PhD students are well known in the field of psychology. For instance, V.V. Pendse, fondly known as 'Appa', had started an institution named 'Jnanaprabodhini' for Gifted Children. Anand Paranjpe, professor emeritus (Psychology and Humanities) at Simon Fraser University, Canada, has written some books on theoretical psychology and Indian psychology. V.P. Sharma was professor and Head, Department of Psychology, R.S. University, Raipur. His research was mainly in the field of educational psychology. Shymla Vanarse had her PhD in experimental psychology. She had also worked in psychology of music and clinical psychology. Sudhir Vanarse was a co-author of the book entitled *Experimental Psychology: A Systematic Introduction*, written by V.K. Kothurkar. P.A. Bhagwatwar, former Professor and Head, Department of Applied Psychology, University of Mumbai, had earned fame in the area of industrial psychology. He is known for his research-based theory 'growth-oriented and comfort-oriented motivational orientations'. This theory has been widely accepted. Ushatai Khire has developed number of tests on Guilford's model of intelligence.

She was a Secretary of 'Jnanaprabodhini Sanstha' for number of years. She is also closely associated with MENSA. V.S. Tahmankar, who worked on achievement motivation, has humanized psychology for excellent rural development at 'Harali' in Solapur district. C.G. Deshpande was professor and Head, Department of Applied Psychology, University of Murnbai. He has developed Indian norms of Raven's Standard Progressive Matrices. His two research-based books, *On Inter-caste marriage* and *Suicide and Attempted Suicide*, gained wide publicity. His other known students, whom he taught for MA includes Suresh Kanekar, former Head, Department of Applied Psychology, University of Mumbai. He obtained record marks in MA examination. He had his PhD degree from Iowa, USA. His research work is on attitudes and applied social psychology.

V.K. Kothurkar wrote eleven books, three independently, three in collaboration and the remaining five were based on his research reports. The three books independent authored by him were *About Learning and Memory* (published by Wiley Eastern Publishers in 1985), आठवण–साठवण (Memory-saving) in Marathi (published by Jnanaprabodhini in 1990) and एक महान मानसशास्त्रज्ञ: बी. ऍफ़. स्किनर (A Great Psychologist: B. F. Skinner, published by Uma Publication, Pune, in 1995). H.S. Asthana translated this book in Hindi. The other three books which were published in collaboration were मानसशात्रा चीमूलतत्वे (Principles of Psychology, published by Messors Joshi-Lokhande in 1960), *Psychology: Normal and Abnormal* in collaboration with Harolikar (published by Orient Longmans Ltd. in 1961) and *Experimental Psychology: A Systematic Introduction* in collaboration with Sudhir Vanarase (published by Wiley Eastern Publishers in 1986). Of all the books he had written, the book entitled *About Learning and Memory* which hit the market was recommended in many universities either as text or reference book. This book was reviewed by the late S.V. Kale.

Besides textbooks and reference books, he had written some research-based reports, which were later published in the form of books. *Report of the Committee on the Indian Examinations Reform Project* was written in collaboration and published by the United States Information Service, New Delhi, in 1959. *A Statistical Analysis of the Failures at the Pre-Degree Examination of the Poona University* was written in collaboration in 1960 and was published by the University of Poona. *Psychological Survey of the Secondary School Children of Poona* was published by the University of Poona in 1962. *Report on Health and Level of Living in Kolhapur Community Project* was also written in collaboration and was published by the University of Poona in 1969. *Abstracts of Research Papers: Experimental Psychology in India* was published by the Indian Council of Social Science Research, New Delhi, in *Indian Psychological Abstracts* in 1973.

## Awards and Recognitions

V.K. Kothurkar has a number of awards and recognitions to his credit. He was awarded research grant for conducting 'An experimental investigation in the modification of social attitudes' by the Government of India in the UNESCO Tension Project, 1951. He was awarded UGC grant of ₹10,000/- to conduct and direct 'An autumn school in experimental psychology' the first of its kind in India, in 1964.

Besides these he represented the University of Poona at the conference of professors of psychology convened by the Government of India in 1951. He was invited to attend the seminar on 'Theories of Personality', conducted by G.W. Allport at Harvard University in 1958. He was an invited nominee of the British Council of Cultural Relations to visit some of the British Universities in 1959. He was a member of the Government of India Committee of ten educators from different Indian universities and was deputed in 1958 for studying and reporting on evaluation techniques in the American universities. He was also deputed by Government of India to visit the Department of Psychology, University of Bukharest, Romania, in 1970. He was a president of the section on education and psychology of the Indian Science Congress held at Banaras in 1968. He was founder president of the Indian Association of Human Behaviour which was started in 1992.

## Contribution to the Field of Psychology

His first interest in research was learning and memory, which are very significant in human lives. Human development depends on learning new procedures, skills—verbal and motor—and cognitive maps. Kothurkar's own researches of human learning and memory, through a large number of papers that he contributed to various journals from time to time, has enhanced his prestige in this area of research. Researchers are familiar with his studies of paired associate learning, serial position learning, short-term paradigm, effect of probing, or probability in learning. He was rigorous experimentalist. So far the mnemonics is concerned, he studied number of viewpoints on matters related to learning and memory.

His research on 'Recall of forgotten names' (*Philosophical Quarterly*, 1950) states the reasons as to how we recall them. Likewise, how affectivity, our positive and negative emotions, affect our recall has been thoroughly explained in his paper entitled 'Affectivity and Recall' (1951). The learning of isolated numbers has been clarified through two papers entitled 'Learning and Retention of an Isolated Number on the Background of Meaningful Material' (1956a) and 'Recall of Isolated Number on the Back-ground of Varying Meaningfulness' (1956b).

Some of his known published articles on learning and memory which are useful for understanding human learning and memory processes includes 'Effect of Meaningfulness of Relation on Paired Associate Learning and Retention' (1964b), 'Effect of Interpolated Recall on Recognition of Schematic Faces' (1965, 11–14), 'Effects of Different Kinds of interpolated Activities on Short-term Remembering' (in Professor Sir F.C. Bartlett Celebration Volume, 1968), 'Effect of Similarity of Interpolated Materials on Short-term Recall' (1968, 405–408), 'Effect of Similarity of Run-structures on Transfer in Probability Learning' (proceedings of the 54th session of the Indian Science Congress, 1967) and 'Effect of Some Perceptual and Verbal Factors on Organization of Free Recall' (11th Annual Conference of the Indian Academy of Applied Psychology, 1974).

His other area of research was 'social tension'. They are an integral part of our life because every society is divided into different groups on the basis of standard of living, language, education, class, caste, religion, etc. The members of the same religion, language, or caste have a feeling as 'we', while for members of other religion, language, or caste there is a feeling as 'they'. This feeling centered around 'we' or 'they' creates affection and liking for our group and disaffection and disliking for other group. These feelings for other group are at the root of discriminatory attitude towards other groups, which for certain reasons results into social tension. When two groups, say, two religious groups, or two caste groups, disagree on certain issues, it may lead to social tension. Though we generally endeavour for social cohesion, it may turn into social tension when some staunch people from either groups or communities disagree vehemently on certain issues. This may lead to stereotyping and prejudice mongering. Kothurkar studied stereotypes and their development among children, provincial stereotypes, social attitudes and their development, human relations, anti-Harijan prejudices, communal traits, the problems of Navabuddhas, and the problems of acculturation of the tribal people and social integration.

His third area of research was 'examination reforms'. Initially he studied the reactions of faculty to examination reform. He also worked on objectives of teaching and learning, educational measurement and evaluation, objectives of examination reform, etc. He had been to America in 1958, as Government of India had deputed him, to study the evaluation techniques in the American Universities. His notable research papers published on examination reforms are 'Reactions of Faculty to Examination Reform' (1960), 'New Trends and Approaches in the Educational Reconstruction of Indian Examinations Since Independence' (Social Sciences seminar, University of Poona, 1960), 'A Note on Objectives of Teaching and Learning with Reference to Examination' (1963), 'Educational Measurement and Evaluation' (1964a), and 'Teaching of Experimental Psychology in Indian Universities' (Indian Science Congress, 1966).

## Kothurkar as a Person and a Teacher

He was an excellent human being, affable, modest, conscientious, and academically disciplined. H.S. Asthana, well-known psychologist and former vice-chancellor, University of Sagar, had written an obituary on Kothurkar. It was published in *Shikshan Varta*, a news bulletin of Human Education Society, Pune. He wrote in his obituary,

> Prof. Nirod Mukerjee, first Chairman of the University of Bombay, Psychology Department and a stalwart in Psychology used to call Prof. Kothurkar, 'God-man of Psychology' for his most unassuming nature. A thorough gentleman and extremely polite, he was uncompromising in academic matters. He was a person of exceptionally high intellectual and personal integrity. He was a quintessential teacher.

I may state here the exact words of Nirod Mukerjee as told to me by Kothurkar himself. He used to say, 'there are two God-men in psychology, one is Professor V.K. Kothurkar and other is Professor H.S. Asthana'. Professor Asthana is really very polite and academically sound researcher in his own right.

He was very conscious of his duties and academic activities. I was his student as well as his colleague. I remember the event that took place in the last year of his retirement. Generally he used to teach two courses at the MA level, one for Part I and other for Part II. In the beginning of academic year of his retirement, colleagues in the department requested him to skip teaching of his usual two courses. He declined their request. After much persuasion, he yielded and said he would teach one course instead of two. To our surprise, he taught the course till the last day of his retirement. He taught that complete course and never allowed others to share it. He would never come late to the class; he would never teach without preparation. He would also maintain regularity in teaching. His delivery was slow and it always helped the students to jot down the contents of his lecture.

He was a very genuine person. His nature was non-interfering and non-controversial. He never imposed his views on others, even the family. He had very good aesthetic sense and enjoyed good things in life. He had a very spartan and disciplined way of life. He had a detached attachment with family events. Though he participated in every family event with enthusiasm, he was at the same time quietly aloof.

Psychology was not just a study and research subject for him but was his way of life and a matter of meditation. He was an atheist and his favourite view was if God exists he should be dissectible on the laboratory table. True to his complete faith in science, he donated his body to medical college of Bharati Vidyapeeth, Pune.

# References

Kothurkar, V.K. (1951). Affectivity and recall. *Philosophical Quarterly, 23*(2, 3 and 4).

————. (1956a). Learning and retention of an isolated number on the background of meaningful material. *Indian Journal of Psychology, 31*(1 & 2), 59–62.

————. (1956b). Recall of isolated number on the background of varying meaningfulness. *Journal of Education and Psychology, 14*(2).

————. (1960). Reactions of faculty to examination reform. *Journal of Education and Psychology, 18*(1).

————. (1963). A note on objectives of teaching and learning with reference to examination. *Education and Psychology Review, 1*(1).

————. (1964a). Educational measurement and evaluation. In B. Kuppuswamy (Ed.), *Advanced, educational psychology.* Delhi: University Publisher.

————. (1964b). Effect of meaningfulness of relation on paired associate learning and retention. *American Journal of Psychology, 77*(1), 116–119.

————. (1965). Effect of interpolated recall on recognition of schematic faces. *Journal of Psychological Researches, 9*(1), 11–14.

————. (1968). Effect of similarity of interpolated materials on short-term recall. *The Quarterly Journal of Experimental Psychology, 20*(4), 405–408.

# 13

# Chandra Mohan Bhatia

(1914–2004)

## Ira Das

Chandra Mohan Bhatia, popularly remembered as C.M. Bhatia, was born in 1914. Being a bright student throughout, he graduated from Agra College, Agra, with the highest percentage of marks. After his postgraduation in mathematics and Licenciate in Teaching (LT) from Allahabad, he taught in the Government Inter College for some time. He did his BEd (honours) from the University of Edinburgh, Scotland. Upon his return he, became principal of the Central Pedagogical Institute (CPI) at Allahabad. He again went to Edinburgh and got his PhD degree in psychology under supervision of Godfrey Thomson. During this period, he developed the Bhatia's Battery of Performance Tests of Intelligence and standardized it on illiterate and literate children of rural and urban India.

*C.M. Bhatia*

On the recommendations of the Acharya Narendra Dev Committee, the Government of Uttar Pradesh (UP) established the Bureau of Psychology and Chandra Mohan Bhatia became its founder-director in 1947. It was visited and appreciated by the then Prime Minister of India Pt Jawaharlal Nehru in 1956. The bureau played an important role in providing guidance services to the community at large. Later on, he became the deputy director of education (training) and deputy director of education (finance) in the UP government. In 1964, he became the additional director of education (UP) and took the charge of director of education in 1967. After this, he became vice-chancellor of the University of Allahabad in 1971. He was a life member of a number of psychological and educational organizations of India including the Indian Association of Clinical Psychology and was president (psychology section) of the Indian Science Congress Association in 1979–1980. He has several research papers to his credit. His writings were also published in newspapers. He also authored several books. He contributed to committees of various universities and educational institutes and remained active till 2000. He died in 2004 at his residence in Agra.

*C.M. Bhatia explaining his test to Prime Minister Pt. Jawaharlal Nehru and Shri Lal Bahadur Shastri when they visited Bureau of Psychology, Allahabad*

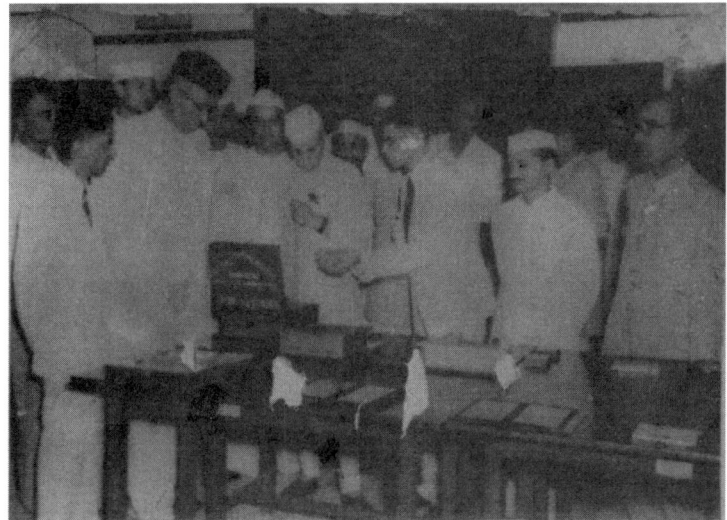

## Research on Intelligence

In the introduction of his book *Intelligence Testing and National Reconstruction*, published in 1948 by Hind Kitabs, Bombay, he wrote:

> This period (1946–48) has seen momentous changes; it has been a period of rapid development too. It is therefore a pleasure to note that the suggestions put forward are already on the way to practical realization- Psychological Institutes are being opened up by almost all provisional Governments.

In this book he had suggested that

> [T]his highly intelligent section of the village population consists of about 7 per cent of the whole (illiterates). We advocate special efforts for the immediate picking out of this superior section and for giving it the proper education and opportunity to enable it to make its rightful contribution to the national life.

In the foreword of his book, *Performance Test of Intelligence under Indian Conditions*, published by Oxford University Press, London in 1955, Godfrey H. Thomson of the University of Edinburgh wrote,

> It is of greatest importance to India, and therefore to the world, that her rising generation should be well educated, each in the way best fitted to his or her talents, and that her manpower, in adulthood, should be helped into those occupations most needed by the nation, most likely to profit by the individual's special abilities, and most likely therefore to make him happy and self-respecting. The object of the testing movement, in which Dr Bhatia is an acknowledged expert, is exactly to forward such aims not by dictatorial direction but by careful assessment of abilities, general and special, and helpful recommendations based on such assessments.

The unique feature of Bhatia's Battery of Performance Tests is the difficult and time-consuming process of data collection on individual basis from different villages located in remote areas scattered over the whole of UP. The geographical distribution of the sample included children of Allahabad, Gorakhpur, Garhwal, Jhansi, Bareilly, and even rural areas of Sultanpur, thus, covering east, west, north, south, and central UP regions. Community-wise distribution included fairly representative samples of Brahmins, Kshatriyas, Kayasthas, Vaishyas, backward communities, Muslims, Christians, Anglo Indians, Sikhs, Parsis, Jains, etc. Occupation-wise distribution of literates included majority of children of middle service class, and proportionate representation of higher profession, lower class services, business and agriculture, and even orphans and children of unemployed parents. Occupation-wise distribution of parents of children from the illiterate group included farmers, petty shopkeepers, artisans and craftsmen such as carpenters, weavers, barbers, washermen, etc., hired labourers, and servants from rural areas. Illiterate children of domestic servants were also taken from urban areas. Communication to the remoter areas of villages during 1947 to the 1950s was possible only through horse-driven carriages (taking 24 hours for covering just 40 km) where roads were not fit for even motor services. It was a time of great political upheaval in India after Partition and, therefore, travelling had its own dangers. Although the villagers were not hostile, they were sceptical and their attitude for outsiders was not favourable. Stay in the village during data collection was very helpful in carrying out the testing work with much scientific rigor. The total number of boys tested for purposes of standardization was 1,154, of which 642 were school-going and 512 were illiterate. The school-going group included a group of 100 boys who were also given the Terman-Merril Intelligence Test Form-L (1937) for the purpose of validation and factor analysis.

The tests included in Bhatia's Battery of Performance Tests of Intelligence were—

1. Kohs' Block Design Test
2. Alexander's Passalong Test
3. Pattern Drawing Test (devised by Bhatia himself)
4. Immediate Memory Test for Digits (with an alternative form suitable for illiterate, devised by Bhatia himself.)
5. Picture Construction Test (devised by Bhatia himself)

Separate norms were provided for literate and illiterate children for calculating IQ.

In the September 1976 issue of *Indian Journal of Psychology,* Vol. 51, Part 3, an article entitled 'The Concept of Intelligence: Its Present Status' by C.M. Bhatia was published in which he said:

There is no denial of heritability of intelligence. Only in the case of this composite and complex trait, the nature of its manifestation is suitably elaborated. Almost 20 years ago, I had echoed the same views when I said, 'We believe that the lower performance of the illiterate group on our battery of tests does not necessarily indicate a lower innate mental ability on the part of this group. The concentration of attention which any test situation requires appears quite foreign to illiterate. Paying attention to essentially abstract situation for any considerable length of time is essentially the result of school practice and the demands of civilization.'

In 1990, Bhatia informally supervised the PhD work of P.K. Mona (then a PhD student of Ira Das, head of the Department of Psychology, Dayalbagh Educational Institute, Agra). The research indicated an important finding that deprived literates scored higher in intelligence, as measured by Bhatia's battery of performance tests, in comparison to deprived illiterates. In the words of Bhatia

> The Indian social set up has a number of deprivations operative, but obviously the most important in the economic, which in its extreme form is called poverty. This is a category of people who are below the poverty line. On account of the features of its educational system, India is still producing billions of illiterate children every year. It is universally accepted that cognitive abilities do not develop properly in the absence of suitable stimulation.

The research results indicated that literate children have significantly higher IQ in comparison to illiterate children, clearly indicating that intelligence lies dormant in illiterates and surfaces up when developmental facilities like education are provided. This effect could be seen more clearly when such comparison between intelligence test scores of literate and illiterate children within the deprived group (below poverty line) was made. A small section of the deprived group who some- how got the opportunity of getting education was compared with the completely illiterate children of equally deprived group (i.e., below poverty line). The literate but economically deprived were significantly higher in intelligence as compared to illiterate deprived group. In the words of Bhatia,

> The trend is clear that schooling and education improves the total intelligence scores of the section of deprived children who go to school. Schooling, which means training of attention and concentration on a task improves performance on an intelligence test'. Bhatia also concluded that, 'the socio-economic grouping and intelligence are on the same pattern in 1990, as they were fifty years ago in 1940s, when Bhatia did his original work.

The results of this research during the 1990s indicate high coefficient of correlation between scores on the sub-tests of the battery and between each sub-test scores with the IQ scores, which proves high content and factorial validity of Bhatia's Battery of Performance tests of Intelligence.

# Reference

Bhatia, C.M. (1976, September). The concept of intelligence: Its present status. *Indian Journal of Psychology*, *51*(3): 205.

# 14

# Fr. Joachim M. Fuster

(1914–2011)

## Satishchandra Kumar and Anjali Majumdar

*Fr. Fuster at Xavier Institute of Counselling (XIC), Mumbai, 2003*

Fr. Joachim M. Fuster was born in Palma de Mallorca, Spain, on 26 October 1914. Growing up with three brothers and a sister, Fr. Fuster had a deeply rooted feeling of community. He grew up in an orthodox joint family surrounding, where he learned respect for elders. From an early age, Fr. Fuster knew he wanted to be a missionary priest. In 1931, when he was 17 years old, the communist party formed the government in Spain. The Jesuits were expelled from the country and so Fr. Fuster moved to Italy. There he received basic training in humanities, Latin, and Greek literature, as well as philosophy for five years, from 1932 to 1937. Thereafter, he got a letter from his superiors to go to India. 'When you live on the level of faith, you don't question. I do it, as it's what God wants me to do' (Sharma, Rashid, Kumar, & Virji, 2004). The quote reminds us of the vows of poverty, chastity, and obedience that all Jesuits take. Till the end of his life, Fr. Fuster was working with the same unflinching dedication, commitment, and self-discipline and was a source of inspiration to all his students (Kumar & Ramaswami, 2005). India became his home away from home, till the day he passed away.

## Affiliations

After coming to India, Fr. Fuster studied philosophy for 3 years in Shembaganur in Tamil Nadu with an international community of 100 Jesuits. Then, he spent 2 years teaching at St. Xavier's School, Mumbai. He enjoyed shaping the innocent and pliable minds of the children during this time. He was then sent to Patna in order to look after the boarding of poor children. It was during his time in Patna that he acquired a BA degree in Hindi. This was consistent with his belief that in order to serve a community one has to understand its culture and language is the best channel to get to the ethos of people. He became a full-fledged priest at Kurseong, Darjeeling.

In 1954, he joined the St. Xavier's College, Mumbai, as a student counsellor. After that, he obtained his master's degree in psychology, pursuing research on the relationship between congruence of self-concept and the self as judged by others and personality adjustment from the American Catholic University in Washington DC. This was followed by his doctorate from the Faculty of Education and Psychology, Maharaja Shivajirao (MS) University, Baroda. His thesis was on the comparative analysis of relationship between acceptance of self and acceptance of others in four Indian college student communities: Hindus, Muslims, Catholics, and Zoroastrians (Sharma, Rashid, Kumar, & Virji, 2004).

From 1958 to 1974, Fr. Fuster was a Professor and Head of the Department of Psychology at St. Xavier's College (Sharma, Rashid, Kumar, & Virji, 2004). His students remember him as a warm and benevolent disciplinarian who could hold the attention of the students for the entire 50 minutes of a lecture. He was also the editor of the *Journal of Vocational and Educational Guidance* from 1962 to 1967, which was published from Mumbai. He became a recognized postgraduate teacher and research guide of the University of Mumbai for doctoral studies in psychology in 1967. In 1966, he attended an eight-day seminar on client-centred therapy under Carl Rogers in Paris (Fuster, 1978). He took a sabbatical in 1971–1972, during which, he was trained as a trainer in sensitivity training or T-group at the National Training Laboratory (NTL) Institute in Bethel, Maine. Since then, he conducted training programmes for psychologist, social workers, counsellors, teachers, and other helping professionals. In 1971, he learned the Carkhuff Model of Counselling under Sidney Wolf in Baltimore, USA (Fuster, 1978). In 1975, he founded the Xavier's Institute of Counselling, which was considered as a beacon of hope by many aspiring counsellors. He insisted that 'as a counselor, if you are not developing the Counsellee's potentialities, making one independent and self-reliant, you are inhibiting one's personal growth'. He was also one of the founding members of the Indian Society for Applied Behavioral Science (ISABS; Sharma, Rashid, Kumar, & Virji, 2004). ISABS is a national, professional organization of behavioural scientists engaged in applying their knowledge to the well-being of persons and organizations. It was registered in January 1972 as a professional body under the Societies Registration Act of 1860 (Sinha, 2004).

In 1978, he received training in the 1977 Carkhuffian model of counselling from Robert R. Carkhuff at the Carkhuff Institute of Human Technology at Amherst, Massachusetts. He worked in the integration of the 1969 model, which emphasized conceptual aspects to a greater extent, with the 1977 model that focused on the application of Carkhuffian principles, especially in the Indian context. Fr. Fuster then continued to train others who were interested in the Carkhuffian model through the Xavier's Institute of Counselling, Mumbai.

Fuster (1978), while responding to the invitation of M.B. Ghorpade, managing editor of *Bombay Psychologist Journal*, wrote an article on his personal experience in India on personal counselling. While writing the article, he explained that he was very interested in seeing the profession of personal counsellors flourishing in India. However, he said that by flourishing, he meant that the quality of their professional services be such that really stimulates the human resource development of their charges. While narrating the experience of 5 years of training counsellor in the Carkhuff's model, he found that a few, roughly one third, are very good; a very few are no good; and the rest need further training. He was very critical of training counselling psychology at the masters level at university set-up in India. Fuster (1978) says

> It is very frustrating, however, to potentially good Indian candidates to this profession to find that the training programmes offered by our Indian universities, are either non-existent or of poor quality. The same could be said of some good professor who would like to use modern ways of training, but are inhibited by the present system and regulations.

He emphasized the need of good and efficient training of counsellors. He concluded by saying that as the American International College, B. Brenson (Fuster, 1978) gave us four characteristics to select counsellor trainees:

1. They can exercise individual moral values
2. They are bright
3. They have a high energy level, and
4. They are open to learning

He said that his experience in India can add two more criteria:

5. They have a high level of maturity and
6. They are keenly interested in stimulating human resource development in India

He concludes by saying that the success of personal counselling depends a great deal on the quality of the person of the counsellor and on the high level on which he functions as a person.

## Fr. Fuster and the Carkhuff Model

Fr. Fuster compares counselling to a computer, 'Counselling is like a computer. You have to put in the right data to get the right output. If the right data is not put in, the outcome will be different' (Kumar & Ramaswami, 2005).

Personal counselling can be conceptualized as the outcome of a very complex interaction between two sets of variables: the counsellor and the counselee. Carkhuff has attempted to spell out some of these variables (Fuster, 1978). In all personal counselling and human resource development, the outcome is some kind of change in behaviour, which is seen in a form of action. There are two broad ways in which this change can be brought into effect:

1) *Manipulate* the change, as done by behaviourists, by conditioning the person to act in a way.
2) Bringing about an *understanding*, or an *insight*, in the person about the change in his behaviour.

It is necessary to integrate the two forms for effective counselling. When understanding precedes action, the goals of the action become relevant to the client. The client goes through three stages during the counselling process:

Exploration → Understanding → Action

A pre-stage to the helping process is involvement, as the client's involvement during the whole process is critical for its success. The cousellor affects or facilitates this change in the client with the help of some counselling skills. The counselling process, as experienced by the counsellor, has four stages—attending, responding, personalizing, and initiating (Fuster, 1978).

In the words of Fr. Fuster:

> [T]he counselor has to function at a higher level in order to be effective, stimulate growth in others, and bring about change in others. This can be achieved through disciplining yourself, training yourself, confronting yourself, reviewing yourself, being clear about yourself, enriching yourself, and working on yourself. (Sharma, Rashid, Kumar, & Virji, 2004)

The Xavier's Institute of Counselling (XIC) provided a certificate course in using the Carkhuff model of counselling, known as the 50 hours counselling course in personal counselling. 'Be Yourself, Know yourself, Develop Yourself'—this is the philosophy behind the teachings of Fr. Joachim M. Fuster and this is exactly what he has helped innumerable people to attain in their lives, through his counselling sessions and lectures over so many decades (Kumar & Ramaswami, 2005). He used to say 'I want to do what God wants me to do. This gives me a lot of fulfilment. God looks at us with love. I live with this faith that God wants me to conduct this counselling course' (Kumar & Ramaswami, 2005), and therefore, one sees that all his personal counselling books are dedicated to Jesus Christ whom he said was the designer and maker of human potential (Fuster, 2008).

After returning from St. Xavier's College as professor and head and then becoming director of XIC, he ran the 50 hours of personal counselling course for almost 35 years and trained more than 2,500 helping professionals through this course. Before accepting students in the course, Fr. Fuster made sure that they were genuinely interested, committed, and had a helping and serving orientation in pursuing the course through a personal interview. During this personal interview, he explained the duration, timings, number of participants, objectives, syllabus, method, learning material, and the eligibility criteria for the certificate during the one-to-one meetings with the candidates. He made sure that the candidates understood that the aim of the course was not to train participants to become professional counsellors. Rather, the aim of the course was meeting the need for continuing formation of professionals in the helping professions. The motto of his counselling course: 'Counselling is as effective as the counsellor is living effectively' (Fuster, 2008). He used to say in the course was 'the best thing you can give a counsellee is yourself functioning at a higher level' (Kumar & Ramaswami, 2005).

The course was made up of 25 sessions of 2 hours each. These sessions were broadly divided into two categories—the training of counsellors and the counsellor's personal growth. The first part included 10 sessions on the Carkhuff model and six sessions on the laboratory methodology (human process/sensitivity training). According to Father Fuster,

> [L]aboratory training is experimenting with self and it is a safe ground to experiment. In order to experiment and explore self, you have to be honest, sincere, and genuine with self. We want to love you and in order to love you, we want to know you as you are. (Sharma, Rashid, Kumar, & Virji, 2004)

The second part of the course consisted of five sessions on self-work and roughly four sessions of tests, distribution of photographs and certificates, and the opportunity for feedback. Fr. Fuster believed in giving explicit attention to the counsellor's personal growth. According to him, 'You are faced with challenges and life is to meet these challenges, pray to God for spiritual strength to meet these challenges'. In one's attempt to solve problems, Fr. Fuster reminded everyone, 'the solution also lies within you, you need to work on self, be yourself, know yourself, and develop yourself' (Sharma, Rashid, Kumar, & Virji, 2004). The counsellor's personal growth included five sessions, which were titled 'Becoming Yourself', 'Mental Health', 'Self-Actualization', 'Conscience and Superego', and 'the Counsellor's Professional Ethics'. The session 'Becoming Yourself' focused on the self-concept. The development in an individual's self-concept is influenced by various factors such as self-esteem, membership and social roles, communication, moral principles, and identification. Even after the individual's self-concept is formed, it remains dynamic, that is, though substantially it remains the same, it is subject to modification as various psychological processes bring better information on various aspects of the self (Fuster, 2008).

During the session 'Mental Health', the focus shifted to maintaining mental health and sources of stress. Mental health includes many aspects ranging from self-acceptance, deriving satisfaction from one's job, and taking reasonable care of one's health to being kind and helpful to others, being interested in the welfare of others, and the capacity to play and have fun. Mental health can be maintained by reducing stress and increasing adjustive resources. Stress arises at four levels—biological, psychological, spiritual, and sociological (Fuster, 2008). Such stress can be reduced by increasing the adjustive resources in the respective areas. For example, taking care of health with appropriate diet, rest, sleep, and relaxation to reduce biological stress; developing a realistic self-concept, increasing self-knowledge and self-understanding, and developing a sense of humour and the ability to laugh at self to reduce psychological stress; having faith, hope, and love to reduce spiritual stress; and having resilience and competence to face difficult times in a group of people to reduce social stress.

Self-actualization includes all the possible aspects of the person. This means, that self-actualization is a life process of self-improvement which will end only with death (Fuster, 2008). To be a self-actualized person, it is necessary to know yourself and your strengths and weaknesses, and accept yourself as you are; try seriously to develop your strengths and minimize your weaknesses; profit from the opportunities for self-improvement that come your way; learn how to get on smoothly with others and stimulate them to grow; be honest with yourself and with others; be responsible and reliable; control yourself and be generous with others; and have a sense of direction in life and know where you are going (Fuster, 2008). The next session focused on defining conscience and differentiating it from superego. Every human being has the ability to reason, and reason has an inbuilt law, the natural law, that distinguishes right from wrong (Fuster, 2008). Conscience is reason applying the natural law to a concrete situation, and judging its goodness and sinfulness (Fuster, 2008). The final session was 'The Counsellor's Professional Ethics'. Fr. Fuster was also among the first people to emphasize the importance of ethics in every profession, especially those related to the service of others. Ethics mean a lot to a counsellor and Fr. Fuster ensured that all the potential candidates to the course took a vow of confidentiality of information regarding self and fellow batchmates. The last session of the course was devoted to professional ethics, values, and how and when to break professional secrecy, counsellor's relationship to counselee and to himself, and the counsellor's influence on counselee.

In addition to these sessions on self-development, Fr. Fuster also provided access to his students to his excellent personal library. As part of the requirement of the course, three tests were conducted in order to judge the participants' learning (Sharma, Rashid, Kumar, & Virji, 2004). To make his course available to people, Fr. Fuster penned *Personal Counselling*, which had 12 editions. The book focuses on human technology and the five-stage counselling process based on the Carkhuffian model, which includes attending skills, responding skills, personalizing skills, initiating skills, and evaluating skills. Even for his training course, Fr. Fuster insisted on knowing these steps by rote. Fr. Fuster described the Carkhuff as follows: 'The Carkhuff Model of human technology is direct and hard-hitting like a gun. Also, the problem should not be like a mosquito, otherwise you are using a gun to hit the mosquito' (Sharma, Rashid, Kumar, & Virji, 2004).

At the end of the 50 hours personal counselling course Fr. Fuster gave a truly inspiring message to the trainees.

> When I am writing these lines at the end of the book, I feel very close to you, reader, man or woman; Asian or African or European, American or Australian; rich or poor; Catholic or non-Catholic. In the light of my Christian faith, I perceive you as a child of God with a unique personality and a unique mission in life. My keen wish is that you understand yourself in depth as to where you come from and where you are going, and that you exploit your human potential in fulfilment of your God-given mission in life. I very much wish that you make the contribution which is expected of you in God's Plan by recycling the learning process over and over again, and that you help others to do the same in order that they, also, make their own contributions. (Fuster, 2008)

Fr. Fuster's pursuit for knowledge was perhaps guided by his belief that 'to pursue knowledge as a means to serving the community is the highest form of *gnyana yoga*'. But all the degrees and academic achievements that he held sat lightly on his shoulders as he was a humble person.

Fr. Fuster's life has not been without sufferings and setbacks. At the age of 45, he was diagnosed with melanoma, which is a malignant tumour of melanocytes. He underwent surgery and other therapies at St. Elizabeth's nursing home. Although the doctors had only given him 2 months to live, his faith and resilience helped him survive the near fatal ailment. He was grateful to God for his recovery as is clear from his statement, 'I really don't know what worked, but it was God's will that I live and so the cancer disappeared' (Sharma, Rashid, Kumar, & Virji, 2004). Even though the cancer was cured, it left its mark on Fr. Fuster. He had difficulty in walking as his right leg was often swollen and painful. But that did not stop him. His undying spirit endured the pain and he moved on to the next challenge.

Fr. Fuster passed away at the age of 96 on 9 January 2011, but his legacy lives on in the form of his teachings to his many students, dedicated to the progress of the various fields of psychology.

## Awards and Recognitions

One of the greatest awards that Fr. Fuster received was the inclusion of his biography in *Men of Achievement*, 12th Edition, Cambridge, England in 1980. He was also awarded the Lifetime Achievement Award by the Bombay Psychological Association for his contribution to counselling psychology (Sharma, Rashid, Kumar, & Virji, 2004). The personal counselling course of 50 hours of Fr. Fuster became so popular that he was invited to Damascus House, London, England, for nine years. For three years, he conducted these courses at the Institute of Ignatian Spirituality, Rome, Italy, Scotland, Spain, Hong Kong, Australia, Guyana (South America), Pakistan, and Sri Lanka to give lectures and conduct the courses.

Fr. Fuster is fondly remembered by all of his students. The editorial team of the St. Xavier's college magazine published an article about him, 'In Fond Remembrance...Father J.M. Fuster' in its 2010–2011 edition. Father Fuster lived life to the fullest and emphatically declared that he had no regrets (editorial team, St. Xavier's college magazine, 2010–2011). Fr. Fuster is truly a legend and one who had always practised what he preached, always contributed towards the individual and social development, and worked for the humanity at large. Having given so much to society throughout his life and by continuing to do till his death, he was definitely a true 'karmayogi' and *aam aadmi* psychologist who has definitely lived up to his belief that '[t]rue happiness lies not in receiving but in giving' (Kumar & Ramaswami, 2005). Students of Fr. Fuster brought out a book *Enriching Lives* in appreciation of Fr. J.M. Fuster on the occasion of his 90th birthday on 26 October 2004 took up the assignment of writing a tribute to Father Fuster to document his course, the process, and the must-be-known facts of one of the stalwarts in the counselling profession. The preface also said that it is the need of the hour to salute Fr. Fuster's discipline, his attempt at taking psychology to common person through his counselling course, and his selfless service to a country where he finds himself by sheer accident and not birth (Sharma, Rashid, Kumar, & Virji, 2004).

# References

Editorial Team. (2010–2011). *In fond remembrance.* St. Xavier's College Magazine.

Fuster, J.M. (1978). Personal counseling. *Bombay Psychologist, 1*(1), 55–59.

———. (2008). *Personal counselling.* Updated edition with training programme, 14th print. Mumbai: St. Paul Press, Better Yourself Books.

Kumar, S., and Ramaswami, A. (2005). *Beyond the ordinary: Stories that inspire and challenge.* Mumbai: St. Paul Press, Better Yourself Books.

Sharma, A., Rashid, F., Kumar, S., and Virji, Z. (2004). *Enriching lives: In appreciation of Fr. J.M. Fuster on the occasion of his ninetieth birthday.* Mumbai: Arihant Art.

Sinha, D.P. (2004). *T-Group team building and organisation development.* New Delhi: Raj Press.

# 15

## Syed Mohammad Mohsin

(1914–1999)

Mithila B. Sharan and Ram R. Tripathi

*Syed Mohammad Mohsin*

Syed Mohammad Mohsin was born on 30 July 1914. He obtained BA (honours) and MA in philosophy from Patna University. He started his career as a government research scholar in Patna College, but was later appointed as a lecturer in the same college in 1938. He went abroad on study leave in 1946 and obtained his PhD degree in psychology from the University of Edinburgh in 1948 under the guidance of James Drever. On his return, he joined Patna College again as assistant professor of psychology. In 1956 he became the founder-director of the Bihar State Educational and Vocational Guidance Bureau. During his stewardship of the bureau, he authored the book *Handbook of Educational and Vocational Guidance*. In 1960, he was appointed as university Professor and Head of the Department of Psychology, Patna University, where he continued till his retirement in 1974. Even after his retirement, he was attached to the Department of Psychology as UGC professor till 1976.

On the recommendation of his thesis supervisor, Drever, Mohsin visited some of the European universities after submitting his PhD thesis where experimental and applied psychology was introduced as the most recent discipline. He had very fruitful discussions in Switzerland with C.G. Jung, the renowned psychologist, and at Geneva with Jean Piaget, the then UNESCO consultant for developmental education. He also stayed at Cambridge for a week and devoted most of his time in contacting F.C. Bartlett, head of the Department of Experimental Psychology. He visited the psychological laboratory for acquainting himself with experimental techniques then unknown in Indian universities. At Edinburgh, Mohsin equipped himself with the most recent and sophisticated statistical methods, factor analysis, and analysis of variance, by regularly attending classes of Sir Godfrey Thomson, head of the Department of Education. Thus, Mohsin was the first to introduce these statistical techniques in psychological and educational research in India.

While teaching in the classroom, he used to reiterate and emphasize very often on 'scientific aptitude', 'objectivity', 'validity', 'reliability', 'meaningfulness', 'controls', 'variables', 'tight design', etc. As a result, for his every student, these words became the keywords for designing a study and using statistical methods. Not only that, a paper like statistics and mental measurement became a popular subject for many of his students in Patna and other universities in Bihar. Credit goes to him that he made every student understand how to collect data and use suitable statistics including factor analysis and analysis of variance.

Mohsin was elected to the Academic Council in 1952 when Patna University became a teaching university and to the Patna University Senate and Syndicate in 1955. He was ex-officio member of the Syndicate in 1963, and the chancellor's nominee in 1984. He was nominated as a member of the Board of Control of the A.N. Sinha Institute of Social Studies when it became a statutory body as a representative of Patna University for two consecutive terms, each of two years, and also of the state government for two terms, each of three years. Thus, he served for the longest time since the institute was created, and the social psychology division of this institute was added to its present three divisions only on his initiative.

Mohsin, as the founder-director of the Bihar Educational and Vocational Guidance Bureau, was very closely associated with the Directorate of Employment and Rehabilitation of the state government. By his contribution, Mohsin had firmly established the role of psychology in scientifically spotting talented children, correcting delinquency among the adolescents, and also restoring normalcy among pre-delinquent children. He assisted the state government in starting the Netarhat Residential School for gifted children and was involved in devising and implementing the procedure for selection and admission in the school. The results were startling, to the extent that V.K.R.V. Rao, the then Education Minister, Government of India, deputed the education secretary, Mr Saraf, to prepare an authentic report about the school. The Saraf Report was published by the ministry concerned recommending that such schools should be established in every state of India. The establishment of the Orthogenic School (auxiliary home) for the reform of pre-delinquent children was also established at Hazaribagh as per his initiative by the then education Secretary, J.C. Mathur. It was another validation of psychological counselling by Mohsin. The pilot centre for the correction of juvenile delinquents at Hazaribagh was another feather in his cap. He also suggested the state government to create the post of chief psychologist in BES Class 1 to act as its head, and that was done. He had also been instrumental in the creation of departments of psychology in the central universities such as Delhi and Aligarh Muslim University and assisted the setting up of the National Council of Education, Research and Training (NCERT). He served as Chairman of the Central Advisory Committee of the National Test Library of the NCERT. He was also research consultant of the University Grant Commission (UGC), NCERT, and the Indian Council for Social Sciences

Research (ICSSR) for many years. This shows how much involvement he had for the development of psychology in India, particularly in Bihar, not only as a subject but as a promise to solve social and educational problems. He had been the founder-president of the Bihar Psychological Association, president of the section of psychology and educational science of the Indian Science Congress Association in 1957 and of the All-India Educational and Vocational Guidance Association in 1960. In recognition, the UGC appointed him as national lecturer in psychology during 1973–1974.

## Contribution to Psychology

A close look at his research papers shows a fascinating trend—Freudian psychology, intelligence testing, mental measurement, laboratory experiments, guidance and counselling, and finally social psychology. He initially wrote on Freudian psychology (1938a), fear instinct (1938), defences against ego-threat in self-judgment (1955b), ego-defences in self-adjustment (1954c), ego-threat (1960d), and emotional maturity (1960a), and went ahead to transfer of training (1939b), nature and measurement of intelligence (1938b), psycho-analytical theory of play (1939a), mental set in associative reproduction (1942), Spearman's tetrad difference criterion and the group factors (1943), and effect of frustration on problem-solving behavior (1954b). A large number of his published work focused on guidance and training/selection. This includes comparative evaluation of the achievement (1954a), revaluation of the traditional system of examination (1955a), psychological tests in vocational guidance (1957), vocational selection and vocational guidance (1958), guidance personal training (1959c), industrial selection (1959d), scientific aptitude (1959e), comparison of the inventoried and observed interests (1959a), counselling pupils (1960b), discovery and development of talent (1960c), diagnostic and prognostic value in school guidance (1960e), incidental learning and personality variables (1968), and learning as a function of habit strength and drive level (1972). In the later part, he focused on attitude (1973b), attitude towards nationalization (1969), attitude strength (1973a), and attitude formation and change (1976).

He authored *A Practical Handbook of Educational Guidance* (1959b), *Elementary Psychology* (1966), *Experiments in Psychology* (1975), *Research Methods in Behavioural Sciences* (1984), and *Attitude: Concept, Formation, and Change* (1990). He also contributed to *Advanced Educational Psychology* (Kuppuswamy, 1964) and *'Third Indian Year Book of Educational Research'* (Adaval, 1968). He also has several tests to his credit—The Hindusthani Group Test of Intelligence (1939), The Bihar Test of General Intelligence (1954), Clerical Aptitude Test Battery (1958), Test of Emotional Maturity (1959), Science Aptitude Test, Forms A and B (1959), A Scale for Measuring Attitude towards Nationalisation, Forms A and B (1968), A Test of Conservatism (1972), and A Test of Self-concept (1975). He also adapted the Bell's Adjustment Inventory (Mohsin-Shamshad Adaptation of Bell's Adjustment Inventory, 1970).

An appraisal of these books is the need of the time. The book on experiments is a model of conducting experiments in psychology with specific details of framing hypotheses, steps in the conductance of experiment, statistical treatment of data, interpretation of results, and preparing reports. The book on research methodology is an unparallel research volume in which research strategies such as field study, field experiments, and quasi-experimental designs with clear distinction among them along with suitable examples in the Indian context are given. The appendix regarding statistical methods in behavioural research is another unique addition to the volume. The statistical techniques with appropriate examples and detailed calculations following the steps given in the formula are very useful.

Establishing the need and utility of psychology in effectively improving the well-being of human life, Mohsin rather explicitly demonstrated the role of selection of talent. Providing guidance to students to choose an appropriate stream of learning to turn out suitable manpower to the nation is well established. Introducing the programme for the correction of pre-delinquent children in the Orthogenic School is a brilliant example of the use of psychological techniques to shape the academic growth and healthy personality of wayward children. All this filled up the gap between theory and practice of psychology in India.

His sad demise on 1 March 1999 was an irreparable loss to psychology.

# References

Adaval, S.B. (Ed.). (1968). *Third Indian year book of educational research.* New Delhi: NCERT.

Kuppuswamy, B. (Ed.). (1964). *Advanced educational psychology.* Delhi: University Publishers.

Mohsin, S.M. (1938a, July). Freudian Psychology. *Calcutta Review.*

———. (1938b). Intelligence: Its nature and measurement, a series of three articles. *Indian Journal of Education,* (September, October, November).

———. (1938c, December). The instinct of fear. *Calcutta Review.*

———. (1939a, January). A psycho-analytical theory of play. *Indian Journal of Education.*

———. (1939b, August). Transfer of training. *Science and Culture.*

———. (1942, May & June). Mental set in associative reproduction. *Hindusthan Review.*

———. (1943, July). Spearman's tetrad difference criterion and the group factors. *Indian Journal of Psychology,* XVIII.

———. (1950, January). A study of the relationship of evaluating attitudes to sex difference, intellectual level, expressed occupational interest and hobbies. *Indian Journal of Psychology,* XXV.

———. (1954a). *A comparative evaluation of the achievement of basic and traditional school children* (Report of Enquiry on Basic Education). Bihar Government Publication.

———. (1954b). Effect of frustration on problem solving behavior. *Journal of Abnormal and Social Psychology,* 49, 152–155.

———. (1954c). Ego-defences in self adjustment. *Patna University Journal.*

———. (1955a, January). A revaluation of the traditional system of examination. *The Bihar Education.*

———. (1955b, January–June). Defences against ego-threat in self-judgment: A factorial study. *Indian Journal of Psychology,* XXX.

———. (1957). Place of psychological tests in vocational guidance. *Indian Journal of Psychology,* XXXII (Part I–II).

———. (1958). Vocational selection and vocational guidance. *Journal of Vocational and Educational Guidance,* 4, 166–171.

———. (1959a). A comparative study of the inventoried and observed interests of secondary school students. *Journal of Educational and Vocational Guidance,* 6, 1–7.

———. (1959b). *A practical handbook of educational guidance.* Patna, Bihar: Secretariat Press.

———. (1959c, August). Guidance personal training. *Journal of Educational and Vocational Guidance,* V(1).

———. (1959d, February). Industrial selection. *Journal of Educational and Vocational Guidance,* V(3).

———. (1959e). Plea for a scientific aptitude test. *Indian Journal of Psychology,* XXXIV(Part I).

———. (1960a). A measure of emotional maturity. *Psychological Studies,* 5, 78–83.

———. (1960b). Counselling pupils. *Teacher Education.*

———. (1960c). Discovery and development of talent. *Journal of Educational and Vocational Guidance.*

———. (1960d, January). Retroactive inhibition: A reaction to ego-threat. *Psychological Studies,* 5(1).

———. (1960e). The diagnostic and prognostic value in school guidance of high and low intelligence test scores. *Journal of Educational and Vocational Guidance.*

Mohsin, S.M. (1967). *Elementary psychology*. Calcutta: Asia Publishing House.

———. (1968). Incidental learning and personality variables. *Journal of General and Applied Psychology*.

———. (1969). A balanced scale for measuring the attitude towards nationalization and suggestion of a method to assess intra-attitude consistency. *Journal of General and Applied Psychology*.

———. (1972). Transfer in PA learning as a function of habit strength and drive level. *Psychological Studies*, *17*, 36–40.

———. (1973a). An empirical evaluation of the concept of attitude strength. *Psychological Studies*.

———. (1973b). The scale product method of scoring an attitude test. *Journal of Economic and Social Studies*.

———. (1976). Reinterpretation of the dynamics of attitude formation and change. *Indian Journal of Psychology*, *51*, 1–60.

———. (1981). *Research methods in behavioural sciences.* Calcutta: Orient Longman.

———. (1982). *Experiments in psychology* (2nd ed.). Motilal Banarsidass.

———. (1990). *Attitude: Concept, formation, and change*. Wiley Eastern.

# 16

# Awadh Kishore Prasad Sinha

(1918–2009)

## Ran Bijay Narayan Sinha

*Awadh Kishore Prasad Sinha*

Awadh Kishore Prasad Sinha (popularly known as A.K.P. Sinha) was an internationally acknowledged psychologist from India. His work, spanning more than half a century, has influenced the academic as much as it has the practicing professionals. He was born on 6 June 1918 at village Tekanpura, then a part of district Monghyr and now a part of Begusarai district of Bihar. He was the youngest of four children of the late Hito Rai, advocate at Monghyr. His parents were quite wealthy and his mother, Nanho Devi, was a religious woman. From a very early age, Sinha excelled as a student. He married Ramrati Devi at the age of 20, passed the matriculation examination from Zilla School, Monghyr, in the year 1935, and enrolled the same year in Patna University, Patna. He obtained an MA in philosophy (1941) with gold medal from Patna University, Patna.

In 1941, A.K.P. Sinha was appointed as a lecturer in philosophy in Rajendra College, Chapra. In 1942, he was appointed as a lecturer in philosophy in Greer Bhumihar Brahmin (GBB) College, now known as Langat Singh College, Muzaffarpur. In 1947, he moved to Patna College, Patna. Availing the Government of India Scholarship for higher studies, in 1948, he went to the University of Michigan, Ann Arbor, and obtained his master in science in 1949 and PhD in 1951. He specialized in the area of social psychology, experimental psychology, and psychology of personality. He worked as the director and senior professor of psychology, Institute of Psychological Research and Service, Patna University (1959–1968). He took over the charge of the institute as its director on

13 May 1958 from Durganand. He was elected Fellow of International Council of Psychologists. Subsequently he was elected Fellow of the National Institute of Science, India. He left the institute on 5 July 1968 to join the post of chief psychologist and director (Grade I), Directorate of Psychological Research (now Defence Institute of Psychological Research), Defence Research and Development Organization, Ministry of Defence (1968–1976). He joined as senior professor and head, Department of Psychology (1976–1977) and director, Center for Research in Humanities, University of Rajasthan, Jaipur (1976–1977). He worked as dean, Faculty of Social Sciences (1978–1980) and head, Department of Psychology, at Ravi Shanker University, Raipur (1977–1980).

A.K.P. Sinha was bestowed the Lifetime Achievement Award by Prestige Institute of Management and Research (2005), National Award by SP Psychology Trust of India (1983), Best Book Award by SP Psychology Trust of India (1990), and the first SP Eastern–Western Psychology Lecture Award (1982). He delivered the Jamuna Prasad Memorial Lecture in 1982. He was president of Indian Psychological Association (1961–1967), Indian Psychometric and Educational Research Association (1969), and section of psychology and educational sciences, Indian Science Congress (1958). He also presided over the Fifth Plenary Session of the International Round Table for the Advancement of Counselling (IRTAC) held in Paris (1972), Loussaine, and Vienna. He was elected fellow of the International Council of Psychologists (1963).

In addition to his other pursuits, Sinha has made a lifelong commitment to the study of psychological research. It could easily be said that in India, Sinha set a standard for experimental work and was instrumental in promoting experimental thinking as far as social psychology is concerned. He experimentally demonstrated how anxiety could be induced in human subjects by exposing them to conditions of uncertainty and how physiological changes in them could be recorded, which is a rare distinction. He received recognition for his outstanding research in experimental psychology and his works are internationally cited in books and journals. Sinha (1958, 1970, 1978a) emphasized the need for multidisciplinary research in India and also the need for coordination in research. He also emphasized the need for more meaningful and purposive dialogue between researchers and practitioners. He was of the view that both should become more sensitive to their mutual interdependence and, thereby, enhance the quality of education. Action research must be encouraged, as opposed to the personal experience as presently used by some educators. Research is needed to formulate a programme of education for teachers, indicating what things should be taught to perspective teachers and what action they should take as teachers.

His research publications include the study of prejudice among university students (A.K.P. Sinha & R.P.N. Sinha, 1960), extracurricular interests of university students (Sinha & Roy, 1960), illusion in low and high anxiety conditions (Sinha & Sinha, 1967) and psychology and national development (Sinha, 1978b, 1991). He has many tests to his credit, such as a comprehensive test of anxiety (A.K.P. Sinha & L.N.K. Sinha, 1969, 1995), scientific aptitude test (SAT; Sinha & Sinha, 1991), and adjustment inventory for school students (Sinha & Singh, 1980). He also developed a scientific creativity scale for 10th grade students (Sinha & Singh, 1987). A comprehensive test of anxiety was developed by him and L.N.K. Sinha (A.K.P. Sinha & L.N.K. Sinha, 1969, 1995) on the basis of the symptoms of anxiety. The test comprised of 75 items with forced choice response (Yes/No). The possible scores ranged from 0 to 75. A higher test score was indicative of greater level of anxiety. An SAT was also developed by A.K.P. Sinha and L.N.K. Sinha consisting of 45 items that covered different areas such as experimental bent, ability to reason and solve problems, detection of inconsistencies, caution and thoroughness, accuracy of observation, and so forth. Adjustment inventory for school students (Sinha & Singh, 1980) was especially developed for Hindi speaking students for segregating well-adjusted secondary school students from poorly adjusted students in three areas of adjustment—emotional, social, and educational. The inventory consists of 60 items, 20 items in each of the three areas of adjustment. Using Yes/No response format, high scores in any of three areas indicate unstable emotional adaptation in that specific area.

During the later years of his career, he stressed on the need for a synthesis of Eastern and Western psychotherapies (Sinha, 1984). According to him, the Western psychotherapies could profitably incorporate the essential elements involved in Yoga and Zen Buddhism with a view to achieve the aim of radical cure of the clients. He authored two books—*Employee Counseling* (1990) and *Human Intelligence in Organizations* (2003).

A.K.P. Sinha designed and developed new programmes for the management of human resources to meet aspirations of the people. He elaborated the role of motivation in armed forces (Sinha, 1976), emphasizing positive motivation as an important factor for high standards of performance, both in peace and in war. He also found that rigidity of behaviour was an important factor of neuroticism and change in perception was less frequent in neurotics than in normal population (A.K.P. Sinha & S.N. Sinha, 1959).

He served as editor, *Indian Journal of Psychology* and chief editor, *Indian Psychometric and Educational Research*, the official journal of the Indian Psychometric and Educational Research Association. He was member of the executive committee of International Round Table for Counselling. He also served as convener of the national committees for economics, education, and social sciences, and the Pan-Indian Ocean Science Association. He was admitted as member of merit for life by the Confederation of Chivalry, Sydney (1988). In 1999, the American Biographical Institute conferred on him honorary appointment to the research board of advisors. Prestige Institute of Management and Research bestowed the Lifetime Achievement Award in 2005.

At the age of 90, he died on 24 April 2009 in Delhi. He fondly remains in the memory of his students as an exceptional mentor.

## References

Sinha, A.K.P. (1958). Planning psychological research in India. *Indian Journal of Psychology*, *33*, 1–20.

———. (1970). A need for coordination in research. *Indian Journal of Psychometry and Education*, *1*(1, 2), 5–10.

———. (1976). Motivation for the armed forces. *Defence Management*, *3*(1), 10–14.

———. (1978a). Strategies for applied psychological research. *Indian Journal of Applied Psychology*, *15*(1), 1–3.

———. (1978b). Need educational research. *Indian Journal of Psychometry and Education*, *9*(1), 1–6.

———. (1984). Eastern and Western psychotherapies. *Indian Psychological Review*, *27*(1), 1–16.

———. (1990). *Employee counseling*. New Delhi: Prachi Publisher and Distributors.

———. (1991). Psychology and national development. *Indian Journal of Psychology*, *66*(1, 4), 1–12.

———. (2003). *Human excellence in organizations*. New Delhi: UBS Publishers Distributors Pvt. Ltd.

Sinha, A.K.P., & Roy, S.K. (1960). A study of extracurricular interests of university students. *The Indian Journal of Psychology*, *35*(3), 125–135.

Sinha, A.K.P., & Singh, C. (1987). Measurement of scientific creativity. *Indian Journal of Psychology and Education*, *18*(1), 1–13.

Sinha, A.K.P., & Singh, R.P. (1980). *Adjustment inventory for college students*. Agra: National Psychological Corporation.

Sinha, A.K.P., & Sinha, L.N.K. (1969). A comprehensive test of anxiety. *Journal of Psychological Researches*, *13*(1), 58.

———. (1995). *Sinha's comprehensive anxiety test (SCAT)*. Agra: National Psychological Corporation.

Sinha, A.K.P., & Sinha, L.N.K. (1991). *Scientific aptitude test for college students.* National Psychological Corporation.

Sinha, A.K.P., & Sinha, R.P.N. (1960). A study of prejudice among university students. *Indian Journal of Psychology, 35*(4), 159–166.

Sinha, A.K.P., & Sinha, S.N. (1959). An experimental study of reversible perspective and neuroticism. *Journal of Education and Psychology, 17*(2), 83–87.

———. (1967). Muller–Lyer illusion in subjects high and low in anxiety. *Perceptual and Motor Skills, 24*(1), 194–195.

# 17

# Hari Shanker Asthana

(1922)

## Vinod K. Kool and Rita Agrawal

*Hari Shanker Asthana*

We normally consult a dictionary when we do not know the meaning of a word. But what happens when we find that the dictionary meaning provides a very routine description and fails to conjure an appropriate mental image? For some words, images of people from real life often provide better descriptors and act as exemplars par excellence. So seems to be the case with the word 'gentleman'. The *Oxford Dictionary* defines the word gentleman as 'a chivalrous, courteous, or honourable man'. You could think of an English knight as one good example but how many of us have met and interacted with British knights? But there is one living example, one person from among us who fits the bill completely. He is a living epitome of the word 'gentleman' in all forms of human expression, be it in his thoughts, his positive emotions, or even his behaviour, which has always been loaded with courtesy and warmth. As far back as we could track our memory, spanning no less than four decades of our association with him, we fail to come across even a single incident that tended to deviate from the highest level of composure and civility that personifies such elegance of human personality. Couple this to profound scholarly pursuits that were virtually non-existent on the scene of psychology when he began his career, and the result is Hari Shanker Asthana. One could only wish that there was one word that could incorporate both sets of qualities. The closest that we could get to was the expression 'a gentleman and scholar', a classic British expression, which got popular from the novel *The Catcher in the Rye* or as the French would say *T'es un gentleman et un e'rudit* (You are a gentleman and a scholar).

Born in northern India on 24 August 1922 to parents settled in Lucknow, he seems to have inherited the scholarship of his father, a professor of chemistry at the University of Lucknow. Hari Shanker Asthana received his early education at the former DAV school and later joined Christian College to prepare for his graduate studies in philosophy at the University of Lucknow. Psychology was either just not taught or was offered merely as a part of the curriculum of philosophy and/or education in most Indian universities, and it is as if by serendipity that psychology in India got the boost it did from this scholar.

A Wikipedia search on Asthana gives us some inkling about his entry into psychology:

Sen Gupta was appointed Professor of Philosophy at the University of Lucknow in 1929. He introduced psychology into the philosophy curricula, and soon established the Department of Experimental Psychology, which focused primarily on social and experimental psychology. By the mid-1930s, he began mentoring students in experimental psychology, including Indian psychologists Raj Narain and H.S. Asthana.

*Hari Shanker Asthana in Chicago (1950), Harvard (1965), and Lucknow (1997)*

Chicago (1950)    Harvard (1965)    Lucknow (1997)

Asthana, too, very frankly states that he was not fortunate enough to receive formal training in psychology per se (that is, in psychology as an independent science). In 1944, the University of Lucknow appointed him as a lecturer in the Department of Philosophy against the leave vacancy of Edward Ahmed Shah, who had been appointed by the then viceroy to the National Defense Council as representative of Indian Christians. Asthana taught metaphysics and moral philosophy for four years and also published his first paper, 'Bergson's Ethical Outlook' in the *Philosophical Quarterly* in 1944. When education was introduced in the then Department of Philosophy four years later, he was asked to teach educational psychology and educational guidance and counselling. His transition to the formal domain of psychology was initiated when he started to teach courses in the burgeoning field of psychology, which grew under the patronage of the late Kali Prasad as a landmark field of study throughout the country. Asthana was instrumental in developing a curriculum of psychology of such a high standard that it was soon emulated by other universities that were beginning to establish their own independent departments of psychology. In 1963, Asthana moved to the Institute of Social Sciences at Agra in the capacity of Reader, but stayed there for only a few months. Very shortly, Sagar University (formally known as Dr Harisingh Gour University) gave him the honour of starting the Department of Psychology as professor and head. Here he remained until his retirement in 1983, with the added distinction of serving Sagar University first as dean, School of Arts and Sciences and later, as its vice-chancellor. We saw the fruition of his hard work and dedication that resulted in the establishment of a modern laboratory of psychology, an advanced postgraduate curriculum, the introduction of psychology as a paper in the Madhya Pradesh Public Service Examination, and seminal experimental work in the field of perception, personality, and testing. It was his foresight which made him establish a centre for neuropsychology at Sagar University when very few psychologists in India were even thinking about it. He trained students who received coveted positions in the field of psychology around the globe. For a short duration of one academic year, he also served as professor and head of the psychology department at the University of Gorakhpur.

The Fulbright programme in India was established in 1950 and young Asthana was one of the first four Fulbright scholars selected from India on the basis of a national competition to pursue research work in social sciences at American universities. During his visit to the USA, he worked very closely with veteran scholars such as L.L. Thurstone (the University of Chicago), W. Kohler, E.C. Tolman, and the Rorschacher, S.J. Beck. In 1966, he was offered another Fulbright assignment to work at Harvard University as an honorary research associate and, subsequently, as a visiting professor at George Washington University in Washington DC. Time spent with Cora du Bois, distinguished professor of social anthropology at Harvard, and a chance discussion with anthropologist Margaret Mead in London attracted him to 'political psychology' (which later led to the publication of a book on the topic). On the occasion of the passing away of George Miller, a cognitive psychologist of '7 plus/minus two' fame, he recalled his experiences at Harvard University and wrote as follows (paraphrased for smooth reading):

Dear Professor Kool:

Thanks. You may feel free to share my letter as you deem fit. However, I hope it is not taken as my self-advertisement!

Miller was the chairman and I had many occasions to meet him.

A few anecdotes:    .

Skinner's lab and his personal office were located adjacent to each other. Someone wrote on his door: Prof. Skinner, the psychologist and Prof. Skinner, the rodent on them!

Once I sought half an hour's appointment with Boring to ask about phenomenology in psychology. But I enjoyed about 2 hours lecture from him! He had a remarkable memory, as his History attests. And at the conclusion of the talk he told me that he was busy translating Fechner's *Elements of Psychophysics* then. (I felt that indeed Fechner was the founder and not Wundt—I am trying to write about three contested 'facts' in the history of psychology). Boring's office was located on the third floor (of Wm. James Hall Building). While we would wait for the elevator, he did not have patience to wait; at his age he would run up the stairs!

I had closer contacts with Gordon Allport owing to my interest in personality psychology. While I participated in his post-doc seminars on some social psychological issues, I wrote for him a paper on Indian theories of personality (summarizing half of my doctoral dissertation of 1950), the other half working out western theories—behaviouristic, psychoanalytical, field theory, etc.—about 7 years prior to Hall & Lindzey's *Theories of Personality*! (The dissertation was evaluated by external referees: Gardner Murphy and Haridas Bhattacharya (of Dacca University).

My close contact with Hadley Cantril both when he came to Lucknow, following Clyde Kluckhohn's visit, and later at Delhi and Princeton brought me closer to Allport—once he took me to a movie: Bernard Shaw's *Pygmalion*!

I had the privilege of meeting Ralph White, Kurt Lewin's student at Washington D.C....and it was fun testing some aspects of Lewin's theory of group dynamics by investigating in real life situation race relations in the residential areas adjoining the University of Chicago with support from one of Lewin's students, Herbert Thelen.

Participating in Wolfgang Kohler's experiments in perception in a tilted room and with acceleration of movement in the 1950s enabled me appreciate their significance for space travel later. But it was Heinrich Kluver (famous for his work on behavior mechanisms of monkeys) from whom I learnt what experimentation means and how to design...

I had learnt and even taught psychophysics for some years (!), but only after learning it from Thurstone, I seem truly to understand it and appreciate that all measurement in social sciences is based on it. And his law of comparative judgment is a remarkable solution. Once, after one of his seminars on multiple factor analysis (I gave up later because of my poor knowledge of Calculus, set theory and matrices, etc.), I asked him what he considered to be his most important work (orthogonal centroid multiple factor method, primary mental abilities, psychophysical law, scaling techniques, etc.), his reply was that it was a short paper he had published in the *Psychological Review* in 1927 on 'discriminal dispersion'! Indeed, it is an original idea providing a unique solution to the psychophysical problem. I then realized that a good fresh idea merits a short paper.

Well, these are lingering old memories! Sorry to have wasted your time and bored you with my anecdotes, knowing full well that if I applied for a lectureship in psychology today, I will disqualify because all my degrees are in philosophy and not in psychology!

Best regards,

H.S. Asthana

His reminiscences bring to the fore that this young Fulbright scholar had the rare opportunity to interact at a very personal level with people who have become legends in psychology and who are known to us only through their books and theories. Yet, just see the humbleness of this man! While many would have talked about such discussions with great pride, Asthana ends the letter by writing that he is sorry for wasting the present author's time and for boring us! We have known him for over 40 years, but never had he shared these anecdotes with us. Is this humbleness not the hallmark of a true scholar?

One can only imagine what happened to Asthana's learning by having discussions and close personal contact with such legendary figures. One can just remark 'wow!' And, he reciprocated these learnings by giving so much not to just all his students but to anyone who came in contact with him and showed the propensity to learn. What an inspiration!

The Fulbright Award was just one of the many other awards he has received. Besides having the distinction of being the first Fulbright scholar in social sciences from India, he was a post-doctoral Fellow at the University of Chicago (1950–1951), where he was awarded the Smith-Mundt and Watumal Awards. He was also the recipient of the Fulbright-Hays Award and the Commonwealth Foundation Award. He served as honorary research associate at the prestigious Harvard University followed by a visiting professorship at Washington University in 1965–1966 and was awarded honorary citizenship of the city of Baltimore, MD, USA, by the mayor of the city in 1986.

The Indian psychological fraternity was not to be left behind in honouring him. He was the recipient of many prestigious Indian awards, including the UGC National Lecturer Award (1976), the Sir H.S. Gour Memorial Award for Social Sciences by the Madhya Pradesh government (1987), and the S.P. National Psychological Award, S.P. Trust (India) in 1986. Other awards include the

Platinum Jubilee lecturership award, Indian Science Congress (1990); Fellow, National Academy of Psychology (1994); Special Felicitation Award, Gurukul Kangri University (1994); S.C. Mitra Memorial Award, Asiatic Society (formerly, the Royal Asiatic Society) (2004); and the Distinguished Alumnus Award, University of Lucknow, in 2006.

Asthana remained active even after his formal retirement such that we often wondered whether he had, indeed, retired. Realizing the potential of this person and not wanting to lose his services, the Government of Madhya Pradesh went all the way to create a special position for him after his retirement. For about 3 years, he was stationed at Bhopal to work as advisor for social sciences in the Council of Science and Technology. On the other hand, Sagar University did not want to lose him either. Through some hefty donations from a business magnate, he had been able to set up a centre for neuropsychology and counselling at Sagar University and he was requested to continue to direct the activities of this centre, which, in fact, he continued as honorary director till 2006. These two positions made him commute between Sagar and Bhopal for almost three years.

Apart from this, his scholarship was well-known to all, and throughout his career and even after his retirement, he was invited to visit, lecture, and deliver keynote addresses at various departments of psychology, not only in India but also in Japan, China, some European countries including the USSR; some African, mid-eastern, and South-East Asian countries; and the neighbouring countries of Sri Lanka and Nepal. He was convener of the UGC panel on psychology from its inception to 1985. Wanting to take advantage of his prolific reading and writing, he was much sought after by various research journals of psychology. Among others, he was editor of *Indian Journal of Psychology*, joint editor of *Diversity and Unity in Cross-Cultural Psychology* and joint editor of *Political Psychology*. His research acumen is clear from the many research projects he has to his credit, from funding agencies such as the UGC, the prestigious National Institute of Mental Health (NIMH), and TCM of the USA and other Government of India projects. Even after his retirement, he continued his academic pursuits and was engaged as consultant to RDSO, Ministry of Railways, Government of India, wherein his services have always been applauded and remembered.

Finally returning to Lucknow, his hometown, in 1986, Asthana continued to dedicate himself to writing and consolidating his thoughts. He has to his credit several books, book chapters, and a large number of research papers. He continues to preside over plenary sessions at psychology symposia and conferences and deliver keynote addresses. Given the limitations of experimental procedures, he realized the need for employing projective techniques in research and was a forerunner in the application of the extremely difficult Rorshach and TAT tests in India. For him, in the pursuit of the study of behaviour, the science of psychology needed support from a wide variety of techniques, and undermining one procedure, he believed, in preference to another, would limit the scope and range of an investigation. When one of the authors of this chapter (Kool) requested him to contribute an article in the book *Perspectives on Nonviolence*, later published by Springer-Verlag, USA (1990), he took a unique route, collecting data by administering TAT on violent and non-violent subjects. It was a solid move to bolster some of the empirical work that was beginning to surface in a relatively new field of psychology of non-violence. In short, Asthana has always surprised us with his wide reading and his ability to deploy hitherto unchartered avenues of investigation to enrich the subject matter of psychological science.

In 2006, a group of his students and colleagues organized a function in collaboration with the Fulbright Foundation in India and the then chairperson of the USEFI felicitated him. It was an extremely nostalgic occasion for one and all, with each person talking about his/her association with Asthana and attempting to find words for the quality of mentoring they had received and were, in fact, still receiving from him. Whether it be for the design of experiments, the use of certain psychometric measures, the interpretation of complex data, or the unravelling of even more complex behaviour, a discussion with him always bore and continues to bear fruit. His tremendous contributions to the field of psychology are recalled along with the manner in which he has touched the hearts of his students and colleagues with his warmth and his courteous behaviour. How can one forget him and, even more so, his twinkling eyes and ever-smiling demeanour?

Another landmark in the post-retirement activities of Hari Shanker Asthana, in defiance of his age, is his genuineness in tracking the relatively newer trends in psychology. For three years, that is, during the period 2009–2011, and being almost 90 years of age, he began to explore issues related to the concept of quality of life and published several papers on this topic in international peer-reviewed journals. Two highly acclaimed papers written during the same period are entitled 'Defining Psychology' and 'Modern Psychology in India: Reminiscences and Reflections'.

A couple of years later, Asthana moved to the USA with his wife to join his son Rajiv, currently a professor at the University of Wisconsin, and daughter Manjari, a psychiatrist in the state of Illinois. However, much to the consternation of all who know him, he not only continues to read and write but is always ready for a serious academic discussion. Whenever he gets time, he writes scholarly articles and offers his comments through various electronic media. Last year (2014), at the young age of 93, he communicated two papers on the founder of modern psychology (arguing for Fechner) and on Wundt (as a 'pure scientist'). His basic training in philosophy keeps him interested in a variety of academic disciplines including philosophy of science. He enjoys reading Kuhn, Popper, Fereyaband, Husserl, and others, and relishes the return to positivism. People much younger would find it difficult to emulate his scholarship, his personal values, or his energy level. For him, the word retirement has no meaning in life. His contribution to psychology, along with his life and lifestyle, will continue to serve as a source of inspiration for people, both young and old.

# 18

# Radhanath Rath

(1926–2014)

## Namita Mohanty and Ajit Kumar Mohanty

*Radhanath Rath*

Understanding human mind and behaviour has always remained a challenge to human intellect. Psychology has been in the forefront of the disciplinary endeavours to explain human functioning in all its diverse manifestations. Thousands of years of Indian knowledge systems and the scriptures sought to give us a rich understanding of various facets of the human mind and society. Unfortunately, the traditional Indian discourse on the human psyche could not become a part of the modern scientific psychology which developed in the Western knowledge systems. Ironically, in the Western as well as in much older Indian traditions, the early psychology grew within the broader fields of philosophy. While the Western scientific psychology maintained a smooth trajectory of severance from psychology, making the crystallization of the new discipline appear to be a natural and spontaneous development, in India, the beginning of scientific psychology during the early decades of the twentieth century was marked by horizontal and vertical décalage from its rich philosophical traditions. While philosophy as a knowledge system and as a modern discipline of study continued to engage in its reflections on the human mind, the 'modern' psychology in India as an academic discipline seemed somewhat keen on disowning its philosophical traditions. For the world of British colonial scholarship at the time, the new science approach of the West was too overpowering to ignore. Strange as it may seem, many of the early academic psychologists in India had their scholarship and intellectual training rooted in academic philosophy in Indian tradition, but, despite this background, there seemed to be some zealousness of the early converts to assert a modern 'scientific' status of psychology in the new Western appeal, partly by an implicit rejection of the philosophical traditions of the country and partly by an emphasis on experimental and objective approaches. As a result, research, development, and expansion of psychology in India in the 1930s and 1940s started with the introduction of Western methodology and replication of studies conducted in the West. Sinha's (1986) study of the history of psychology in India shows that the early developments in psychology in India were clearly marked by Western influences and theories such as the Freudian psychoanalysis and experimental psychology of the West. Sinha also points out that it took the psychologists in India a few decades to realize the limitations of the Western theories and methods in understanding the human mind and society in our indigenous contexts. There were many pioneers in asserting Indianness of the discipline of psychology—Durganand Sinha, Shiv Kumar Mitra, J.B.P. Sinha, Radhanath Rath, and Udai Pareek—to name a few. All those who contributed to the emergence of an international identity of the discipline of psychology in India approached the task from very different perspectives working in different areas of the discipline. But all of them had one thing in common—they combined robust research and scholarship with strong and assertive leadership contributing to building a sustained future of the discipline in the country.

Radhanath Rath (1926–2014) was one of the makers of contemporary psychology in India, a leader who stood tall among his peers and had the vision to shape the future of psychology in India in many ways. His studies on inter-group prejudices, caste stereotypes, attitude, status of women, and social tension are considered milestones in social psychological research in India. Equally significant were his studies on the educational problems of the disadvantaged (scheduled castes and scheduled tribes), and his intervention studies for the enhancement of cognitive abilities in the socio-culturally disadvantaged children, which shaped the discipline of educational psychology and led to the foundations of the psychology of the disadvantaged as a specialized academic area in psychology in India. At the same time, Rath had a seminal role in popularizing psychology as an academic subject in higher education in India and in expansion of the discipline during the last three decades of the last century.

## Emergence of Psychology from Philosophy in India and Odisha

Psychology gradually evolved out of a long tradition of broader philosophical discourse and developed an identity as a separate discipline. Wundt laid the foundation for experimental psychology by establishing the first laboratory at Leipzig in 1879 for the scientific study of psychological phenomena. Although it is generally believed that modern Western psychology began with the Leipzig lab, its development outside the mother discipline was slow and gradual. Wundtian approach gained popularity and spread far and wide across the globe. Psychology in India was highly influenced by Western developments in the discipline, and in 1905, psychology was introduced as an independent subject in the postgraduate course in the University of Calcutta. The first laboratory was set up in 1915, almost after 10 years of opening of the discipline. G.B. Bose (1938) has pointed out in his review of the progress of psychology in India that it took 30 years for this new psychological movement to reach India. There were two major strands in the early developments of psychology in India. One was the work of a group of psychoanalysts influenced by the Freudian wave and the other was the early contributions of a group of experimental psychologists inspired by the post-Wundtian developments. Early experimental research in India included studies on perceptual errors leading to a theory of illusion (Bose, 1926a cited in Sinha, 1986), physiological studies on perception (Mitra, 1927 cited in Sinha, 1986), tactual sensation (Mukherji, 1936 cited in Sinha, 1986; Roy, 1937), learning and memorisation (Gopalswami, 1926a cited in Sinha, 1986), learning curve in feeble minded children (Sinha, 1936 cited in Sinha, 1986), and the relationship between memory and intelligence (Jalota cited in Sinha, 1986, 1936a; Maiti, 1931 cited in Sinha, 1986). Psychoanalysts in India used psychoanalytic theory and concepts in their work (Haldar, 1935, 1937 cited in Sinha, 1986) and they focused on clinical application of psychoanalysis taking up related research topics such as conflicting wishes, defence mechanisms and dreams (Bose, 1920; 1922 cited in Sinha, 1986). Some of the Indian Psychologists started taking keen interest in the adaptation and administration of intelligence test and thus, it became a popular research pastime of Indian psychologists (Berkeley-Hill, 1927; Chatarjee, 1927; Bose, 1944; Kapat & Bhattacharje, 1948; Menzel, 1956).

Inspired by the new wave of psychology with a strong experimental focus and the positive steps taken by the University of Calcutta establishing psychology as an academic discipline, departments of psychology were opened in different universities both at undergraduate and postgraduate levels in Dacca, Mysore, Lahore, Lucknow, Aligarh, and, gradually, in many other universities. Unfortunately, in the early psychological studies and research in India, our own traditional philosophical insights into the human mind remained a missing link.

Radhanath Rath established the first Department of Psychology at Ravenshaw College in 1953 and was the only teacher who started teaching psychology in Odisha. Though he had a postgraduate degree in philosophy, having studied psychology only as a paper at the masters level in Patna University, he trained himself in the new experimental approaches to study human behaviour including psychophysics and opened an experimental psychology laboratory in the department where students conducted laboratory-based practicals on learning, memory, perception, personality, intelligence, and psychophysics. The emphasis on experiments helped cultivate a scientific attitude to study of behaviour.

## Radhanath Rath: Life and Leadership

Born in 1920, Radhanath Rath was educated in a village primary school situated at Tallaram Palli in the southern part of Odisha. He lost both his parents at an early age and was brought up by his elder brother and other family members. He completed his high school education in 1937 from Ravenshaw Collegiate School, Cuttack, passed intermediate arts from the legendary Ravenshaw College, Cuttack, in 1939, and then went to Patna to pursue graduation. He graduated with philosophy honours in 1941 and completed his master's degree in philosophy from Patna University in the year 1943. He started his teaching career as a lecturer in philosophy in Ravenshaw College in

1944 where he had studied for his intermediate degree. Thereafter, he went abroad for his doctoral work and was awarded a PhD degree from the University of London in 1949. He stayed in London from 1946 to 1949 and, on his return to India, continued teaching and research in Ravenshaw College. It was a historic move when he established the Department of Psychology as an independent department in 1953, literally separating himself and the new discipline from the mother Department of Philosophy in Ravenshaw College. The department shifted to Utkal University, Bhubaneswar, in 1958 and he became the first professor in psychology in Odisha in 1960. He continued as the head of the department till 1981, the year of his formal retirement. Thereafter, he was honoured by the Indian Council of Social Science Research (ICSSR) as a national Fellow. During his tenure as a professor and head of the department in Utkal University, Rath brought many laurels to the Department of Psychology and one of them was obtaining the UGC recognition of the department as a centre of advanced study (CAS) in psychology in 1976, the first such centre of psychology in India and the only CAS in Odisha. This special status not only made psychology quite popular in this part of the country, leading to the opening of the subject of psychology in a number of colleges in Odisha with a large student population, but also prompted a climate of advanced and trend-setting psychological research in diverse fields originating from the centre in Utkal University.

Rath was a regular practitioner of *yoga* and *pranayam* for over a period of 60 years and remained active and in good health for 94 years. We lost him on the 29 September 2014 after a brief period of illness. He lived a fulfilled life and enriched the lives of many who came in contact with him. His life is an important chapter in the history of psychology in India, and he would be remembered as a pioneer and as one who shaped the course of the discipline in India.

Rath was not only an avid reader, he was a prolific writer too. Besides numerous research papers and discipline-specific books, he wrote a large number of popular articles in Odia based on the day-to-day happenings in the society. He regularly contributed articles to widely circulated local newspapers and magazines. He was also a novelist, with a psychological orientation in his stories which focused on human relationships, emotions, family bonding, and social issues. He has written a large number of books—29 novels, 9 travelogues, and an autobiography *Mo Swapna, Mo Jibana* (My Dream, My Life) in Odia language which was his mother tongue. All his literary creations are extensively read and appreciated by the people of Odisha and earned for him the prestigious Odisha Sahitya Academy award. He won several regional, national, and international awards for his achievements in academics and literary and social work. Some of them include the National Scholarship (University of London, 1946–1949), Soviet Land Nehru Award (1966), National Fellowship (ICSSR, 1981–1983), Odisha Sahitya Academy award (1993), Vigyana Prachara Samiti award (for Popularization of Science, 1998 and 2002), Bharat Excellence Award Gold Medal (2005), and Personalities of India Award Gold Medal (2005) by International Penguin Publishing House. Rath was elected as the local secretary of the Indian Science Congress in 1962 and 1977. He was also elected as the president of psychology and education section of the Indian Science Congress in 1966 and as the president of the Academy of Applied Psychology, India, for a period in 1972–1974. It must be pointed out that Rath was influenced by Marxist philosophy and was an atheist. It seems his early development under conditions of hardship and his personal struggle for achievement may have affected such orientation in his personal and professional life. He lived the life he preached, and his approach to study of psychology and his personal life style were deeply rooted in his belief in Marxism and atheism. He edited and published by his own singular efforts an influential Odia literary monthly magazine called *Samukhya* which was known for its liberal and Marxist policy.

# Research Contributions of Radhanath Rath

Rath was primarily a social psychologist who studied the problems of people across caste, class, gender, socio-economic status, age, and rural–urban settings. The ICSSR survey of research in psychology published in 1972 carried his scholarly review 'Social Psychology: A Trend Report'. It was a pioneering effort to compile and analyse the research work in social psychology in India. In his analysis, Rath categorized social psychological research under eight broad areas, namely, (a) cultural and social processes, (b) attitudes and opinions, (c) group and interpersonal processes, (d) communication, (e) aesthetics, (f) sexual behaviour, (g) smoking, drug, and alcohol use, and (h) methodology. Prior to 1940, as he pointed out, there were only 55 research publications, but the research activities increased in the next decade (1940–1950) and there were 64 publications. The number further increased to 102 during the period 1950–1960 and, thereafter, there was a leap forward with the number going up to 306 in the decade from 1960 to 1970. The highest number of publications were in the area of cultural and social processes and the second highest was on attitudes and opinions. These were the major areas in which the contributions of Radhanath Rath were quite seminal.

In his review of research on social psychology in India, Rath pointed out the need for problem-oriented research in India and emphasized theory building and adopting more appropriate methodology to study social behaviour and processes. He maintained that methodological rigour, random sampling, and rigorous statistical techniques would be helpful for the generalization of research findings. He was in favour of multidisciplinary and integrative approaches to research in this field with a focus on social issues and problems.

Rath, like some of his contemporaries, did not believe in replication or 'foreignness' of psychological studies (Sinha, 1977). By using well-known scaling techniques such as the social distance scale, Likert and Thurstone scales, and established measures, several issue-focused researches on stereotypes towards various socio-cultural groups and attitudes towards socio-economic and political issues in Indian society were taken up by him and his associates (Rath, 1957, 1959; Rath & Das, 1957, 1958; Rath & Sircar, 1960; Dandekar & Rath, 1971). As Sinha (1986) observes, studies by Rath on prejudices and stereotypes were significant contributions fostering understanding of the genesis, dynamics, and evolution of inter-group relations and social tension in Indian society.

Rath's studies on the impact of disadvantage and poverty on cognitive and perceptual processes of children and the adverse effects of socio-environmental disadvantages on the cognitive ability of primary school children belonging to scheduled castes and tribes in terms of poor academic performance have been quite influential, leading to a very popular and well-cited monograph in the field (Rath, Dash, & Dash, 1979). Through a number of intervention studies, Rath showed the positive impact of well-designed training in facilitating some cognitive abilities of disadvantaged children (Patnaik & Rath, 1982; Rath, 1982; Rath, Dash, & Dash, 1979; Rath & Patnaik, 1978). Earlier, in 1969, he took up a statewide study in schools in Odisha on the impact of the mid-day meal programme (the Cooperative for Assistance and Relief Everywhere [CARE] Feeding Programme) with the Council of Social Development, New Delhi. This large-scale, path-breaking study was multidisciplinary in its approach, bringing in different disciplines of psychology, education, sociology, anthropology, health, and nutrition as well as economics. The evaluation of the CARE mid-day meal programme showed some positive effects of the feeding programme on children's classroom performance and attendance. This was perhaps the first ever study in India on mid-day meal and its impact.

# International Research, Collaborations and Academic Leadership

With Rath's initiative and support from the UGC, the CAS in psychology at Utkal had research collaborations with a number of international universities including the psychology departments of the University of Birmingham, UK; Malmo University, Sweden; and the University of Amsterdam, the Netherlands. Rath also participated in several national delegations to different countries. These included visits to the USA in 1957 as a member of the visiting team to observe the general education programmes run by American universities and to the USSR in 1966 and 1968 as a member of Indo-Russian cultural delegation. He visited a large number of universities in Canada, the UK, Sweden, China, Japan, Thailand, and many other countries presenting his research and exchanging ideas.

Rath was a great leader and a successful organizer. Many national and international conferences were organized by the Department of Psychology under his leadership. He successfully organized the International Congress of the International Association of Cross-Cultural Psychology (IACCP) in Utkal University, Bhubaneswar, Odisha, and edited the publication of selected papers presented in the Congress along with H.S. Asthana, D. Sinha, and J.B.P. Sinha (Rath, Asthana, Sinha, & Sinha, 1982). The Bhubaneswar IACCP is still remembered as a successful Congress, and till date it is the only major international Congress of IACCP held in India. Rath was the local secretary for organizing the first Indian Science Congress at Ravenshaw College in 1962 and again in 1977 at Utkal University, Bhubaneswar. He organized many other national and international conferences, seminars, and symposiums including the annual conference of the Indian Association of Applied Psychology (IAAP).

It will not be an exaggeration to speak of Rath as an institution builder as he was not only engaged in the infrastructural expansion of the department he headed for over two decades but was also very meticulous in adding potentially effective human resources to the department. Even though he started the department single-handed, it had 19 teaching faculty members including three professors and 44 research scholars when he retired from his profession in 1981. The psychology faculty at Utkal under Rath had the singular distinction of having the largest number of PhD holders from universities abroad, many with prestigious scholarships (Commonwealth Scholarship, Killam Scholarship, etc.). Out of 19 faculty members, 14 had doctoral degrees from Canada, the UK and the USA. Students and faculty members from the Department of Psychology at Utkal, under Rath's leadership and inspiration, bagged the largest number of Commonwealth Scholarships in psychology till about the late 1970s. Rath always emphasized on the holistic development of children and took steps that contributed immensely towards early childhood education. Through this process, a new feather was added to the cap of the department in 1980 when a model preschool was opened in the department as a Demonstration and Research Centre for Early Education (DARCEE) with three trained teachers, six caretakers, and an annual intake of 60 three-to-five-year-old children. DARCEE was recognized and lauded by the UGC which sanctioned teacher's positions for this early childhood education programme. The Department of Psychology was also running a one-year diploma course for training prospective nursery teachers. Rath was the chairman of the Odisha Child Care Organization and academic director of the Early Childhood Education and Care Programme of Odisha. At Cuttack, where he resided, he established a nursery school and introduced a one-year diploma course in child care and education for women having graduate degrees. During his tenure as the head of the Department of Psychology, an animal laboratory, one of a few such labs in the country, was set up at Utkal.

# Rath in the History of Psychology in India

In conclusion, it can be said that Rath's professional development as a teacher and researcher in psychology for over four decades is, in many respects, a story of how the discipline evolved in India. Like him, psychology in India originated as a departure from philosophy with early emphasis on experimental approach. Soon, psychology in India grew in showing some awareness of the need to focus on indigenous problems and contemporary social issues—a development to which Rath had significant contributions. His work on the cognitive development of disadvantaged children not only showed applications of psychological tests for understanding of the poor performance of the scheduled tribe children compared to those of the scheduled castes and upper caste groups, it also sought to analyse the dynamics of disadvantage and poor cognitive and educational performance. Although this influential research and arguably pioneering monograph (Rath, Dash, & Dash, 1979) giving the details of the research had some major limitations in its interpretations of the data and understanding children's test performance (Mohanty & Prakash, 1993), it became an important source of reference in the field of psychology of the disadvantaged. Incidentally, the CAS in psychology at Utkal started the first specialization area of psychology of the disadvantaged in India in the masters programme in psychology at Utkal, and the credit for this must go to Rath's research in the area and his leadership. Despite the limitations of his formal training in psychology, lack of comprehensive exposure to the diverse areas of the discipline including modern statistical techniques, and the limited resource conditions of a new area of teaching in higher and university education in India, Rath was driven by a desire to establish a strong foundation of research and scholarship in psychology in India. His initiatives for a firm grounding to the discipline through problem-oriented social research, successful expansion of teaching programmes in Odisha and in the country, pioneering role in strengthening educational psychology and psychology of the disadvantaged, and his overall contributions to the early phase of psychology in India make him a tall figure in the history of the discipline in India. He was a man of dedication, discipline, strong will power, and creative vision tempered with practical sense. His contributions to psychology, his leadership, and his pioneering role in shaping the discipline in India make him eminent among the makers of the history of psychology in India.

# References

Berkeley-Hill, O. (1927). Employment of intelligence tests in school in India. *Indian Journal of Psychology*, 2.

Bose, G. (1938). Progress of psychology in India during the past twenty-five years. In B. Prasad (Ed.), *The progress of science in India during the past twenty-five years*. Calcutta: Indian Science Congress Association.

———. (1944). Nature of intelligence and its measurement. *Indian Journal of Psychology*, 19.

Chatterjee, G.C. (1927). Intelligence test for college freshmen. *Indian Journal of Psychology*, 2.

Dandekar, V.M., & Rath, N. (1971). *Poverty in India*. Poona: Indian School of Political Economy.

Kapat, G., & Bhattacharje, C. (1948). Some critical observations on pass along test. *Indian Journal of Psychology*, 21.

Menzel, E.W. (1956). *The use of new type tests in India* (4th ed.). London: Oxford University Press.

Mohanty, A.K., & Prakash, P. (1993). Theoretical despairs and methodological predicaments of developmental psychology in India: Some reflections. In T.S. Saraswathi & B. Kaur (Eds), *Human development and family studies in India* (pp. 104–121). New Delhi: SAGE Publications.

Patnaik, N., & Rath, R., (1982). Effect of cognitive training on the achievement of socially disadvantaged low achievers. In R. Rath, H.S. Asthana, D. Sinha, & J.B.P. Sinha (Eds), *Diversity and unity in cross-cultural psychology* (pp. 87–96). Lisse: Swets and Zeitlinger, B.V.

Rath, R. (1957). Attitudes of university students towards some socio-cultural and educational issues. *Journal of Educational Psychology*, 214–224.

———. (1959). A comparison of attitude scores on some socio-cultural and educational issues between two samples of college students after an interval of four years. *Journal of Social Psychology*, 50, 57–64.

———. (1972). *Social psychology: A trend report*. A survey of research in psychology. New Delhi: ICSSR.

———. (1982). Problems of integration of the disadvantaged to the mainstream. In D. Sinha, R.C. Tripathy, & G. Mishra (Eds), *Deprivation, its social roots and psychological consequences*. New Delhi: Concept Publishing Company.

Rath, R., Asthana, H.S., Sinha, D., & Sinha, J.B.P. (Eds). (1982). *Diversity and unity in cross-cultural psychology*. Lisse, the Netherlands: Swets, Zeitlinger, B.V.

Rath, R., & Das, J.P. (1957). Study in stereotypes of college freshmen and service holders (of Orissa) towards seven Indian groups. *Indian Journal of Psychology*, 3, 239–252.

———. (1958). Study in stereotypes of college freshmen and service holders in Orissa, India, towards themselves and four other foreign nationalities. *Journal of Social Psychology*, 47, 373–385.

Rath, R., Dash, A.S., & Dash, U.N. (1979). *Cognitive abilities as school achievements of the socially disadvantaged children in primary schools*. Bombay: Allied Publishers.

Rath, R., & Patnaik, N. (1978). Effect of training on some cognitive abilities. *Journal of Psychological Research*, 23, 81–92.

Rath, R., & Sircar, N.C. (1960). Inter-caste relationship as reflected in the study of attitudes and opinion of six Hindu caste groups. *Journal of Social Psychology*, 51, 3–25.

Roy, S. (1937). An experimental study of certain qualities of sense of touch. *Indian Journal of Psychology*, 12.

Sinha, D. (1977). Orientation and attitude of social psychologists in a developing country. *International Review of applied Psychology*, 26, 1–10.

———. (1986). *Psychology in a third world country: The Indian experience*. New Delhi: SAGE Publications.

# 19

# T.E. Shanmugam

(1921–1997)

## Vadakkupet Swaminathan and Velusami Kaliappan

*T.E. Shanmugam*

T.E. Shanmugam was born on 8 April 1921. As psychology formed an integral part of philoso-phy, he did his graduation and subsequent postgraduation in philosophy with psychology at Pachaiappa's College, Chennai, during the 1940s. He was awarded an MLitt in psychology in the year 1946 for the thesis entitled, 'An Analytical Study of Juvenile Delinquents and Adult Criminals' and a subsequent PhD (psychology) in the year 1952. His area of research for the doctoral programme was psychology of adolescence. As per the record available at the Department of Psychology, University of Madras, his guide for doctoral research (PhD) was G.D. Boaz and he was the first person to receive a PhD in psychology at the University of Madras. After a brief stint in Pachaiappa's College, Chennai, as a faculty in the Department of Philosophy, he joined service in the Department of

Psychology at the University of Madras in 1950 as senior lecturer. Subsequently, he was promoted as Reader and later as professor of psychology. After the death of G.D. Boaz, the founder professor in the Department of Psychology, Shanmugam became the head of the Department of Psychology in the year 1966.

In the early part of his career, he did postdoctoral research at the Institute of Psychiatry, University of London. He visited the Universities of Oxford, Sheffield, Liverpool, and Manchester in the UK. He was a visiting professor of psychology at the Universities of Moscow and Tbilisi in the erstwhile Union of Soviet Socialist Republic and the Universities of Rutgers and Pennsylvania in the USA.

T.E. Shanmugam belonged to a family of academicians and doctors. His elder brother T.E. Gnanamoorthy was a professor of Tamil, while his wife Mrs Ambika Shanmugam was a professor of biochemistry in Madras Medical College. His children are also doctors. Owing to this strong academic as well as medical background, Shanmugam's views in psychology were always marked by objectivity with a well-balanced orientation of science as well as humanities. His proficiency in Tamil (his mother tongue as well as the regional language in Tamil Nadu from where he hailed) and English was always widely appreciated across the state of Tamil Nadu. Being a sportsman who played hockey during his college days and tennis up to his middle age, he always maintained the sportsman's spirit in all his endeavours, both in professional and personal relationships.

## Affiliations

Shanmugam was one of the founder pillars of criminology in India and a significant contributor to its growth, particularly to the study of crime and delinquency from a psychological perspective. During his tenure as professor and head of the Department of Psychology (1965 to 1981), he brought the discipline of criminology to the University of Madras from Madras Medical College. This could be considered as a significant step in promoting criminology as a subject of study in higher education. Otherwise, the academic programme pertaining to the field of criminology would have been discontinued in the mid-1970s. He played an instrumental role in creating the Department of Criminology at the University of Madras in 1983. Though it became an independent department, he continued to lend his academic support to the fields of criminology and psychology in various possible ways till his last breath.

Shanmugam was associated with quite a number of professional organizations. He was the president of the Madras Psychology Society, Indian Academy of Applied Psychology, Indian Psychological Association, Section on Psychology and Educational Services of the Indian Science Congress, Indian Society of Criminology, and a host of other related organizations. He was a member of the British Psychology Society and a Fellow of Tamil Nadu Academy of Sciences. He served as the honorary director of the Juvenile Guidance Bureau, Chennai. He was the editor of the *Journal of Psychological Researches*, *Indian Journal of Applied Psychology*, and *Indian Journal of Experimental Psychology*, published by the Madras Psychology Society. As mentioned previously, Shanmugam was one of the founders of the Indian Society of Criminology and continued as its chairman for 11 years from 1970 to 1981. Working closely with criminal justice professionals and like-minded academicians, he took special care of the Indian Society of Criminology during its initial stages of growth, thus providing a strong foundation on which it stands today.

## Awards and Recognitions

T.E. Shanmugam was elected a Fellow of the Indian Society of Criminology in the year 1975 and received the prestigious ISC–Kumarappa–Reckless Award in the year 1985 for his contributions in the field of criminology. As a member of the editorial board of the *Indian Journal of Criminology* from its inception right up to his last day, he was very quality conscious and maintained high standards in a non-compromising manner while evaluating articles sent for publication in the journal. He had the honour of getting 'Best University Teacher Award' in the year 1982 from the Tamil Nadu government. In his honour, the Madras Psychology Society has instituted the Professor T.E. Shanmugam Award for Excellence in Research.

Shanmugam received a UGC National Research Fellowship which enabled him to carry out research in community psychology. The book entitled *Community Psychology* received one of the most prestigious awards, namely, the UGC–Swami Pranavananda Saraswathi Award. Shanmugam was a recipient of the International Man of the Year Award given by the International Biographical Center, UK.

## Contribution to the Field of Psychology

During his teaching and research career which spanned over a period of four decades, Shanmugam published many books, and research and popular articles. Out of these publications, many were in the field of delinquency. His book entitled *Psychosocial Factors Underlying Juvenile Delinquency* (published by the University of Madras in the year 1980) ought to be mentioned specially. His postdoctoral research at the Institute of Psychiatry, University of London, with Hans J. Eysenck had an everlasting impact on him. On his return to India, based on Eysenck's theory of criminality (as explained in the book *Crime and Personality* authored by H.J. Eysenck), he undertook many research studies with his research scholars exploring the relationship of personality factors to various forms of crime and delinquency. Though he had an inclination to formulate his hypotheses for various research studies, mainly on the basis of Eysenck's conception of human personality, he was not averse to other viewpoints. As a prelude to this work, he has systematically presented studies on delinquency from psychological and sociological points of view comparable to the studies carried out by Glueck and Glueck, and Sbeldon and Brown. Some of the psychological aspects such as creativity, cognitive dissonance, level of aspiration, and suggestibility have been given due attention along with the basic dimensions of personality based on Eysenck's theory while explaining psychosocial features of juvenile delinquents in India.

Prior to this research study, Shanmugam made a scientific study for his doctoral research on adolescent personality with a focus on emotional instability during adolescence. Materials collected in the years between 1948 and 1953 were subjected to statistical analysis, and a book entitled *Adolescent Personality* was written on the basis of this rigorous research work. The book was published by the University of Madras with a foreword from N.D. Sundaravadivelu, the then vice-chancellor of the University of Madras. Though references cited in the book may be termed as 'old,' the findings of this study are relevant to social conditions even today. The important contributions made through this book to the field of psychology are construction and validation of two tests of personality for the Tamil-speaking adolescent pupils. The author has said that these tests have been adapted in different languages and are being used for research at predoctoral and doctoral levels. These two tests are briefly described in the following paragraphs.

(i)  *The Personality Inventory (TPI):* Though the original version of this inventory was in Tamil, the author, T.E. Shanmugam, has translated it into English and verified the psychometric aspects of the test thoroughly. It has a total of 100 items in the inventory which assesses 10 aspects of adolescent personality, namely,

1. Somesthenic tendency (6 items)
2. Neurasthenic tendency (10 items)
3. Socially inactive (tendency) or Social inactivity (14 items)
4. Anxiety (14 items)
5. Depression (9 items)
6. Paranoid tendency (13 items)
7. Orientation towards reality (11 items)
8. Sleep difficulties (5 items)
9. Excitability (9 items)
10. Hypersensitivity (6 items)

(Though Shanmugam has not mentioned in his book, some of the items could be buffer because the number of items which are mentioned above when added do not make the total as 100; moreover, some of the items are found to overlap across the 10 aspects). For those who are interested in knowing about this inventory, it is suggested that they could directly refer to the book *Adolescent Psychology*, pp. 26–29). According to Shanmugam, these items have been extracted from *Personal Data Sheet* by R.S.Woodworth (1920), *A Neurotic Inventory* by Thurstone and Thurstone (1930), and *Medical Questionnaire* by H.J. Eysenck (1948). Having selected 100 items from these three sources, the inventory was tested for reliability using the methods of test-retest, split-half, and rational equivalence. Reliability coefficients computed based on these three standard methods ranged between 0.89 and 0.94. The student $t$ values were also worked out, perhaps to determine the discriminant power of items and $t$ values varied from 101.9 to 134. As part of the validation process, the inventory was administered to a sample of delinquents and a sample of non-delinquents'; mean scores of these two groups were compared for statistical significance of difference. Similarly, statistical significance of mean differences across these 10 aspects of personality between adult criminals and adult 'non-criminals' was also ascertained. Critical ratio values were found to be 5.69 and 12.22 respectively for adolescent and adult groups.

(ii)  *Verbal Projection Test (VPT):* The VPT is originated from the Word Association Test by Carl Gustav Jung and the Thematic Apperception Test by Morgan and Murray. Instead of presenting the items in a non-verbal form, such as a picture, Shanmugam carefully selected 35 statements for the VPT. A total of 11 situations were identified with the help of senior professors, and these 35 items were pertaining to any of these 11 situations. The 11 situations covered in the VPT are as follows:

1. Relationship with father, mother, and siblings
2. Relationship with friends
3. Relationship with opposite gender
4. Fear
5. Anger
6. Home life

   7. Masturbation, homosexuality
   8. Relationship with teacher
   9. Loneliness, shyness
 10. Fear of the dead and
 11. Attitude towards authority

Some sample items from the VPT are—

1. A boy is standing alone, while other boys are playing.
2. A boy with books in his hand is walking slowly away from the fields, where people are looking downwards.
3. Mother embraces a child and kisses the child. Father is there and a boy is looking at him.
4. Father and son are facing each other; Father is with stern face; Mother is by their side.
5. In the operation theatre, a figure is found lying; instruments are there.

These 35 items were further reduced to 20 items based on the observations made during the pilot study at Juvenile Guidance Bureau, Chennai. The observations were discussed with Gardener Murphy who was on a visit to Madras (the earlier name for Chennai) in 1950. The suggestions of Murphy were acknowledged to be useful in reducing the number of items from 35 to 20 and the areas to be assessed through the VPT to be reduced from 11 to 5. The five areas which have been retained in the final version of the VPT are mentioned below:

1. Family,
2. Sex,
3. Sociability,
4. Religion, and
5. Health.

Items have been prepared both in English and local vernacular (Tamil). However, Shanmugam has added that the English translation did not bring out the true atmosphere created by the Tamil version of the test. In the analysis of the stories, though the emphasis was on the contents of the stories, the 'formal' characteristics were also considered. Among a few storing schemes available at that point of time for projective tests, the one prepared by R.M. Clarke for TAT (Thematic Apperception Test) was found suitable for the purpose of quantifying the contents of the stories given as responses to these 20 items in VPT. Even the scheme provided by Clarke was modified considerably to suit the purpose of the author of VPT. In the preparation of the final scoring scheme, Shanmugam had the privilege of suggestions and help from Robert Holt of New York University (USA), A.H. Maslow, Brandeis University (USA) and Jean Cummings, the University of Nottingham (UK). The final scoring scheme had the following features:

1. Assessment of Needs (in terms of Achievement, Affection, Belongingness, Recognition and Sensory gratification).
2. Influence of Environment on the Organism or Individual as (a) Frustrating, (b) Helpful and (c) Neutral.
3. Reaction of the Organism (Individual) to the Environment either as (a) Neurotic symptoms showing frustration and insufficiency or as (b) Reactions of self-sufficiency and emotional stability.

4. Adequacy of the Principal Character as shown by Central Themes and Dominant Tones of the Stories and

5. Ending (whether satisfactory or not).

Through test-retest method, reliability coefficient was worked out for VPT. As the respondents were found to give identical stories with very little variation, reliability coefficient was increased to 0.96. But the reliability coefficients became less when the difference between test and retest was increased by a couple of months. Then the reliability coefficient was found to be 0.80. The reliability further declined when the time gap was increased to 10 months. Validity of the VPT was established by adopting the following three procedures:

6. Comparison of VPT results with the TAT results.

7. Comparison of the estimates of parent and teachers of the respondents on the responses of the respondents to VPT.

8. Comparison between 'normal adolescents' and 'juvenile delinquents' on responses to VPT.

By following the procedures mentioned above, discriminant validity was established for VPT. Critical ratios were calculated for each of the three procedures and all the critical ratio values were found to be significant thus indicating high validity of the test, that is, VPT.

Research studies carried out by using the aforementioned two tests clearly brought out the fact that puberty affected the emotional stability of the youth. At the fantasy level, puberty intensified their needs. Psychological needs such as succorance, aggression, and security were found to be crucial importance like hunger. The need for sex was found to be of average importance, while the need for achievement occupied negligible place. Though many more studies on the population of adolescents have been done after these studies by Shanmugam, due credit should be given to him for injecting the spirit of empiricism in the minds of scholars of next generations.

With a grant from the University Grants Commission under the Retired Teachers Scheme for a 2-year period, Shanmugam wrote a book *Community Psychology* and published it in the year 1987. The foreword for this book has been written by world-renowned economists Malcolm S. Adiseshiah (ex-vice-chancellor of the University of Madras). This book has five chapters. Chapters I and II include the definition, nature, and scope of community psychology with a note on existing models at that point of time. Chapter III presents eight social indicators, namely, population, poverty, beggary, unemployment, under employment, and problems of education under which section three social problems such as wastage, mental retardation, and giftedness are included. Problems of women, alcoholism and drug addiction, delinquency and crime, mental illness, and mental health form the basis of the other part of this chapter. In Chapters IV and V, intervention strategies and training-cum-research programmes are explained. In the absence of a well-structured book with a definite focus on Indian scenario, this publication of Shanmugam is like an oasis. This book is a prescribed textbook in many educational institutions across India for academic programmes in psychology. Shanmugam has written another textbook for young students of psychology titled *Abnormal Psychology*.

Two of several significant research projects which he carried out ought to be mentioned. They were (a) Effect of transcendental meditation on prisoners (funded by Mahesh Yogi Research Foundation) and (b) Psychological assessment in the recruitment of police personnel.

Contributions of T.E. Shanmugam were quite seminal in upgrading the quality of teaching psychology with 100 per cent research orientation at the Department of Psychology, University of Madras. His expertise and special interest in personality brought worldwide recognition to the

Department of Psychology, University of Madras, where he served as professor emeritus till his last breath. He was a thorough gentleman to the core and he bore no ill will against anybody. His informality had endeared him to all his colleagues and students alike. He never wielded his superiority maliciously either in knowledge or position. Officially, 20 research scholars had the pride and pleasure of acknowledging the guidance of T.E. Shanmugam in their respective doctoral theses as their research supervisor. It is quite needless to add that each of these 20 research scholars and other research scholars who had the privilege of receiving exceptionally excellent guidance from Shanmugam infuse transcendence and enlightenment in the minds of those with whom they interact day in and day out, just as how Shanmugam used to do when he was alive. The alphabets T and E which Shanmugam has got as his initials perhaps to signify the fact that he transcended to the highest level of thinking for enlightening himself and subsequently others. Hence he was Triumphant for Ever Shanmugam—T.E. Shanmugam.

Shanmugam died on 5 August 1997 at his residence in Chennai. The end was so sudden that it was unbelievable for those who had met him at the Department of Psychology, University of Madras, a few days before his demise.

# 20

## Anwar Ansari

(1922–1978)

Akbar Husain

*Anwar Ansari (second from left)*

The Department of Psychology, Aligarh Muslim University, enjoys the privilege of being one of the oldest departments in the subcontinent. During the period when the subject was rooted within philosophy, the department was called the Department of Philosophy, although psychology formed part of the syllabus in every examination. In 1932, experimentation in psychology was introduced at the BA level and a psychological laboratory was set up by M. Umaruddin. This was a momentous event in the history of the department. M. Umaruddin became head of the Department of Philosophy and Psychology in 1947 and continued in that capacity till his demise in 1964. During this period, the department developed in various spheres and became prepared to function as a distinct and separate department.

In 1964, the Department of Philosophy and Psychology were bifurcated and the Department of Psychology came into existence. Anwar Ansari became the first head of the Department of Psychology. With the foundations firmly laid in the traditions initiated by M. Umaruddin, the independent department of psychology began to move towards the assimilation of contemporary, modern directions in the field and many significant areas emerged and developed. The areas of social psychology, personality, clinical psychology, educational psychology, industrial psychology, and experimental psychology came to the fore. Broadly speaking, this covers most of the fields of applied psychology. Research activities increased in the department at Aligarh with significant contributions in various areas. Experimental-personality psychology appeared to be the area where most research work was done by Anwar Ansari.

A.M. Mohd. Anwar Ansari was born in Lucknow on 10 July 1922 in the house of Farangi Mahal (aka Firangi Mahal) scholars. He had his primary education at Lucknow and obtained BA and MA degrees from the Aligarh Muslim University and a PhD degree from London. During his studies in London, he was a newsreader in BBC Urdu service. He also spent about a year at the Department of Psychology, University of Calcutta, under the noble and scholarly guidance of Girindrasekhar Bose and S.C. Mitra. He joined Aligarh Muslim University as lecturer in psychology in the Department of Philosophy in 1954 and was selected as Reader in 1956. He was the first head of the independent Department of Psychology, when it was created in 1964, and soon became the professor. He was a member of several national and international professional bodies and was the elected president of the section of psychology and education of Indian Science Congress in its session of 1971–1972. He was honoured as UGC National Lecturer in 1977–1978 and 1978–1979. The LA coding test and value-orientation scale are the significant contributions in the field of experimental-personality psychology by Anwar Ansari. He also served as the dean of students' welfare and was the dean of the faculty of social sciences at the time of his demise on 30 July 1978. In him, Indian psychology has lost a reputed, dignified and friendly teacher who combined in himself scholarliness with nobility.

# 21

# Bishwa Bandhu Chatterjee

(1922–1983)

## Giridhar Prasad Thakur

*Bishwa Bandhu Chatterjee*

Bishwa Bandhu Chatterjee was born on 3 October 1922 in Varanasi. After completing his MSc degree in chemistry from Banaras Hindu University, he began his career as a research chemist at Delhi Cloth Mill (DCM), Delhi. Thereafter, he joined Union Academy Higher Secondary School in New Delhi and Vidya Bhavan Teachers Collage in Udaipur. Later, he shifted to psychology, completed his PhD in psychology from the University of Illinois, and also worked at the University of Michigan as a postdoctoral fellow.

He served various institutions in different capacities. During 1962–1963, he was professor and head of the psychology department at Balwant Rajput College, Agra. From 1963 to 1966, he served the National Institute of Community Development, Dehradun, as joint director. He then shifted to the Gandhian Institute of Studies, Varanasi, and worked there for a decade (1966–1976). In 1976, he joined Utkal University, Bhubaneshwar, as a professor of psychology. After superannuation, he joined North-East Hill University, Shillong, as a senior professor. His interest was in diverse fields such as learning without awareness, structural analysis of projective outputs, multivariable approach to measurement, sociometric data, games-decision and behaviour, non-violent conflict resolution, and so forth.

He has 80 research papers and a few books to his credit. His books *Riots in Rourkela, Challenge of Famine, Impact of Social Legislation on Social Change, Community Approach to Family Welfare, Candle in Woodland, Taxonomy of Behavioural Data,* and *Conflicts and Their Resolution* seem to cross the boundary of psychology to encompass sociology and other areas.

He died of a heart attack on 16 December 1983 in Aizwal. He was posthumously conferred with the Swami Pranavanand Award.

# 22

# Durganand Sinha

(1922–1998)

## Ramesh Chandra Mishra

Durganand Sinha was one of the psychologists whose passion for knowledge and unremitting productivity for almost five decades presents before Indian psychologists a model which shows how one can do culturally appropriate, socially relevant, and academically respectable research with very limited resources. He gave a new direction to psychology in India, prepared at least three generation of psychologists for excellence in research and teaching, laid the foundation of the Department of Psychology at the University of Allahabad, and elevated it to the level of a centre of advanced studies. In countless international conferences and meetings held in the developed world, he served as the ambassador of the Third World Psychology.

*Durganand Sinha*

He was born on 23 September 1922 in the princely family of the state of Banaili in Bihar. He received his BA honours (1943) and MA in philosophy (1945) from Patna University with specialization in psychology. A year later, he went to the University of Cambridge where he received advanced training in scientific psychology by Sir F.C. Bartlett. On return from Cambridge in 1949, Sinha joined Patna University as a faculty member. In 1958, he moved to the Indian Institute of Technology, Kharagpur. The fame of his scholarship grew all around so quickly that in 1961 he was invited as professor to establish the Department of Psychology at the University of Allahabad where he stayed until his superannuation.

During his stay at Allahabad, Sinha also held visiting assignments for short periods at several institutions in India (such as M.S. University of Baroda, Jawaharlal Nehru University, and the University of Delhi) and abroad (such as, Educational Testing Service, Princeton, USA; Queen's University, Canada; and the University of Hong Kong). In the mid-1980s, he served as the director of the A.N. Sinha Institute of Social Studies, Patna. His love for the Department of Psychology at the University of Allahabad brought him back, and he spent his time there working with his colleagues and students on a variety of projects until his last breath on 23 March 1998.

Sinha's contributions to psychology brought him several honours, awards, and fellowships. In 1979, he received the Wilhelm Wundt Centenary Award. The International Association for Cross-Cultural Psychology conferred on him an honorary fellowship. The University Grants Commission and the Indian Council of Social Science Research awarded him with national fellowships. The Government of Madhya Pradesh honoured him for his distinguished contributions to research in social sciences. In 1996, a special symposium on 'applications of psychology in social change and development' was organized at the International Congress of Psychology in Montreal in his honour. Berry, Mishra, and Tripathi (2003) brought out a festschrift volume entitled, *Psychology in Human and Social Development: Lessons from Diverse Cultures* in his honour. The National Academy of Psychology (India) offers the Durganand Sinha Medal for the best piece of doctoral thesis every year.

Durganand Sinha supervised 30 doctoral students from Bangladesh, India, Iran, and Nepal. He collaborated in research programmes with Gustav Jahoda, Jan Deregowski, John Berry, and Henry Kao. Traveling, enjoying new cultural experiences, developing contacts, and maintaining relationships with people worldwide were part of his nature. He participated in different roles in about 200 national and international conferences, seminars, and symposia worldwide.

Sinha's charismatic personality had strong academic and social components. Naidu (1992) considered him as an 'institution of psychology in India' (p. 1), a scholar who 'has facilitated the process of indigenization of psychology in India' (p. 2) and a person who 'has carried on a one-man crusade of being a representative of the Indian and Third World points of view in international congresses' (p. 3). In Misra's (1998) view, Sinha 'changed the framework and climate of doing research by advocating a dialogue between text and context, theory and practice, and culture and psychology' (p. 8). Pandey (1998) wrote, '[N]o description of the life of Sinha can be complete without stressing his powerful influence on the people with whom he interacted and collaborated' (p. 694). Berry (2006 remarked, '[H]e was a close friend and great scholar with whom I was privileged to collaborate. He … inspired all those who came in contact with him: in fact I have often said that I learned something new every time he spoke' (p. 1).

## Contributions to Psychology

Sinha's contributions to psychology are multifarious. What we have seen him doing and talking about can be situated in the field of cross-cultural psychology. This field of psychology is broad ranging in its interest, including basic psychological processes (e.g., perception, cognition, emotion, and personality) and their application to several areas of human concern (e.g., social change and development, psychopathology, and health). No cross-cultural psychologist in the world other than Sinha has seemingly addressed so many of these topics in his lifetime work. His concern for application of psychological research to the solution of social and national problems was stronger than engagement in research for academic fun.

Mishra (2006) has summarized Sinha's vision of psychology and his contributions to psychology. In the following pages, we will focus on some of these aspects to appreciate the spirit Sinha nurtured for the development and expansion of psychology.

## Struggle Against Colonial Impact on Psychology

In his student days, Sinha was exposed to the colonial educational system both in India and at Cambridge. This impact was reflected in his early studies on memory (Davis & Sinha, 1950a, 1950b). While teaching psychology to engineering and technology students at Kharagpur, he developed interest in the study of industrial problems such as job satisfaction, absenteeism, group morale, and anxiety. His work on job satisfaction is considered to have predated Herzberg's two-factor theory. However, in the course of these studies, Sinha felt uncomfortable with the blind use of Western theories and models, and he started looking for alternatives.

## Culturally Sensitive and Appropriate Psychology

Sinha's disenchantment with Western theories and models of behaviour grew out of his sensitivity and experience of the realities of the life of grassroot-level populations (e.g., farmers in villages). In the 1960s and 1970s, about 80 per cent of the Indian population lived in villages under conditions of poverty. He considered the promotion of national development as his moral responsibility, and carried out classical studies of villager's needs, hopes, and aspirations. The eventual publications (Sinha, 1969a, 1974), demonstrate his courage to propose an alternative approach to the understanding of a villager's motivation.

## Macro-approach to Behaviour

A main feature of the Western scientific psychology is the analysis and understanding of behaviour in artificially created laboratory conditions. Sinha clearly realized that behaviour of people was embedded in their ecological and cultural contexts. Before an eco-cultural framework (Berry, 1976) to the understanding of human behaviour was formally proposed, Sinha (1952) had studied human behaviour in relation to earthquakes, which was an ecological factor, but never talked about in psychology at that time. His early studies on anxiety (Sinha, 1962) and perceptual differentiation (Sinha, 1979, 1982) demonstrated the role of ecological and cultural factors in human behaviour. This approach finally got full representation in his book (Mishra, Sinha, & Berry, 1996) in which the roles of ecology and acculturation were clearly identified in cultural and psychological adaptations of the Adivasi groups.

## Problem-oriented Research

Social concerns were the driving force in Sinha's academic journey, both within India and internationally. These concerns are reflected in his early studies of absenteeism, work frustration, job satisfaction, and motivation in industrial settings (Sinha, 1972a) as well as in his later works on poverty

(Sinha, 1976, 1990a), deprivation (Sinha, Tripathi, & Misra, 1982), health (Sinha, 1990b), and social values (Sinha & Kao, 1988). Not only did he outline a programme of Adivasi children's education (Sinha & Mishra, 1997) and management of acculturative stress of the Adivasi peoples (Mishra et al., 1996) but he also prepared a module for sensitizing field functionaries about the strength of Adivasi culture and life (Mishra & Sinha, 1998). He advised psychologists to draw their research problems from the field rather than from research journals. No other scholar seems to have shown such a wide range of concerns about applied issues.

## Integration of Indian and Western Traditions

Sinha's grounding in philosophy always engaged him with Eastern and Western perspectives in psychological inquiries. He was against indiscrete borrowing from the West for research and practice of psychology in India, and he was also against declaring all Western psychology as useless. What he wanted was an integration of both the perspectives. He advocated careful examination of the appropriateness of Western concepts, tools, models, and theories before using them in research or practice in the Indian setting. He also believed that, through integration of Indian concepts, methods, and practices, Western psychological knowledge could be greatly enriched in several areas (Sinha, 1965). The dichotomy created by terms like 'Indian psychology' or 'Western psychology' could never receive Sinha's appreciation. He firmly believed that knowledge could not be conditioned by national boundaries, and it could also not be tied to the apron strings of a particular method. For him, objectivity in knowledge was not all that psychology should aspire for. He argued for integration of empirical and experiential approaches to generate a unified and universal psychological science.

## Indigenizing Psychology

The main reason for Sinha's disappointment with Western Academic Scientific Psychology (WASP) was that culture had not got place in it. Psychologists, who were using culture as a variable in their studies, were also not happy with each other. The contrast in their viewpoints was reflected in the use of emic and etic approaches to the study of human behaviour. Those who supported emic approach argued that human behaviour could and should be understood only in local cultural context, and not in comparison with others. Grounded in this idea were the approaches of indigenous psychology, ethnopsychology, societal psychology, and cultural psychology. Those who followed the etic approach argued in favour of comparison of different cultural groups in order to discover similarities and differences in behaviour. This approach was reflected in cross-cultural, acculturation, and intercultural psychology.

Sinha (1965, 1986) made a significant contribution to this debate. While he recognized the importance of local cultural perspectives in understanding behaviour, he also argued that the local should be viewed in the broader cross-cultural perspective. This idea was strongly reflected in his effort towards 'indigenization of psychology' (Sinha, 1989, 1997) rather than creating an 'indigenous psychology'. Berry (2006) has remarked that in order to be cross-cultural, one has first to be cultural. Sinha demonstrates the rare quality of being both. His studies on change in villages (1979b), rural leadership (1969a), intergenerational differences (1972b), first-generation learners (1969b), child socialization (1981; Sinha & Mishra, 1999), and cognitive development (Mishra et al., 1996) provide clear examples of indigenization of psychology instead of transplantation of Western psychology. He made a distinction between 'cosmetic indigenization', and 'paradigmatic indigenization', and sincerely argued in support of the latter (Sinha, 1997).

## Methodological Innovations

Sinha's research with farmers in villages and Adivasi populations in forests revealed many problems in the use of standard methods (Sinha, 1983; Sinha & Mishra, 1993). In village studies, he noted that illiterate villagers experienced great difficulty in rating objects or events on point scales. He developed a 'ladder-rating scale' in which a difficult process of rating was reduced to a familiar and simple activity. The 'grain sorting' method developed for the study of level of aspiration and 'happy life test' for the study of the needs of the villagers also reflect his creative innovation. Story-Pictorial and Indo-African Embedded Figures Tests (Sinha, 1984) bear testimony to his methodological innovations for the study of cognition.

In all these methods, the contents and procedures were developed in ways so that they reflected the realities of people's day-to-day life. Sinha placed great confidence in activity-based measures and he used every opportunity to introduce them in his studies. His mind was so innovative that he could create ideal tests for the study of psychological phenomenon anywhere by drawing upon local resources (Mishra, 2006).

## Distribution of Knowledge

Very few scholars combine the qualities of a sensitive researcher, teacher, and writer. Sinha was all in one. He was productive until his last breath. Some of his unfinished works were completed and published by his colleagues and students after his death (e.g., Mishra, Sinha & Berry, 1999). He published more than 150 research papers and articles in national and international journals of psychology and edited volumes. He also wrote or edited 18 volumes of psychology addressing a variety of themes of national and international concerns.

The brief account of the life and work of Durganand Sinha presented in this chapter indicates that he was an institution of psychology. As a global psychologist and true social scientist, he drew perspectives from economics, sociology, political science, history, and anthropology and integrated them in the psychology he did, practiced, encouraged, and pleaded for. The development of new concepts, methods, and theoretical approaches characterize the advancement of any science. Sinha contributed to psychology in all these respects. Generations of psychologists will remember him through his work, which has given new directions to academic psychology in India and also made its pursuits worthwhile for the human society.

## References

Berry, J.W. (1976). *Human ecology and cognitive style.* New York: SAGE/Halstead.
———. (2006). Noble thoughts come from all directions: An appreciation of the scholarship of Professor Durganand Sinha. *Psychology and Developing Societies, 18* (1), 1–14.

Berry, J.W., Mishra, R.C., & Tripathi, R.C. (Eds) (2003). *Psychology in human and social development: Lessons from diverse cultures*. New Delhi: SAGE Publications.

Davis, D.R., & Sinha, D. (1950a). The effect of an experience upon the recall of another. *Quarterly Journal of Experimental Psychology, 2*(2), 43–52.

———. (1950b). The influence of an interpolated experience upon recognition. *Quarterly Journal of Experimental Psychology, 2*(3), 132–137.

Misra, G. (1998). Professor Durganand Sinha (1922–1998). *Cross-Cultural Psychology Bulletin* (September), 6–10.

Mishra, R.C. (2006). Durganand Sinha: His vision for psychology in the Third World. In K.M.S.R. Murthy, R. Subramanian, P. Sumangala & V.K.R. Kumar (Eds), *The great social scientists of India* (pp. 242–255). Chennai: Emerald Publishers.

Mishra, R.C., & Sinha, D. (1998). Role models, socialization patterns and cognitive strength of tribals. In K. Sujatha (Eds), *Modules for tribal education* (pp. 47–71). New Delhi: NIEPA.

Mishra, R.C., Sinha, D., & Berry, J.W. (1996). *Ecology, acculturation and psychological adaptation: A study of Adivasis in Bihar*. New Delhi: SAGE Publications.

———. (1999). Meeting the challenges of fieldwork in cross-cultural psychological research. *Psychology and Developing Societies, 11*(1), 91–104.

Naidu, R.K. (1992). Professor Durganand Sinha: A legacy for psychology in the developing world. *Psychology and Developing Societies, 4*(1), 1–2.

Pandey, J. (1998). Obituary: Durganand Sinha (1922–1998). *Journal of Cross-Cultural Psychology, 29*(6), 691–694.

Sinha, D. (1952). Behaviour in catastrophic situation: A psychological study of reports and rumours. *British Journal of Psychology, 43*(3), 200–209.

———. (1962). Cultural factors in the emergence of anxiety. *Eastern Anthropologist, 15*(1), 21–37.

———. (1965). Integration of modern psychology with Indian thought. In A.J. Sutchi & M.A. Vick (Eds), *Readings in humanistic psychology* (pp. 265–279). New York: Free Press.

———. (1969a). *Indian villages in transition: A motivational analysis*. Delhi: Associated Publishing House.

———. (1969b). Level of aspiration of villagers in certain community development areas. *Journal of General and Applied Psychology, 11*(1), 50–56.

———. (1972a). *Studies in industrial psychology*. Agra: Sri Ram Mehra Publisher.

———. (1972b). *The Mughal syndrome: Psychological study of intergenerational differences*. New Delhi: Tata McGraw Hill.

———. (1974). *Motivation and rural development. Two studies on Indian framers*. Calcutta: Minerva Associates.

———. (1976). Study of psychological dimensions of poverty. *Journal of Social and Economic Studies, 4*, 167–200.

———. (1979). Perceptual style among nomadic and transitional agriculturalist Birhors. In L. Eckensberger, W.J. Lonner, & Y.H. Poortinga (Eds), *Cross-cultural contributions to psychology* (pp. 83–93). Lisse: Swets & Zeitlinger.

———. (1981). *Socialization of the Indian child*. New Delhi: Concept Publishing Company.

———. (1982). Socio-cultural factors and the development of perceptual and cognitive skills. *Review of Child Development Research, 6*, 441–472.

———. (1983). Human assessment in the Indian context. In S.H. Irvive & J.W. Berry (Eds), *Human assessment and cultural factors* (pp. 17–34). New York: Plenum.

———. (1984). *Manual for Story-Pictorial E.F.T. and Indo-African E.F.T.* Varanasi: Rupa Psychological Corporation.

———. (1986). *Psychology in a third world country. The Indian experience*. New Delhi: SAGE Publications.

———. (1989). Cross-cultural psychology and the process of indigenization: A second view from the Third World. In D.M. Keats, D. Munroe, & L. Mann (Eds), *Heterogeneity in cross-cultural psychology* (pp. 24–40). Lisse: Swets & Zeitlinger.

Sinha, D. (1990a). Intervention for development out of poverty. In R. Brislin (Ed.), *Applied cross-cultural psychology* (pp. 77–97). Newbury Park, CA: SAGE Publications.

———. (1990b). Concept of psycho-social well-being: Western and Indian perspectives. *NIMHANS Journal*, 8(1), 1–11.

———. (1997). Indigenizing psychology. In J.W. Berry, Y.H. Poortinga & J. Pandey (Eds), *Handbook of cross-cultural psychology* (Vol. 1, pp. 129–169). Boston: Allyn & Bacon.

Sinha, D., & Kao, H.S.R. (1988). *Social values and development: Asian perspective.* New Delhi: SAGE Publications.

Sinha, D., & Mishra, R.C. (1993). Some methodological issues related to research in developmental psychology in the context of policy and intervention programmes. In T.S. Saraswathi & B. Kaur (Eds), *Human development and family studies in India: An agenda for research and policy* (pp. 139–150). New Delhi: SAGE Publications.

———. (1997). Some personality, motivational and cognitive characteristics of tribals and their implications for educational development of children. *Indian Journal of Educational Planning and Administration*, 17(3), 283–295.

———. (1999). Socialization and cognitive functioning. In T.S. Saraswathi (Ed.), *Culture, socialization and human development* (pp. 167–187). New Delhi: SAGE Publications.

Sinha, D., Tripathi, R.C., & Misra, G. (1982). *Deprivation: Its social roots and psychological consequences.* New Delhi: Concept Publishing Company.

# 23

# Hosur Narayana Murthy

(1924–2011)

## Indira Jai Prakash

Hosur Narayana Murthy, H.N. Murthy, was born in Bangalore in 1924. His parents were Hosur Ramaswamaiah Subba Rao and Smt. Rajamma. His father, Mr Subba Rao, was an official at the Bhadravathi Iron and Steel Plant. Murthy finished his basic schooling at Bhadravathi town and then went to Mysore city for his college education. While in Mysore, he joined the university to pursue his bachelor's degree (BA) in psychology.

*Hosur Narayana Murthy*

At that time, M.V. Gopalaswamy was a prominent figure in the academic and cultural scene of the erstwhile princely state of Mysore. He was one of the founding fathers of the University of Mysore. Gopalaswamy had worked under Charles Spearman for his doctoral degree in London. After his return, he established the psychology department in 1924. Till then, psychology was considered part of the philosophy department. The University of Mysore had the distinction of having one of the earliest independent departments of psychology, thanks to Gopalaswamy. A brilliant intellectual with deep interest in both ancient Indian and modern psychology, Gopalaswamy shaped the interests of young Murthy to a considerable extent. Under the guidance of this eminent teacher, for his bachelor's degree, Murthy submitted a dissertation titled 'National Stereotypes' (a comparative study of how Indians perceive foreigners and how foreigners perceive Indians). He was judged as the best scholar in psychology and philosophy and was awarded the 'Bhabha Memorial Gold Medal' in 1952. He also secured a master's degree (MA) in psychology in 1954 from the University of Mysore. For a while after his MA, he worked at the Mysore State Mental Hospital at Bangalore before relocating to Ranchi European Lunatic Asylum (later renamed as Central Institute of Psychiatry) at Ranchi, Bihar.

Murthy was impressed by Joseph R. Nuttin, whose work on motivation he considered superior in providing insight in to human behaviour, both normal and abnormal. On an educational scholarship, he joined the Institut De Psychologie Et De Pedagogiques of Universite Cathololique De Louvain, Belgium, to work under Nuttin. His doctoral thesis 'A Study of Human Motivation in the Indian Context' was submitted in 1963. The thesis had three annexes—papers titled 'Relation of Cyclothymia: Schizothymia to Extroversion-Introversion; 'Psychotic Dimension: A Study with Objective Tests'; and 'Existence of Common Superstitions in Normals and Schizophrenics'. Murthy's doctoral work was liberally cited by Nuttin in a paper 'Future Time Perspective in Human Motivation and Learning' published in *Acta Psychologica* in 1964. While in Europe, Murthy was exposed to the emerging field of behaviourism and advances in behaviour therapy.

On his return to India, Murthy joined the All India Institute of Mental Health and Neurosciences (now a deemed university, called National Institute of Mental Health and Neurosciences, NIMHANS). He guided and shaped the future of clinical psychology in India for the next two decades. He was a visionary and expanded the scope of psychologists' work by introducing new areas of clinical service. He, along with N.N. Sen, has been considered instrumental in introducing behaviour therapy in India. Both were brilliant academicians who ignited the imagination of a generation of students.

Murthy was a prolific researcher. As early as 1954, he had published a paper, 'Clinical Manifestation of Fear, Anger and Jealousy in Children'. The range of his interest was vast and varied. There are publications on Indian contribution to psychology and relating it to modern psychology (1960, 1961), intellectual deficit (1965, 1966, 1967), national character (1961), role of family in mental illness (1961), psychological study of paintings of psychotics (1965, 1966), vocational guidance (1965), crime and temperament (1966), student selection and guidance (1965), group therapy (1959, 1966), effect of ECT (1966), use of objective tests (1966, 1967), ecological aspects in schizophrenia (1967), and a variety of psycho-physiological topics such as arousal (1967, 1968, 1970, 1975), to name a few. He contributed a chapter on counselling and therapy to the survey of research in psychology, Part I of ICSSR (1980). At a rough count, there were more than 140 papers listed against his name in 1977. This was apart from popular articles, talks, and unpublished papers. Being a senior professor at a prestigious institution, he was on the boards of several university bodies and committees, too numerous to be enumerated. He played a major role in all governmental policies and programmes related to mental health, being on the faculty of the NIMHANS, which is a leading institute for training mental health professionals.

At NIMHANS, one of his major projects was to develop diagnostic tests. Over several years, along with his colleagues, he attempted standardizing different diagnostic scales modelled after the MMPI (Minnesota Multiphasic Personality Inventory). From 1964 to 1970, different scales were standardized and published in *Transactions* the in-house journal of the then All India Institute of Mental health and Neurosciences. The outcome was the multiphasic questionnaire (MPQ), probably the first indigenous clinical scale for diagnostic purposes. He had the ability to anticipate emerging trends in the field of psychological disorders and therapy and encourage research in those areas. Under his leadership, research in neuropsychology, behaviour modification, biofeedback, suicide behaviour, criminal behaviour, psychological disorders, test development, claims of reincarnation, and Indian thoughts on personality were initiated. His work examining ayurvedic concepts in mental health opened a new area of understanding the relevance of ancient Indian medical concepts in treating mental disorders. He visualized and implemented a holistic approach to patient care by involving family and the social groups in both diagnosis and therapy. Research collaboration with foreign universities, notably with the University of Virginia School of Medicine, stimulated investigation into parapsychological phenomena. He was perhaps one the first psychologist in India to study the personality and adjustment pattern of *yogis*, paving way for scientific study of yogic claims. His presentation 'Psychology of Yoga' in a seminar on Yoga and science in 1975 is considered as one of the earliest efforts at psychological analysis of that practice.

Murthy was one of the pioneers in founding and shaping the destiny of the Indian Association of Clinical Psychologists (IACP), a professional body that guides the mental health services rendered by psychologists in the country. It also sets standards for their education and training. He provided much needed leadership at a time when clinical psychologists were fighting to establish their identity in a field clearly dominated by psychiatry. He was also the president of IACP for a term. In his presidential address to the IACP in 1972, he gave a clarion call to members to maintain high professional standards, humanize their services, and assume social responsibility. IACP honoured one of its founding fathers by instituting the 'Dr H.N. Murthy Oration'. At every IACP conference, a clinical psychologist is selected to speak on the latest issues in the field of behavioural medicine and bio-feedback—a fitting tribute to the master who initiated students into this field.

Many consider his effort to link Indian philosophy with modern psychology to be his most enduring legacy. In 1959 and 1960 itself, he had presented his views on contribution of India to modern psychology and the relevance of ancient Indian psychology to modern research. But laying a solid foundation for behaviour therapy in clinical field was not a mean achievement. The credit for encouraging the development and adaptation of psychological tests suitable for Indian context also goes to him. He was a source-well for seekers trying to push the boundaries of knowledge through research. His presentations at sessions of the Indian Science Congress used to provide novel ideas to potential researchers paving way for exploration of new areas.

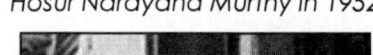

*Hosur Narayana Murthy in 1952*

Coming to his personal life, Murthy was a bachelor and lived with his brother and his family in Jayanagar, Bangalore. He was an ardent devotee of Sri Ramakrishna Paramahamsa and was closely associated with the Ramakrishna Matt in Bangalore. His keen intellect and versatile knowledge combined with his approachability attracted people. Since he was such a well-read person with wide interests, his office at the institute used to be crowded with scientists, spiritual gurus, students, and artists engaged in lively discussion on various topics. As a person, he was what could be best described as a 'humanist and existentialist'. Not many of his generation embraced the deviant and deficient with as much compassion as Murthy. People who knew him remember his gentle manner, kindness, impish humour, and non-judgemental attitude more than his brilliance. He was an excellent mentor, role model and father figure for many of his students. He guided several research students in their doctoral work, who in turn became pioneers in their chosen field of specialization. He inspired a generation of clinical psychologists to excel in their profession. In his later years, he spent most of his time in spiritual pursuits and limited his social contacts. An avid reader, he has left behind a rich collection of books on varied subjects which found a place in the private collection of one of his students.

# 24

# Shrikrishna Vasudeo Kale

## (1924–2012)

### Satishchandra Kumar, Heena Kamble, and Anjali Majumdar

*Shrikrishna Vasudeo Kale, Columbia University, New York, USA*

Shrikrishna Vasudeo Kale was born in Jamkhindi, a town in Karnataka, on 24 April 1924. He did his schooling from the Nutan Marathi Vidyalaya, Pune, followed by Shikshana Prasarak Junior College, Pune. After completing his school and junior college, he pursued further studies and acquired a master's of arts degree in philosophy, from Sir Parashurambhau College (S.P. College), where he was a student of Shankar Vaman Dandekar—also fondly known as Professor Sonopant Dandekar. For further studies, he went to the USA, where he pursued a master's degree and doctorate in psychology. In 1953, he submitted his doctoral dissertation entitled 'Learning and Retention of English-Russian Vocabulary under Different Conditions of Motion Picture Presentation' (Sinha, 1986). His dissertation was published by University of Pennsylvania in 1953–1954 (Kale & Grosslight, 1953). On finishing his studies in the USA, he received a recommendation letter from C.R. Carpenter who was the head of the Department of Psychology and director of Instructional Film Research Program at the time. In this letter, Carpenter recognized Kale as a 'diligent, systematic, and intelligent investigator'. Carpenter also recommended Kale's contribution as 'in a university doing both teaching and research. He has much to offer that India greatly needs in the area of complex social-psychological research'.

After returning from the USA, he joined S.P. College, Pune, and was the Head of the Department of Philosophy. During this period, he was also the visiting postgraduate faculty of the University Department of Psychology, Poona University. In the college, he was known as a sharp-minded professor and student-friendly teacher. In the earlier days, psychology and science of reasoning were an integral part of philosophy and Kale strived hard for the inclusion of psychology as an independent subject at the college level. He was appointed as the secretary of Shikshan Prasarak Mandal on 1 March 1957. He remained a lifelong member of the Mandal. On the occasion of the platinum jubilee celebration in 1958, he, along with Dattovaman Potdar, was elected as the president of the Mandal.

*Recommendation Letter from C.R. Carpenter, Head, Department of Psychology, Instructional Film Research Program*

THE PENNSYLVANIA STATE COLLEGE
SCHOOL OF EDUCATION
STATE COLLEGE, PENNSYLVANIA

INSTRUCTIONAL FILM RESEARCH PROGRAM

re: Shrikrishna Vasudeo Kale

To Whom It May Concern:

Dr. Kale completed his dissertation research on vocabulary instruction and film methodology with this University and the Instructional Film Research Program. We became well acquainted with him as a person and as a professional investigator and scholar.

We are delighted to give Dr. Kale the highest commendations. He is a diligent, systematic and intelligent investigator. In a short time he mastered systematic western psychology -- even complex quantitative statistical concepts. His mastery of the relevant scientific literature is outstanding.

Dr. Kale is most socially acceptable to his colleagues. He has poise and self-assurance, tending to be slightly submissive according to western standards. He works well with groups being cooperative and adaptable to a wide range of social-personal demands. Withal he has integrity of a high order.

In our opinion Dr. Kale should find his field of greatest usefulness in a university doing both teaching and research. He has much to offer that India greatly needs in the area of complex social-psychological research. It has been our hope that when Dr. Kale returned to India he would find opportunities to help develop extensive educational and informational programs using sound motion pictures, radio, and later, television. His pioneering explorative research in language instruction, using the film, may prove of great value when applied in India. Also he would be a very valuable person for cooperating with the many kinds of mass media information programs of UNESCO, the United Nations or of other nations who have guest programs in India.

C. R. CARPENTER
Head, Department of Psychology
Director, Instructional Film Research Program

Kale served the Mandal till 3 November 1959, after which he was appointed as Reader in the University Department of Applied Psychology which was situated in Bombay University (now known as the University of Mumbai) in the academic session 1958–1959. He was appointed officiating professor and head of the department, when Nirod Mukherjee, professor and head of the department, resigned on 18 March 1968 (University of Bombay Annual Report 1967–68). On 15 November 1968, Kale, who was officiating as head of department, was appointed professor and head of the University Department of Applied Psychology (University of Bombay Annual Report 1968–69) which he continued and occupied till his retirement on 30 April 1984 (University of Bombay Annual Report, 1984–85).

## Affiliations

Through the efforts and the vision of Kale, the Department of Applied Psychology, earlier provided the space of a few hundred square feet in East Wing Seminar rooms of the Fort Campus, Churchgate on its inception on 26 July 1959 (Kale, 1984), was shifted from South Mumbai to the new university Campus, on the first floor of Ranade Bhavan (Vidyanagari) Kalina, Santacruz (East), Bombay from June, 1972 (University of Bombay Annual Report 1971–72).

With the vision of subsequent heads of the department, such as Suresh Kanekar, P.A. Bhagwatwar, C.G. Deshpande and others, it was housed in a separate building of ground-plus-one floor at CD Deshmukh Bhavan on 26 January 1995. Now the Department of Applied Psychology has the modern state-of-the-art infrastructure and community-oriented counselling centre.

'Dr Kale was a person of mild manners, unassuming by temperament, strong of convictions and addict of hard work', was how he was described on his retirement in the personalia of *Bombay Psychologist* 1984 issue (Kale & Ghorpade, 1984). He worked tirelessly throughout his life for the cause of psychology and earned for himself a respectable name and status in the city. Since the establishment of the Department of Applied Psychology 55 years ago, he has played a significant role in its development and made tremendous contribution by building an adequate infrastructure during his tenure. It is only hoped that his achievements are further reinforced and made effective use of, in the times to come.

Through archival research, it was also found that five students completed their PhD theses under his guidance. These five students thanked Kale in the acknowledgements of their theses as follows:

1. Blanche, L. Barnes, 1981. *Mental Health of the Officer Personnel in Indian Merchant Marine*: 'I would like to express my deep sense of gratitude to my guide, Dr. S.V. Kale for his invaluable guidance and ready assistance, but for which I would not have been able to prepare and complete this thesis. I shall never forget his painstaking efforts and eternal patience in going through the manuscripts of my thesis'.

2. Barthakur, Pradeep Kumar, 1982. *Small Group's Reaction to Frustration as a Function of Leadership Behaviour: An Experimental Investigation and a Theoretical Analysis*: 'His (Dr. Kale's) patience has given me the chance to complete this investigation. Dr. Kale's eye for details has forced me to examine my omissions and brought out the hasty and ill-considered notions. But what I am most grateful for is his allowing me the freedom to grow. He never imposed rigid intellectual frames to curb my spontaneous intellectual pursuits'.

3. Thatte, S. Shubha, 1982. *Attentional Deficits in Psychiatric Disorders (in Relation to Arousal and Pathology Level)*: 'I am deeply indebted to Dr. S.V. Kale, Head of the Department,

Department of Applied Psychology, University of Bombay, whose perennial encouragement helped me through this venture'.

4. Barve, Anagha, 1986. *A Psycho-Social Study of Vocational Planning with Special Reference to Choice, Decision and Indecision*: 'It was indeed a privilege and pleasure to have been a student of Dr. S.V. Kale earlier in my career. Hence, being his doctoral student was natural and even more rewarding. His intuitive perception and painstaking approach to the subject was a constant source of inspiration. My deep gratitude to him for his guidance'.

5. Deosthale, P.G., 1986. *Doordarshan: A Psychological Study*: 'Sincere gratitude to my guide, Dr. S.V. Kale, for his constant untiring and valuable guidance at every step in this research study'.

## Marathi Manasshashtra Parishad (MMP)

A new organization called Marathi Manasshastra Parishad, with Kale as the president and with an ad hoc executive committee formed out of the representative cross-section of the academic as well as professional psychologists, scholars, and researchers in psychology who were interested in the dissemination and application of knowledge of the twentieth century science of psychology and it's spread among the Marathi speaking local, rural and tribal people (whether living in Maharashtra or anywhere in India or abroad) was formed in December 1982 at the University Department of Applied Psychology, University of Mumbai. Kale and Ghorpade (1985) reported the details of the first conference of the Marathi Manasshastra Parishad, which was held in Aurangabad (once called Pushpanagari) on 28 and 29 June 1985, in *Psychological News Bulletin*, a column of news about the happenings in the field of psychology in India and abroad. Some of the interesting topics on which deliberations were made were 'Buddhi and Bhavana' and 'Psychology in Muslim Saints' literature. Kale, who was the president, released the souvenir. In his presidential address he discussed the antecedents of the formation of the Marathi Manasshastra Parishad, and the ways in which it can and should develop. With supporting facts and figures, he elaborated upon how psychology would contribute to such important areas as socio-economic development, national unity and integration, social reforms, and enrichment and harmonization of the day-to-day life of the individuals and the society among Marathi-speaking people of today and tomorrow.

Interestingly, the 25th conference of Marathi Manasshastra was held in the University Department of Applied Psychology and Counselling Centre, University of Mumbai, on 22 and 23 December 2010. On 3 and 4 May 2013, the 28th conference of Marathi Manasshastra Parishad was held in Solapur, Maharashtra. Today, the membership of Marathi Manasshastra Parishad is approximately 300.

## Bombay Psychological Association

From 1968 to 1980, Kale served as the president of Bombay Psychological Association (BPA), which was founded in 1945 as a quasi academic organization with a main objective to unify psychologists, psychiatrists and share and exchange their view on the subject of psychology. He fulfilled his dream of BPA having its own journal, *The Bombay Psychologist*, in October 1978. He became the first general editor and founder of the journal. The other members of the Journal who helped in its publications were M.B. Ghorpade as managing editor and the team of editorial committee consisting of

N.N. Shukla, T.A. Desouza, P.K. Ghosh, R.B. Naik, M.D. Bengalee, Joseph Battu, and Anil Roy. He remained its general editor till 1983–1984.

During his tenure as general editor, eminent psychologists both from India and abroad contributed to the journal and enriched its publications. Some of the eminent international psychologists were H.J. Eysenck, Pittu Laungani, J.M. Fuster, J. Filella and some eminent Indian psychologist who contributed were B. Kuppuswamy, Udai Pareek, P.K. Muttagi, A.M. Dolke, R. Kundu, G.K. Valecha, Rehana Ghadiali, Durganand Sinha, Omer Bin Sayeed, S.K. Verma, V.K. Kool, P.H. Prabhu, P.V. Ramamurthi, Girishwar Misra, and M.N. Palsane to name a few. His vision and contribution is felt by the present generation as *Bombay Psychologist* is in the 35th year of publication with 28 volumes, and the number of members who prescribe the journal are 678. Kale was also the president of the Indian Academy of Applied Psychology (IAAP) from 1979–1981 (*Journal of the Indian Academy of Applied Psychology*, 2011).

## Contribution to Psychology

Kale was always aware of the social situations existing in the environment. It is also evident from his work that he thought ahead of his time. Through his articles, he tried to spread awareness about many social issues such as education, progress of psychology, and corruption, which are important issues even today. He worked on the editorial committee of a publication and was actively associated in compiling 'The Directory of Psychologists and other personnel active in the field of Psychology in Greater Mumbai and the rest of Maharashtra State (India)', which was printed by Bombay Psychological Association (BPA) and published in May 1972 (University of Bombay: Annual Report 1972–73).

## March of Psychology

'March of Psychology' is amongst the many publicized works of Kale. It was a series of articles which was published in *Bombay Psychologist* between 1978 and 1980. Through these articles, Kale brought to light the journey of psychology in India and around the world. In his work, he also spoke about civic and political consciousness, as well as adolescent behaviour.

The first article was published in the first volume of *Bombay Psychologist*, Issue 1, October 1978. Kale wrote this article speaking about the important psychological research of the time near Mumbai and research in social psychological topics such as aggression, crime, and group performance conducted in Bombay University (Kale, 1978). Other interesting research investigations included cross-cultural differences in the meaningfulness of AV values, behaviour of workers, supervisors in industrial settings, and differences in need hierarchies between workers and supervisors. This article also mentioned the growth of psychology in other parts of India, thereby asserting that from the emergence of strong centers of experimental and comparative psychology in universities such as Poona, Nagpur, and Calcutta, to the increasing amount of work in various subfields of psychology such as educational psychology, counselling and vocational psychology, and developmental psychology, the growth of awareness, and importance of psychology as a social science was phenomenal. Kale also mentioned the progress of psychology around the world.

Through 'March of Psychology,' he also tried to spread awareness about the progress in the field of psychology. The second part of 'March of Psychology' was published in the second issue of Volume 1 of *Bombay Psychologist* in April 1979. The year 1979 marked the centenary of the first laboratory of experimental psychology established in Leipzig (Germany) in 1879. Thus, the article was mostly devoted to the life, work, and achievements of Wilhelm Wundt, the father of experimental psychology and also to the newer laboratories of 1979. Kale also gave an account of other memorable events in and around 1879. Galton's questionnaire on ideational types, Maudsley's 'Pathology of Mind', Ebbinghaus' studies of memory was also important events of 1879. As the year 1979 was International Child Year, Kale also cited the contribution of child psychology to the reassertion of importance of child in human family and in human society.

In the third article in 'The March of Psychology' series, published in Volume II of *Bombay Psychologist* in October 1979, Kale focused on the research done on adolescent behaviour, and psychology of civic consciousness. The article described the studies made at that time in adolescent psychology on the susceptibilities that a teenager student is likely to develop in the age of over-stimulation and the debilitating effects it may have had on their relevant goal-seeking and self-actualizing behaviour. Regarding the psychology of civic and political consciousness, Kale mentioned that even though the local self-government tried their best to promote civic consciousness among children, due to overcrowding in large urban areas and due to influx of population from areas where civic consciousness was not well trained; there was a general break-down of rules of civic behaviour and their observance. He also stressed the importance of creating an urgent need for examining the psychological basis of social, civic, and political behaviour due to the situations of civic and political instability at that time.

The fourth article of the series was published in Issue 2 of Volume II of *Bombay Psychologist* in April 1980. The article focused on the correlation between relevance and research interest. Kale noted that even though ideally the relevance of a problem and research interest should be perfectly correlated, in reality, they are at best moderately correlated because of various factors such as the degree of interest and preference for pure research, choice to stay within the arena of a particular conceptual and methodological orientation, etc. He also discussed mental health as a research area. Kale then discussed psychology of sports in the article, bringing to light the considerable research in the psychology of sport accumulated in different parts of the world and the useful lessons that could be drawn from them to change the situation of Indian sports. He also discussed the difference between the leadership functioning of the captain of a team and the leadership functioning in other situations like that of an executive or an army general, ending the article with a small reference to helping behaviour (altruism) as a research area.

## Corruption or 'Brhashtachara'

The article was published in Volume VII of *Bombay Psychologist* in July 1985. Through this article, he presented some ideas that are relevant in the present era too, which shows his ability to think beyond the boundaries of time. He used this article to provide the readers a psychological view of corruption and an idea of how the cancer of corruption could be surgically removed from our systems. Kale elaborated that behaviour of an individual is seldom in vacuum. Even in solitude, the behaviour of an individual is stimulus-instigated and stimulus-sustained behaviour.

'Interbehavior between two such poles or ends and a certain kind of degree of mutuality, reciprocity, give-and-take, contractual—implicit contractual or explicit contractual—understanding is something which makes human behaviour a fascinating subject of study for psychologists, sociologists, economists, political scientists of national or international relations, management scientists, jurisprudence scholars, administrative science experts, journalism science students as well as experts of security defense, military operations and many others' (Kale, 1984). Inter-behaviour is an appropriate descriptive label for normal social or group behaviour, and the degenerate forms of inter-behaviour can be called 'corruption'. According to Kale, reward proportionate with response in a given situation was not the cause of corruption, but the disproportionate reward—either being too high or too low—might lead to corruption, exploitation.

Kale suggested that in a Third World country which is so densely populated like ours, in order to eradicate corruption from its root, it is necessary to stress and promote the importance of stimulation and resulting cognition as its own reward, rather than depending on external and material rewards (Kale, 1984). The article showed Kale's great insight into one of the most burning social problems of India.

## Child Psychology and Child Guidance

Kale also edited the book *Child Psychology and Child Guidance* published from Himalaya Publishing House. The first edition of the book was published in 1978 and was sold for ₹16 only. The book was the first of its kind in India. It attempted to cover the details of the syllabus prescribed by Indian universities and projected the fundamentals of the subject in a lucid and comprehensive manner. Having collective authorship, the book included chapters contributed by esteemed child psychologists of India such as Premla S. Kale (Kale's wife), Pradeep K. Barthakur, Usha Khire, Ramola Kakkar, Suman O. Kapoor, and Mrinal A. Chaukar. It was a comprehensive volume which offered not only theoretical knowledge but makes a practical approach to the problems that may be uncovered by a study of the subject.

The book contained 15 chapters which covered a range of topics like the nature of child psychology, principles of development, adjustment, child guidance, behavioural problems, methods of examination and treatment, etc. The book is still prescribed as a reference book in many universities such as Osmania University, Andhra University (Vishakhapatnam), and Bharathiar University (Coimbatore).

## PSYCHRON

Kale also developed a psychometric instrument, PSYCHRON, along with Shri S.B. Bhosale for the research students working in the area of experimental psychology. It measures human reaction time, movement time, and the time perception by sensing person's response on being subjected to controlled audiovisual stimuli of different frequency, amplitude, intensity, and colour. The PSYCHRON received nationwide acceptance and was made available by Western Region Instrumentation Centre (WRIC), University of Mumbai, to the Departments of Psychology of about 12 different universities, colleges, and other institutions. Defence Institute of Psychological Research (DIPR) has used it to study the time taken for verbal responses of subjects to visual word stimuli presented using a slide projector interfaced to PSYCHRON. It was also used by H.V.P. Mandal's Degree College of Physical Education, Amravati, Maharashtra, to study the responses of sports personnel under stress conditions. PSYCHRON also found its applications for studying the movement and reaction time of BEST drivers (Mumbai road transport) to road traffic signals. It has potential to be used for monitoring the effect of pharmaceutical drugs on patient's motor response (University of Bombay, Annual Report 1979–80).

## Awards and Recognitions

Kale was appointed a member representing the Maharashtra State on the Executive Committee of Indian Psychological Association (University of Bombay, Annual Report 1974–75), and was elected as the president of the Indian Psychological Association (1983–1984) (University of Bombay, Annual Report 1983–84). In 1978, he was elected as sectional president of the section of psychology and educational sciences of the 65th session of the Indian Science Congress held in January 1978 (University of Bombay: Annual Report 1976–77). He was also elected as a member of the sectional committee of psychology and educational sciences of Indian Science Congress Association for the year 1974 at Nagpur in January 1974 (University of Bombay: Annual Report 1973–74).

In 1979–1980, Kale was elected as the president of the Indian Academy of Applied Psychology (University of Bombay, Annual Report 1979–80). He was also an expert member of psychology on the University Grant Commissions Panel on Psychology (University of Bombay, Annual Report 1979–80). He was also the editor of the *Bombay Psychologists* and guest editor of *Psychology*, Vishwakosha, Wai (University of Bombay, Annual Report 1983–84). Kale was an expert at the Defence Institute of Psychological Research, Government of India (University of Bombay, Annual Report 1983–84). He was also the visitors nominee of Banaras Hindu University and Aligarh Muslim University (University of Bombay, Annual Report 1983–84).

Kale was the chairman of the Psychology Terminology Committee of the Directorate of Languages, Government of Maharashtra (University of Bombay, Annual Report 1983–84). He also worked as chairman of the sub-committee appointed by Marathwada University to prepare a list of scientific and technical terms for the subject of psychology in Marathi, so that it could be readily consulted by students of Marathwada University studying the subject in Marathi medium. The committee prepared a list of nearly 1,500 scientific and technical terms (in Marathi) and submitted it to the Marathwada University for approval and publication in suitable form (University of Bombay, Annual Report 1974–75). Kale was given a Lifetime Achievement Award by the Bombay Psychological Association (BPA) for his contribution to the field of psychology.[1]

He passed away on 8 March 2012, at the age of 87. Kale was a pioneer psychologist who had a distant and grand vision for the development of psychology in India. His contribution to psychology is vast, respected, and remains unparalleled.

## References

Kale, S.V. (1978). March of psychology in India and around the world. *Bombay Psychologist: A Journal of the Bombay Psychological Association, 1*(1), 17–21.

———. (1984). A brief historical note on the development of the department of applied psychology and a look into future. *Bombay Psychologist: A Journal of the Bombay Psychological Association, 6,* 24–26.

Kale, S.V., & Ghorpade, M.B. (1984). Psychological News Bulletin. *Bombay Psychologist. A Journal of Bombay Psychological Association, 6* (1), 29–34.

---

[1] See http://www.bpa-india.org/donation-membership, retrieved on 17 April 2017.

Kale, S.V., & Ghorpade, M.B. (1985). Psychological News Bulletin. *Bombay Psychologist. A Journal of Bombay Psychological Association, 7*(1), 32–36.

Kale, S.V., & Grosslight, J.H. (1953). Learning and retention of English-Russian vocabulary under different conditions of motion picture presentation. Pennsylvania State University. Philadelphia: USA.

Sinha, D. (1986). *Psychology in a third world country: The Indian Experience.* New Delhi: SAGE Publications.

University of Bombay. (1967, 1 April–1968, 31 March). *Annual report for the year 1967–68* (pp. 103–104). Bombay: Author.

———. (1968, 1 April–1969, 31 March). *Annual report for the year 1968–69* (pp. 154–157). Bombay: Author.

———. (1971, 1 April–1972, 31 March). *Annual report for the year 1971–72* (pp. 143–145). Bombay: Author.

———. (1973, 1 April–1974, 31 March). *Annual Report for the Year 1973–74* (pp. 88–91). Bombay: Author.

———. (1974, 1 April–1975, 31 March). *Annual report for the year 1974–75* (pp. 83–85). Bombay: Author.

———. (1976, 1 April–1977, 31 March). *Annual report for the year 1976–77* (pp. 75–76). Bombay: Author.

———. (1979, 1 April–1980, 31 March). *Annual report for the year 1979–80* (pp. 74–75). Bombay: Author.

———. (1983, 1 April–1984, 31 March). *Annual report for the year 1983–84* (pp. 101–104). Bombay: Author.

———. (1984, 1 April–1985, 31 March). *Annual report for the year 1984–85* (pp. 103–104). Bombay: Author.

# 25

## Lal Bachan Tripathi

(1925–2012)

### Girishwar Misra

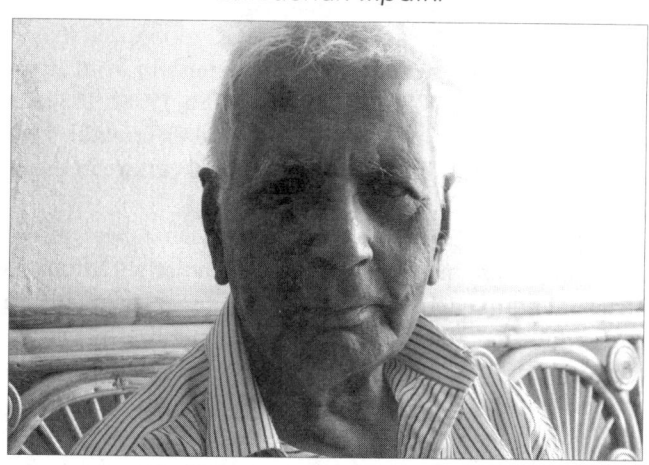

*Lal Bachan Tripathi*

Lal Bachan Tripathi was a distinguished scholar and professor of psychology. As a teacher and researcher, he was unsurpassed by many of his generation. He started his professional journey in an era when fostering and maintaining a scientific image was the core concern. As such the effort was guided by the motivation to follow a path of inquiry that may offer unambiguous, dependable, and objective approach to appreciate, understand, explain, and predict various aspects of psychological reality. It was held that such a move shall bring in certainty in this otherwise very fuzzy domain of psychological knowledge. In this context, the scientific way of conducting psychology was expected to remove the ignorance due to non-scientific and faith-oriented explorations into the functioning of mind-related matters (Tripathi, 2000c, 2003). The scientific procedure of empirical engagement with unbiased, detached observation was accepted as the key to knowledge creation.

---

[1] This article is a revised version of a piece written by the author for Introduction in Misra (2007).

It was supposed to furnish necessary ground in consonance with a deterministic and mechanistic paradigm. This was the only way to pursue a value-free and objective inquiry leading to discovery of facts. A strong commitment to this position became the defining feature of the academic and professional endeavours of L.B.Tripathi.

L.B. Tripathi appreciated the value of science and maintained its spirit in his academic approach. He believed in gaining knowledge through empirical techniques. He was keen to map the objectively verifiable domains of psychological life which set the contours of reality and knowledge. In the foreword to K.D. Broota's (1989, p. v) *Experimental Design in Behavioral Research* he articulated his methodological position in the following words:

> Experimental method is the mainstay of social science research in general and psychological research in particular, mainly because it is considered to be the most dependable way of determining causal relationships between the antecedent and the consequent variables.

L.B. Tripathi held psychological theorization capable of explaining the increasingly greater domain of an area of study as the prime concern of any scientific pursuit. He viewed science as an exercise in building theories that has potential of a greater degree of generalization (Tripathi, 1966, 1984). It is not a mere coincidence that he designed, introduced, and offered a course on psychological theory at the masters level at the University of Gorakhpur and opted for theoretical psychology as one of the fields of specialization for the department when the UGC recognized it as a department of special assistance (DSA). This theoretical orientation did not deter him from attending to social issues such as deprivation (Misra & Tripathi, 1975, 1977, 1978a, 1978b, 1978c, 1980, 1982; Tripathi, 1982), parenting (Tripathi, 1999a), future time perspective (Agarwal & Tripathi, 1978, 1979), vocational preference (Gupta, Tripathi & Agarwal, 1994) and professional culture in the community of teachers (Tripathi, 1986, 2000a, 2000b, 2002).

He was born on 15 September 1935 in a village named Dharahara in Balia district of Uttar Pradesh, a region famous for achievements in the Indian scholarly traditions as well as contributions to the freedom struggle and Indian polity. His father, late Sri Jagannath Tripathi, was a farmer by profession. After early education at a Sanskrit *pathshala* in a nearby village, he received higher secondary education in Azamgarh and moved to Banaras Hindu University, Varanasi, for higher education. There he studied under scholars such as B.L. Atreya and S.S. Jalota. After doing a masters in psychology with the distinction of being first-class first in 1955, he started a career in the professional world at a PG college at Barot near Meerut in western Uttar Pradesh. After staying for a very short period of two months, he was selected as an assistant professor at the newly created University of Gorakhpur in 1957 by Sri B.N. Jha, an educationist of great repute. He along with Madan Mohan Sinha and Sri S.B.L. Bhardwaj established the Department of Psychology at the University of Gorakhpur, now rechristened as Pt Deen Dayal Upadhyay University.

The turning point in the academic career of Tripathi came when he left for Canada as a Commonwealth Scholar. He received rigorous training in psychology at McGill University, Montreal, under the mentorship of scholars such as Donald O. Hebb and Dalbir Bindra. He earned a doctorate in human cognitive psychology based on his research on concept formation under Bindra in 1963. After completing his doctoral studies, he joined the University of Gorakhpur in 1963 and moved to Jodhpur University and served there as Reader and head of the psychology department for a year. He returned to Gorakhpur as Reader in 1964 and became professor and head in 1968.

Teaching became a passion for him. As a university teacher, his goal became training the young minds with a zeal. He committed himself to the mission of teaching and research of psychology and nurtured the students and colleagues in a selfless manner. His presence in the department helped create an atmosphere of sincerity and dedication. After serving the university for 39 years in various capacities including dean, pro vice-chancellor, and acting vice-chancellor he retired in 1996. On the invitation of R.C. Tripathi, he joined the Centre for Advanced Studies (CAS) in psychology at the University of Allahabad and served there from 1999 to 2001 as a visiting professor. Subsequently, Janak Pandey requested him to be associated with the newly founded UGC Centre for Behavioral and Cognitive Sciences (CBCS) as a visiting professor. He continued in that capacity during 2002–2003.

L.B. Tripathi initiated his students, colleagues, and peers in methods, theorization, and different domains of research and equipped them to pursue research and apply the resulting knowledge in addressing various problems. Commitment to scientific reasoning coupled with critical and comprehensive understanding constituted his motto. At the University of Gorakhpur, 22 students earned doctorate under his supervision. They worked in various fields of psychology including *time perception* (Sidha Nath Rai), *person perception* (Bhaskar Deo Mishra), *prolonged deprivation* (Girishwar Misra, Ashtanand Tiwari, and Sushil Kumar Tripathi), *social motivation* (Narendra Kumar Mani Tripathi, Rashmi Gupta, and Pushpa Sharma), *time perspective* (Adesh Agarwarl), *learning and memory* (Sheela Singh, Ramji Lal Srivastava, Veera Srivastava, and Anupam Nath Tripathi), *religiosity* (Achal Nandini Srivastava), *group polarization* (Rajendra Tiwari), *dependence proneness* (Banarasi Das Tiwari and Ramesh Mani Tripathi), and *child rearing and socialization* (Renu Singh and Madhulika Srivastava). It is gratifying that most of these students are now senior faculty and some of them have extended the domains of research and have earned a place in the academic world.

He undertook a number of research projects including calibration of materials in Hindi for research purposes (ICSSR), psychological consequences of prolonged deprivation (with Girishwar Misra, ICSSR), learning disability in a deprived society (with Achal Nandini Srivastava, NCERT), and psychological outcomes associated with severe iodine deficiency (With Banarasi Das Tiwari, ICMR).

His presence at the UGC as member of subject panel and UGC national lecturer was widely appreciated. He was part of the editorial committee of the first ICSSR survey of research in psychology under the editorship of Shiva K. Mitra. Subsequently, he wrote a review chapter. 'Higher Mental Processes' in the third ICSSR survey edited by Janak Pandey.

He was contributing to ensure the quality of research in psychology as a member on the editorial boards of many journals including *Indian Journal of Psychology, Indian Psychological Review, Indian Psychologist, Indian Journal of Current Psychological Research, Personality Study and Group Behavior* and *Psychological Studies.*

In his professional life, he was associated with the Indian Science Congress Association and was on the executive board of Indian Psychological Association (IPA). He took the initiative to organize the psychology community in Uttar Pradesh. He was the founder president of the UP Psychological Association (UPPA). Looking at the political and personal diversions in the professional organizations, psychologists gathered at Bhopal University in 1988 and decided to form the National Academy of Psychology (NAOP) India. On that occasion, L.B. Tripathi was unanimously nominated as the convener of advisory committee for drafting the constitution of the organization.

He excelled as a teacher and became a role model for many. As Hindi became the medium of instruction, he along with his colleagues took the initiative to bring out a series of standard textbooks in Hindi for undergraduate students. His *Modern Experimental Psychology* (Tripathi, Agarwal, Srivastava, Srivastava, Misra & Mishra, 1994a) has gone into 10 editions. He also wrote and edited Hindi textbooks with colleagues on social psychology, physiological psychology, research methods (Tripathi, Agarwal, Saxena & Misra, 1994), and psychological statistics. He translated the Hulse,

Deese, and Egeth's *Psychology of Learning* into Hindi which was published by Tata Mcgraw-Hill (India).

Tripathi started his university career when the challenge was to develop an identity for the newly emerging discipline of psychology and create a space for it in the university community. To this end, he worked hard to establish this discipline in the academic world of higher learning. He became instrumental in opening psychology courses at numerous institutions. He established a model centre of higher learning in psychology. Under his dynamic leadership, Gorakhpur department was elevated by the UGC to the status of DSA.

In addition to teaching and research, L.B. Tripathi was a source of inspiration. Scholars often sought his advice in academic matters. Thus, when late Anima Sen was writing the monograph *Attention and Distraction*, which was subsequently published (1983), and did not give the historical context of the domain of research, she asked none other but L.B. Tripathi to write the foreword of the book. He happily obliged her by providing a lucid and in-depth analysis of cognitive psychology in general and attention in particular. This is a very precise and conceptually rich piece. To have a feel of his style of exposition I would like to quote from it. He observes:

> Gradual realization of the failure of the behaviouristic paradigm, and irresistible upsurge made by the cognitive psychology provided the necessary impetus and ideas for revival of some older mentalistic concepts with more readily operationalizable definitions. Great strides made in the field of information processing technologies and communications proved extremely fertile for yielding new models for under-standing the functions of human brain.... By the end of the 60s psychology had gone a full circle from the point of abandoning mentalistic concepts to reaccepting them. (Sen 1883, pp. x–xi)

When L.B. Tripathi was asked to review research in higher mental processes in the third ICSSR survey, he had to organize the chapter and develop a conceptual scheme. As such the term 'higher mental processes' (against lower cognitive processes!) does not occur in psychological vocabulary. So, Tripathi (1988, p. 289) had to articulate one such notion that can have legitimacy in scientific discourse. He proposed that

> [H]igher mental processes are those psychological activities in which mediational processes go beyond the direct constraints of sensory input and motor output, are predominantly determined by neurophysiological processes of the brain, and are explicable in terms of either reductionistic neurophysiological processes or special constructs.

> (Higher mental processes. In Janak Pandey, 1988)

It is because of clarity of concepts and expository style that L.B. Tripathi became one of the most frequently sought-after resource persons at national seminars and refresher courses in psychology and UGC orientation programmes for university teachers. He is regarded as an undisputed scholar in the field of experimental psychology and research methods. His concern for viewing themes in historical perspective and relating them to the broader conceptual context made him a central figure in the academic debates and discourses.

A champion of panhuman psychology, Tripathi's scholarship continued to enrich students and researchers learning scientific psychology. Informed by the vision that foundational psychological processes are the common building blocks of psychological discourse, he viewed neuropsychological and cognitive processes as basic (Misra & Tripathi, 1978d; Tripathi, 1988). He was convinced that these processes are potent enough to explain the socio-cultural processes. With an open but critical mind, he came out with a critical scrutiny of many of the assumptions, beliefs, values, and preferences held by the majority or masses (Tripathi, 1999b). He believed in parsimony and found many concepts not only theoretically superfluous but scientifically untenable.

Tripathi commanded unmatched respect from friends, peers, colleagues, and students. Those who have visited him cannot forget his affection, care, and generosity during such interactions. During a long inning as a leader in the discipline of psychology at the national scene spanning over a period of four decades, he has been a constant source of inspiration and a guiding force for a large number of colleagues and students. As a guru, L.B. Tripathi has nurtured several generations of psychologists. Engaged in the endeavour of institution building and pursuing the dharma of a mentor, he invested his entire energy in teaching and helping people learn psychology.

Tripathi left for his heavenly abode on 5 October 2012 at his residence in Allahabad. He is survived by his wife, three sons—Anand, Vibhav, and Vivek—and two daughters—Pragya and Manisha. He will be remembered as a gentle and affectionate human being with a professional approach and humanitarian thinking.

# References

Agarwal, A., & Tripathi, L.B. (1978). Time perspective: I. Theoretical considerations. *Psychological Studies, 23*(2), 61–68.

———. (1979). Time perspective: II. Development and empirical validation of a new tool. *Psychological Studies, 24*(1), 59–65.

Broota, K.D. (1989). *Experimental design in behavioral research*. Delhi: Wiley Eastern.

Gupta, R., Tripathi, L.B., & Agrawal, A. (1994). Development of power motive and related vocational preferences. *Indian Journal of Applied Psychology, 31*(1), 14–20.

Misra, G. (Ed.). (2007). *Psychological theory and teaching profession: Select essays by Professor L.B. Tripathi*. New Delhi: Concept.

Misra, G., & Tripathi, L.B. (1975). Cognitive activities as a function of prolonged deprivation. *Psychological Studies, 21*, 54–61.

———. (1977). Psychological consequences of prolonged deprivation. *ICSSR Research Abstracts Quarterly, 7*, 94–111.

———. (1978a). *Manual of prolonged deprivation scale*. Agra: National Psychological Corporation.

———. (1978b). Prolonged deprivation and motivation. *Journal of Psychological Researches, 22*, 171–179.

———. (1978c). Prolonged deprivation and status perception. *Indian Journal of Social Work, 39*, 113–121.

———. (1978d). The psychology of perception: A curricular approach. *Journal of Education and Psychology, 25*, 129–143.

———. (1980). *Psychological consequences of prolonged deprivation*. Agra: National Psychological Corporation.

Pandey, J. (Ed.). (1988). *Psychology in India: The state of the art* (Vol.1, pp. 289–328). New Delhi: SAGE Publications.

Sen, A. (1983). *Attention and distraction*. New Delhi: Sterling.

Sinha, D., Tripathi, R.C., & Misra, G. (Eds). (1982). *Deprivation, its social roots and psychological consequences* (pp. 49–71). New Delhi: Concept.

Tripathi, L.B. (1966). Information theory in contemporary psychology. *Indian Psychological Review, 2*, 109–118.

———. (1982). Some methodological problems of deprivation studies. In D. Sinha, R.C. Tripathi & G.Misra (Eds), *Deprivation, its social roots and psychological consequences* (pp. 49–71). New Delhi: Concept.

———. (1984). *Foundations of recent developments in experimental psychology*. Agra: Dayalbagh Educational Institute.

———. (1986). 'Some motivational aspects of university teachers'. A key note address at a seminar on motivation in educational context organized at Bhopal University, Bhopal.

Tripathi, L.B. (1988). Higher mental processes. In Pandey, J. (Ed.), *Psychology in India: The state of the art* (Vol.1, pp. 289–328). New Delhi: SAGE Publications.

———. (1999a). On reward and punishment in Indian universities. *University News, 37*(10), 1–5.

———. (1999b). Some erroneous beliefs of parents about their children. *Praachi Journal of Psycho-cultural Dimensions, 15*, 91–94.

———. (2000a). Indian universities: Underlying assumptions and consequences. *Amity Business School Review, 2000, 1*, 6–12.

———. (2000b). Roles and responsibilities of university teachers. *Zenith*, 9–13.

———. (2000c). Some reflections on contemporary psychology. *Psychological Studies, 45*, 14–18.

———. (2001). Culture as a psychological construct. *Psychology and Developing Societies, 13*, 129–140.

———. (2002). My concept of a university. *Zenith*, 12–21.

———. (2003). Knowledge and faith in contemporary psychology. *Psychological Studies, 48*, 516.

———. (2004). Extra remunerative assignments in the universities. *University 42*(30), 1–4.

Tripathi, L.B., Agarwal, A., Saxena, A.K., & Misra, G. (1994). *Adhunik prayogik manovigyan,* (10th ed.). Agra: H.P. Bhargava.

Tripathi, L.B., Agarwal, A., Srivastava, A.N., Srivastava, A.N., Misra, G. & Mishra, B. (1994). *Manovigyanick anusandhan padhati.* Agra: H.P. Bhargava.

# 26
# Piara Singh Hundal

(1925–1983)

## Anuradha Bhandari

Piara Singh Hundal is renowned for his distinguished career in the field of psychology. Born into a family of agriculturists on 7 May 1925, Hundal grew up to be a brilliant student. He completed his MSc in psychology from Aligarh Muslim University in 1958. Following this, he earned his PhD from the Department of Psychology at Panjab University, under the guidance of S. Jalota, and was awarded the degree in 1963. Subsequently, Hundal served as research assistant, lecturer and Reader at Panjab University from 1959 till 1973. Thereafter, he joined the Guru Nanak Dev University as a professor of psychology in 1973. There he occupied various eminent positions, such as the dean, Faculty of Arts and Social Sciences, and the head, Department of Psychology, from September 1973 until his untimely demise on 27 January 1983. During his academic lifetime, he was a member of the Indian Psychological Association and the Indian Science Congress.

*Piara Singh Hundal*

Hundal was awarded the UGC National Fellowship to continue his research at the Institute of Advanced Studies, Shimla.

Hundal's major areas of research interest in the field of psychology were intelligence, personality, and motivation. He was a strong advocate for the use of multivariate techniques in research. He published several research papers in prestigious journals and guided more than a dozen masters and doctoral dissertations. He started the journal *Personality Studies and Group Behavior* which was published from the Guru Nanak Dev University and indexed in the psychological abstracts. Hundal (1967) prepared the Punjabi version of the 'General Mental Abilities Test' and a scale to measure 'attitude towards labour unions.' In 1969, Hundal assessed the purely motivational effects of knowledge of performance in a repetitive industrial task. The subjects of his study were low paid workers with 1–5 years of experience on the job. The experimental task was to grind a metallic piece to a special size and shape. Results showed increased output with increases in degree of knowledge of performance (Hundal, 1969).

In 1971, Hundal and Brar looked at the impact of reformatory education on the manifest behaviour and some psycho-social aspects of juvenile delinquents in a Borstal institute in Punjab. The study was limited to measureable aspects of human behaviour such as delinquency proneness, manifest behavioural difficulties, and attitudes towards institutionalization (Hundal & Brar, 1971).

Hundal's work in the area of intelligence and personality also led to a series of publications. In 1965, a paper was published in the *Psychological Studies* regarding the stability of item indices of the General Mental Ability Test (Hundal, 1965). The test was administered on students of Grades 7–11 from the same school. The results for both item difficulty and discrimination suggested the usefulness of the test items at Grades 7–11. Hundal, Singh, and Singh (1970) found anxiety to be unrelated to measures of academic achievement in postgraduate male students. Continuing their work in personality, Hundal and Singh (1971) in a paper published in *Multivariate Behavioral Research* explored the factorial structure of intellectual and non-intellectual characteristics now taking a sample of teacher-trainees. They found Eysenck's MPI factors of neuroticism and extraversion were not factorially similar to the second-order factors of anxiety and extraversion of Cattell's 16 PF.

Establishing psychometrics as an important field of research in India, Hundal did significant research on Raymond B. Cattell's model of intelligence. He guided a doctoral dissertation on the biological concomitants of fluid and crystallized intelligence. Collaborating with John Horn of the University of Denver, he published a paper in *Applied Psychological Measurement*. In 1977, Hundal and Horn studied the relationships between short-term learning, fluid, and crystallized intelligence.

He further supervised doctoral research on projective and psychometric indices of creativity and their relationship with crystallized and fluid intelligence. In a research paper co-authored with L.S. Minhas in 1982, postgraduate male students were administered psychometric and Rorschach measures of creativity and those of fluid and crystallized intelligence (Hundal & Minhas, 1982). In another research paper in the same year, Hundal, Minhas, and Singh (1982) administered projective and psychometric measures of creativity to students along with indices of intelligence, personality, and motivation. They found human movement to be a unique index having strong significance and relevance for the 'meaning' dimension of creativity.

Hundal played an important role in initiating work on achievement motivation in India. In 1972, Hundal and Jerath studied the personality, intelligence, and ability correlates of projective measure of achievement motivation and their factorial structure.

Apart from concentrating on research projects at an academic level, Hundal (1971) conducted seminal work at a social level on the entrepreneurs of Punjab. Using Rogers' scale of n-achievement motivation for a psycho-social experiment among Indian small-scale entrepreneurs in Ludhiana,

Punjab, from 1963–1964, Hundal reported in an unpublished monograph that a certain group of entrepreneurs called *Ramgarhias*, primarily engaged in metal work, who had been observed to take more financial risks by ploughing back profits into industry, had significantly higher n-achievement than another group of entrepreneurs, mostly Jains, who were primarily engaged in the hosiery business and who had been observed to be much more cautious in business, tending to save their profits instead of spending them for the expansion of their businesses. He conducted a second study on n-achievement motivation among the same group of small-scale entrepreneurs from Punjab by applying McClelland's Test of Insight to 40 of 200 subjects studied. In this investigation, he found the mean n-achievement scores of the 'metal' group to be significantly higher in comparison to the 'hosiery' group (Hundal, Unpublished Monograph).

Persisting on the study of achievement motivation, Hundal supervised Satvir Singh's doctoral work on the personality characteristics and motives of the fast and slow progressing farmers of Haryana. In 1978, Hundal and Singh studied correlates of progressive farm behaviour to determine motives and personality characteristics associated with differential rates of farm output. The study indicated that the need for achievement and a few related variables were positively associated with progressive farm behaviour, while anxiety and religious interest were negatively linked to the same (Hundal & Singh, 1978).

Hundal also established the Word Association Test to be an important diagnostic test for clinical research in India. In 1974, Hundal and Upmanyu studied emotional indicators in word association and their relation with psychometric measures of anxiety and neuroticism. They found significant links between emotional indicators in word association and guilt, suspiciousness, and neuroticism. In 1981, Hundal and Upmanyu reported in a paper that the characteristic of the stimulus word is an important variable in accounting for personality differences in word association behaviour.

Hundal's contribution has tremendous significance, especially in the 1960s and 1970s, when the discipline of psychology was beginning to command respect in the whole of northern India. Not only through his publications did he garner national and international recognition for the departments of psychology at Panjab University and Guru Nanak Dev University, he went on to establish important linkages with eminent American psychologists such as Raymond B. Cattell, John L. Horn, and David C. McClelland. The knowledge and the rigorous training he gave his students have helped them to grow, contribute meaningfully, and strengthen cross-cultural research in the field. A prolific researcher and psychologist with depth and vision, Hundal has left back a formidable legacy for the students of psychology and young psychologists of India.

# References

Hundal, P.S. Socio-psychological aspects of small-scale industrial entrepreneurship in northern India. (Unpublished monograph).

———. (1965). Stability of the general mental ability test item statistics at different grade levels. *Psychological Studies*, *10*(2), 104–114.

———. (1967). A study of attitude of small scale entrepreneurs towards labour unions. *Indian Journal of Applied Psychology*, *4*(1), 28–32.

———. (1969). Knowledge of performance as an incentive in repetitive industrial work. *Journal of Applied Psychology*, *54*(3), 224–226.

———. (1971). A study of entrepreneurial motivation: Comparison of fast- and slow-progressing small-scale industrial entrepreneurs in Punjab, India. *Journal of Applied Psychology*, *55*(4), 317–323.

Hundal, P.S., & Brar, H.S. (1971). Measuring the impact of reformatory education on the manifest behaviour and some psycho-social aspects of juvenile delinquents. *Applied Psychology*, *20*(2), 149–155.

Hundal, P.S., & Horn, J.L. (1977). On the relationships between short-term learning and fluid and crystallized intelligence. *Applied Psychological Measurement*, *1*(1), 11–21.

Hundal, P.S., & Jerath, J.M. (1972). Correlates of projective measure of achievement motivation and their factorial structure. *Indian Journal of Psychology*, *47*(1), 15–27.

Hundal, P.S., & Minhas, L.S. (1982). Overlapping components of psychometric and projective indices of creativity and those of crystallised and fluid intelligence. *Personality Study and Group Behaviour*, *2*(1), 28–35.

Hundal, P.S., Minhas, L.S., & Singh, A. (1982). A study of Holtzman and Rorschach ink-blot responses as measures of creativity. *Personality Study and Group Behaviour*, *3*(1), 67–83.

Hundal, P.S., & Singh, M. (1971). A factor analytical study of intellectual and non-intellectual characteristics. *Multivariate Behavioral Research*, *6*(4), 503–514.

Hundal, P.S. & Singh, S. (1975). Structure of personality characteristics and motive patterns of farmers. *Indian Journal of Psychology*, *50*(1), 33–43.

———. (1978). Some correlates of progressive farm behavior. *Journal of Occupational Psychology*, *51*(4) 327–332.

Hundal, P.S. & Upmanyu, V.V. (1974). Emotional indicators in word association and their relation with psychometric measures of anxiety and neuroticism. *Applied Psychology*, *23*(2), 111–119.

———. (1981). Nature of emotional indicators elicited by Kent-Rosanoff Word Association Test: An empirical study. *Personality Study and Group Behaviour*, *1*(2), 50–61.

Hundal, P.S., Singh, A., & Singh, M. (1970). Factor analytical study of tests of anxiety. *Psychological Reports*, *26*(3), 875–878.

# 27

## Udai Pareek

(1925–2010)

### Dinyar M. Pestonjee and Surabhi Purohit

*Udai Pareek*

Udai Pareek was born in 1925. After completing a BA from St. John's College, Agra, in 1944 and a BT from Teachers' Training College, Ajmer, in 1945 (both affiliated to Agra University), he shifted to the University of Calcutta for doing an MA in psychology and completed it in 1950. He also did an MA in philosophy from Agra University in 1952. In 1956, he completed his PhD in psychology from the University of Delhi.

Udai Pareek served several institutions starting his career as a teacher of psychology at S.T.C. Training School, Jaipur (July 1945 to July 1948 and January 1951 to June 1952). He joined Teachers Training College, Bikaner, as a lecturer in psychology and worked there for a year (June 1953 to June 1954). He was associated with the University of Delhi from July 1955 to June 1957 as a visiting lecturer in psychology. In June 1956, he joined the National Institute of Basic Education, New Delhi, as a psychologist and worked there till January 1962. Thereafter, he worked as an education psychologist at the Indian Agricultural Research Institute, New Delhi (February 1963 to February 1964) and then shifted to Small Industry Extension Training Institute, Hyderabad, as director (February 1964 to August 1966). During this period, he was also a visiting associate professor of psychology (with joint appointment in the Carolina Population Center), University of North Carolina (September 1966 to June 1968). In July 1968, he became professor and head of the Department of Social Sciences, National Institute of Health Administration and Education, New Delhi, and remained there till August 1970. He then joined the University of Udaipur as director, School of Basic Sciences and Humanities, and chairman, Faculty of Social Sciences (September 1970 to June 1973). From May 1973 to January 1985, he was professor of organizational behaviour (L&T Chair) at the Indian Institutes of Management, Ahmedabad. Besides these, he served as USAID Management Training System Development Advisor to the Ministry of Health from April 1985 to May 1987 and USAID Organization Development Advisor, Ministry of Health, Republic of Indonesia, from June 1987 to June 1988. At the time of his demise in 2010, he was a distinguished visiting professor at the Indian Institute of Health Management Research, Jaipur.

He specialized in management, specifically OB, OD, HRD, organisation structuring, and training. In his lifetime, Pareek served and provided guidance to several organizations, institutions, and professional bodies in the area of HR. He was the chairman of the Human Resource Laboratory of Applied Behavioural Sciences at EMPI Business School, New Delhi; chairman of the Governing Board of the Institute of Developmental Research and Statistics, Jaipur; advisory member for Asia and the Middle East of Human Resource Development International; member of the Academic Advisory Board of the Global Committee on the Future of Organization Development (sponsored by the OD Institute in collaboration with the OD Network and the International OD Association); chairman of the governing boards of the Institute of Development Studies, Academy of Human Resource Development (promoted by the National HRD Network of India), the South Asian Association of Psychologists (SAAP); founder-president of the National HRD Network and the Indian Society of Applied Behavioural Science; chairman of the Scientific Advisory Committee; and vice president of the Management Board of IIHMR. He was on the governing boards of several institutes and companies, including Globarena, Hyderabad, and the National HRD Network.

Some of his consultation/professional activities include team development of holding companies of Egypt, Cario, and Alexandria; UNIDO Organization development consultant to the Institute of Computer Development of Hungary, Budapest; UNIDO consultant on Transfer of Training Technology, MIDF, Malaysia; Organization development consultant to Bank Pertanian, Malaysia; USAID Organization development advisor, Rural Development Programme of NTT, Province of the Republic of Indonesia; organization designing (and restructuring) of some Indian organizations, including Bharat Coking Coal Ltd., Kothari Industries Ltd., Bharat Earth Movers Ltd., State Bank of India, Industrial Development Bank of India, Punjab & Sind Bank, Unit Trust of India, Petrofils Ltd, and CASP-PLAN, organization development in several Indian organizations, including State Bank of India, Indian Airlines, HMT, Lersen & Toubro, BCCL, ICI, Holy Family Hospital, and Medical Mission Sisters RPG Transmission, and team building in several companies such as Rickett & Coleman, Swed Forest, Red Barna (Sri Lanka), Kidavari (an NGO working for out-of-school adolescents), and a group in Malaysia (with NTL of the USA and ORI of Malaysia). He has been US-AID HRD/OD advisor to the Ministry of Health, Government of Indonesia. He was also HRD advisor to the Bank of Baroda.

He had worked in the fields of education, agriculture, small industry, and public health.

His publications include *Training for Organizational Transformation* (co-authored with Rolf P. Lynton, 2000). He was editor of the *Journal of Health Management* and consulting editor of the *Journal of Applied Behavioural Science*. He was on the editorial/advisory boards of *Human Resource Development International, Indian Journal of Clinical Psychology, Indian Journal of Training and Development, Human Capital, Abhigyan, IBAT Journal of Management, LBS Journal of Management, Prestige Journal of Management, Journal of Community Guidance and Research*, etc. He was the first editor of *Vikalpa* and was on the editorial boards of *Administrative Science Quarterly, Organisation and Group Studies*, and *Psychologia* between 1973 and 1985.

Udai Pareek Human Resource Laboratory for Applied Behavioural Sciences (UPHR-LABS) was launched on 3 May 2004 under his chairmanship. EMPI honoured him with the Lifetime Achievement Award.

## Contributions in the Field of Psychology

He was the only Asian to become Fellow of the National Training Laboratories (NTL), and the only Fellow from India of the Society for the Study of Social Issues (SPSSI). He was Fellow of the Indian Society of Extension Education. He was one of the foremost experts on training and organizational behaviour in India. Together with T.V. Rao, he established the first dedicated department of human resources development at L&T in the mid-1970s, much before HRD was known, and made it popular.

Any history of the HRD movement of India would be incomplete and irrelevant without mentioning the contributions of Udai Pareek. Popularly known as the 'pioneer of HRD in India' and 'Father of HRD movement of India', Udai Pareek changed the thought process of many organizations and individuals. He influenced the life of thousands of HR professionals as mentor, coach, and scholar, who kept in touch with the worlds of academia, industry, management, and research.

After his doctoral work, he worked as a psychologist for several years in 'basic education', a name given by Gandhi to education that is designed to make students self-sufficient by giving them an education more relevant to the Indian society. During this period of work with teachers and headmasters, he became interested in the work of Kurt Lewin and his associates and began to see action research as a key—almost Gandhian intervention to help them help themselves to solve their problems.

He had authored or edited about 60 books and more than 360 papers. He has been given several national and international awards and has been cited in a large number of national and international biographical reference books. Some of these are India's *Who's Who, Delhi; Who's Who in the World; Dictionary of International Biography*, London; *Writers Directory*, London; *Men of Achievement*, Cambridge, England; *All India Educational Directory*, Chandigarh; *Contemporary Authors*, USA; *Famous India; Reference Asia; Leaders of India*, etc.

A new human resource development system emerged in India in 1974 with T.V. Rao and Udai Pareek heading the movement. It was started as a 'review exercise of the Performance Appraisal System' for Larsen & Toubro by, the duo from IIM, Ahmedabad, which resulted in the development of a new function—the human resources development function. Rao and Pareek were instrumental in setting up the HRD department for L&T and making it the first company in this part of the world to have a fully dedicated HRD department

Udai Pareek gave the concept of role efficacy and extension motivation. He has listed ten major reasons for role conflict and stress—self-role distance, role stagnation, inter-role distance, role ambiguity, role expectation conflict, role overload, role erosion, resource inadequacy, personal inadequacy, and role isolation. What is remarkable is that Udai was not satisfied with merely suggesting an idea. He was concerned about application and solutions. He, therefore, offered the Organisational Role Stress Scale (ORS Scale) which helps measure role stresses. Having defined role stress and helped measure it, he goes on to define and explain role efficacy. He defines role efficacy as the potential effectiveness of a role or the psychological factors underlying role effectiveness.

The concept of extension motivation simply means a need or a desire to extend oneself or the ego to others and relate to a larger group and its goals. It means a motivation for helping others, working for larger goals that benefit larger groups or society. It also means an ability to sacrifice one's own comforts and desires for the sake of others. It is this powerful motivation that has led to many great people to make sacrifices for the good of the larger community.

Pareek proposed that it is extension motivation that causes any given society to develop. 'A super-ordinate goal probably arouses this motive. Such goals may therefore be important not only in developing harmony but also in sustained motivation of people in development'. He has left a lasting impression through his innovative writings of various books and articles. His ideas and thoughts would continue to live amidst all HR lovers.

# 28

# E.I. George

(1926–1989)

## V. George Mathew

*E.I. George*

E.I. George was born in a village named Thumpaman in southern Kerala on 1 May 1926 in a well-known Syrian Christian family. His father was in financial business and had suffered reversals. Therefore, they were not doing well financially, and that may be the reason for George as a young student joining the seminary training to be a priest. He was supported by the church to continue his education. He was popularly known as clergy George those days. He was bright in studies and passed the MA in philosophy with credit. He became a lecturer in philosophy in the most reputed government college in the state. He discontinued his theological studies and married the daughter of T.K. Koshy, a well-known educationist who was director of public instruction in the state. George secured scholarship to go to England and do his PhD. He worked under H.J. Eysenck of the University of London on political attitudes and personality. He explored the relation of political attitudes to Eysenck's personality variables.

On his return to India, he was appointed as the head of the Department of Psychology of the University of Kerala. It was his task to organise this new department funded by the UGC. Soon, the department had two more teachers. The department was formally inaugurated in 1957 and an MA course in psychology was started; the first course devoted entirely to psychology in the state. Eminent professors of south India such as Major S. Parthasarathy, B. Krishnan, and Hafees were those who helped the department to organise the course of study, conduct examinations, and so on. Soon the PhD programme also started. I joined the department as a student in the MA course in 1961. After passing out, I joined George as a research scholar. Later I became research assistant and member of the teaching faculty in the same department.

George was a very handsome person. He was always well groomed and impeccably dressed. He was very dynamic and impressive. He could speak fluent English. His infectious laughter was well known. He was very sociable and quick-witted. He managed to be the centre of attention everywhere he went. He used to travel very frequently and people used to remark that he spent more time in the plane than on the ground. He published several papers and books.

He held additional charge as honorary director of youth welfare in the university for several years. Several incidents come to my mind when I think about George's ability to rise to the occasion and his quick-wittedness. A new vice-chancellor had taken charge. He was visiting the departments and checking whether the staff, particularly the heads of departments were coming on time. The working time started at 10 AM but George habitually came at 11 AM only. The vice-chancellor, perhaps hearing about this, one day came at 10.45 and sat in George's chair, waiting for him to come. George, as usual, came at 11 AM. He saw the vice-chancellor's car parked in front of the department building. Without any hesitation, he entered the head's room and saw the vice-chancellor sitting in his chair. George laughed, addressed the vice-chancellor by name and said 'good morning'. There were several people in the room waiting to see what would happen. Without losing his cool George said, 'I am on leave today. I am on my way to my native place. I just dropped in to check my mail'. He asked for his mails, collected his letters, and without even sitting down, left in a hurry. The vice-chancellor looked like a fool and went away as soon as George left. It is said that many other heads of other departments in similar predicaments shivered, went on their knees apologising and begging for pardon.

George was one among the pioneering psychology professors in the country. He was one of the stalwarts in the Indian Psychological Association. He was the founding president of the Kerala Psychological Society and still later the founding president of the Kerala Manasasthra Parishath. He was instrumental in organising the psychology department in Calicut University. George guided a large number of students for their PhD. He was a teacher of all the early psychologists in Kerala.

George worked on several research projects funded by the UGC, ICSSR, and so on. The very first research project was on psychological correlates of academic achievement. Another one funded by the National Council of Educational Research and Training was on developmental norms for children. One of the projects funded by the National Family Planning Institute was on psychological consequences of vasectomy, which studied people undergoing vasectomy in large-scale vasectomy camps held in the state and served to understand misconceptions regarding vasectomy among the general public. In an interesting project, he compared the 10th and 11th Standard children who were subjected to 10- and 11-year streams in the state of Kerala, respectively. This was carried out during the time when schooling years was reduced from 11 to 10 and both the streams took the same examination. The study showed that there was very little difference in psychological character-istics and academic achievement between the two streams of students and, therefore, supported the reduction of number of school years from 11 to 10. George had several projects surveying the needs and problems of school and college students in the state of Kerala sponsored by different organ-isations in the state. The university senate gave him a project to collect public opinion regarding examination reforms in the university. Based on the results of the survey, the university introduced several examinations reforms like starting the policy of revaluation of examination papers. Most of the early psychological tests in Malayalam (including tests of intelligence, temperament, and motivation) were developed in connection with these research projects. George published several research papers and made chapter contributions in books.

George was the first person in Kerala to speak on topics of popular interest over the radio. He also wrote several popular articles on psychology. He was largely instrumental in making psychology a popular subject in Kerala and generating public interest in the same.

Around 1990, I was on tour in the Himalayas and I chanced upon the Indian Institute of Social Sciences at Shimla. I had heard that they give accommodation to academicians. I telephoned the director. As soon as he heard my name, he invited me to stay in the institute for a few days. When I went there, I found that the best room was arranged for me as per instructions from the direc-tor. Long back, it was the master bedroom where the viceroy slept in summer. I was told that the director wanted to meet me after I had checked in. When I entered his room, the director looked surprised and disappointed. He asked, 'Are you Dr. George from Kerala?' Then I understood that he had mistaken me for E.I. George. I explained that I was a different person. The director had met George somewhere and was greatly impressed. Anyway, I could live in the royal bedroom of the Institute for a few days because someone had mistaken me for E.I. George!

George retired from the University of Kerala in 1986. He was put in charge of organizing the School of Behavioural Sciences in M.G. University. He passed away at his residence because of a heart attack in 1989 at the age of 63. His smiling portrait hangs in the head's room in the psychology department of the University of Kerala. To new students in the department he is just a picture, but to us who have known him, he is the father figure of psychology in the state and a living forceful memory.

# 29

# Madhavrao Babasaheb Ghorpade

(1926)

## Satishchandra Kumar, Anjali Majumdar, and Tejal Dhulla

Born on 31 July 1926 at Kolhapur, Maharashtra, Madhavrao Babasaheb Ghorpade (alias, Jay Ramrao Ghorpade) has done much for the growth of psychology in India. As the managing editor of *Bombay Psychologist*, he was quite aware of the developments in psychology in India and as such played a very vital role in maintaining records of those happenings.

*Madhavrao Babasaheb Ghorpade in 1962*

# Early Life and Career

Ghorpade's father, a senior officer in Kolhapur state government, passed away in 1927 when Ghorpade was only a year old. After that he studied up to the 3rd standard under the care of his elder brother in Navatihal. He then went back to Kolhapur to pursue his further education. There, he stayed with his uncle, Shri Ganpat Rao, who was the assistant police commissioner of the maharaja of Kolhapur. After passing his matriculation exam from Nagoji Rao Patanka High School, Kolhapur, he joined the Rajaman College of Kulti from where he got his bachelor of arts (BA) degree. Thereafter, he became a school teacher at NP High School, where he served till his marriage in 1954. Then, with the support and encouragement of his wife, he went to the University of Pune to pursue postgraduation, that is, MA in psychology, in 1956. Ghorpade's wife, Neela Ghorpade, played a very important role in his academic life. As it is said, behind every successful man is a great woman; Ghorpade brought out the truth of that statement. Neela Ghorpade was a school teacher and supported the whole family, including the finance of Ghorpade's education, throughout the 2 years while Ghorpade pursued his higher education.

Ghorpade described his difficulties while pursuing higher education in a handwritten note as follows:

> When I was in BA, one of the papers was Psychology of Religion, which I liked so much that many a times I thought of doing MA only in Psychology. But Rajaram College had no provision and I have to go to Pune for pursuing MA with Psychology. So [for] four years, till I married I had to wait up to 1954 for going to Pune for doing my MA in Psychology.

After completing his masters in 1958, he was appointed as a lecturer of psychology at St. Xavier's College in Mumbai where he served for 9 years. Ghorpade has sweet memories of St. Xavier's College, Department of Psychology, where he worked with Father Fillela and Father Fuster. Both were Spanish priests, excellent teachers of psychology, and good human beings. Ghorpade says that he came from a Marathi school, studied in Marathi, and did his masters from the University of Pune; still they recruited him as a fresh lecturer in psychology in one of the internationally renowned college. They coached him, mentored him, and developed his skills and abilities, not only as a teacher but also as a human being. In true sense, he learnt that Xavier's followed the grassroots level of psychology and that the subject has to go to the natives if it is to be meaningful and socially relevant. Fathers Fillela and Fuster demonstrated these qualities. Ghorpade is very indebted to the college and both of his colleagues that a rural Maharashtra, Marathi speaking person, was recruited, then shaped and transformed in an encouraging, enriching, secular, professional, and talented culture like that of St. Xavier's College.

Later, in 1969, he was appointed as head of the psychology department in the newly established RD National College, Bandra, Mumbai. He was a well-respected and dearly loved head of the department. His colleagues recognized him as 'the man who built up the Psychology Department and moulded the students and staff in Psychology…with his abilities, discretion and pleasing manners' (Parekh, Correa, & Vipin, 1987). The college started its psychology association under his headship. He served at RD National College till his retirement in 1986. He was succeeded by Durga Parekh as the new head of the psychology department. On the occasion of his retirement, S. Paivaidya, editor of the college magazine described him as a person with 'generous, amiable and soft-spoken nature' (Paivaidya, 1987). He also worked as a visiting postgraduate teacher of the Department of Applied Psychology of Bombay University (now known as the University of Mumbai) for more than 15 years (Ghorpade & Kumar, 1988). He was also the managing editor of *Bombay Psychologist*, since the publication of its first volume on 28 October 1978 till 1986. In 2003, he received the Lifetime Achievement Award from the Bombay Psychological Association, along with the founding members. His brief biography was also mentioned in the *Asia's Who's Who of Men and Women of Achievement.*

Ghorpade was far sighted and was ahead of his time. Much of his work was about recording the events in the growth and development of psychology in India, so that future generations could be aware of the journey of this discipline of study. Ghorpade is a self-motivated and self-contained person. He has always been interested in arts and music. He also plays the *sitar*. He taught himself how to play the sitar, without receiving any lessons. The high level of his creativity is also visible in his beautiful works of art.

*Madhavrao Babasaheb Ghorpade at the age of 89*

## Publications

Ghorpade's publications have been both illustrious and diverse. He published reading material on psychological testing as well as abnormal psychology besides contributing research papers and articles in journals. In 1964, he published his first book, *An Introduction to Experimental Psychology*. In 1975, he wrote *Essentials of Psychological Testing*. This was followed in 1977 by *Essentials of Psychology*, the revised editions of which were also published in 1980 and 1985. He wrote these books 'with a view to providing students with a simplified, straightforward, yet precise and intelligible account of the major concepts in contemporary psychology and preparing them thoroughly for a more advanced study of the subject' (Ghorpade, 1977). In 1978, he penned another book titled *Essentials of Social Psychology*. His objectives while writing this book were, first, to present anyone concerned or interested 'a book that will enable them to understand and evaluate the latest developments in social psychological research without losing the sight of its former moorings'; and second, 'to introduce the readers to the basic concepts and ideas in social psychology' (Ghorpade, 1978). Along with this book, he was also involved in the conception and publishing of the first volume of *Bombay Psychologist* in 1978. He continued to be the managing editor of *Bombay Psychologist* till 1986.

In 1980, he co-authored another book with P.K. Ghosh. This book was titled *Industrial Psychology*. Through this book, the authors wanted to make the readers 'aware of the complex relationships that exist between the man, the machine and the organization in the present technological and highly industrialized civilization' (Ghosh & Ghorpade, 1981). This book was revised and published in 1981, 1985, and 1986 as well; in 1991, it was published as *Organizational Psychology* (Ghorpade, 1983). In 1983, he wrote the psychological news bulletin for Vol. V (1) of the *Bombay Psychologist*. This was a regular article in *Bombay Psychologist* which mentioned the ongoing events, activities, and conferences (both national and international). He wrote the psychological news bulletin for Vol. VI (2) of in 1984 (Kale & Ghorpade, 1984).

In 1988, he co-authored another book with Vipan Kumar titled *Introduction to Modern Psychotherapy*. The book discussed the ideas, viewpoints, and concepts of the major Western and Eastern psychotherapies. It introduced the therapies in their respective theoretical frameworks and with special reference to treatment procedures of each one of them (Ghorpade & Kumar, 1988).

In 1984, in the combined publication of Vol. V (2) and Vol. VI (1) of *Bombay Psychologist*, Ghorpade's article 'A Chronicle of Psychology in Bombay 1914–1984' was published. 1984 marked the silver jubilee year of the Department of Applied Psychology of the University of Bombay; and so, through this article, Ghorpade traced the history of important events that led to the establishment of the department (Ghorpade, 1984). One of his wishes was that psychology should have its own identity in India with a grand building like the William James Hall at Harvard. He is saddened by the lack of efforts in maintaining archival records in psychology in India. Even as the world celebrates International Archival Day on the 9 June[1], Ghorpade's effort in charting the progress of psychology in India is appreciated.

## Acknowledgements

Special thanks to Manjula Ghorpade, Professor Ghorpade's eldest daughter, and Jay Ghorpade, Professor Ghorpade's son, for providing us with the details of his personal life, and allowing us to capture the glimpses of Professor Ghorpade's life on camera.

## References

Ghorpade, M.B. (1977). *Essentials of psychology*. Bombay: Himalaya Publishing House.
———. (1978). *Essentials of social psychology*. Bombay: Himalaya Publishing House.

---

[1] See http://www.ica.org/1561/international-archives-day/celebrate-the-international-archives-day.html

Ghorpade, M.B. (1983). Psychological news bulletin. *Bombay Psychologist: A Journal of Bombay Psychological Association, V*(1), 59–63.

———. (1984). A chronicle of psychology in Bombay 1914–1984. *Bombay Psychologist: A Journal of Bombay Psychological Association, V*(2), *VI*(1), 9–17.

Ghorpade, M.B., & Kumar, V.B. (1988). *Introduction to modern psychotherapy*. Bombay: Himalaya Publishing House.

Ghosh, P.K., & Ghorpade, M.B. (1981). *Industrial psychology* (2nd rev. ed). Bombay: Himalaya Publishing House.

Kale, S.V., & Ghorpade, M.B. (1984). Psychological news bulletin. *Bombay Psychologist: A Journal of Bombay Psychological Association, V*(2), *VI*(1), 29–34.

Paivaidya, S. (1987). Editor's note. *National College Arts & Science Magazine 1986–87*. Bombay: Express Stationary Service.

Parekh, D., Correa, R., & Kumar, V.B. (1987). Psychology association. *National College Arts & Science Magazine 1981–82*. Bombay: Express Stationary Service.

# 30
## Sharadchandra Shankar Kulkarni

(1926)

## Vishnu Vasant Gavraskar

*Sharadchandra Shankar Kulkarni*

India has produced many psychologists who have contributed significantly to the enrichment of science—through their voracious writings, teachings, and commendable research. There are few who have contributed immensely to the noble task of development of this science to its perfection through their relentless research activities and also through practising the principles themselves, albeit with a difference. And that difference is in creating—and not following—history. Sharadchandra Shankar Kulkarni is one of those rare psychologists and educationists who have the passion to create history. He has been a dynamic force that has transformed challenges into opportunities and pitfalls into solutions. Many renowned academicians, social workers, and leaders are generally religious followers and staunch advocates of some established ideology propagated by their 'idol'. They have strong faith in that established ideology and, therefore, continue to cherish and meticulously practise those preachings. There are few who believe in eclectic model—meaning thereby—accepting all 'good' ideas from various ideologies—at times conflicting also—and blending all of them into an elixir. S.S. Kulkarni has been one of those few respectable exceptions who have critically studied various cultures—including preachings by saints; religious leaders transcending creeds, castes, and religions across the globe; various ancient and modern social scientists, educationists, and psychologists.

Born on 7 May 1926 in Koloshi, a remote drought-stricken village in Kanakavali Taluqua of Sindhudurg district of Maharashtra, Kulkarni did his MA in philosophy in 1950 at a time when psychology was not even recognised a separate discipline of study in most of the Indian universities. With an intense flair for higher learning and matching competence, he moved to the USA for a doctoral programme in psychometry in 1958. Constructively channelizing the initial ridicule by his white professor, Dr Kulkarni, through his relentless efforts coupled with a sharp analytical mind, succeeded in winning profound praise from the same professor. He completed all his doctoral assignments with flying colours and in a record time and was awarded a PhD in 1960. By virtue of his completion of PhD in psychometry with a distinction, he was offered a position of faculty in the Educational Testing Service (ETS), Princeton, New Jersey, USA, which was internationally acclaimed as the unique organization conducting psychological testing all over the world for admissions to reputed undergraduate and graduate management and other schools in the USA, and also for recruitment to the federal services. Kulkarni worked in ETS for 1 year and returned to India to accept a job in the National Council for Educational Research and Training (NCERT), Delhi, the apex-level educational body dedicated to the cause of educational research and training in India.

His 9-year-long career at NCERT from 1963 to 1971 was full of almost insurmountable challenges in the area of education. India needed an educational system of its own to help Indians rise above the abysmal level of poverty and unemployment and to attain financial independence, breaking the shackles of slavery. Managing the things with resource crunch and, more importantly, with inadequate trained teachers to evolve the educational reforms was a gigantic task. However, Kulkarni accepted the challenge and addressed it with a three-pronged strategy:

1. A nationwide educational survey to fathom the educational needs; to start with, in mathematics, of the students who differed in their socio-economic background, language (medium) of instructions, geographical diversities, and cultural variations,
2. Undertaking preparation of programmed learning material to be used by the learners on their own, without any need for intervention of a teacher, and
3. Implementing the methodology and receiving feedback to ascertain whether fetched the desired results.

During the nationwide mathematical achievement survey, he arranged simultaneous administration of tests all over the country for the students at three levels—end of primary school, end of elementary school, and end of secondary school. These paper-pencil tests were objective (multiple choice) type. Correctly identifying the problem of linguistic diversity, the tests were made language-free, that is, the questions were designed on various mathematical operations, such as addition, subtraction, multiplication, division, using the mathematical signs and symbols, inverse operations involving the fundamentals, squares, square roots, etc., and were presented in non-verbal format. The survey threw light on relative performance of various groups afflicted with diversities, such as gender differences, socio-economic variations, geographical (rural, semi-urban, urban, metropolitan, etc.), parental education, linguistic variations among the students, that is, groupings based on medium of instructions at school, namely: English, vernacular, Hindi, etc. The comprehensive study revealed very significant findings having long-term implications from policy-making viewpoint. For example, one of the findings of the study was that female children of literate mothers had significantly higher performance on the test of mathematics than their other counterparts. It was Kulkarni who laid the foundation of several other studies which highlighted the unintended discrimination against certain groups of students vis-à-vis others. Obviously, the study underlined dire need to review and revise certain policies so as to effectively tackle the undue discrimination and provide a level-plain field to all, thus neutralizing the impact of the variation due to the influence of extraneous factors and forces. Because of the criticality of the findings, NCERT subsequently replicated the study in various other subjects in the curriculum and made important policy changes for betterment.

The country's educational system in those days had not come out of its deep slumber. It was in total disarray and needed total revamping. There was a dearth of schools to accommodate the vast student population, dearth of even basic educational aids, and above all dearth of teachers. The challenge before the country was to evolve a technology that would be able to address all these deficiencies and still help the budding students gain the most updated knowledge, acquire scientific outlook and develop desired skill sets. Impressed with Kulkarni's intellectual potential of high order, intense analytical ability, flair for true research, openness to accept new technology, keenness to experiment with these novel ideas and technologies, and more importantly, deeper psychological insights, NCERT entrusted him the gigantic task of developing self-learning material using educational technology. The term 'self-instruction material' was substituted with 'self-learning material', as the former was (mis)interpreted as a rather autocratic imposition. S.S. Kulkarni accepted the challenge and proved how worthy he was to handle the assignment effectively. The outcome of his relentless efforts and optimum utilization of the then available technology, he developed learning frames. These frames were arranged in graded manner that would build foundation and also enhance curiosity of the self-learner to proceed further on to a more difficult frame. Thus, each frame was suitably designed to impart knowledge, provide a launching pad for the higher cognitive skill in the next frame and also raise interest and intellectual curiosity of the learner. The work of S.S. Kulkarni had been a confluence of content knowledge and technology and, therefore, was duly acknowledged as a path-breaking exercise in the field of education.

In the year 1965, Kulkarni founded a professional body named 'Indian Association of Programmed Learning (IAPL)'. This was later transformed into 'Indian Association of Educational Technology (iAET)'.

During Smt Indira Gandhi's prime ministerial tenure, banks were recognized as an effective tool of socio-economic upliftment of the country's gigantic population. Banks were, therefore, nationalised in two lots and as a natural corollary they were required to expand in the nook and corner of the country. However, the banks lacked the most important resource to expand, that is, quality human resource. Banks needed some methodology of testing that could be utilized to select youth with right kind of knowledge, skills, and attitude. Banks looked up to National Institute of Bank Management (NIBM) which was set up as an apex-level institute for research and training for the banking Industry. However, NIBM was not equipped—neither academically nor administratively—to take up the mass-scale psychological testing activity for recruitment of the required workforce in the banks. Being aware of the nationwide survey conducted by Kulkarni under the aegis of NCERT, the then Director of NIBM approached Kulkarni for his services to set up the mass-scale and scientifically propelled recruitment activity that should be fair, objective, impartial and unbiased, and also to be perceived so.

During his tenure at the National Institute of Bank Management, Kulkarni envisioned a scientific methodology of psychological testing that was fair for the diverse cultural, language, and socio-economic groups of the country. The four most important dimensions that he propagated for this achievement were—(a) accuracy, (b) secrecy, (c) freedom from biases, and (d) speed. The critical competencies of analytical reasoning, numerical aptitude, moderate level of linguistic proficiency, aptitude for perceptual speed and accuracy, sensitivity to and concern for social issues, empathy for the under-privileged groups, and general awareness of national and international happenings etc. were identified through a systematic job-analysis process and tests of objective type were designed to differentiate the candidates on these competencies. He not only played an important role in establishing the system but also monitored it constantly to evolve it into a foolproof, scientific methodology. It is worth mentioning that his novel ideas of using non-verbal tests to assess intelligence and reasoning, and numerical aptitude, keeping the test of English language as only 'qualifying' and not reckoning its marks in the aggregate for merit ranking, has paid rich dividends in ensuring that the tests do not unduly favour candidates with a different medium of instruction.

His work had been duly recognised at the international level. He was invited by IMF and UNESCO as a consultant to work in Bangladesh, Sri Lanka, and Thailand. In the field of selection and training of the senior-level positions, particularly in industries, he initiated the use of techniques like simulation exercises and management games. He also brought the idea of 'quality circle' to improve the quality in organization in the Indian context. As a true researcher, he always held research activity in high esteem. The District Development Council of Sindhudurg district invited him to conduct survey regarding the limitations and their solutions for the improvement in banking system in order to promote agriculture and other agro-based and related rural industries.

His openness to receiving a dispassionately novel idea, contemplating on its probable impact for the welfare of mankind and accepting and implementing it with passion are the hallmarks of his work culture. While reading Freud, Jung or Binnett with passion, he is equally passionate to read with rapt attention the preachings of Saints like Dnyaneshwar, Ramdas, Kabir, Tulsidas and Tukaram. Unlike the many 'renowned' contemporary scientists who take pride in branding with scorn and ridicule the valuable mythological teachings as 'mere myth', Kulkarni takes a lot of pains to go, with an absolutely open mind, to the root of the preachings by the Indian saints, religious scriptures and mythologies to explore and interpret the teachings in today's context.

Kulkarni has not only tried to explore the hidden treasure of these mythologies and preachings of the saints, but has been leading the life of an ascetic, contributing generously to the society to the best possible extent. Accepting both agonies and ecstasies of life with a balanced mind is not an easy matter. But Kulkarni has been taking both as realities of life with balanced judiciousness. He has neither shown any undue elatedness while being at the zenith of glory, nor indicated even the slightest discomfiture when confronted with irreversible and abysmal grief. He has been leading the third stage of his life, Vaanprasthashram, renouncing home and family for lonely meditations in the wilderness, but with a striking difference. And that difference is in his indomitable spirit of making valuable contribution to the society—to the under-privileged, to the needy women, to make them financially independent—to empower them financially, and of course, emotionally. To realize this dream of imparting financial independence to the womenfolk and the poor, under-privileged units of the society, he founded a service-oriented institution for rural reconstruction, Narayan Ashram, donating his own land in Koloshi in Sindhudurg district of the Konkan Division of Maharashtra, money, and most importantly, his conceptual treasure of thoughts and toiling physical efforts. The institution—the brainchild of Kulkarni—founded initially with seven dedicated volunteers inspired by his concept of social service, zeal and enthusiasm of this then '66-year young', passionate social servant, has now hundreds and hundreds of volunteers—all flared by Kulkarni's motivating and invigorating interactions. The *ashram* had started activities in the crucial areas of irrigation to tide over age-old water scarcity in that area, issues of health—especially of the poor and the women—and education of the rural poor. In the area of health, the ashram undertook health check-up for the children, pre- and post-natal care for women, infant and child development programmes, camps for cataract surgery, and artificial limbs for the physically/orthopedically challenged. These activities of free and most essential social services were made available to the rural area people of Sindhudurg district. Kulkarni, being a world-famous educationist himself, started several educational activities such as workshops and programmes for orientation of the primary and secondary school teachers, workshops for students, etc. However, these activities were not confined only to health and education, but have covered diverse areas such as insurance, journalism, horticulture, women empowerment etc. and implemented them for rural reconstruction.

# 31

## Sheo Dan Singh

(1930–1979)

## Raghubir Singh Pirta

*Sheo Dan Singh*

Sheo Dan Singh was born in the year 1930 in a village named Chajjupur in Aligarh District, Uttar Pradesh. After finishing his early education at a small town called Khair, he joined Aligarh

Muslim University for higher education. He passed the master's degree in psychology with a gold medal and went to England for his doctoral work. In 1959, after earning a PhD from the University of London, he returned to India. After working for some time as a teacher in a college at Agra, Singh joined Panjab University situated at Chandigarh in 1962 as a professor of psychology. From 1967 to 1971, he was in the USA for advanced research work. After serving as associate professor in Canada for a while, Sheo D. Singh came back to India and joined Meerut University (now Chaudhary Charan Singh University) in 1971 where he initiated research on non-human primates. A decade later, when his hard work was bearing fruits, he succumbed to a fatal disease in 1979. His wife, Vimal Kumari Singh, a psychologist, had assisted Sheo D. Singh in his research during the early years. The couple was blessed with three children and all of them are well established and well settled in life.

## Contributions

When Sheo D. Singh joined the Department of Psychology at Panjab University after returning from England, his primary subject of study was the behaviour of non-human primates, specifically that of the common monkeys of India. His research has close parallels to that of Sir Solly Zuckerman, who had similar understanding of the South African baboons long before planning naturalistic studies on these monkeys. In *The Social Life of Monkeys and Apes* by Zuckerman (1981), the work of Sheo D. Singh finds a prominent reference. Within the cognitive domain of psychology, Sheo D. Singh (1969) selected research problems which had their ramifications reflected in all aspects of the discipline, starting from laboratory to public debates, for example, on schooling and reservations for deprived groups.

Foreign experts such as Harry F. Harlow and his colleagues at the University of Wisconsin in the USA found that the infant monkeys reared in impoverished environments (IE) were not intellectually inferior to those nurtured in enriched environments (EE). These psychologists show a leaning on Sheo D. Singh's work in order to support their thesis (Harlow & Mears, 1979).

Sheo D. Singh received doctoral degree on his thesis 'A Study of the Constitutional and Situational Determinants of Conditioned Emotional Response in the Rat, and Its Modification by Drugs' from the University of London under Professor H.J. Eysenck in 1958. This research (Singh, 1959, 1961; Singh & Eysenck, 1960) was of considerable significance as is evident from its citation in scientific literature.

The thesis was amongst the earliest works on the two strains of rat developed at the Animal Psychology Laboratory in Maudsley Hospital, University of London. These lines of rat, now being used in different parts of world, were named as Maudsley Reactive, measured by high anxiety-related response, and Maudsley Non-reactive, measured by low anxiety-related response. Although the two lines were developed by P.L. Broadhurst, a senior colleague, it was Sheo D. Singh who adapted the method of assessing anxiety in rats (Broadhurst, Sinha & Singh, 1959; Eysenck, 1960/2013; Eysenck & Rachman, 1965/2013).

*The testing environment*

*The rearing environment*

As soon as Singh joined Panjab University, Chandigarh, in 1962, he initiated a research programme to study the effect of urban environment on the behaviour of rhesus monkeys (Singh, 1966a, 1966b, 1966c; 1968a, 1968b). Of particular interest in this work are his findings on the cognitive behaviour or 'intelligence' of these non-human primates (Singh, 1969). While focusing on the paradigm of environment enrichment and enhancement of 'intelligence' or cognitive behaviour, Sheo D. Singh thought urban environment might have improved 'intelligence' in rhesus monkey. But the study revealed that the forest monkeys (IE) were as good as the urban monkeys (EE) in mastering learning problems. These experiments were cited as examples of good research design in the textbooks on experimental psychology (e.g., Beauchamp, Bruce & Matheson, 1970; McGuigan, 1983).

At the same time, though studies in psychopharmacology on H.J. Eysenck's hypothesis partly continued (Singh, 1962, 1964; Singh, Sharma & Manocha, 1965; Singh & Singh, 1961).

In addition to this, Singh also visited the USA and collaborated with Professor Harry F. Harlow and his colleagues (Singh & Lewis, 1974) at the Wisconsin Regional Primate Research Center (WRPRC; now Wisconsin National Primate Research Center), University of Wisconsin, to work on his research projects. During this period, he acquired the necessary skills to dissect the brain of the rhesus monkey and performed some ingenious experiments on the effects of selective prefrontal cortical lesions on their social behaviour. At a broader level, Sheo D. Singh took the initiative to introduce primate behaviour research in India. Not only did he return to India with a new vision of experimental research, but also borrowed essential equipment to initiate research as soon as he could locate a place at Meerut University. The equipment included a stereotaxic machine, Wisconsin General Test apparatus, a Skinner box, and a number of other necessary items.

For a functional approach to evaluate the role of the frontal lobe in social behaviour of the primates, it became imperative to observe operated animals in social groups. This was the focus of experiments carried out during the visit of Sheo D. Singh at the WRPRC. In *The Prefrontal Cortex*, Fuster (2008) specifically noted that though the effects of the frontal lobe damage had been previously observed in laboratory, they were most vividly confirmed from observations in social groups (e.g., Deets, Harlow, Singh & Blomquist, 1970; Singh, 1976). Such contributions of Sheo D. Singh drew considerable attention from investigators (e.g., Anderson, 2007; Reite & Field, 1985).

A complete understanding of the functional significance of the frontal lobe in territorial defence, sexual behaviour, dominance hierarchies, and social signalling, which Singh predominantly wanted to achieve, was possible only under natural conditions. This was the primary focus of research at the Primate Research Laboratory at Meerut University in India. After joining the psychology department at the Meerut University in 1971, Singh took upon himself the task of preparing a natural setting for these primates. After some trial and error, the outdoor enclosures for the monkeys were in place. The Primate Research Laboratory, located in a serene environment under the canopy of mango (*Mangifera indica*) and *bel* or wood apple (*Aegle màrmelos*) trees was indeed a major achievement as no other university in India had such facilities for testing and housing primates at that time. A significant addition to this achievement was launching a field study site at Asarori Forest in 1973 about 150 km away in the Siwalik Hills near Dehra Dun. The first two papers that emanated from the studies at the Asarori Forest highlight the programme on social development of rhesus monkey infants in a free-ranging environment (Singh, 1977, 1980).

Unfortunately, Sheo D. Singh died untimely on 26 June 1979 due to a fatal disease and his dream which had started taking shape in the Primate Research Laboratory at Meerut University remained unfulfilled. However, the enthusiasm and interest that he could kindle in the minds of few talented researchers regarding study of primate behaviour (see Pirta, 2009) is undoubtedly a ray of hope.

# References

Anderson, G.S. (2007). *Biological influences on criminal behavior.* New York, NY: Taylor & Francis.

Beauchamp, K.L., Bruce, R.L., & Matheson, D.W. (Eds). (1970). *Current topics in experimental psychology.* New York, NY: Holt, Rinehart and Winston.

Broadhurst, P.L., Sinha, S.N., & Singh S.D. (1959). The effect of stimulant and depressant drugs on a measure of emotional reactivity in the rat. *Journal of Genetic Psychology, 95*(2), 217–226.

Deets, A.C., Harlow, H.F., Singh, S.D., & Blomquist, A.J. (1970). Effects of bilateral lesions of the frontal granular cortex on the social behavior of rhesus monkeys. *Journal of Comparative and Physiological Psychology, 72*(3), 452–461.

Eysenck, H.J. (Ed.). (1960/2013). *Experiments in personality (Psychology Revivals): Volume 1: Psychogenetics and psychopharmacology.* New York, NY: Routledge.

Eysenck, H.J., & Rachman, S. (1965/2013). *The causes and cures of neurosis (Psychology Revivals): An introduction to modern behavior therapy based on learning theory and the principles of conditioning.* New York, NY: Routledge.

Fuster, J.M. (2008). *The prefrontal cortex* (4th ed.). London: Academic Press.

Harlow, H.F., & Mears, C. (1979). *The human model: Primate perspectives.* New York, NY: John Wiley & Sons.

McGuigan, F.J. (1983). *Experimental psychology: Methods of research* (4th ed.). Englewood Cliffs, NJ: Prentice-Hall.

Pirta, R.S. (2009). Biological and ecological bases of behavior. In G. Misra (Ed.), *Psychology in India. Volume 1: Basic psychological processes and human development* (pp. 1–67). Delhi: Pearson.

Reite, M., & Field, T. (Eds). (1985). *The psychobiology of attachment and separation.* New York, NY: Academic Press.

Singh, S.D. (1959). Conditioned emotional response in the rat: I. Constitutional and situational determinants. *Journal of Comparative and Physiological Psychology, 52*(5), 574–578.

———. (1961). Conditioned emotional response in the rat: Effects of stimulant and depressant drugs. *Journal of Psychological Research, 5,* 1–11.

———. (1962). Effects of stimulant and depressant drugs on physical persistence. *Perceptual and Motor Skills, 14*(2) 270.

———. (1964). Habit strength and drug effects. *Journal of Comparative and Physiological Psychology, 58*(3), 468–469.

———. (1966a). Effect of human environment on cognitive behavior in the rhesus monkey. *Journal of Comparative and Physiological Psychology, 61*(2), 280–283.

———. (1966b). The effects of human environment upon the reactions to novel situations in the rhesus. *Behaviour, 26*(3–4), 243–249.

———. (1966c). The effects of human environment on the social behavior of rhesus monkeys. *Primates, 7(1),* 33–39.

———. (1968a). Social interactions between the rural and urban monkeys, *Macaca mulatta. Primates, 9*(1), 69–74.

———. (1968b). Effect of urban environment on visual curiosity behavior in rhesus monkeys. *Psychonomic Science, 11*(3), 83–84.

———. (1969). Urban monkeys. *Scientific American, 221*(1), 108–115.

———. (1976). Sociometric analysis of the effects of the bilateral lesions of frontal cortex on the social behavior of rhesus monkeys. *Indian Journal of Psychology, 51*(2), 141–160.

———. (1977). Effects of infant-infant separation of young monkeys in a free-ranging natural environment. *Primates, 18*(1), 205–214.

———. (1980). Xenophobic reactions of free-ranging rhesus infant groups raised in natural habitat. *Primates, 21*(4), 492–497.

Singh, S.D., & Eysenck, H.J. (1960). Conditioned emotional response in the rat: III. Drug antagonism. *Journal of General Psychology, 63*(2), 275–285.

Singh, S.D., & Lewis, J.K. (1974). An evaluation of transfer suppression phenomenon at different stages of learning-set formation. *Primates, 15*(2–3), 205–208.

Singh, S.D., Sharma, S., & Manocha, S.N. (1965). Habit, drive and drug effects. *Psychological Studies, 10*, 38–44.

Singh, S.D., Singh, V. (1961). The effect of stimulant and depressant drugs on the latency of autokinetic illusion. *Acta Psychologica, 18*, 354–359.

Zuckerman, S. (1981). *The social life of monkeys and apes* (2nd ed.). London: Routledge & Kegan Paul.

# 32

# Jagannath Prasad Das

(1931)

## Rauno Parrila

*Jagannath Prasad Das*

Jagannath Prasad Das was born in Puri, Odisha, in 1931. His early education took place in Cuttack, then the capital of Odisha, where he studied from elementary grades to BA (honours), the latter in Ravenshaw College. He has later noted (Das, 2015) that his academic ambitions and idealism were greatly fostered by his philosophy and psychology teachers in Ravenshaw, including R. Rath, G. Mishra, S. Sahu, P.S. Sundaram, B.B. Das, and O.P. O'Brien.

Following the honours degree in philosophy and psychology, he moved to Patna University for an MA in experimental psychology. In Patna, he came in contact with several inspiring professors, especially S.M. Mohsin who encouraged him to focus on empirical research and to avoid writing review papers at least for the first 5 years of his academic career, an advice that J.P. Das took to heart—already his first publication (Das, 1954) was an experimental study.

## Early Academic Career

Upon receiving his master's degree in 1953, J.P. Das returned to Ravenshaw College as a lecturer in the newly opened Department of Psychology under the leadership of R. Rath. Two years later, he was awarded the Indian Government's Overseas Scholarship to study for a doctorate degree in England at the University of the London Institute of Psychiatry under the guidance of H.J. Eysenck. His dissertation research focused on the relation between hypnosis, eyelid conditioning, and reactive inhibition, all topics that stayed with him during his early career. While in England, he started an influential collaboration with Neil O'Connor on issues related to disadvantage and developmental disabilities in children. O'Connor, who could read original Russian articles that were only infrequently translated to English, introduced J.P. Das to Russian psychology, particularly the works of Alexander Luria. This had very significant consequences to his later career.

*Jagannath Prasad Das*

After obtaining a PhD in 1957, J.P. Das returned to Ravenshaw College where the MA programme in psychology had just been launched. In 1961, the department of postgraduate psychology was transferred to Utkal University and he moved to its new campus in Bhubaneswar, where he still maintains a residence and a clinic that provides services for individuals with developmental and learning disabilities. His early research in India focused mainly on verbal conditioning, but he also expanded his interests to cross-cultural psychology and the effect of adverse environment and nutrition on cognitive skills. His first major academic book, *Verbal Conditioning and Behaviour* (Das,

1969), was based on the early experiments conducted in India and examined topics such as verbal learning and symbolic processes relating to language, hypnosis as selective inhibition, and verbal deficits in people with mental retardation.

In 1963, J.P. Das was invited to Peabody College in Vanderbilt University as a Kennedy Foundation professor, followed by a year in the University of California, Los Angeles, as a visiting associate professor. These 2 years in the USA were influential for his career by focusing his interest in both intellectual development, perhaps not least due to his new friendship with Arthur Jensen, and in intellectual disabilities. Three years after returning to Utkal University in 1965, he was offered a position at the University of Alberta in Canada as a research professor at the newly formed Centre for the Study of Mental Retardation (later renamed after him as J.P. Das Centre for Research on Developmental and Learning Disabilities). J.P. Das arrived in Edmonton, Alberta, in January 1968 in the middle of a bitterly cold prairie winter and started to build the centre's research programme on mental retardation.

At the University of Alberta, he continued his research into learning and cognitive processes of individuals with mental retardation and of disadvantaged children. Much of the early work in Alberta focused on orienting response, a fundamental aspect of attention, in individuals with mental retardation. These studies (see e.g., Das, Dyer & Bower, 1969) suggested that typically developing children and children with mental retardation showed minimal differences in the evocation or maintenance of the orienting response, or in extinction following no reinforcement when the orienting response ceased to signal anything important for the children to attend to, in instructed learning situations; in fact, children with mental retardation were shown to have a remarkable sensitivity to the demands of the situation. However, where learning had to occur without instruction, the typically developing children were better. Significantly, none of these early studies suggested that children with mental retardation had a generally depressed orienting response—as summarized in Das (2015), they were not unusually distracted, unable to inhibit responding to non-signals, nor did they lack habituation to signals no longer worthy of attention.

In terms of disadvantaged children, J.P. Das's (1973a) research on the effects of cultural deprivation on cognitive processes of tribal, rural, and urban children was published in 1973. It was among the first studies showing the significant impact environment had on the differences between the advantaged and disadvantaged groups: low caste disadvantaged children in rural villages did poorly in cognitive tasks when compared to high caste Brahmin children, but the gap between the two groups in cognitive performance was drastically reduced when both groups lived in the city—a result suggesting that urban life offered the disadvantaged children various channels for enriching their knowledge. Subsequent studies in Sri Lanka (Das & Pivato, 1976) expanded this work and showed that poor nutrition associated with chronic poverty resulted in poor cognitive performance with most disadvantaged children; however, the negative effect of malnutrition was mitigated somewhat if the mothers had even primary school education. In other words, better home literacy practices and openness to new information did partially offset the effect of poor nutrition and poverty.

## Mid-career: The PASS Theory

During the 1970s, J.P. Das visited the renown Russian neuropsychologist Alexander Luria in Moscow and begun his highly influential work first on simultaneous and successive cognitive processes, and then on PASS (planning, attention, simultaneous, and successive) processes leading to the PASS theory of intelligence. As Robert Sternberg (2015, p. xiii) recently noted, at the time

J.P. Das proposed the PASS theory, 'the field of intelligence was lost in a theoretical swamp' in trying to distinguish between or synthesize various psychometric theories. Building on Luria's (and earlier work by Pavlov and Sechenov) work on the functional organization of the brain, he (Das, 1973b; Das, Kirby, & Jarman, 1975, 1979), took distance from psychometric theories and, instead, proposed one the first theories of intelligence that was genuinely 'brain-based,' an approach that is now the norm in the field.

As the PASS theory of intelligence is Das's best known contribution to psychology, I will provide a short overview of the theory here (for a recent more thorough description, see Das, 2015). The overview is decidedly not chronological in that, besides research on orienting response, the third unit—comprising simultaneous and successive processing—was the focus of most of the early work, only to be later complimented with research on planning and attention.

The PASS theory proposes that cognition is organized in three systems and four processes borrowed from Luria (1973). The first system, or functional unit, is the attention-arousal system. It is responsible for maintaining arousal levels and alertness, and for ensuring focus on relevant stimuli. Arousal maintains the cortical tone that allows for the focus of attention. Attention consists of the mental processes needed for a person to selectively attend to some stimuli in the environment and to ignore others. It includes such aspects as focused attention, selective attention, resistance to distraction, orienting response, and vigilance. According to Luria (1973), the attention-arousal system is located primarily in the brainstem, the diencephalon, and the medial regions of the cortex. In Luria's model, this unit provided the brain with the appropriate level of arousal or cortical tone, and directive and selective attention. Luria stated further that optimal conditions of arousal are needed before the more complex forms of attention involving 'selective recognition of a particular stimulus and inhibition of responses to irrelevant stimuli' (Luria, 1973, p. 271) can occur. The cognitively-oriented PASS model, and the Das–Naglieri cognitive assessment system (see further) assessment battery based on it, emphasize the more complex attention functions of selection and inhibition as significant sources of individual differences, while acknowledging at the same time that proper levels of arousal are a necessary precondition for all PASS processes to operate efficiently (e.g., Das, 2015).

The second system in the PASS model is planning, which Luria (1973) broadly located to the frontal lobes of the brain. Planning consists of the deliberate mental processes by which a person determines, selects, and deploys efficient solutions to problems of all kinds. Planning involves higher level cognitive functions responsible for controlling and organizing behaviour, forming mental representation, selecting and constructing strategies, retrieving relevant knowledge, and monitoring performance. Planning actions and executing those plans are both part of planning, although plans do not necessarily have to be executed; they can be, and often should be, discarded on the basis of anticipated outcomes. Planning as defined in the PASS theory includes many executive functions, but it also includes future-oriented behaviours that are frequently not captured by descriptions of executive functions. The wide-ranging nature of planning as well as its applications to education and management are covered in more detail in two books Das, Kar, and Parrila (1996) and Das and Misra (2015).

The third system is the information processing system that employs two distinct processes to encode, transform, and retain information. Both of them can operate on multiple different types of stimuli—numbers, words, pictures etc.—and the distinction between content and how it is processed is inherent to the third system. We engage in simultaneous processing when we need to focus on the relationships between the items and their integration into groups, in other words, to form a gestalt and see the stimuli as a whole where each piece is related to others. Examples include recognizing figures, such as a triangle within a circle versus a circle within a triangle, or recognizing the difference between 'he had a shower before breakfast' and 'he had breakfast before a shower'.

According to Luria (1973), simultaneous processing is broadly associated with the occipital and the parietal lobes of the brain.

Successive processing is engaged in when organizing separate items into a coherent sequence with a specific serial order is required for information to be understood and usable. Examples of this include remembering a sequence of words or actions exactly in the order in which they were perceived, or a child reading out loud a long word and trying to keep all the sounds in the correct order in their memory to blend them at the end. When we engage in successive processing, we either organize the input into a chain-like progression or maintain the order of the items in the original stimuli—in both cases the specific order of the items matters. In Luria's model, successive processing was associated mainly with the frontal-temporal areas of the brain. Luria's ideas on simultaneous and successive processing had their origins in Sechenov's (1968) earlier research on physiological processes of the brain and in Vygotsky's (1962) ideas of the relationship between language and thinking; Das, Kirby and Jarman (1975, 1979) expanded these ideas to understanding individual differences in cognitive and academic performance.

Figure 32.1 provides a summary of the PASS theory of intelligence. Input and output can both be external and observable (such as speech or actions), or internal and unobservable (such as thoughts and emotions). Further, all cognitive processing requires some knowledge of the content of the stimuli to start with—otherwise it would not be recognized as such. Figure 32.1 reminds us that cognitive processes operate in the context of an individual's already existing knowledge base, including their memories, emotions, and motor skills, stored in long-term memory. In Das's (2015, p. 29) own words, '[m]etaphorically, knowledge base is the water on which cognition floats'.

**Figure 32.1**
*The PASS Theory of Intelligence*

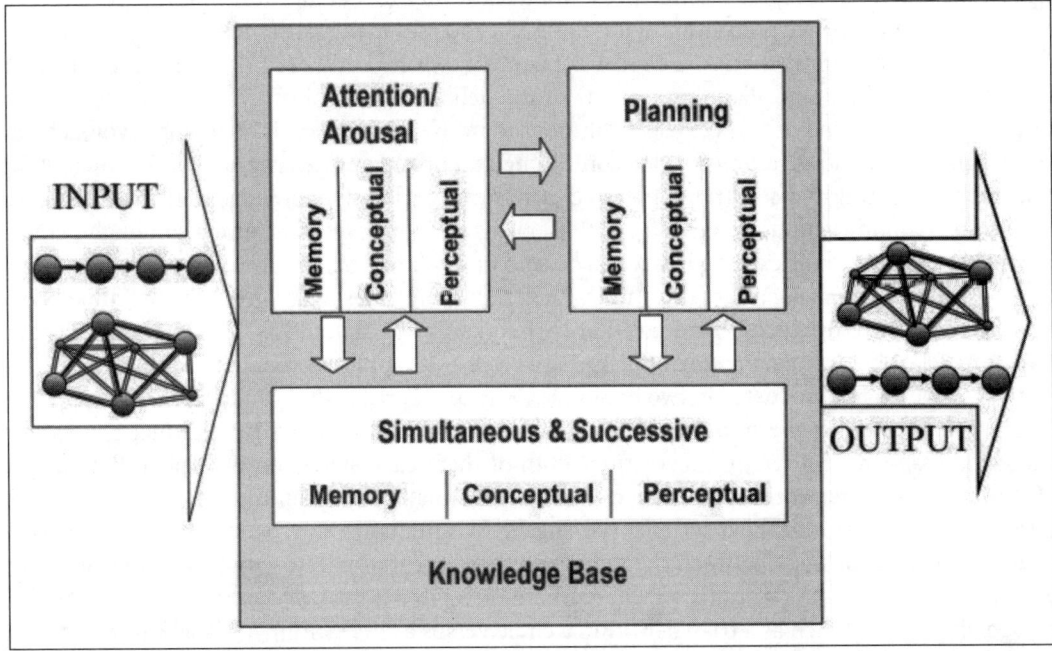

*Source:* Modified from Das, Naglieri & Kirby (1994).

# Later Career: Applications of the PASS Theory

Since its initial formulation, J.P. Das has continued to develop the PASS theory itself as well as engage in multiple different lines of applied work extending the theory. Perhaps the most prominent of these has been the development of a standardized assessment battery for the PASS processes: Das-Naglieri cognitive assessment system (DN-CAS; Naglieri & Das, 1997) and, recently, cognitive assessment system–second edition (CAS2; Naglieri, Das & Goldstein, 2014). Traditionally, construction of psychometric tests of intelligence grew as an enterprise mostly separate from psychology, a state of affairs that McNemar (1964) had already 50 years ago observed as a problematic trend that needed correction. Development of DN-CAS was driven by the idea that constructs, not individual differences, define a theory and for a test to be able to explain behaviour, it needs to be based on valid constructs. The value of individual differences is in the prediction of behaviour, not in explaining the construct or the behaviour.

Based on Luria's neuropsychological investigations and more recent advances in psychological sciences, Das and his colleagues developed and tested multiple tasks to assess each of the PASS constructs, starting with the simultaneous and successive processing (e.g., Das, 1973b; Das & Molloy, 1976) and later expanding to planning and attention (e.g., Ashman & Das, 1980; Das & Dash, 1983; Das & Heemsbergen, 1983; Naglieri & Das, 1988). These tasks formed the basis for the initial DN-CAS (Naglieri & Das, 1997), the first norm-referenced assessment battery with tasks assessing all functional units proposed by Luria. When it was published, DN-CAS provided the first construct-driven and cognitive-processing-based alternative to traditional psychometrically driven IQ tests that largely focused on verbal/non-verbal distinction; notably, many other tests have since moved towards the same direction and now provide multiple cognitive processing indices. DN-CAS has been adapted to multiple languages and generated research across the globe (for examples, see Papadopoulos, Parrila & Kirby, 2015) and CAS2, a revised version of CAS, was recently published with updated norms (Naglieri, Das & Goldstein, 2014).

Returning to his deep interest on disadvantaged children, much of Das's later research has focused on extending the PASS model to designing interventions to remediate cognitive difficulties and poor academic achievement of learning disabled and culturally disadvantaged children. This line of research builds also on Soviet psychology, most notably on Luria's and Vygotsky's research on cultural disadvantage, learning, and the role of inner speech in regulating behaviour. Throughout his career, Luria argued that assessment and diagnosis are never goals to themselves but tools for prognosis of the individual's developmental potential to move through their 'zone of proximal development', a concept borrowed from Vygotsky (Carlson & Hunt, 2015). The first intervention programme, PASS Reading Enhancement Programme (PREP; Das, 1999) was significantly influenced by these ideas and developed to improve reading abilities by enhancing the information processing skills that affect reading. More specifically, PREP was designed for use in one-to-one instructional settings for those who fail to learn to read through typical classroom instruction, avoiding the explicit teaching of specific reading skills. The PREP tasks involve a global training component and an additional curriculum-related bridging component. The global components include materials and activities designed to enhance the PASS processes with non-threating content. The bridging component involves the same cognitive demands as the global component and provides training in how to apply the successive and simultaneous processing strategies to academic content, such as reading new words.

Over the past 30 years, PREP has been translated to different languages and used successfully in both clinical and research situations (see e.g., Brailsford, Snart, & Das, 1984; Carlson & Das,

1997; Das, Mishra, & Pool, 1995; Mahapatra, Das, Stack-Cutler, & Parrila, 2010; Papadopoulos, Das, Parrila, & Kirby, 2003; Papadopoulos, Ktisti, Christoforou, & Loizou, 2015). While most of the studies have involved children with specific learning disabilities functioning in their first language, Mahapatra et al. (2010) recently used PREP to successfully remediate reading comprehension difficulties among English language learners in India. They suspected that the PREP training provided the children enough cognitive strategies and language analysis skills to push them over the threshold for comprehension in their second language (English). Following acquisition of the strategies, the children could apply the strategies and skills and likely benefited more from regular classroom instruction.

Cognition Enhancement Training (COGENT; Das, 2004) follows the same principles of interactive teaching and learning as PREP but is designed for younger children (ages 4 through 7) with normal and atypical developmental histories. The latter can include children who are at-risk for developing reading and other learning difficulties; these could include those who have limited exposure to literacy, mild developmental delay, and/or language impairment. COGENT is designed to enhance cognition, phonological awareness, language skills, and automatic recognition of letters and simple words; all skills that are linked to early literacy and school learning. Like PREP, it may be particularly useful in compensating for the disadvantages of poverty and cultural deprivation. Although COGENT is a newly developed programme, the early reports on its efficacy have been favourable (e.g., Das, Hayward, Georgiou, Janzen, & Boora, 2008; Hayward, Das & Janzen, 2007).

## Continuing Research Interests

True to the advice he received from his professor S.M. Mohsin 60 years ago, J.P. Das has been a prolific producer of empirical studies throughout his distinguished career, with more than 300 papers and book chapters to his name (in addition to the 25 books). While he formally retired in 1996, he has continued to make significant contributions, both empirical and theoretical, to psychological sciences. At the time of writing this short research biography, he continues to examine and develop the PASS processes; for example, his ongoing research examines the relationship between executive functions and planning, and between speed of processing and the PASS processes. Similarly, the application of PASS to remedial work with disadvantaged children is ongoing; here his main focus has recently been to develop a math intervention/booster programme for struggling children. His life work presents itself as that of a scientist, a humanist, and, as I can personally attest, a teacher and a mentor to a new generation of scientist both in India and beyond.

## References

Ashman, A.F., & Das, J.P. (1980). Relation between planning and simultaneous-successive processing. *Perceptual and Motor Skills, 51*(2), 371–382.

Brailsford, A., Snart, F., & Das, J.P. (1984). Strategy training and reading comprehension. *Journal of Learning Disabilities, 17*(5), 287–290.

Carlson, J.S., & Das, J.P. (1997). A process approach to remediating word-decoding deficiencies in Chapter 1 children. *Learning Disability Quarterly, 20*(2), 93–102.

Carlson, J., & Hunt, E. (2015). A Janus view: J.P. Das's ideas in retrospect and prospect. In T.C. Papadopoulos, R.K. Parrila, and J.R. Kirby (Eds), *Cognition, intelligence, and achievement: A tribute to J. P. Das* (pp. 51–77). San Diego, CA: Elsevier.

Das, J.P. (1954). Effect of a completely dissimilar interpolated learning on 'retroactive inhibition.' *Indian Journal of Psychology, 29,* 161–167.

———. (1969). *Verbal conditioning and behaviour.* Oxford: Pergamon Press.

———. (1973a). Cultural deprivation and cognitive competence. In N.R. Ellis (Ed.), *International review of research in mental retardation* (vol. 6, pp. 1–53). New York, NY: Academic Press.

———. (1973b). Structure of cognitive abilities: Evidence for simultaneous and successive processing. *Journal of Educational Psychology, 65*(1), 103–108.

———. (1999). *PASS Reading Enhancement Program* (PREP). Edmonton, AB: J.P. Das Centre on Learning and Developmental Disabilities. Retrieved 17 April 2015, from http://www.childlearningprogram.com/

———. (2004). *COGENT: Cognition enhancement.* Edmonton, AB: J.P. Das Centre on Learning and Developmental Disabilities). Retrieved 17 April 2015, from http://www.childlearningprogram.com/

———. (2015). Three faces of processes: Theory, assessment, and intervention. In T.C. Papadopoulos, R.K. Parrila, and J.R. Kirby (Eds), *Cognition, intelligence, and achievement: A tribute to J.P. Das* (pp. 19–47). San Diego, CA: Elsevier.

Das, J.P., & Dash, U.N. (1983). Hierarchical factor solution of coding and planning processes: Any new insights? *Intelligence, 7*(1), 27–38.

Das, J.P., Dyer, F.N., & Bower, A.C. (1969). Orienting responses to vigilance signals: A comparison of GSRs of normal and retarded children. Abstracts of XIXth International Congress in Psychology, London.

Das, J.P., Hayward, D., Georgiou, G., Janzen, T., & Boora, N. (2008). Comparing the effectiveness of two reading intervention programs for children with reading disabilities. *Journal of Cognitive Education & Psychology, 7*(2), 199–220.

Das, J.P., & Heemsbergen, D.B. (1983). Planning as a factor in the assessment of cognitive processes. *Journal of Psychoeducational Assessment, 1*(1), 1–15.

Das, J.P., Kar, B.C., & Parrila, R.K. (1996). *Cognitive planning.* Thousand Oaks, CA: SAGE Publications.

Das, J.P., Kirby, J.R., & Jarman, R.F. (1975). Simultaneous and successive syntheses: An alternative model for cognitive abilities. *Psychological Bulletin, 82*(1), 87–103.

———. (1979). *Simultaneous and successive cognitive processes.* New York, NY: Academic Press.

Das, J.P., Mishra, R.K., & Pool, J.E. (1995). An experiment on cognitive remediation of word-reading difficulty. *Journal of Learning Disabilities, 28*(2), 66–79.

Das, J.P. & Misra, S. (2015). *Cognitive planning and executive functions: Applications in education and management.* New Delhi: SAGE Publications.

Das, J.P., & Molloy, G.N. (1975). Varieties of simultaneous and successive processing in children. *Journal of Educational Psychology, 67*(2), 213–220.

Das, J.P., Naglieri, J.A., & Kirby, J. R. (1994). Assessment of cognitive processes: The PASS theory of intelligence. Boston: Allyn & Bacon.

Das, J.P., & Pivato, E. (1976). Malnutrition and cognitive functioning. In N.R. Ellis (Ed.), *International review of research in mental retardation* (vol. 8; pp. 195–223). New York, NY: Academic Press.

Hayward, D., Das, J.P. & Janzen, T. (2007). Innovative programs for improvement in reading through cognitive enhancement: A remediation study of Canadian First Nations children. *Journal of Learning Disabilities, 40*(5), 443–457.

Luria, A.R. (1973). *The working brain.* London: Penguin Books.

Mahapatra, S., Das, J.P., Stack-Cutler, H., & Parrila, R. (2010). Remediating reading comprehension difficulties: A cognitive processing approach. *Reading Psychology, 31,* 428–453.

McNemar, Q. (1964). Lost: Our intelligence? Why? *American Psychologist, 19*(12), 871–882.

Naglieri, J.A., & Das, J.P. (1988). Planning-arousal-simultaneous-successive (PASS): A model for assessment. *Journal of School Psychology, 26,* 35–48.

Naglieri, J.A., & Das, J.P. (1997). *Das-Naglieri Cognitive Assessment System*. Itasca, IL: Riverside Publishing Co.

Naglieri, J.A., Das, J.P. & Goldstein, S. (2014). *Cognitive Assessment System– TX* (2nd Edition). Austin: Pro-Ed.

Papadopoulos, T.C., Das, J.P., Parrila, R.K., & Kirby, J.R. (2003). Children at risk for developing reading difficulties: A remediation study. *School Psychology International, 24*(3), 340–361.

Papadopoulos, T.C., Ktisti, C., Christoforou, C. & Loizou, M. (2015). Cognitive and linguistic dynamics of reading rememdiation. In T.C. Papadopoulos, R.K. Parrila, and J.R. Kirby (Eds), *Cognition, intelligence, and achievement: A tribute to J.P. Das* (pp. 311–343). San Diego, CA: Elsevier.

Papadopoulos, T.C., Parrila, R., & Kirby, J.R. (Eds). (2015). *Cognition, intelligence, and achievement: A tribute to J.P. Das*. San Diego: Elsevier.

Sternberg, R.J. (2015). Foreword. In T.C. Papadopoulos, R.K. Parrila, and J.R. Kirby (Eds), *Cognition, intelligence, and achievement: A tribute to J.P. Das* (pp. xiii–xv). San Diego, CA: Elsevier.

Sechenov, I.M. (1968). *Selected works*. Amsterdam: E.J. Bonset.

Vygotsky, L. (1962). *Thought and language*. Cambridge, MA: MIT Press.

# 33

## Koneru Ramakrishna Rao

(1932)

## Sonali Bhatt Marwaha

Koneru Ramakrishna Rao is a philosopher, psychologist, and educationist with vast experience in national and international arena as a teacher, researcher, and administrator. He studied philosophy under the tutelage of Professors Saileswar Sen and Satchidananda Murthy at Andhra University and with Richard McKeon at the University of Chicago. He worked with J.B. Rhine at Duke University and later headed his Foundation for Research on the Nature of Man and was its executive director from 1988 to 1994.

*Koneru Ramakrishna Rao*

Born in a middle class agricultural family in a small village on 4 October 1932 in Krishna District of Andhra Pradesh, India, K. Ramakrishna Rao was the first to attend college from his then tiny village, and he has since many firsts to his credit. Graduating with a BA (hons) in 1953 and an

MA (hons) in 1955 from Andhra University, he earned a PhD (philosophy) and a DLit (psychology) degree from the same university. As a Smith-Mundt Fulbright scholar and a fellow of the Rockefeller Foundation, he attended the University of Chicago and worked with Richard McKeon during 1958–1960 on Gandhian philosophy and American pragmatism.

Ramakrishna Rao taught philosophy and psychology at Andhra University beginning in 1953 until 1982. From 1984 to 1987, he served as the vice-chancellor of Andhra University from 1984 to 1987. He later headed the Andhra Pradesh Commissionerate of Higher Education and was the adviser to the Government of Andhra Pradesh on higher education (1987–1988) in the rank of chief secretary. As the vice-chairman of the Andhra Pradesh State Planning Board (1994–1995) with the rank of cabinet minister, Rao was instrumental in developing several innovative schemes to take the government to its grassroots and promote district and local-level planning. During his tenure as vice-chancellor, he initiated several curricular and administrative reforms that had far reaching consequences. These include (a) mandatory courses at the undergraduate level to all students on Indian culture and civilization, (b) field work and project reports built into the curriculum, (c) specialized courses on computer application, and (d) establishment of the Institute for Yoga and Consciousness (1985).

As chairman of the Committee on Reorganizing Higher Education in Andhra Pradesh, Rao was instrumental in providing a blueprint for organizing higher education in the state. Following his recommendations, the Andhra Pradesh State Council of Higher Education came into being. The first of its kind, it is taken as a model by several other states. He headed several other national and state-level committees on education. These include the committee on the governance of universities in the state, the committees to establish on Gandhian model the Institute for Professional Studies, and a rural university in Andhra Pradesh. Another committee under his chairmanship prepared a comprehensive report in 1995 on reorganizing school education in the state of Andhra Pradesh. The reports of all these committees were published, extensively discussed, and became the bases for state legislation and administrative action.

Rao began his academic career in the Department of Philosophy of Andhra University, held over a period of 30 years various teaching and administrative positions, and started a number of new programmes there. He also undertook various important academic assignments abroad and taught at several universities in the USA, including Duke University, the University of North Carolina at Chapel Hill, the University of Tennessee at Chattanooga and the California Institute for Human Science. He has travelled widely and lectured at a number of universities and participated in a large number of national and international conferences. He visited and lectured at universities in the USA, Canada, the UK, Germany, France, Greece, Sweden, the Netherlands, Denmark, Iceland, Italy, Japan, China, Pakistan, Thailand, Singapore, and Sri Lanka.

He is considered an authority in the areas of Indian psychology, consciousness studies, Yoga, and psychical research. Reviewing Rao's book *Consciousness Studies: Cross-Cultural Perspectives* (2002), Douglas Stokes, an American psychologist, wrote: 'It is the best and most comprehensive work on the subject of East–West psychology and philosophy that I have ever read, and I would recommend it as must reading to all serious students of the subject'. Larry Dossey, an authority on non-conventional healing, wrote:

> As physician interested in the role of consciousness in healing, I have unfailingly been inspired by Dr. Rao's work over the years. I consider him a giant in science in general and in the fields of psychology and parapsychology in particular. No one in modern science has done so much with more clarity, courage, and insight.

According to Sudhir Kakar, distinguished psychoanalyst and well known author,

> Prof. Rao is much more than an eminent psychologist-philosopher or educationist. When the intellectual history of twentieth-century India comes to be written, his name will occupy an honoured place as one of the few thinkers who did not uncritically accept the dominance of Western scientific discourse but creatively mined the Indian philosophical traditions to raise fundamental questions on the nature of consciousness and attempted to free our thinking from the stranglehold of modern Western discourse.

*The former President of India Smt. Pratibha Patil awarding the Padma Shri to K. Ramakrishna Rao at the award ceremony at Rashtrapati Bhavan, New Delhi*

In recognition of his contributions, he was awarded the Padma Shri (literature and education category) in 2011. He is the first and only psychologist so honoured so far by the Government of India. Additionally, he was awarded honorary doctoral degrees by Andhra University (Doctor of Letters, Honoris Causa, 1990), Nagarjuna University (Doctor of Science, Honoris Causa, 1988), and Kakatiya University (Doctor of Letters, Honoris Causa, 1986). He was elected as Fellow of the National Academy of Psychology (2007) and president of the Indian Academy of Applied Psychology (1987–1989) and the Parapsychological Association (1965, 1978, 1990), an international organization of professional parapsychologists with its headquarters in the USA. Following two terms as chairman of the Indian Council of Philosophical Research (2006–2012), he is presently the chancellor of GITAM University (since 2012) and President of Asian Congress of Philosophy (since 2011). He was Editorial Fellow, Project of History of Indian Science, Philosophy and Culture, (2003–2006). He is currently Chancellor of GITAM University and the Chairman of the School of Gandhian Studies.

## Contribution to the Field of Psychology

Rao's intellectual curiosity, spurred by a combined background in philosophy and psychology, poised him to take a path less travelled, against the then existent behaviourist trend in psychology, and enter into fields of inquiry that looked too esoteric and subjective to be scientifically studied—parapsychology and consciousness studies.

His curiosity about one of the most enigmatic areas of human experiences—extrasensory perception (ESP)—led him to work with J.B. Rhine, the father of modern experimental parapsychology, at Duke University, USA, from 1962 to 1965. On his return, he established the Department of Psychology and Parapsychology at Andhra University (1967). His training at Duke transformed him from being a tender-minded thinker to a tough experimental psychologist. In tune with the research of the day, he contributed to the body of work examining personality and cognitive factors in ESP. In addition, he carried out extensive experimental research into the phenomenon called psi-missing. His presidential address at the Annual Convention of Parapsychological Association held in New York in 1965 reviewed his research, its rational, and significance. Rao's studies of the 'differential effect' provide evidence to one of the best replicated studies in parapsychology. He developed the concept of 'bidirectionality of psi' which has come to be regarded as a very basic aspect of parapsychological phenomena.

As founder-head of the Department of Psychology and Parapsychology at Andhra University (1968–1982), Ramakrishna Rao initiated several new programmes of research. Among them was the establishment of the Dream Laboratory with state-of-the-art equipment to monitor and record the subject's dreams in a laboratory setting. First of its kind in the country, it was started in the early 1970s and several students received their PhD degrees for their work on nocturnal dreaming under Rao's guidance.

In later years, his growing disenchantment with the Western premise of psi phenomenon brought him back to his roots in the Indian philosophical traditions to study philosophical perspectives of psi phenomena in greater depth from the Indian perspective. This naturally led to his renewed interest in consciousness studies and the cross-cultural perspectives on the meaning of consciousness and Indian psychology as an alternate paradigm in psychology. His contribution to the field of consciousness studies, incorporating the Indian philosophical perspectives, is internationally acclaimed. Emphasizing the importance of the Indian viewpoint on consciousness studies, he presented the paper *Consciousness in Indian Psychology* in 1972 at the Third International Conference on Humanistic Psychology in Tokyo. We find the culmination of Rao's work on consciousness in his widely reviewed and referred book *Consciousness Studies: Cross-Cultural Perspectives* first published in 1982 in the USA.

His early recognition of a psychology embedded in the Indian philosophical traditions has blossomed into full-scale professional interest in Indian psychology. Rao has defined Indian psychology as 'a body of psychological knowledge involving coherent model(s) to systematically explain human nature with concepts, categories and models derived from thought native to India' and consciousness is its defining characteristic. His book *Cognitive Anomalies, Consciousness, and Yoga* (2011) is a comprehensive review of relevant areas of consciousness studies, psychic phenomena, and Yoga psychology. It provides a coherent model for developing Indian psychology as a system like psychoanalysis with significant implications for understanding cognitive excellence, transcognitive states of consciousness, and human well-being. Reinterpreting the concept of pure consciousness in Advaita Vedanta, Buddhist psychology of transcendence and yoga practices for controlling mind and cultivating consciousness, he developed a model of the person as a composite of body, mind, and consciousness, with significant research implications for psychology—East and West.

Virtually the leader of the band of scholars in the field of Indian psychology, Rao is the initiator of the 'manifesto of Indian psychology'. He, along with Anand Paranjpe and Ajit Dalal, edited the *Handbook of Indian Psychology* and authored with Paranjpe *Psychology in the Indian Tradition*. The two books together are an important source for teaching Indian psychology to graduate and post-graduate students. His most recent research explorations relate to Mahatma Gandhi. This is a return to his original interest in Gandhi, a topic of his PhD dissertation 50 years ago, but with a difference. He moved away from a pragmatic interpretation of Gandhi to an understanding from a spiritual perspective, from a philosophical study to psychological investigation. His keynote addresses at national seminars held at M.S. University, Baroda, and GITAM University, Visakhapatnam, during 2013 develop the theme of Gandhian dialectic of human development and provide a thorough psychological interpretation of *satyagraha*, going well beyond Joan Bondurant and Erik Erikson.

Rao is the founder editor of the *Journal of Indian Psychology* and the chairman of its current editorial board. He edited the *Journal of Parapsychology* for almost two decades. He has recently started *GITAM Journal of Gandhian Studies,* and serves as the chairman of its editorial board.

Rao has so far published 22 books, nearly 300 research papers, and about 50 book chapters. A complete bibliography of his publications is available in the book *Consciousness, Gandhi and Yoga: Interdisciplinary, East-West Odyssey of K. Ramakrishna Rao*, edited by Sambasiva Prasad (2013). This volume contains extensive reviews of Rao's work by international scholars and experts in consciousness studies, Yoga, parapsychology, and Gandhi, such as Max Velmans, Sudhir Kakar, Anand Paranjpe, and Jean Kristeller.

Eighty-five-years young Rao works full time. With four books to appear in 2017 and half a dozen research papers at various stages in the publication process, he is now as active as he was 50 years ago, travelling around the world and advancing psychological knowledge in an interdisciplinary and inter-institutional setting. As Jean Kristeller, a psychology professor at Indiana State University says 'Rao is one of these rare individuals whose words and endeavours have placed him at the forefront of the revolution in thinking in these areas over the last fifty years'. Girishwar Misra of Delhi University adds, 'Prof. Rao has made seminal contributions to the field of Indian psychology.... His contributions amount to nothing less than bringing a paradigm shift'.

His forthcoming books include *Gandhi's Dharma* (Oxford University Press), *Colonial Syndrome in Modern Indian Mindset* (Springer), *Foundations of Yoga Psychology* (Springer), *Elements of Parapsychology* (McFarland), and *Phenomenology of Violence*, co-edited with Sambasiva Prasad (DK Printworld).

Ramakrishna Rao continues to be an exemplary researcher, an outstanding teacher, and a relentless institutional builder. He is clearly a creative leader among psychologists beyond his native country.

# 34

# Moazziz Ali Beg

(1932–2013)

## Akbar Husain

Moazziz Ali Beg was born in Agra on 27 August 1932 in a family of Mughals who had settled there after migrating from Iran around the time of the battle of Buxar. His ancestor, Mirza Mubarak Ali Beg, settled in Agra and one of his ancestors had joined the array of Nawab Shuja-ud Daula. A short account of his ancestors is available in *Zikr-E-Ghalib* by Malik Ram who had met Nawab Mirza, the elder brother of Beg's maternal grandfather, Mirza Tasadduq Ali Beg, who lived in Gali Hakiman, Agra. Mirza Tasadduq Ali Beg held a high post in the judiciary under the British Rule. Gali Hakiman is almost adjacent to Kala Mahal where Mirza Ghalib had his residence. One of Ghalib's cousin sisters, Moti Begum, was married to Mirza Akbar Ali Beg, one of the ancestors of Moazziz Ali Beg.

His paternal grandfather, Mirza Irfan Ali Beg, was highly honoured by the British Empire and taken as the Companion of our Imperial Service Order by George the Fifth under the royal warrant on 12 February 1912. His father, Mirza Qurban Ali Beg, refused to go in the service of the British Empire and lived in Gur Ki Mandi, Agra, managing his property. His mother, Asghari Begum, came from a Mughal family of Lucknow. She was a highly cultured lady and after the death of her husband, when Beg was a child, she gave him the best education available at that time. The family of his mother lived in Aligarh and her elder brother, Mirza Ibrahim Beg, resigned from the service of the British after he refused to fire at the Indians when a riot had taken place. He was editor of the paper *Surgususht* issued from Aligarh. He was a collaborator of Sir Syed Ahmad Khan as a member of the educational conference. Some members of this Mughal family went to Gwalior in the service of Sciendias. Beg's grandmother—the wife of Mirza Irfan Ali Beg—Nawab Usmani Begum, was the daughter of Usman Khan Suba, the governor of Gwalior. Beg's father was Sufi and had a great reverence for Sri Krishna, and as man of great austerity he was highly respected in the large family of Agra. His lifelong intimate friend was Chaubey Ayoudhya Parshad Chaturvedi of Gur Ki Mandi, Agra, who, after the death of Beg's father, looked after the widow and the child and managed all matters concerning their property. Like his father, Beg subscribed to Sufism and went under Hazrat Maikash Akbarabadi—a descendent of Sufis of Agra coming down there from the time of Emperor Jahangir.

# Education and Contribution to the Field of Psychology

Beg's childhood education was at home under a Hindu teacher, Chokey Lal, who taught him Urdu and English. Chokey Lal loved him like his own child and cared for him in every way. Later on, his early education was completed from Christian and English schools. After passing high school from a Muslim school of Agra, his mother took him to Aligarh where he finished his postgraduate education from Aligarh Muslim University in 1952. In 1956, he went to study at the University of Oregon, USA, and received an MS degree. He completed his PhD from Aligarh Muslim University. His main work since 1973 is treated as unique by the leading American psychologist, Stanley Krippner. He has examined the heuristic power of Vedantic and Sufi concepts and his papers have been published from Delhi, Tokyo, Basel, Munich, Vienna, New York, Hobart, and Buenos Aires.

As a thinker, Beg had exchanged views with leading thinkers such as P.A. Sorokin, F.S.C. Northrop, Lewis Mumford, and Glen Martin. His work has been evaluated and honoured by a host of scholars and recognized by American, German, and Australian scholars. His biography has been published by the American Biographical Institute, North Carolina, USA, and from the International Biographical Centre, Cambridge, England. In India, his biography has been brought out by Asia Publishers. His treatise on world peace, brought out by Global Vision Publishing House, New Delhi, carries the remarks of American and Australian scholars. As Glen Martin has said, 'Perhaps only a scholar from India with its vast intellectual tradition and integrative vision could write with such scope, clarity and insight'. Ian Gold of Monash University, Australia, observes, 'In the light of recent tragic events in America and the events that may follow them, your aspirations and work seem to me more crucial than ever'.

Beg worked for peace under the aegis of the International Philosophers for Peace, University of Virginia. He delivered lectures at many Indian universities, California College and Georgia University. He had also lectured at the University of Munich, Germany. He taught in the Department of Psychology, Aligarh Muslim University; Maharishi Dayanand University, Rohtak; and the University of Engineering, Roorkee.

He passed away on 23 December 2013.

# 35

## S. Anandalakshmy

(1932)

### Nandita Chaudhary

A nandalakshmy is renowned for her distinguished career in the field of child development and related areas of cultural studies, family dynamics, social welfare, and gender studies.

S. Anandalakshmy

A brilliant student, S. Anandalakshmy's career path has been unconventional and deeply inspiring for younger colleagues and students. She earned her bachelor's degree from Queen Mary's college, Madras, where she studied history and economics. Following this, she enrolled herself for a BEd programme in Lady Willingdon College and subsequently for a master's degree in Presidency College, under the University of Madras. She began her career as a schoolteacher in Chennai. She served as the head of this school, Vidya Mandir, for 2 years. An outstanding student with university ranks, Anandalakshmy soon applied for a Fulbright Scholarship and went to the USA to earn a second master's degree in child development and education from Bryn Mawr College, USA, and, following that, a doctorate from the University of Wisconsin at Madison, USA. After completing the doctoral programme, Anandalakshmy returned to India and took up a teaching job at Lady Irwin College, University of Delhi, where she developed and established a master's degree course in child development. Simultaneously, she played an advisory role for prominent bodies such as the UNICEF, Ministry of HRD, and several other academic institutions in India. Anandalakshmy also brought about many changes in the curriculum of the Nursery School that was attached to the Department of Child Development at the Lady Irwin College. Here, she introduced, with some effort, a programme to include and incorporate three-to-five-year-old children with disability into the configuration and curriculum of the school. Later, under her supervision, the faculty members of the Department of Child Development took up the initiative to set up 'The Enabling Centre' which provided primary education and support to children with disabilities.

Apart from this, Anandalakshmy was also actively involved with the NGO sector. After meeting Meera Mahadevan, the founder of Mobile Crèches in 1969, she involved herself in a unique programme run for children of migrant labourers, which continues to function in Delhi and other cities till date. She also participated actively in the ventures of SWRC (Social Work and Research Centre), a foundation set up by Bunker and Aruna Roy, which is now referred to as 'The Barefoot College' in Tilonia, Ajmer district, Rajasthan. She continues to be associated with MKSS, Mazdoor Kisan Shakti Sanghatan, in Dev Doongri, Rajasthan, set up by Aruna Roy, which played a crucial role in initiating the Right to Information, the Right to Food, Rural Employment Guarantee, and Pension Parishad, in rural Rajasthan. While Anandalakshmy was still at Lady Irwin College, she befriended Ela Bhatt of SEWA (Self Employed Women's Association) in Gujarat. Over 40 years, SEWA has genuinely empowered more than 900,000 of its women members emerging from the grassroots level in Gujarat. Anandalakshmy's ties with Lady Irwin College have been abiding, where for over seven years, she served the college as the director. She is a part of the executive committee supporting a number of colleges such as the Barefoot College in Tilonia, Volontariat in Pondicherry, and Bala Mandir in Chennai. She worked with the Bernard van Leer Foundation, helping assess and monitor childcare work in SEWA, Ahmedabad. In the course of assisting the Sarva Shiksha Abhiyan in Tamil Nadu, she made two short documentaries on the innovative methods (ABL and ALM) of teaching practiced in Tamil Nadu schools.

## Awards and Recognition

Anandalakshmy frequently visited universities in the USA, at the invitation of the Asia Society, and spent two summers at the Institute of Advanced Studies in Edinburgh and a three-month period at the Maison des Science de l'homme in Paris. Anandalakshmy applied for and received the East-West Centre fellowship which funded her doctoral studies at the University of Wisconsin, Madison. From the mid-1970s onwards, she was offered the honorary part-time post of screening the applications for grants in psychology at the Indian Council for Social Science Research. For about 10 years, from 1975, she remained on the UNICEF list as an expert in childhood education during which she attended workshops and seminars at Kabul, Kathmandu, Jakarta, the Maldives. and Sri Lanka. In a meeting held at Kathmandu, she met Kathy Sylva working for the education department of Oxford University, with whom she became friends. Collaborations with Kathy Sylva continued and Anandalakshmy was invited a few years later to share her work with the faculty and students of the educational psychology department at Oxford. Anandalakshmy was also invited by Professor

Robert LeVine of the Harvard School of Education to give a talk to a group of his students in and around Cambridge, Massachusetts. In the year 1987, the Ministry of Human Resource Development was developing the National Policy on Education (1987) for which she was invited to attend several meetings under the leadership of the then Secretary of Education Anil Bordia. Anandalakshmy attended several international conferences like the American Psychology Conference in Chicago. Three years after Anandalakshmy returned from Wisconsin, she attended the first conference of the International Association of Cross Cultural Psychology (IACCP) at Hong Kong in 1972. To prepare her paper, she visited the Indian Institute of Advanced Studies, Shimla, where she resided for a month.

In 1973–1974, she attended an Indo-US meet in New Delhi where she got to meet several scholars and teachers from both the countries working in the field of child development. Subsequently, two major South Asia seminars in Chicago and Harvard, in 1981 and 1982 respectively, provided her an opportunity to meet several specialists (anthropologists, psychiatrists, and sociologists) from India and all around the world.

## Contributions

Anandalakshmy has led several research studies in the areas of the girl child, cognitive development in early childhood, and socialization. She edited a book for SAGE, along with two colleagues, on the theme of qualitative research methods. Within the first 10 years of the setting up of the MSc course in child development at Lady Irwin College, Anandalakshmy organized an informal *Homework Help Centre* for the children of the *karamcharis* in the college campus. The masters' students of the Department would teach and administer this centre. The children were assisted mostly in understanding the English language and doing their English homework. While still a doctoral student of Wisconsin-Madison, Anandalakshmy took up the ambitious task of criticizing Arthur Jensen's controversial paper on race and intelligence, where he had propounded the theory that African-Americans lacked the capacity for abstract thinking. This brief critical note was later published in the *Harvard Educational Review*. With a co-student, Jane Adams, she also presented a seminar for the department on Jensen's thesis, in which they argued their case and criticized the theory on the basis of statistics and rational thinking, making it clear that they were attacking it on its methodological grounds as well as on its grossly racist approach.

One of her major contributions has been the establishment of a master's degree course in child development at the Lady Irwin College. The course had already been planned by her in 1966 after reviewing several courses being offered in American universities, and finally with the expert advice and help of Dr Helen Ashby, who was sponsored by the Ford Foundation to help in the task, Anandalakshmy accomplished her goal. One whole year was spent in developing the specific curriculum for the two-year master's degree course in child development, with further inputs from many expert academicians of the University of Delhi. The course envisaged was culturally relevant and interdisciplinary in nature and therefore included elements of other disciplines such as psychology, sociology, anthropology, and social work. The degree to be given for the course in child development was MSc (master of science). Since a science course demands a substantial amount of practical work, the Nursery School attached to the department was to serve as a laboratory for simple experiments and observational studies. Institutions for children with disabilities and other special needs, as well as other schools in the city, had to be located as potential fields for the students' practical assignments.

On her return from Wisconsin, Anandalakshmy was determined to do research with fresh ideas that emerged from the Indian academia and not simply replicate and reproduce the research interests and inferences of the Western world. Her distinctive stance, which her students later imbibed, was not to succumb to the seduction of mainstream psychology, and engage in culturally meaningful work. Anandalakshmy next planned to undertake a study on the socialization of children, taking cues from traditional crafts families. Families engaged in bangle-making, pottery, mat weaving and clay-toy-making in various parts of New Delhi and Old Delhi constituted the first four groups meant for study. These ideas later matured into an ICSSR sponsored project on the 'socialization for competence,' which till date is considered to be one of the landmark studies on socialization. Detailed observations and survey data were collected about the block printers of textiles (Chippa Rajvamshis) of Sanganeer near Jaipur, the Banaras silk weavers of Varanasi (Ansari Muslims), and the farming communities in the villages near Pantnagar, UP. The research findings were later to be published as a chapter in the IACCP proceedings printed in the Netherlands, which was a summary booklet for the ICSSR, and as an article in the journal *Seminar*.

The second major area in which Anandalakshmy has interest and has collaborated with many students and colleagues to do research was on the relationship between cognitive functioning and nutritional status of infants and young children. Children ranging from the age group of toddlerhood to that of 6 years were taken from three different socio-economic levels as subjects. The rationale was to investigate into a claim made by US scientists that protein malnutrition resulted in mental retardation of children, which strangely coincided with the US trade policy of exporting a large amount of soya bean products to India. The results of the study found that there was no perceptible relationship between cognition and nutrition per se, but when the child was very low on nutrition, all other functions were low. This was a definite relationship, but only for cases of severe malnutrition.

While working in the Department of Child Development at the Lady Irwin College, Anandalakshmy supervised a large number of the master's degree dissertations written on themes related to the fields of disability, cognition, socialization, language development and family relationships. The Nursery School attached to the department had several children with mild to moderate disabilities, and was later transformed by Anandalakshmy to form 'The Enabling Centre; which organized a mixed-age, multiple-level primary education programme for children. A survey within a 5 km radius of the college was conducted to identify children who had not attended school at all or dropped out of school due to a physical or mental disability. This centre was funded by the Ministry of HRD under its scope for the promotion of 'innovative and experimental programmes in elementary education'. Later, she also supervised some interesting research projects on adolescents and their relationship with their parents.

After serving Lady Irwin College for a number of years as the director, Anandalakshmy took premature retirement and moved back to her home in Madras. Over the last two decades there, she has been most productive. She travelled to Bellagio (the Rockefeller Centre in Italy) for a month, attended an international conference in Beijing, and contributed a chapter to a book entitled *Making a Difference* in which several eminent authors were featured. As a member of the Knowledge Network set up by the WHO, she attended two meetings in Ottawa and Vancouver in Canada. As a consultant on Doctors@NDTV, she also provided email counselling sessions that were later compiled into a book by Roli Publications. She edited a set of papers on qualitative research along with Nandita Chaudhary and Neerja Sharma which were to be published by SAGE. Another publication by Routledge entitled *Cultural Realities of Being* that Anandalakshmy jointly published with Jaan Valsiner and Nandita Chaudhary was released in the early months of 2014.

Among the other activities that Anandalakshmy has been occupied with is the propagation of Sarva Shiksha Abhiyan in the State of Tamil Nadu. It proved to be an interesting experience for her, and the aim was achievable because of the positive support and co-operation provided by MP Vijaya Kumar. At his request, a document on the innovative methods and materials of teaching and two short documentary films (concept, script, and voice by Anandalakshmy) on activity-based learning (ABL) and active learning methodology (ALM) were prepared. These films have brought visibility to the project of innovative pedagogy steered by Vijaya Kumar.

As an adjunct to the newspaper, *The Hindu*, when the *Folio* magazine was released, the editor of *The Hindu* magazine invited Anandalakshmy to write for the paper. Quite a few short articles on education, childhood, and disability, and at times an occasional book review, have been contributed by her to *The Folio*, the magazine, or the main paper, *The Hindu*. Anandalakshmy continues to work with a number of organizations and is actively involved in their planning and developmental processes. Among these are the Bala Mandir in Chennai, Voluntariat in Pondicherry, Barefoot College in Tilonia, SEWA in Ahmedabad, and the Mobile Crèches in Delhi. She continues to play an advisory role to the Department of (re-christened) Human Development and Childhood Studies at Lady Irwin College.

# 36

# Bishwa Nath Mukherjee

(1933–1997)

Satishchandra Kumar, Anjali Majumdar, Heena Kamble, and Braj Bhushan

Born on 15 October 1933, Bishwa Nath Mukherjee is remembered for his contributions to the field of psychology, psychometry, statistics, and education. Beginning his journey in this discipline with psychology as one of the papers in his bachelor of arts (BA) degree in 1951, he completed a master of arts (MA) in experimental psychology from Patna University in 1953. Thereafter, he did a PhD in qualitative psychology from University of North Carolina, Chapel Hill, in 1964 ("Ideal Role Model for Psychologist," n.d.)

## Academic Career

In September 1962, B.N. Mukherjee was appointed as an assistant professor of psychology at Indiana University, Jeffersonville, USA, where he taught various undergraduate and graduate courses till September 1964. Upon his return to India, he joined the Council of Scientific and Industrial Research, Government of India, as a pool officer and was assigned to the Department of Psychology, Patna University, in October 1964, where he taught statistics and research methods to postgraduate (PG) students till September 1965 ("Ideal Role Model for Psychologist," n.d.).

In September 1965, he joined the Department of Psychology, Nagpur University, as Reader and Head. The department was established in 1963 and B.N. Mukherjee became the third head of the department following P.N. Singh and D.B. Shesh (www.nagpuruniversity.org/links/dep_psychology.htm). He remained head till March 1968. Here also Mukherjee offered PG courses in research methods, statistics, psychological testing, and personality. During his tenure as head, he worked to expand the activities of the University Psychology Association. The professional, social, and cultural activities of the association were inaugurated on 3 August 1965 by Justice N.L. Abhyankar (Annual Report, 1965–66). In April 1968, Mukherjee became the associate director and head at the industrial psychology division at Shri Ram Centre for Industrial Relations, New Delhi. He stayed at this post till September 1968, after which he became an associate professor of psychology at York University in Downsview, Ontario, Canada. There, he taught individual differences to undergraduates, along with multivariate statistical analysis and advanced personality assessment as a part of graduate course till July, 1971. After his tenure at York University, he returned back to New Delhi in August 1971and became the joint director of research, Council for Social Development. He remained at this position till March 1979, after which he was elevated as the director of research, Council of Social Development. In April 1981, he joined the computer science unit of the Indian Statistical Institute (ISI), Calcutta (now named as Kolkata), as a professor in the applied statistics, computing and survey division. He retired from ISI in November 1993 at the age of 60 ("Ideal Role Model for Psychologists," n.d.).

Mukherjee served as statistical consultant to Sir George Williams University in connection with an intensive analysis of students' grades during 1968–1969. He also served as a guest faculty in various training programmes in social science research and behavioural sciences and agricultural management at many renowned institutes. He was also an occasional consultant to CARE India for advising on problems connected with nutritional surveys and programme evaluation. He also served at the Ahmedabad Textile Industries Research Association as the honorary chairman of the panel of experts in human relations from 1974 to 1984 ("Ideal Role Model for Psychologists," n.d.). He served as an expert in the Economic Commission for Asia and the Far East (ECAFE) in February 1974. In February 1978, he was resource person for the meeting on monitoring and evaluation of the social development programme of the UN Asian and Pacific Development Institute in collaboration with United Nations International Children's Emergency Fund (UNICEF) and United Nations Centre for Regional Development (UNCRD) at Manila. Besides being a senior faculty in the United Nations Educational, Scientific and Cultural Organization (UNESCO) sponsored course, he also served as an expert in the World Health Organization (WHO) meeting held at Geneva related to the planning of multi-site studies on relative acceptability of reversible and irreversible sterilization methods ("Ideal Role Model for Psychologists," n.d.). He was also a member of Educational Research and Innovations Committee (ERIC) and National Council for Educational Research and Training (NCERT), New Delhi, from 1980 to 1991. He also served as a senior faculty in the training programmes arranged for junior statistical service and newly recruited officers of the statistical service of the Government of India. In addition to directing three projects, he actively participated in the institute's prestigious National Survey of Foreign Tourists between 1982 and 1985. In 1992, he became a member of the task force on users' perspective on spacing methods at the Indian Council of Medical Research. During his work at ISI, he participated actively from time to time in teaching the International Statistical Education Centre (ISEC) courses as a part of the training activities of the International Statistical Institute, Voorburg, Netherlands. He was also a visiting scientist at Chiba University, Japan, in October 1984. He worked from time to time as a senior consultant to Programme Support Unit, Indo-Dutch Cooperation Programme in Water Management and Community Health at Lucknow ("Ideal Role Model for Psychologists," n.d.).

He supervised PhD theses in measurement and statistics at York University (1968–1971). He was also a research guide for PG students of the Department of Psychology, Patna University, as well as Nagpur University. He also guided several doctoral candidates as well, who obtained their PhD degrees in psychology from Nagpur University; IIT-Delhi; and Jamia Millia, Delhi, and in statistics from ISI, Kolkata. He was a life member of the Indian Society for Medical Statistics and a member of the Biometric Society until he passed away ("Ideal Role Model for Psychologists," n.d.).

## Active Engagements in Projects

Mukherjee provided his expertise to many research projects. At Nagpur University he was the honorary project director of the University Grants Commission (UGC) funded project on juvenile delinquency (Annual Report, 1967–68). While serving as a psychologist at the B.M. Institute of Psychology and Child Development, Ahmedabad (1956–1958), he directed two research projects, namely 'a study of relationship between learning efficiency and ability variables connected with performance in the two-hand coordination test' and 'a Gujarati adaptation of the Wechsler Intelligence Scale for Children'. While in USA, he worked on three projects. The first was on learning efficiency and aptitude patterns which was sponsored by Graduate School of Indiana University, Bloomington. The second project was on achievement motivation and was sponsored by the US Office of Education, Washington DC. The third project was on the status of women and family planning, funded by the Division of Human Rights, UN, New York. He directed a research project at Shri Ram Centre for Industrial Relations, New Delhi, on 'human aspects of shift work in industry' funded by Planning Commission, Government of India. Other projects include comprehensive settlement planning in Ranaghat Block of Nasia District in West Bengal, sponsored by the Department of Science and Technology; 'a quick impact study of the Sircilla Rural Electric Cooperative Society' sponsored by the Rural Electrification Corporation, New Delhi; a study on mass communication and village life, sponsored by the Institute of Mass Communication, University of Leicester, England; 'positive and negative effects of family planning in West Bengal' funded by the Indian Council of Medical Research, New Delhi; 'social attitude towards air pollution in proper Calcutta, funded by the Department of Environment, Ministry of Environment and Forests; and a study of attitude of scientists towards air pollution in proper Calcutta, sponsored by the Division of Applied Statistics, Surveys and Computing, ISI, Kolkata ("Ideal Role Model for Psychologists," n.d.). He was the social psychologist and senior staff member of the Central Research Cell from 1971 to 1974 that worked on the integrated area development, a study funded by the Ministry of Food, Agriculture and Development, Government of India, and Ford Foundation. In 1972, he was also appointed the project director for 'fertility and family planning survey in Haryana and Tamil Nadu states'. This project was undertaken by the Population Council of India and the Council for Social Development, New Delhi, and was sponsored by the Ministry of Health and Family Planning, Government of India ("Ideal Role Model for Psychologists," n.d.).

## Contribution to the Field of Psychology

Mukherjee was perhaps the most prolific writers of his time who contributed many papers on theory, methods, and application of multi-variate analysis. His interests varied from statistical psychology to social and industrial psychology. Besides psychology, he also contributed to the field of education, demography, and women empowerment. His seminal papers on statistical techniques include 'Reliability Estimates for a Modified Two-hand Coordination Test' (1960), 'Statistical Problems Connected with the Efficient Designs of Tests' (1962), 'Factor Analysis of Some Qualitative Attributes of Coffee' (1965), 'Rational Equation Designed to Represent the Forgetting Process (1965), 'Mathematical Contributions to the Psychology of International Politics' (1966), 'Application of Canonical Correlational Analysis to Learning Data' (1966), 'Derivation of Likelihood Ratio Tests for Guttman Quasi-simplex Covariance Structures' (1966), 'Likelihood Ratio Tests of Statistical Hypotheses Associated with Patterned Covariance Matrices in Psychology' (1970),

'Analysis of Covariance Structures and Exploratory Factor Analysis' (1973), 'Circumplex Models in Psychological Research' (1973), 'A Questionnaire Measure of Persistence Disposition' (1974), 'A Factor-analytic Study of Respondent Variability in Demographic Data' (1974), 'Techniques of Covariance Structural Analysis' (1976), 'The Factorial Structure of Wechsler's Preschool and Primary Scale of Intelligence at Successive Age Levels' (1975), 'The Foundations of Multivariate Analysis' (1982), and 'The Reliability and Validity of the So-called "Hard" and "Soft" Data' (1985).

He published on varied topics in diverse areas of psychology such as achievement values, mathematical psychology, social desirability, and industrial psychology. His work focused on topics such as achievement values as related to self-concept and self-image, conceptualization of achievement value construct, social desirability and anxiety, judgments of social desirability, job-related needs, and many more. Mukherjee is one of the very few psychologists from India who published in the *British Journal of Mathematical and Statistical Psychology* and *Psychometrika*. In his paper titled 'Derivation of Likelihood-ratio Tests for Guttman Quasi-simplex Covariance Structures' with two predefined values of covariance matrices, he obtained the maximum-likelihood estimates for covariance matrices which have the Guttman quasi-simplex structure (Mukherjee, 1966). He published three more papers in the *British Journal of Mathematical and Statistical Psychology*—'Invariance of the Guttman Quasi-Simplex Linear Model Under Selection', 'Analysis of Covariance Structures and Exploratory Factor Analysis', and 'The Factorial Structure of Aptitude Tests at Successive Grades'. In 'Analysis of Covariance Structures and Exploratory Factor Analysis,' he discussed the similarities and differences between covariance structural analysis and exploratory factor analysis and addressed 'the relative superiority of the former' (Mukherjee, 1973). In 1960, he published a paper 'Reliability Estimates for a Modified Two-hand Coordination Test' in *Perceptual and Motor Skills,* which spoke about the problems in estimating reliability of learning tasks in which the subject's performance change with practice (Mukherjee, 1960). Another paper titled 'Techniques of Covariance Structural Analysis' was published in the *Australian Journal of Statistics* which discusses the 'scope and important features of covariance structural analysis in which some pattern can be postulated *a priori* for covariance matrix' (Mukherjee, 1976).

Other significant papers by Mukherjee includes 'Reversibility of the Effects of a Patterned Variable Interval Schedule' (1966), 'Extinction of Spontaneous Recovery as a Function of Direction of Shift in Abbreviated Intermittent Schedules' (1966), 'The effect of Shifts in Fixed-interval Schedules on Acquisition, Extinction, Spontaneous Recovery, and Re-acquisition' (1967), 'A Multi-variate study of Immediate Recall of CVC Trigrams Varying in Meaningfulness and Pronounceability' (1971), and 'A Multi-variate Study of Immediate Recall of CVC Trigrams Varying in Meaningfulness and Pronounceability' (1978). Papers pertaining to achievement values include 'Achievement Motivation and Goal-setting Behavior in the Class Room' (1965), 'Social Desirability and Anxiety Variables in Three Measures of Anxiety' (1966), 'Achievement Value, Social Desirability and Endorsement of Trait Names on the Berdie Adjective Check List' (1968), 'Discriminant Analysis of Self-ratings for College Students Having Differential Manifest Anxiety' (1969), 'Multivariate Study of the Relationship Between Manifest Anxiety, Test Performance and Self-ratings' (1969), 'Some Characteristics of the Achievement-oriented Person: Some Implications for the Teaching-learning Process' (1969), 'Multivariate Study of Learning During Initial Stages of Practice in Mirror Tracing Task in Relation to Manifest Anxiety' (1968), 'Factor-analytic Study of Job Satisfaction' (1969), 'The Role of Verbal Factors in a Test of Achievement Value' (1969), 'Achievement Values as Related to Self-concepts and Stability of Self-images' (1970), 'Achievement Values and Self-ideal Discrepancies in College Students' (1970), 'Multivariate Relationships Among Measures of Achievement Motive and Achievement Values' (1972), and 'Towards a Conceptualization of the Achievement Value

Construct (in *Motivation and Organisational Effectiveness,* edited by S.K. Roy and A.S.K. Menon, 1974).

His publications bearing importance for the area of industrial and organizational psychology includes 'Human Aspects of Shift Work in Industry' (1968), 'Importance Ranking of Job-related Needs by Indian Textile Mill Workers' (1968), 'Personality Characteristics and Intra-individual Variability in Industrial Output' (1969), and 'Background Factors and Mass Media Exposure as Predictors of General Awareness Level Among Factory Workers in Five Developing Countries' (1977). His paper 'Importance of Job-related Needs by Indian textile mill workers' published in the *Indian Journal of Industrial Relations* (1968) explored the importance of hygiene factors for factory workers employed in a progressive textile mill. He mentioned that 'there is not one single factor which determines workers' satisfaction with their jobs but a set of factors differing between employees and between those engaged in different levels of occupation' (Mukherjee, 1968). This study established earnings and job security as predominant factors associated with the expectations of Indian workers. 'Adequate personal benefits' was the least important factor. A similar study titled 'a factor-analytic study of job satisfaction' was published in the *Indian Journal of Industrial Relations* (1969) which examined the 'extent of generality of job satisfaction across different aspects of job'. He countered Vroom's view of considering job satisfaction as a generalized affective orientation in an individual to various aspects of his work situation. Through this study he identified three meaningful factors that influence the job satisfaction of textile mill workers in India— satisfaction with management, feeling of achievement, and job involvement (Mukherjee, 1969).

In his paper titled 'Personality Characteristics and Intra-individual Variability in Industrial Output,' published in the *Indian Journal of Industrial Relations*, he and his collaborator explored the relationship between consistency of output rates and psycho-pathological aspects of individuals, such as anxiety, conflict pressure, neuroticism, and job dissatisfaction. They attempted to study the effectiveness of incentives by comparing the median intra-individual variability index and the average ratio of the range of intra-individual performance. 'Incentivation was conceived as the drive within the individual to work up to his optimum efficiency in order share his gains in monetary terms' (Mukherjee & Menon, 1969). They found no relation between production trends and personality characteristics.

His work focusing on the contemporary social issues include 'A Comparison of the Results of Family Planning KAP Surveys in Haryana and Tamil Nadu, India' (1974), 'Restrictions on Married Women's Activities and Some Aspects of Husband-wife Relations in Khasi Culture' (1974), 'A Multidimensional Conceptualization of Status of Women' (1975), 'Awareness of Legal Rights Among Married Women and their Status' (1975), 'Some Needed Social Science Research for Fertility Decline in India' (1975), 'Status of Women as Related to Family Planning' (1975), 'Reliability Estimates of Some Survey Data on Family Planning' (1975), 'Role of Husband-wife Communication in Family Planning' (1975), 'A Simple Method of Obtaining a Health Hazard Index and its Application in Micro-regional Health Planning' (1976), 'Planning Value and Unplanned Pregnancy' (1977), and 'Prediction of Family Planning and Family Size from Modernity Value Orientations of Indian Women' (1978).

While comparing the family planning surveys in Haryana and Tamil Nadu, Mukherjee attempted to evaluate the knowledge of contraceptive methods, attitudes toward the family planning programme, and reasons for not using contraceptive techniques in samples from Haryana and Tamil Nadu. He stated that the main reason for non-adoption of family planning methods, apart from wanting additional children and having religious or ethical objections, was inadequate or improper knowledge of the methods (Mukherjee, 1974a). In yet another study of husband-wife communication in family planning, data from Haryana, Tamil Nadu, and Meghalaya were compared to determine the relationship between husband-wife communication and knowledge, attitude, and practice of family planning. He found that adoption of family planning techniques was significantly related to the frequency of husband-wife communication (Mukherjee, 1975). In his paper 'Restrictions on Married Women's Activities and Some Aspects of Husband-wife Relations in Khasi Culture' he tried to shine some light on the extent of patriarchal beliefs in the Khasi culture. He tried to gauge various attitudinal dispositions of the Khasi society about married women such as decision-making, marital satisfaction, degree of restrictions, and dominance. He believed that even in the matrilineal tribal groups in Meghalaya, females did not have a better position as compared to the males. Through this study, Mukherjee broke the myth of female superiority in the Khasi community (Mukherjee, 1974b).

The work of Mukherjee clearly indicates his awareness and interest in the social culture beliefs and practices of India. He wrote papers such as 'Mass Media Exposure and Individual Modernity' (1978), 'Political Modernity and Mass Media Exposure: An Empirical Study in Five Developing Countries' (1978), and 'A Comparative Analysis of Some Indian Experience in Monitoring and Evaluation of Social Development Programmes' (1978). In the book *A Perspective on Psychology in India,* edited by Bimleshwar De and Durganand Sinha (1977), he reflected his concern for the social conditions of world in his chapter 'Background Factors and Mass Media Exposures as Predictors of General Awareness Level Among Factory Workers in Five Developing Countries'. He elaborated the effect of mass media exposure on the relationship between formal and informal education and general and political awareness of male factory workers in India, Nigeria, Chile, Bangladesh, and Israel (Mukherjee, 1977).

Mukherjee also contributed to the assessment of educational system. His contributions in this area includes 'Quality Control in Indian Educational Research' (1992), 'Needed Research in Psycho-educational Assessment in India' (1993), 'Toward a Rapprochement Between the Two Basic Paradigms of Educational Research' (1993), and 'Educational Assessment and Evaluation' (1997). His article 'Needed Research in Psycho-educational Assessment in India' published in *Psychological Studies* (1993) mentions the neglect of proper conceptualization and theoretical underpinning as well as methodology in the literature pertaining to Indian psycho-educational assessment. He criticized the haphazard and unsystematic manner in which the foreign tests and tools were adapted stating that 'the whole field of psycho-educational assessment in India is almost virgin and we need to start from the scratch if we are at all serious about indigenisation' (Mukherjee, 1993a). He described various areas of psycho-educational assessment as relevant, including research for identifying gaps, research in reconceptualization, selection for relevant theoretical framework, research for building up of a large pool of items, and multi-variate methods for assessing psychometric properties. His paper titled 'Toward a Rapprochement Between the Two Basic Paradigms of Educational Research' published in *Quality and Quantity* (1993) brings forth the advantages of an approach towards education that combines the scientific as well as the humanistic approach. While the natural-science approach promotes the hypothetico-deductive paradigm, the humanistic approach uses the more interpretive/symbolic paradigm. 'For enriching educational research, we need both analytical and synthetic orientations, micro and macro data, statistical and clinical predictions, deductive and inductive inference, as well as theoretic objectivity and practical valuations' (Mukherjee, 1993b). In 1997, Mukherjee published a chapter 'Educational Assessment and Evaluation' in the fifth survey of educational research (1988–92). He discussed the various trends in assessment and evaluation of education during that era, describing the rise in the development of assessment tests to measure different abilities other than academic intelligence such as criterion-reference tests, reading tests, achievement tests, aptitude tests, and so forth. He gave a detailed description of the important tests developed during that period, highlighting the pros and cons of each test (Mukherjee, 1997). He also analyzed the trends, gaps, and priority areas in assessment. He criticized the test-developing scenario of that time because most of it was focused on 'one-shot' studies (Mukherjee, 1965).

Critically examining the contemporary work done in the country, he contributed a chapter titled 'Psychological Theory and Research Methods' in the book *A Survey of Research in Psychology 1971–76 Part-I* edited by Udai Pareek. Besides summarizing the relevant work done in various areas of psychology with special reference to theoretical work done by Indian psychologists, he also reviewed conceptualization, reconceptualization, and measurement of psychological concepts, including mathematical models of human behaviour, attitude measurement, psychophysics, and development in the area of multivariate statistical analysis. He endorsed that Indian research lack seriousness in developing appropriate theoretical framework and giving adequate theoretical explanations to the empirical findings. He emphasized the need to 'draw out comprehensive research proposals before executing their studies' just like architects and engineers (Mukherjee, 1980). He also published three books—*A Laboratory Guide in Psychology* (1956), *Human Problems of Shift Work* (1971), and *Foundation of Multivariate Analysis: An Advanced Textbook* (1981).

He has the credit of developing seven tests—sentence completion test for measuring achievement values, incomplete sentence blank for measuring achievement motive, persistence disposition questionnaire, job attitude inventory, scale for measuring self-perceived and group-perceived status of women, self-insight test for measuring self-ideal discrepancies, and environmental preservation value inventory. In 1974, he published an article titled 'A Questionnaire Measure of Persistence Disposition' wherein he defined persistence as 'a personality trait characterized by a drive to remain steadfast in a chosen line of action in spite of opposition' (Mukherjee, 1974a). He developed a 20-item true-false persistent disposition questionnaire (PDQ).

## Editorial Work

Mukherjee was a consulting editor of *Multivariate Behavioral Research*, a quarterly journal published by the American Society of Multivariate Experimental Psychology, University of Colorado, Boulder, USA, from December 1956 to December 1968. In January 1972, once again he became the consulting editor of *Multivariate Behavioral Research* when its publication began from the University of Chicago. He also served as the consulting editor of *Social Change*. He was ad hoc reviewer of *Snakhya*, *Psychometrika*, *Indian Journal of Agricultural Statistics*, and the *British Journal of Mathematical and Statistical Psychology*. He was member of the editorial board of the second survey of *Research in Psychology* from 1971 to 1976 which was funded by the Indian Council of Social Science Research, New Delhi. He was also the founder editor of the newsletter of the Indian Society for Medical Statistics (1968–88). He was a member for the editorial board of the Social Change and Monograph Committee, National Psychological Corporation. Along with being a member of the editorial board, he also contributed a chapter to the fifth survey of educational research in India ("Ideal Role Model for Psychologists", n.d.).

## A Man of Varied Interests

B.N. Mukherjee is remembered for his interests and contributions to various fields of psychology and other allied areas. His fields of specializations included advanced statistics with special reference to multivariate statistical techniques, mathematical foundation of quantitative social science, personality assessment with special reference to cross-cultural problems, environmental psychology, population dynamics and demography, and evaluation and monitoring of social action programmes (Mukherjee, 1974c). He always endorsed the importance of developing theory and practices that are conducive to the Indian culture, rather than blindly adopting the Western theories. In one of his papers he mentions that 'psychology has to go native if it has to be creative and relevant in society' (Sinha, 1986). While reviewing research done in psychology between 1971 and 1976 in India, Mukherjee mentioned that 'in India, Psychology is in greater crisis because…it has failed to establish a meaningful linkage between practical needs of our country and the haphazard direction of psychological research in India' (Mukherjee, 1980).

Mukherjee bemoaned the lack of professional approach but was hopeful about the future of psychology in India. He encouraged the younger generation of psychologists to explore things from an inter-disciplinary standpoint, looking at applied social problems from sociological and anthropological, as well as economic points of view. The flame of inspirations became silent in 1997, but left behind an ever-inspiring story of hard work and excellence.

## Acknowledgements

Professors Gautam Gawali, R.V. Khubalkar, A.V. Kulkarni, and P. Dhare for providing information about B.N. Mukherjee.

## References

Ideal role model for psychologists (n.d.). Retrieved from Dr. Gawali.

Mukherjee, B.N. (1960). Reliability estimates for a modified two-hand coordination test. *Perceptual and Motor Skills, 11*(1), 13–14.

———. (1966). Derivation of likelihood ratio tests for Guttman quasi-simplex covariance structures. *Psychometrika, 31*(1), 97–123.

———. (1968). Importance ranking of job-related needs by Indian textile mill workers. *Indian Journal of Industrial Relations, 4*(2), 162–185.

———. (1969). A factor-analytic study of job satisfaction. *Indian Journal of Industrial Relations, 5*(4), 429–439.

———. (1973). Analysis of covariance structures and exploratory factor analysis. *British Journal of Mathematical and Statistical Psychology, 26*(2), 125–154 (IPA, 8:6).

———. (1974a). A questionnaire measure of persistence disposition. *Indian Journal of Psychology, 49* (December), 263–278.

———. (1974b). Restrictions on married women's activities and some aspects of husband-wife relations in Khasi culture. *Indian Anthropologist, 4*(2), 104–130.

———. (1974c). A comparison of the results of family planning KAP surveys in Haryana and Tamil Nadu, India. *Studies in Family Planning, 5*(7), 224–231.

———. (1975). The role of husband-wife communication in family planning. *Journal of Marriage and Family, 37*(3), 655–667.

———. (1976). Techniques of covariance structural analysis. *Australian Journal of Statistics, 18*(3), 131–150.

———. (1977) Background factors and mass media exposure as predictors of general awareness level among factory workers in five developing countries. In B. De and D. Sinha (Eds), *A perspective on Psychology in India* (pp. 210–247). Allahabad: Eagle Offset Printers.

Mukherjee, B.N. (1980). Psychological theory and research methods. In Udai Pareek (Ed.), *A Survey of Research in Psychology* (1971–76) Part I (1). Bombay: Popular Prakashan, 1–135.

———. (1993a). Needed research in psycho-educational assessment in India. *Psychological Studies, 38*(3), 85–100.

———. (1993b). Toward a rapprochement between the two basic paradigms of educational research. *Quality and Quantity, 27*(4), 383–410.

———. (1997). Educational assessment and evaluation: A trend report. In *Fifth survey of educational research: 1988–92,* New Delhi: NCERT, 670–694.

Mukherjee, B.N. & Menon, A.S. (1969). Personality characteristics and intra-individual variability in industrial output. *Indian Journal of Industrial Relations, 4*(4), 462–481.

Nagpur University. (1965, 1 April–1966, 31 March). *Annual report for the year 1965–66* (pp. 100–103). Nagpur: Author.

———. (1966, 1 April–1967, 31 March). *Annual report for the year 1966–67* (pp. 89–90) Nagpur: Author.

———. (1967, 1 April–1968, 31 March). *Annual report for the year 1967–68* (pp. 44–46). Nagpur: Author.

Sinha, D. (1986). *Psychology in a third world country: The Indian experience.* New Delhi: SAGE Publications India Pvt Ltd.

# Website Reference

www.nagpuruniversity.org/links/dep_psychology.htm

# 37

# Mohan Chandra Joshi

(1933–2010)

## Rama Charan Tripathi

*Mohan Chandra Joshi*

One of the first concerns of psychologists in India, after psychology made an entry into the university system 100 years back, was with the measurement of individual differences. The first test of intelligence in India by Rice was actually an adaptation of the Binet-Simon test and was constructed in the middle of the first decade of the twentieth century. The concern with the development of psychological tests continued well into the 1950s. Mohan Chandra Joshi belonged to this pioneering group of psychometricians.

He was born to Kumaoni Brahmin parents in a village in the district of Almora in 1933. His family traced its ancestry to Maharashtrian Brahmins like many other Kumaoni Brahmins do. His parents were relatively poor but valued education highly. It was because of this reason that after he completed primary education he was sent to the government intermediate college, Nainital. His school was considered an excellent school in the region and getting admission to such a school itself was considered quite an achievement. He passed out his high school and intermediate examinations obtaining a first division, considered something of a rarity in those days. It was not only education that he cared about but also about how young people could contribute in the process of nation building. India's struggle for independence had made a deep impression on his young mind. Largely due to this reason, he decided to pursue his higher studies at the Banaras Hindu University (BHU) which was established by Pandit Madan Mohan Malviya. The mission of the university was to train Indian minds in the best of the Indian tradition while they pursued modern education. Mohan Chandra Joshi's excellent academic background got him a scholarship but the amount was not enough to meet his boarding and other expenses at Banaras. He, therefore, decided to undertake tuitions to support his education. He completed his BA (honours) in 1952 and was among the top three students of his batch. His economic situation had eased a bit because one his professors in the Department of Philosophy and Psychology, B.L. Atreya, had become fond of him and took care of his accommodation. This, along with the merit scholarship that he got, permitted him to continue his postgraduate education in psychology at the BHU. The department at BHU, like many departments in India, was basically a department of philosophy which also offered an MA programme in psychology. The department, however, was recognized for some big names in philosophy including, Sarvapalli Radhakrishnan, T.R.V. Murti and B.L. Atreya. Very few of the philosophy faculty had received any formal training in psychology, though they had developed interest in studying psychological phenomena. Among these were Haridas Bhattacharya and B.L. Atreya. Atreya had supervised students for their doctoral studies in Indian psychology. He also was recognized for his work on parapsychology. Among the faculty was S. Jalota who had obtained his degree in psychology from a British university. He was recognized for his work in the area of intelligence testing. Mohan Chandra Joshi's interest lay in the emerging science of psychology. This drew him close to his teacher S. Jalota. Joshi completed his master's degree in 1954 and was awarded a gold medal for being the best student in his class. He was hired as a faculty soon after he completed his MA from BHU. In the meanwhile, he also enrolled for his PhD under S. Jalota. A number of students had completed their doctorate under him on psychological testing. Mohan Chandra Joshi also decided to work in the area of intelligence testing and decided to develop a group verbal test of primary mental ability. The submission of his PhD got delayed because he was awarded a Rotary Foundation Fellowship to pursue higher studies in psychology at Stanford University. He chose Stanford because that gave him a chance to study under some of the most distinguished psychometricians of his time, namely, Lewis Terman, Maud Merrill, L. Cronbach, and Quinn McNemar. It may be recalled that it was at Stanford University that the famous Stanford-Binet test was constructed by L. Terman which got used throughout the world. He returned to teach at BHU in 1957 after obtaining another master's degree in psychology from Stanford. His master's dissertation related to studying the influence of rural-urban differences, SES and caste on intelligence (Joshi, 1959).

Mohan Chandra Joshi moved to Sagar University in the latter half of 1959 as an assistant professor. In February 1960, he married Meera Katre, one of his former classmates and a niece of the famous Indian linguist, S.M. Katre. She too joined the Department of Psychology as an assistant professor. His stay at Sagar was for a brief period. He moved back to BHU in 1963 to his old department, which by then had become an independent department of psychology, as a Reader in clinical psychology. The years at Sagar were spent in contributing towards establishing a new department of psychology which was trying to find its moorings as a new discipline all over India after separating from its parent department of philosophy. He was among the first ones among the psychologists to publish technical papers in Hindi in the journal of Sagar University called *Madhya Bharti*. His second innings at BHU was a short one. He left after he was offered a professorship at Ravishankar University, Raipur, in 1969. He moved to Jodhpur National University in 1972 as professor and chair of the Department of Psychology where he also served as the dean of the faculty of arts before superannuating from the university in 1993. Soon thereafter, he became the vice-chancellor of Kumaon University. Besides being an excellent teacher, he was a true mentor and a great motivator and kept in regular contact with his students long after they had ceased to be his students. I was fortunate to be one of them. He was a great humanist, someone who always stood up for the underdog. These values also found reflection in his research as we will discuss later.

Mohan Chandra Joshi was deeply committed to the cause of the development of psychology in India and was part of several such initiatives. One such initiative was starting of a new psychology journal called *Indian Psychological Review*. This initiative was significant because there were not even half a dozen good psychology journals published out of India in those days. He was passionate about publishing only in Indian journals and always expected his students also to do the same. His argument was that the quality of psychological research in India will improve if good quality papers were published in the Indian journals. He had an inherent dislike for professional rivalries in the academia. His efforts to harmonize the relationship between the two major factions which operated then within the Indian Psychological Association (IPA) may be recalled in this context after he became its president. He tried to reenergize IPA by taking several new initiatives and giving a fresh lease of life to the association's journal, the *Indian Journal of Psychology*. His abiding interest in addressing social issues led him not only to working on problems of the socially excluded and marginalized sections of the Indian society in the context of intelligence and personality but also in lending support to the establishment of an association of community psychologists in India.

## Major Academic Contributions

A major issue that confronted psychologists in the 1950s related to investigating the role that was played by the environmental factors in the shaping of psychological dispositions and their stable attributes including intelligence. The studies carried out on identical twins may be given as an example. Such an interest was largely due to the issues that got raised subsequent to the treatment that was meted out to the Jews in the Nazi Germany. The Second World War also had led psychologists to investigate the significance of social factors and issues of social, economic, and political equality and, in general, of social justice in relation to personality attributes. Mohan Chandra Joshi's work that he had carried out at Stanford University fittingly addressed some of these issues. He was able to show that rural people and low socioeconomic status (SES) respondents scored low on intelligence tests. The caste-based differences in intelligence, however, were found to be non-significant. A major contribution that was to follow was the test he developed for the measurement of general mental ability (Joshi, 1960). The test consisted of seven sub-tests, namely, synonym, antonym, number series, classification, best answers, reasoning, and analogies, all which showed high amount of saturation on the 'g' factor. It was, perhaps, the first verbal group test of intelligence in India which employed the psychometric rigour expected by the APA in the case of educational and psychological tests. The test was standardized and norms developed on a sample of close to 4,000 respondents from six Hindi speaking states of the country (Joshi, 1960; 1981). The test has been widely used on Hindi speaking subjects and is basically a power test. Setting a time limit does not change the relative scores of the respondents very much (Joshi, 1956). Joshi followed up his group verbal test of intelligence with a non-verbal group test of intelligence for use with children (Joshi & Tripathi, 1968). This test too measured general mental ability and correlated highly with his verbal test of intelligence. It had four sub-tests, namely, classification, pattern recognition, analogies and picture arrangement. It provides age-wise and grade-wise norms. Joshi's major contribution lay in developing diagnostic instruments that could be used for the purposes of educational and clinical counselling. He was involved in developing an Indian adaptation of the Minnesota Multiphasic Personality Inventory (MMPI) for use with clinical population at SS Hospital of BHU (Joshi & Singh, 1966). This effort led further to the development and standardization of another diagnostic instrument called Jodhpur Multi-phasic Personality Inventory (JMPI) that he developed with one of his students, A.K. Malik (Joshi & Malik, 1981). JMPI has been widely used for research as well as for clinical purposes in India.

As assessment of human attributes was an abiding interest of Mohan Chandra Joshi. He also became interested in understanding how the differences in such attributes came about. Some of the research studies that he carried out focused on how child-rearing practices influenced the development of personality (Joshi & Dhaliwal, 1977; Joshi & Tiwari, 1977) and the impact of cultural heroes in the development of ego-ideals (Joshi & Joshi, 1967).

Unfortunately, not only has the tradition of psychological measurement which flourished in India well into the middle of the twentieth century waned considerably but so has the rigour which is required in the construction of such instruments. This is largely due to the fact that construction of psychological instruments is not seen as a proper research activity in the academic circles.

# References

Joshi, M.C. (1956). A study of intelligence scores with and without time-limit. *Indian Journal of Psychology*, *31*, 27–29.

———. (1959). The influence of rural-urban, socio-economic and caste differences on intelligence scores. Master's dissertation. Stanford, CA: Stanford University.

———. (1960). Construction and standardization of a group test of general mental ability in Hindi for school and college going students. Unpublished doctoral dissertation. Banaras Hindu University, Banaras.

Joshi, M.C., & Dhaliwal, A. (1977). Child rearing practices and personality of Satnamee children. *Indian Psychological Review*, *15*, 7–12.

Joshi, M.C., & Joshi, Meera M. (1967). Ego-ideals as symbolised by cultural heroes. *Indian Psychological Review*, *3*(2), 140–146.

———. (1981). *Manual of directions and revised norms for test of general mental ability*. Varanasi: Rupa Psychological Corporation.

Joshi, M.C., & Malik, A.K. (1981). *Jodhpur multiphasic personality inventory*. Varanasi: Rupa Psychological Centre.

Joshi, M.C., & Singh, B. (1966). Influence of socioeconomic background on the scores of some MMPI scales. *The Journal of Social Psychology*, *70*(2), 241–246.

Joshi, M.C., & Tiwari, J. (1977). Personality development of children in relation to child rearing practices among socio-economic classes. *Indian Psychological Review*, *14*, 5–15.

Joshi, M.C., & Tripathi, R.B. (1968). *Manual of directions and norms for non-verbal group test of intelligence*. Varanasi: Rupa Psychological Corporation.

# 38

## Prabhakar Anandrao Bhagwatwar

(1934)

Satishchandra Kumar, Anjali Majumdar, Tejal Dhulla, Heena Kamble, and Aarti Ramaswami

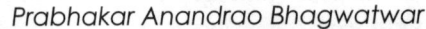

*Prabhakar Anandrao Bhagwatwar*

Prabhakar Anandrao Bhagwatwar was born on 28 June 1934 in Talodhi (Balapur) district of Chandrapur, Maharashtra. He spent the first 6 years of his life in Talodhi village and in 1940 his parents moved to Nagpur for their children's education. He was the youngest of four sons. His education, both in school and college, was completed in Nagpur. He studied in New English High

School in Nagpur and completed his college graduation from S.B. City College, Nagpur, in 1956. He came to Pune to do his masters in psychology from the Department of Experimental Psychology, Pune University, and completed it in 1958.

Bhagwatwar had always been interested in the applied value of psychology and wanted to have the connection between psychology and the world of work. In 1966, he enrolled for a PhD under V.K. Kothurkar of Pune University and completed his doctoral thesis in 1969.The topic of his research work was 'Comparative Study of the Impact of Community Development Programme on Personality Dynamics, Attitudes and Social Change in Maharashtra with Special Reference to Mulshi and Purandhar Taluka'.

In 1960, Bhagwatwar joined S.P. College, Pune, as a lecturer. He remained at that post till 1966 after which he became the head of psychology department, S.P. College, and remained its head until 1987. He later moved to the University Department of Applied Psychology as professor and head from 1987 till 1994. While sharing his journey of psychology he says 'When I joined S.P. College it was a one person department and there was no provision for psychology, especially at the graduation level. From that stage he transformed the department into a recognized postgraduate centre, renowned for Industrial and Organizational psychology'. When he left the department in 1987, its strength was 10. He says,

> I insisted and always went to V.K. Kothurkar in Pune University to start Industrial Psychology, and on my request he started the same in Pune University. I was the first student of the first batch of Industrial Psychology, and from 1961 the responsibility of teaching Industrial Psychology was handed over to me till 1972, when I started the postgraduate center in S.P. College in Pune; all syllabi till 1972 of Industrial Psychology were framed, developed and revised either by me or under my leadership.

Bhagwatwar was also a visiting faculty at Symbiosis Institute of Management, Pune, from 1979 to 1984 and Institute of Management Development and Research (IMDR), Pune, from 1976 to 1984.

He joined the University of Mumbai on 29 June 1987 as professor and head of the University Department of Applied Psychology (UDAP). Bhagwatwar believes that industrial psychology has tremendous applied value. According to him, 'an Industrial Psychologist should first identify the industrial problem and then work on it'. In an educational university, a person identifies their problems, collects data, and so on; however, this endeavour is for selfish individualistic purposes and not for applied purposes. During his tenure in the University of Mumbai, he tried to make the curriculum more applied by changing the syllabus and also changing the examination pattern. In 1988, the department unofficially started a counselling center in August under the headship of Bhagwatwar (Annual Report, 1987–1988). Even though the center was officially established in 1995, Bhagwatwar is credited for working on the proposal to the University Grant Commission to start the counselling center in UDAP, University of Mumbai. This center extended various types of services to adults, students and children, and old people in areas such as family therapy, marriage counselling, adjustment problem, psychological disorders, psychotherapy, vocational choice, vocational adjustment, problems of old age, and post-retirement problems (Annual Report, 1987–1988). This counselling center was not a teaching activity, but the application of psychology to help the people to have a correct understanding of their problems and suggest the remedial measures or help them to identify the remedial measures themselves (Annual Report, 1987–1988).

During his tenure at the University of Mumbai, he organized two conferences. The first, 'Intervention Strategies for Human Resource Development' was held from 24 to 26 February, 1989 (Annual Report, 1988–1989). Durganand Sinha, who was the head of the department, Department of Psychology, University of Allahabad, at that time, and Fr Romuald D'Souza, director of XLRI (Xavier School of Management, formerly Known as Xavier Labour Relations Institute), Jamshedpur, were guests of honour at this conference. The other conference, 'Leadership Challenge for Human Resource Development', was held from 14 to 16 December, 1990 (Annual Report, 1990–1991). It was attended by Udai Pareek and D.M. Pestonjee, who were both associated with Indian Institute of Management (IIM), Ahmedabad, at the time.

It was the vision of Bhagwatwar, along with Mehroo Bengalee, vice-chancellor of the University of Mumbai, and the faculty of UDAP, that led to the official attachment of the counselling center on 10 October, 1995. The center was placed in a building near the Jawaharlal Nehru Library, which was named C.D. Deshmukh Bhavan. The building was formally inaugurated by the then vice-chancellor Shashikant Karnik on 26 January 1995. The counselling center which was housed at the Fort campus was shifted to the Deshmukh building, Kalina Campus, Santacruz (East), in July 1995 (Annual Report, 1995–1996).

Bhagwatwar has a mixed opinion about psychology on the whole. On one hand, he feels that psychology has great value for the society; on the other hand, he feels it is not truly applied in the Indian society. He reasons that this is so because psychology and society are mutually exclusive; psychology is not interested in society, and neither is society interested in psychology. He mentions 'all applied field of psychology is without application in Indian context'. In order to have an impact in Indian context, this mutual exclusivity must change. If psychology, as a profession, wants to make an inroad in all walks of our life, it must be connected to the social milieu. He feels that theory and application of psychology should go hand in hand.

In his write up on remembrance (A Collection of Psychological Episodes) which was published by Indian Association of Human Behavior, Pune, V.K. Kothurkar remembers Bhagwatwar as a psychologist with splendid obsession for the teaching facilities for industrial psychology in the department of experimental psychology (Kothurkar, n.d.). Kothurkar mentioned that he yielded to these demands, and taught him from the only book available to him which was written by Viteles. He praised Bhagwatwar for mastering the subject on his own, and making a name for himself in the subject. Kothurkar also praised his insightful psychology.

## Professional Affiliations

Bhagwatwar has been affiliated to various associations and institutions. He has been a member of Indian Science Congress from 1969 to 1975, Indian Psychological Association, and American Psychological Association (APA). He is a lifetime member of the Indian Academy of Applied Psychology, Bombay Psychological Association (BPA), Marathi Manasshastra Parishad, Indian Association of Mental Health, and Indian Association of Human Behaviour. He chaired one session at the Marathi Manasshastra Parishad– III Session, held on 30–31 January, 1988, Sholapur (Annual Report, 1987–1988).

He has also conducted many assessment and training programmes for various organizations such as Larsen and Toubro (Bombay), Indian Oil Corporation (Bombay), Siemens India Limited (Bombay), Railway Staff Training (Baroda), Land Development Bank (Pune), and Maharashtra Agro-Industries Development Corporation (MAIDC). He also conducted training programmes in educational institutes such as Goa University, Karnataka University, National Institute of Training in Industrial Engineering (NITIE, Mumbai; Annual Report, 1988–1989), and Training Program College of Agricultural Banking (Pune).

He has also held many respected administrative and advisory positions at various institutions. Bhagwatwar was the area chair (Western Maharashtra) of International Council of Psychologists (ICP) from 1990 to 1993. He was a member of the advisory committee of Yashwantrao Chavan Maharashtra Open University, Nasik, from 1990 to 2000, the Institute of Banking Personnel Selection (IBPS, Mumbai) from 1988–1994, and the Indian Council of Social Science Research (ICSSR) from 1987 to 1990. When the Railway Ministry, Government of India, formed a committee to look into the causes of railway accidents in 1993, he was a member of that committee. This committee was chaired by D.P. Sen Majumdar, who was the director of the psychology wing in defence services. The report showed findings that the main cause of accidents was incompatible selection which resulted in human errors. They included suggestions for abilities required by motormen as well as vigilance functions of motormen.

## Research and Publications

Bhagwatwar has extensively published throughout his career. His project 'Pre-Medicine and Pre-Engineering Aptitude Test' was funded by the ICSSR, New Delhi, in 1970. This test was published in 1973. He was also a senior research fellow for ICSSR (New Delhi) for 2 years post his retirement (December 2000). During that duration he worked on *Organizational Effectiveness: An Information Processing Model*. He guided eight PhD candidates as well as six MPhil and 20 MA dissertations. In 1972, he published *Community Development Programme: A Psycho-Social Study*. This book covered social psychology in rural places in Maharashtra. Between 1975 and 1980, he authored seven books. These include *Sugam Manasshastra, Samayojan Manasshastra, Samajik Manasshastra, Samanya Manasshastra, Upayojit Manasshastra, Psychology of Industrial Behavior,* and *Psychology of Industrial Behaviour* (Revised). Other books written by him include *General Psychology, Organizational Behaviour,* and *Psychology of Industrial and Organizational Behaviour*. His book *Industrial and Organizational Psychology* was published by Sheth Publishers in June 1987 (Annual Report, 1986–1987). He has also authored a monograph titled, 'Organizational Excellence', published by the Indian Association of Human Behaviour (Bhagwatwar, 2008). He also developed and published three widely used questionnaires, 'Pre-Medicine and Pre-Engineering Aptitude Test', 'Organizational Efficiency Questionnaire (OEQ)', and 'Stress Questionnaire'.

## References

Bhagwatwar, P.A. (2008). *Organizational excellence monograph*. Pune: Indian Association of Human Behaviour.

Kothurkar, V.A. (n.d.). *Remembrances (A collection of psychological episodes)*. Pune: Sawkar Art Service. Obtained from C.G. Deshpande.

University of Bombay. (1986, 1 April–1987, 31 March). *Annual report for the year 1986–1987* (pp. 51–52). Bombay: Author.

———. (1987, 1 April–1988, 31 March). *Annual report for the year 1987–1988* (pp. 66–68). Bombay: Author.

———. (1988, 1 April–1989, 31 March). *Annual report for the year 1988–1989* (pp. 57–58). Bombay: Author.

———. (1990, 1 April–1991, 31 March). *Annual report for the year 1990–1991* (pp. 67–68). Bombay: Author.

———. (1995, 1 April—1996, 31 March). *Annual report for the year 1995–1996* (pp. 22–23). Bombay: Author.

# 39

## Suresh Kanekar

(1934)

## Chithprabha Kudlu

*Suresh Kanekar*

'I plead guilty to being a psychologist' is the opening line of Suresh Kanekar's satirical essay where he describes the travails faced in his interactions with the lay public. Recounting several hilarious encounters including a bizarre request for palm reading, he states tongue-in-cheek, 'I am really surprised by the fact that many people mix me up with Freud. I do not like it; nor would Freud, I am sure'. In his characteristic style laced with self-deprecatory humour Kanekar writes about how even admirers were 'scandalized' by his 'professional incompetence' on discovering his inability to offer solutions to their problems. An experimental social psychologist's difficulty in conveying his job description in lay terms comes as no surprise, but Kanekar finds he has to battle similar stereotypes in professional circles. As he observes in another essay, 'the social scientist is sometimes confused with a social worker and is expected to contribute to the solution of social problems'. A behaviourist who firmly believes in the positivist approach to the study of human behaviour, Kanekar is critical of social scientists mixing up their personal agendas with research. In his opinion, 'the job of the social scientist is to analyze and understand social phenomena, not to reform criminals or to promote family planning'. Value neutrality, in his eyes, is a prerequisite for an objective understanding of social phenomena.

In keeping with his philosophy of science, Kanekar's academic work is by and large restricted to empirical inquiry and quantitative analysis of social phenomena, but the deeper philosophical questions that motivate this inquiry get expression in his semi-academic and popular writings. A prolific writer, Kanekar has published scores of analytical articles, poems, and satirical pieces in national dailies like the *Times of India* and reputed literary magazines like the *New Quest*. The writer in him effortlessly switches from a dry, formal academic style to a lucid, readable style targeted at a popular audience. Far from being an ivory tower scientist, Kanekar brings to bear his psychological expertise on a variety of socially relevant subjects ranging from love to violence, and intelligence testing to sexual aggression. This deep engagement with society came naturally to Kanekar whose formative years were shaped by his involvement as an activist at the forefront of the Goan liberation movement.

# Evolution of a Spirited Freedom Fighter into a Committed Academic

The regularity of Kanekar's exemplary academic career belies an unconventional youth. Born in 1934 in Ponda, in the then Portuguese territory of Goa, Suresh Kanekar spent his early childhood in Panaji and Mapusa, studying in Marathi, Portuguese, and English schools in succession. As a student of intermediate arts in Karnatak College, his attention was divided amongst a multitude of activities ranging from table tennis to dramatics. In his memoirs, Kanekar describes himself as being an indifferent student during his early schooling and an irresponsible one during his college years. Indecisive and aimless after emerging from college with a BA (honours) in philosophy in 1953, he found himself drawn to the Goan freedom movement that had just then begun to gather steam. Little did he know then the significance of this whimsical decision which he describes as being 'escapism at worst and romanticism at best'. Nevertheless, Kanekar appears to have had the right attributes of a freedom fighter—unflinching commitment to principles and infinite supply of guts that more than made up for his avowed deficiency of patriotism, qualifying him for five years of rigorous imprisonment. Ironically, the Portuguese unwittingly provided a fertile training ground; the prison environment in Fort Aguada provided him with opportunities to interact with the stalwarts of the Goan liberation movement. The 25-year-old who emerged from the prison in 1959 was deeply committed to the patriotic cause for which he continued to work until the Goan independence.

Once outside prison, Kanekar had to find a way to earn his daily bread. Capitalizing on his BA degree, he garnered a headmaster's position in Damodar Vidyalaya, one of the largest and reputed schools in Goa. This period of Kanekar's life was relatively peaceful, though eventful. He had to suffer one more arrest and imprisonment, though brief. It was also during this time that he met his future wife, Kumud Kakodkar, the sister of Mitra Kakodkar alias Bir, a renowned freedom fighter. In keeping with his commitment to the patriotic cause he had joined the National Congress (Goa). By the time of Goa's liberation in 1961, Suresh Kanekar had become a well-known public figure in the state. A career in public life would have been the next logical step to take, but Kanekar felt that academics suited his aptitude better. In 1962, he resigned both from his job and the National Congress to pursue graduate studies at the University of Poona. Psychology, a subject to which he was exposed in his undergraduate years, seemed a logical choice. Though he intended to specialize in educational psychology, the very first course he took impressed him so much that he changed his preference instantly to social psychology. The professor who taught this course was the renowned experimental psychologist V.K. Kothurkar, who after graduating from the University of Cambridge had set up the Department of Experimental Psychology in Poona in 1950. Kothurkar continued to be an important influence all through Kanekar's academic career.

This time around, Kanekar had decided to take his studies seriously and was determined to do well in exams. But given the penniless state in which he had arrived in Poona, a good amount of his time was lost in odd jobs such as tutoring and administrative assistance. Moreover, extra-curricular activities of various kinds including sports, dramatics, music, and debating took away some of his attention. In spite of the distractions, Kanekar not only broke previous performance records in psychology but also stood first for the entire social science division in the university. The next three years went into undergraduate teaching at Chowgule College and graduate teaching at Nagpur University. Meanwhile, he had begun to work towards his dream of pursuing doctoral studies in the USA. In 1966, Kanekar was awarded both the Fulbright Travel Grant and the highly competitive US Government Scholarship. Soon after, he left for the USA to enrol in the social psychology doctoral programme in the University of Iowa. Here he worked on the experimental study of group performance under the mentorship of Milton E. Rosenbaum. At Iowa, Kanekar had the opportunity to interact and learn from a number of senior psychologists including Judson Brown, Rudolf Schulz, and Harold Bechtoldt. An important intellectual influence on him was Gustav Bergmann, a renowned philosopher and psychologist, previously one of the youngest members of the Vienna Circle. While working towards his doctorate, Kanekar also gathered teaching experience as a part-time faculty member  as a full-time visiting faculty member at Lawrence University in Appleton, Wisconsin.

In 1972, after completing his doctorate, Kanekar returned to India. Soon after, he joined as Reader in the Department of Applied Psychology in the University of Bombay. His two decades of tenure here as teacher and researcher were highly productive, not in the least dampened by the inefficient and hostile bureaucracy and a mediocre academic environment that he describes in his memoirs. Though there were many individual academicians and administrators of integrity who supported Kanekar, politicking often came in the way of work and nepotism won over considerations of merit. Kanekar attributes some of his difficulties to his individualistic attitude and outspoken nature. Nonetheless, the university's failure to grant professorship to an academician of such outstanding accomplishment is not something that can be easily explained away. While we remember, acknowledge, and celebrate Kanekar's life and accomplishments, we must bear in mind that he achieved what he did in spite of the uninspiring institutional environment that prevailed around him at that time.

## Contributions to the Field of Psychology

Kanekar is an social experimental psychologist interested in various aspects of human behaviour in social settings. Along with various collaborators, Kanekar has conducted empirical studies on most of the major areas in the field of social psychology including attribution, affiliation, helping behaviour, group performance, social learning, attitudes, interpersonal attraction, ethical norms, and gender bias. He has also briefly touched upon topics such as academic performance, romantic love, personality attributes, and so on. Kanekar's work has to be read in the context of the topical and methodological orientation of American experimental social psychology in the 1970s–1980s, which had its ideological moorings in behaviourism at the University of Iowa.

In the area of group performance, Kanekar formulated two useful concepts for classifying groups, namely, 'quasi-group' and 'pseudo-group'. His most significant theoretical contribution is in the area of 'attribution of responsibility', an area pioneered by Fritz Heider and later elaborated by Bernard Weiner. Kanekar established a distinction between moral and causal responsibility on the strength of evidence gathered by a series of research studies conducted in the 1980s. The studies investigated determinant influences played by various demographic, personal, and situational characteristics on responsibility attribution. Studies conducted by Kanekar and associates set a trend that was followed by researchers working on the area of attribution in India in the ensuing decades.

Kanekar is a pioneer in the social psychological study of attitudes towards sexual aggression in India. He deserves special mention for applying his mind to an issue that had until then received little academic attention. In fact, the largest chunk of his empirical research examined responsibility attribution behaviour in the context of various forms of sexual aggression. The programmatic research initiated by Kanekar on rape attributions had its beginnings in his personal misgivings of the counterintuitive findings of a 1973 study by Jones and Aronson. The study found that a more respected rape victim (a married woman) was blamed more for her rape than a less respectable victim (a divorced woman). Over the years, Kanekar along with his research students and associates conducted several studies, none of which substantiated the findings of Jones and Aronson. Among other issues examined in the experiments were the rape victim's causal versus moral responsibility, the rapist–victim relationship, the gender-adversary perspective, and the ambiguity about victim's consent. The studies consistently demonstrated that victims of sexual aggression were viewed more harshly by the dominant male segment in the Indian society when compared to findings of similar studies in Western societies. In terms of judgmental variations obtained as a function of rapist–victim acquaintance and participant's gender, they reflected the relatively low status of women and the patriarchal dominance of men in Indian society. Kanekar describes the context and relevance of his findings in a semi-academic essay. Though there has been much progress on the legal front over the past two decades, issues raised by Kanekar are of much relevance today given the increasing incidence of sexual violence against women in India.

Kanekar's scholarly contribution is not limited to empirical-study-based research reports. He has also dealt with issues of theoretical and methodological significance in various analytical articles. Of special mention are his essays on Skinner. Kanekar, who comes across otherwise as an unabashed admirer of Skinner's behaviourist doctrine, makes some incisive observations that question the epistemological foundations of radical behaviourism. He identifies inherent contradictions in Skinner's thinking, pointing out that,

> Skinner's eminently justifiable deterministic position regarding the lawfulness and controllability of human behaviour makes nonsense of his Cassandraesque prediction that human cultures will fail in the absence of better designs, especially in the absence of objective criteria for 'better' designs outside of the evolutionary process.

An important conceptual analysis provided by Kanekar is the distinction between as-is and as-if approaches to the problem of determinism versus freedom of will. This approach allows for fixing moral responsibility on individual actions without departing from the philosophical framework of determinism. Kanekar's other important analytical articles include a discussion on the relevance of social science, a critical evaluation of Freud, a critical review of the scientific understanding of romantic love, and an analytical appraisal of the concept of non-directive generalized drive.

At the University of Bombay, Kanekar taught a range of courses including social psychology, history and systems of psychology, and research methods and statistics. Kanekar is remembered by his students for his informative and intellectually stimulating classes. In a lucid description of his philosophy of teaching, Kanekar makes his commitment to teaching loud and clear saying that he believed 'the function of creating knowledge' to be more important than 'the mere imparting of knowledge'. He states that despite being more inclined towards research, a pure research career would not have appealed to him because 'A young mind, brimming with curiosity, wonder, and questioning, can stimulate as well as invigorate more determined and sustained efforts toward conceptual cleansing and intellectual integrity'.

During his tenure, Kanekar had also supervised four PhDs, nine MPhils, and seven masters' dissertations. Among his research students, he was known as a tough and meticulous taskmaster who would not tolerate even a single comma being out of order. A research student recollects being sent back for being 45 seconds late for an appointment, pointing out that he 'never settled for less than perfect'. At the same time, she remembers him as an exceptional mentor who encouraged even master's students to publish papers in reputed peer-reviewed journals. She says, 'What I liked most was being treated like a thinking adult who would have to come up with her own learnings. He didn't teach ever, he either role modeled or inspired'.

## Accomplishments and Affiliations

When he retired from the University of Bombay in 1995, Kanekar had over 115 academic articles to his credit. These were published in a variety of reputed journals including the *American Psychologist*, *Journal of Social Psychology*, *Journal of Applied Social Psychology*, *British Journal of Psychology*, *European Journal of Psychology*, *Australian Journal of Psychology*, *Human Relations*, *Psychonomic Science*, and *Behavioral and Brain Sciences*. He has also served as a reviewer for several American and European journals. Kanekar has published two academic books, one based on his doctoral thesis and the other on the subject of attitude formation, a product of an unsolicited UGC grant for a university-level book.

During his tenure in the University of Bombay, Kanekar had also served in advisory and administrative capacities for the University Grants Commission (UGC), the Indian Council of Social Sciences Research, the Union Public Service Commission, the Ministry of Defense, the Maharashtra Public Service Commission, and so on. He also worked as chairman of the board of studies in psychology of the University of Bombay in 1984–1985 and 1986–1987.

Kanekar is currently an international affiliate of the American Psychological Association. In the past, he has been a member of various professional bodies including the Indian Academy of Applied Psychology, Midwestern Psychological Association, Western Psychological Association, Sigma Xi, and New York Academy of Sciences.

Though two decades have passed since his official retirement, Kanekar has never really retired from academics. Soon after his retirement from the University of Bombay, he migrated to the USA where he continued to work as adjunct faculty member in various universities including the University of Phoenix, United States International University, San Diego State University, and California School of Professional Psychology.

Meanwhile, he managed to make good use of his spare time to accomplish his long standing dream of writing a novel. The novel, *Mangoes and Monsoons*, set in pre-liberation Goa, is partly biographical. Subsequently, he also published a book of his memoirs which includes a view of Goa during his childhood, a personal narrative of the Goan liberation movement, and a brief account of his graduate student days in the USA and his academic career in India.

In brief, Kanekar's life and accomplishments stand testimony to a motto that his students have often heard him citing, 'Strive for perfection and settle for excellence'.

Suresh Kanekar currently works as a research professor at Alliant International University in San Diego, California. A young man in his 80s, Kanekar divides his time among research, teaching table tennis, and playing bridge. The puzzle of determinism versus free will, biological basis of behaviour, epistemology, and such other philosophical issues continue to occupy his inquisitive mind.

# 40

# Gurpur Gaurishankar Prabhu

(1935)

## Ahalya Raguram

*Gurpur Gaurishankar Prabhu*

Clinical psychology as an independent discipline was established about 65 years ago. However, its early formative years were overshadowed by the larger field of psychiatry. G.G. Prabhu is among the foremost contributors towards shaping of this field, enabling it to emerge from the shadow of psychiatry and crystallize an identity of its own. He made an indelible mark on this field during his professional career spanning over 55 years and continues to do so thereafter. He has taught and mentored scores of trainees from the fields of clinical psychology, psychiatry, nursing, and several other disciplines as well. What were the origins of his interest in psychology and how did he gravitate towards clinical psychology? What were the major influences that determined his choices and how did they unfold?

## The Journey Begins

Gurpur Gaurishankar Prabhu was born on 2 September 1935 and raised in Madras (now Chennai) in a family with high academic and intellectual attainments. His childhood was uneventful except for the fact that even before he reached adolescence, he was perceived as a person of strong views and very decided preferences, attributes that persisted all through his life. As a voracious reader, he encountered several seminal works published around that time excited his adolescent curiosity and interest—Freud's writings on the workings of the psyche and the newly published Kinsey report which was the most detailed exposition for the first time of human sexual behaviour. As these books delineated ideas that were new, revolutionary, and perceived by some to be even shocking, they were often read surreptitiously. It was another book given to him by his uncle, a colonel in the British army, titled *Psychology for the Fighting Man* that opened up for him the vast possibilities for the application of psychological principles. As an adolescent, the idea of using psychology in the field of defence was at once novel and thrilling.

The steady course on which he had embarked was disrupted by an unexpected turn of events. This came in the form of the completely unanticipated and premature death of his father to whom he was deeply attached. Death was to play another significant and life-altering role later on as well. Already, by then, a person of strong views and very decided preferences, the natural rebelliousness typical of adolescence was fuelled by the loss of this very significant relationship. Unsettled by the turbulence, the family decided that a change of scene and the presence of a calming influence would be beneficial for his future. A decision was made by the family to send him to Calcutta, to reside with his father's elder brother who was a monk (Swami Vireswarananda) at the Ramakrishna Mission, who later on became its president for nearly two decades. This sojourn and the wise counsel provided by his uncle had its desired effect and young Prabhu became more 'manageable,' though in his own words 'the rebelliousness has never completely died down'. He describes an incident of some significance that occurred during this period, though its import became evident to him only much later on. Every few days, a black car would come to take his uncle on a visit and Prabhu was usually taken along. They would go over to the house of a man who Prabhu remembers as being 'very tall and huge'. There, this person and his uncle would converse for an hour or two at a time. As the conversations were in Bengali, Prabhu could not follow the content; in any case, his attention was more drawn to the large platter of sweets that were offered at every visit! This man would usually pat and ruffle his hair when they left. It was more than a decade later that Prabhu discovered the identity of the person whom they regularly visited and its enormous significance—Girindrasekar Bose, the father of psychoanalysis in India and about whose contributions Prabhu was to write about in later years. Though oblivious at that time, he believes that that gesture of Girindrasekar Bose was a blessing bestowed on him.

By the time he completed his inter-science (current pre-university level), he had decided to pursue psychology for his undergraduate studies at the University of Calcutta. Two factors weighed in his choice of the University of Calcutta. First, it was one of the centres in India where psychology was a vibrant and thriving discipline and second, his earlier exposure to Calcutta. However, family compulsions intervened and he applied for and obtained a seat in engineering under the sports quota, having represented the university as a strike bowler. This stint lasted precisely 18 days—the idea of pursuing a course which he had got into on criteria other than merit was anathema to him. It resulted in his quitting the course much to the disappointment of his mother. However, the conviction that merit should be paramount in higher education endured all through his career. Thus, the first steps in the long journey were initiated in 1953 by his joining the newly introduced psychology (honours) programme in 1951 by the University of Madras. A brief but significant encounter during this period further strengthened this resolve. The department organized a talk for the students by a visiting professor—a rare occurrence in itself. The professor, a short man about 5 feet 4 inches in height, simply attired in a dhoti, kurta, and shawl, made a deep and lasting impression in his short talk on whole group. The professor raised the pertinent question as to why they were all pursuing psychology. He pointed out that if it was to enable them to find jobs as lecturers, they would then only be teachers, not psychologists. One has to render psychological services to the society in order to be a psychologist in the true sense of the term. This short interaction, however, lingered in Prabhu's mind for many days and decisively influenced his subsequent choices. The professor whom he never met thereafter was Raj Narayan of the University of Lucknow.

For a young person aspiring for a career in psychology in India, the early 1950s seemed an opportune moment to ride the wave and the prospects seemed limitless—expansion in the universities, the government's interest and commitment to expand psychological services for the public, the corporate support for this venture, albeit short-lived, as well as the previously mentioned possibilities of its role in the defence services of the country. The die was cast and Prabhu firmly set foot on the path to a career in psychology. Clearly, the decision was not due to chance or lack of merit; psychology for many years was considered to be the last refuge of those whose marks were not sufficient to allow them to join other courses, especially for young men. For him, it was an informed choice and psychology seemed to draw him into its fold, offering limitless opportunities.

On completion of his studies at the University of Madras in 1956, Prabhu joined as a tutor in psychology at the government college (now known as the university college of the Mangalore University) of the Karnatak University, a position on which he worked for two years. Incidentally one of his early students in the BA class was Malavika Karanth who later on as an assistant professor (1981, Malavika Kapur) became his colleague at NIMHANS and who, as an additional professor, took charge of the department from him in 1995 when he superannuated. However, the spark ignited by Raj Narayan, to strive to use psychology for alleviating the problems of the common man continued to glow. Therefore, when the opportunity presented itself, he went over to the All India Institute of Mental Health (AIIMH) at Bangalore to pursue a diploma in medical psychology (DMP) as clinical psychology training was then called. He joined the course in 1959, the fifth batch to undergo training. The training programme there, however, had several lacunae, foremost among them being the fact that while there were several notable persons on the faculty, none of them had been specifically trained in clinical psychology. Thus, trainees acquired skills in interviewing techniques and arriving at a diagnosis and were exposed to psychological theory and psychodiagnostic assessment. They were taught the theoretical aspects of psychotherapy and psychoanalysis, but there was a glaring lack of practical experience or training in therapeutic techniques.

On completion of the DMP course, an opportunity arose in the form of an assistant professor's post at the Central Institute of Psychiatry (CIP) at Ranchi. At the same time, he was also selected as a lecturer at the Annamalai University. As there were great opportunities to pursue his passion for cricket at the latter place and none in Ranchi, he seriously considered accepting the position at Annamalai University. However, on the sane advice offered by a family friend T.E. Shanmugam, who later became professor at the University of Madras, that 'cricket would last for another 4–5 years but psychology was for life', he abandoned that idea and went over to Ranchi to take up position as an assistant professor. The department there too had its own set of problems as the other post of psychologist was vacant and the only other staff member of the department was an assistant psychologist. Prabhu rose to the onerous challenge of running the training programme with nine students virtually single-handedly, including providing guidance for their dissertation work. At the same time, he involved himself more seriously in psychotherapy, making copious notes of the sessions and the processes involved and discussing them later with Dr Bhaskaran who was then the deputy medical superintendent of CIP, a form of informal supervision. The tireless efforts that he put in to keep the training programme going received endorsement from a completely unexpected source. The functioning of the AIIMH, Bangalore, reached a nadir and, hence, Erna Hoch, a WHO consultant and mental health advisor to the Government of India, was requested to assess the functioning of both centres of mental health in the country and submit her recommendations. She spent 15 days each at Bangalore and Ranchi, intensively observing all the activities including the lecture classes, case discussions, etc. She outlined several sweeping changes to be made, including a shift of the Bangalore centre to Ranchi. In her report to the government, she also alluded to the fact that while the functioning of the Bangalore centre itself was far from satisfactory, yet a person trained there and working at Ranchi was doing a highly commendable job in running the training programme. This was a true accolade indeed coming from the highest echelon of the Ministry of Health. During his stint at Ranchi, Prabhu began to delve into the Rorschach Inkblot Test by way of both training and research. He corresponded with Klopfer who was highly appreciative of his work. At the same time, he also registered for his PhD with the Rorschach Test as the subject of enquiry. One of his major international publications, 'A Rorschach Profile of Normal Indian Subjects,' was an outcome of this endeavour. Several other papers on various aspects of the Rorschach followed, spanning the period between 1962 and 1978.

After spending a little less than 2 years at CIP, Prabhu contemplated a move to the All India Institute of Medical Sciences (AIIMS) in New Delhi. He was advised against this move for several reasons. First, the post was that of a clinical psychologist and not a faculty level one as per the prevailing rules of the Medical Council of India. Second, the setting was that of a general hospital and doubts about the sustainability of providing mental health care in such a setting were persistently voiced. Third, his PhD registration could not be continued due to the shift. Despite all these drawbacks, he chose to go ahead with the move. He encountered new challenges working in an environment very different from the mental hospital setting that he had trained and worked in earlier—a widely prevalent ignorance about the scope of clinical psychology, a completely different type of (non-psychotic) clientele, and the need to evolve a distinctive approach to assessments that would be suitable and relevant for the setting. He threw himself into the task of addressing these issues with characteristic vigour. As a guiding principle, he decided that rather than looking westwards for inspiration, clinical psychology could make an indelible mark in the country and establish its relevance only by focusing upon indigenous needs and issues and finding solutions. Among the first of such tasks that he undertook was the adaptation and standardization of several questionnaires and inventories that were required for use in the new clinical setting. He began by establishing norms derived from the Indian population for the Eysenck's Personality Inventory, Crown and Crisp's Middlesex Hospital Questionnaire, Beck and Hamilton's rating scales for depression, and others. With these tools, he was able to demonstrate to the medical fraternity that many psychological constructs could be objectively and systematically measured and the findings utilized to inform interventions. Gradually, referrals began from various departments including neurology, paediatrics, dermatology, and even ophthalmology to deal with a case of 'cataract psychosis.' The endocrinology department had initiated a major project of enormous public health significance to examine iodine deficiency in the country and its consequences. Prabhu played a key role in the evaluation of intelligence of the population studied, to estimate the prevalence of intellectual backwardness. These efforts resulted in many publications and laid the foundation for the emergence of health psychology in the country; in fact, Prabhu can well be described as the first health psychologist of the country.

Despite these developments, he felt that clinical psychology needed to expand its reach even further. This came about through a very different path. AIIMS had introduced the teaching of behavioural and social sciences for the undergraduate students for the first three semesters. Prabhu discovered that while a syllabus for teaching these subjects existed, it was not comprehensive or well thought out for the context. His first task, therefore, was to conceptualize and structure the syllabus with the objectives clearly spelt out, then followed the task of operationalizing it, monitoring and evaluating its impact, and making the necessary modifications. These classes became very popular with the undergraduate students and drew students from medical colleges as well. It was a well-formulated presentation of psychology as a base not just for psychiatry but for medicine as a whole. There was a lot of emphasis given by the WHO and other medical schools abroad, including Harvard, to humanizing medicine and these classes gave the impetus to inculcate this spirit in the trainees. Apart from these reasons, many of the undergraduates who were aspiring to go abroad had to take the Educational Commission for Foreign Medical Graduates (ECFMG) examination which had a large component of psychology. They had a ready option offered by these classes to help their preparations for the exam. Once the programme was consolidated, Prabhu published an article based on this experience in the *Indian Journal of Medical Education*. This caught the attention of the director general of health services who asked the director of AIIMS to depute Prabhu for a workshop being organized jointly by the ICSSR, UGC, and Ministry of Health for professors on the teaching of psychology and social sciences in the undergraduate medical curriculum. This, and the fact that his paper was used as one of the background papers at the workshop, invoked much ire in the group owing to his relatively junior status at the time. It was also noticed by Henry Walton, who was the WHO advisor for undergraduate training of psychiatry and behavioural sciences at the South East Asia regional office. This recognition led to Prabhu being invited as an advisor when, in 1972, the regional office organized a workshop for South Asian countries on the teaching of psychiatry for undergraduate medical students.

A parallel stream began when RAK College of Nursing requested him to provide guidance for the dissertations of their MSc students as well as deliver lectures in psychology. Prabhu had already had some experience doing this since he had been assigned to teach the diploma in psychiatric nursing (DPN) trainee nurses while a student himself at AIIMH (he accepted the task since it came with the promise of a small addition to the meagre stipend that was being paid!). AIIMS itself started the post-certificate course in nursing in 1975 and, given his ongoing association with the nursing colleges, he was the natural choice for coordinating the newly commenced course as well as the BSc nursing course which started in 1978. Then (as also perhaps even now), many would pay lip service to the importance of the nursing profession but delegate the lectures to juniors. Prabhu demonstrated his firm commitment to the idea that all parallel and related professions should be treated with respect by taking the classes himself. This was another conviction that remained all through his career, continuing even after he moved to NIMHANS. He used these classes to demonstrate to the postgraduate psychiatry trainees whom he would take along, the method of communicating concepts and theories for those who had little familiarity with the subject being taught. It was his belief that the hallmark of a good teacher was her/his ability to simplify concepts so that students across all disciplines and levels of training would be able to comprehend them. In the midst of all these developments, Prabhu also obtained his PhD registering afresh at AIIMS.

Another area which Prabhu was drawn into with utmost reluctance was mental retardation. There were referrals for assessment of IQ from the departments of neurology and psychiatry which were within manageable limits. Over a period of time, however, the referrals from the paediatrics department increased markedly to the extent that appointments were available only several weeks later. The irate head of the paediatrics department complained about this to the head of psychiatry and it was decided to designate one afternoon a week solely for the IQ assessments. This arrangement too did not ease the problem as within a short time a back log of cases once again built-up . It was in this uneasy situation that an incident occurred which greatly perturbed Prabhu and initiated a wholly new sequence of actions. A model school for mental retardation close to AIIMS would refer children for assessment of their IQ, disabilities, functional abilities, and so on before they were admitted to the school. A parent who had brought his child for the assessment was seen by Prabhu. The child's father who was about the same age as Prabhu sat with tears silently rolling down his face. Prabhu realized that the father needed more support and counselling than just psychoeducation alone. After a few sessions, the father told Prabhu,

> [D]oc, I have got the appointment after two and a half months, and I have a certificate…now just as I came here, I will go to model school, and put my daughter's name on the waiting list. Their intake is 4–5 per year…her name will be there for another 5 years…you know, if by that time an opening comes, she gets in…otherwise they will say that she's above 14, now we can't take her, they will take her name from this list. I was reading somewhere that nobody has the right to die without a doctor's prescription…. no child with disability has a right to grow without a psychologist's certificate. I wish in this country at least there are a handful of people who understand the problems of the parents of those with mental retardation.

These words from a distraught father shook him up thoroughly, the impact remaining for a few days after that. It also overcame his disinclination to work in the area of mental retardation. He then approached the head of the department of psychiatry with a proposal to reorganize the services for mental retardation which would be more comprehensive and not restricted to just issuing certificates and brief psychoeducation. The head was surprised as he was aware of Prabhu's earlier reluctance, but did not oppose the plan. These services expanded very rapidly because Prabhu realized that there were limitations to the care that could be provided at AIIMS and looked for other resources. He joined hands with an NGO, the Okhla Centre School for children with special needs. He became the technical advisor for several other NGOs and then tied up with the Federation for the Welfare of the Mentally Retarded (FWMR), which had centres all over India. In the later years, he was invited to become the vice-president of this national body. Prabhu impressed upon the chairperson of his department the need to start a specialty clinic for mental retardation with postgraduate students being posted there. In another first for AIIMS, Prabhu, a non-medical person, was appointed as the chief consultant of this clinic. This did not go down well with some consultants and a representation against his appointment was given to the then director of AIIMS, Dr Ramalingaswami. He summarily dismissed the representation stating that if the WHO South East Asian regional office could have Prabhu as a consultant there was no reason why AIIMS could not use its available expertise. The Ministry of Social Welfare (currently Social Justice and Empowerment) took note of the developments in this sector and started seeking Prabhu's advice and guidance in its plans to set up a national institute for mental handicap as part of its new initiatives for the International Year of

Disabled Persons in 1981. He was asked to advise the government in the setting up of this institute and was intimately involved at every stage of policy-making and planning. It was assumed in official circles that because of his close involvement with the project, he would be appointed as the first director. However, since he declined the offer, he was requested to continue to provide guidance for the fledgling institute. He remained a member of the governing council from its inception to 1997 and chairman of the Academic Committee and Executive Committee till 1990.

Another area in which Prabhu was actively associated with from 1972 onwards was substance abuse. This again arose in response to a felt local need. Late one evening, he received a call from a professor of IIT, Delhi, who told him that one of their students was in an agitated state and was being brought to the emergency service of AIIMS. Prabhu facilitated his treatment there, mainly in the form of detoxification. A few days later, the scenario repeated itself with another student and within 2 months, many more cases were brought to his notice. He approached a colleague in the department, Dr Davinder Mohan, and mooted the idea of carrying out a survey among the student population to understand the extent of the problem in Delhi. A MD student was assigned this topic for his thesis work and the results were astounding. Realizing that this was going to be a major problem in the years ahead, Prabhu and Dr Mohan applied for a grant from the health ministry to carry out a large-scale survey to examine the prevalence and patterns of drug use. This was turned down as the health secretary refused to accept that the problem existed on such a large scale. They had better luck with the Ministry of Social Welfare which agreed to fund the project. A number of studies on various aspects of substance use and abuse were published between 1974 and 1984, beginning with the Bulletin of Narcotics International. These studies provided the impetus for setting up the National Drug Dependence Treatment Centre in 1988 with Dr Mohan in charge.

By the late 1960s, there had been considerable progress in his career. However, the sense of unease at not being adequately equipped with therapeutic skills continued to dog him. This situation was remedied when Dr Erna Hoch came to AIIMS as a visiting professor for 1 year and 6 months. He approached her with the aim of improving his therapeutic competencies and the opportunity arose when she asked him to join her in her sessions, as a co-therapist. These sessions helped him learn the principles of existentially oriented psychotherapy. Yet, it also highlighted another difficulty that he experienced in practicing therapy—a sense of alienation from his clients. He believed that his background contributed in some measure to this feeling—the fact that he was the fourth generation to be educated in his family and growing up with a father who was far ahead of his times on many issues and held very liberal views. Above all his background was totally urban as his first exposure to the rural setting was at the age of 19 while in a NCC camp. Thus, he felt that he could not share the worldview of majority of his clients on many issues. Convinced that studying sociology would help him bridge this gap, he enrolled for evening classes to pursue a postgraduate degree in the subject. While he obtained another degree, it did not help him find the answers that he was looking for. He was 43 at the time and had been an examiner at MA (psychology) level for 15 years and had examined 14 doctoral theses. However, as a participant observer (!!) he obtained an inside view of the futility and hollowness of the practical utility of the Indian educational system which, later, he personally shared with Dr Madhuri Behn Shah when she was the chairperson of the UGC.

The next turning point came around 1975. Death intervened yet again, with the tragic accident of his beloved wife Dolly. Having been his colleague in the department at AIIMS, Prabhu found it difficult to continue there as there were many memories associated with the place which were painful reminders of the loss every day. He began actively planning for a complete change of environment and three possibilities arose—as director of the Defence Institute of Psychological Research, a short-term assignment as a WHO consultant in Sri Lanka, and the chairperson's position at the

Department of Clinical Psychology at NIMHANS. After debating the impact of the move on his two young children, he ultimately decided to accept the position at NIMHANS. One of the main factors that weighed in this decision was the chance for him to develop a world-class training programme, having been thus far a vocal critic of the existing programmes. When he took charge of the department in 1981, the programme was being run in a rather 'routine' manner. There was no comprehensive document that laid down the training objectives, mode of delivery, and methods of evaluation apart from the annual examinations. As he had done with the earlier training programme on behavioural sciences at AIIMS, he set about formalizing the training by clearly defining the training goals, specifying how the goals were to be achieved, and introducing an objective method of continuous evaluation of the performance of trainees over the 2-year MPhil course. With the structuring of the training programme, a greater sense of accountability ensued, both for the trainees as well as the faculty. The programme was consolidated within a few years with regular reviews and modifications as required. The immediate fallout of these changes was that clinical psychology was able to assert its identity as a specialization among the other departments at NIMHANS, and soon these departments began to incorporate some of the monitoring and evaluation methods into their own programmes. Another distinctive idea that he facilitated was the development of specializations within the realm of clinical psychology. At that time, there were only two specialized areas that offered training and services in the department: neuropsychology and behaviour therapy. Prabhu encouraged faculty members to identify areas of interest to them and build up research and training in those areas. This led to the emergence of newer areas such as child mental health, stress, coping and adaptation, substance abuse, community psychology, family and couple therapies, psychosocial aspects of mental illness, and psychosocial and neuropsychological rehabilitation. Training in psychotherapy, formal supervision, and test development also received a boost. Trainees had placements in all these specialized areas. Thus, the final 'product' was a professional who had the competencies to be able to independently function in any setting and who also had a sound foundation in several specialized areas which they could pursue further.

Prabhu also brought in several administrative changes, emphasizing discipline and accountability. He was a strong proponent of democratic functioning and collective responsibility and, hence, ensured that departmental faculty meeting were held regularly every month so that all issues could be discussed in a frank and transparent manner and decisions taken. In his own words,

> If I may use an oxymoron, I was a democratic autocrat. Total democracy is to be practiced till a policy decision is arrived at. Once it is reached, it is to be implemented and practiced uniformly without fear or favour except the rarest of the rare issues on compassionate grounds.

He advocated for the system of a rotating headship of departments at the institute level with 5-year tenure, an idea that did not find favour with some of existing heads of the departments, but was subsequently introduced after his retirement as per the requirements of the UGC. He was of the firm conviction that the role of the chairperson had go beyond just administering the department. He believed that, fundamentally, the role of a chairperson lay in framing policies and planning that would drive the activities of the department. The chairperson's role also required him/her to take cognizance of the strengths of the department, build on them, and create awareness among other departments. He was able to successfully accomplish all of these during his tenure as the chairperson of the department spanning 15 years. His vision was to establish a three-tier academic structure. The first tier, which he considered to be the foundation, was the MPhil training programme. The second, a system of identifying, nurturing, and mentoring promising trainees so that they could be shaped to take on leadership roles in the future. The third tier was the PhD programme which would advance high quality research. In retrospect, he believes that the first tier has been very successfully established and consolidated. The MPhil training programme in clinical Psychology is at par with other international programmes and is far ahead of similar training programmes in the country. Clinical psychologists, on completion of their training at NIMHANS, are highly sought after for various positions within the country and are able to get into PhD or other advanced training programmes abroad with ease. With regard to the second tier, he believes that the department has advanced sufficiently to be able to provide academic leadership with scope for increasing the contribution in national policy-making. Likewise, he is of the opinion that the bar could be raised higher for the PhD programme.

G.G. Prabhu was associated with several organizations. Besides being Member, International Expert Advisory Panel (1984–1990) of the World Health Organization (WHO), he was WHO Consultant on Classification of Mental Disorders, Mental Handicap and Life Style and Mental Health. For the Indian Council for Medical Research (ICMR) he was Member, National Advisory Committee on Mental Health, Neurological Sciences, Coronary Prone Behaviour, and Convener, Committee on Ethics in Mental Health Research. He was Member, Governing Council (1984–1997) of the Rehabilitation Council of India. He was also its Member, Executive Council and Chairman, Committee on Mental Retardation (1986–1998). He extended help to the Government of India as advisor to Ministries of Defence, Home Affairs, Civil Aviation Security, Social Welfare (now Social Justice and Empowerment), Health and Family Welfare, and Sports and Youth Affairs, Planning Commission (Social Welfare Sector). He was Member, National Committee for the formulation of Mental Health Program and Central Mental Health Authority (1994–1997). He was also Member Karnataka State Mental Health Authority. He also served as Member, Perspective Planning Committee of National Institute of Hearing Handicap and National Institute of Visual Handicap. Some of his international assignments includes International League of Societies in Mental Handicap (ILSMH), Member, MORE (Mobilization of Resources) Committee (ILSMH), Member, Asian Affairs Committee, Invited Honorary Member, Japan League for Mental Retardation, and Executive Committee member of the Asian Federation for Welfare of Mentally Retarded Persons.

In summing up his contributions to the profession of clinical psychology, several facets stand out distinctly. First, his efforts in introducing behavioural sciences to undergraduate medical students and other mental health related disciplines in ways that would be meaningful and relevant to them. The second major contribution can be discerned in his commitment towards developing services for persons with mental handicap, in policy-planning and advocacy, culminating in the setting up of a national institute to address the problem of mental handicap. Likewise, his sustained efforts through research and at the policy level paved the way for the setting up of a dedicated centre to tackle the problem of substance abuse. Above all, his most significant contribution lies in the evolution of a rigorous training programme in clinical psychology. His tireless striving well after he laid down office. During the 1960s, the Indian Psychological Association was collapsing and becoming dysfunctional. The newly emerging profession of clinical psychology had several issues that needed addressing and was in dire need of a professional body. Prabhu played the cardinal role (1965–1970) in the formation of the Indian Association of Clinical Psychologists (IACP) of which he is the founder general secretary. The year 2018 is the golden jubilee year of this robust professional organization. For the last two decades, Prabhu has been practicing detached participation with the IACP as he gets fully involved only when approached for advice and guidance. His philosophy: the younger active generation should be responsible to manage all the affairs of the profession.

The hallmark of all his endeavours is his passionate commitment to the causes that he espouses. Colleagues and former students remember him as strict disciplinarian, who set high standards of performance, as much for himself as he expected from others. Generous in his praise but equally ruthless in his criticism when something was not up to the mark, his is a presence that cannot be ignored. He enjoys being with young trainees and in most conferences that he attends, he can be found surrounded by them, all eager to interact with him. His involvement with the field of clinical psychology remains as intense today as it was when he first started out. It remains for the profession to carry forward his vision for the field.

## Acknowledgements

I am deeply grateful to G.G. Prabhu for permitting me to interview him at length on which this narrative is based. I am greatly indebted to my doctoral students, Ms Suruchi Sonkar and Ms Suvarna Joshi who helped with the background research and the onerous task of transcribing the interview.

# 41

# Jai Ballabha Prasad Sinha*

(1935)

## Dharm P.S. Bhawuk

*Jai Ballabha Prasad Sinha*

While growing up in Kathmandu, Nepal, I had the privilege of hearing many inspiring stories from my lifelong mentor, Narsingh Narayan Singh, about one of his peers, Jai Ballabha Prasad Sinha. They had studied at Langat Singh College, Muzaffarpur, Bihar. Singh himself has very high standards, and is not given to easy praise. But he always spoke of J.B.P. Sinha in the superlative and with the highest regard, often referring to him as 'the world famous professor' or 'a big professor'. It was fascinating to know that even in Patna one could do world-class research, and it inspired me to excel in whatever I did in Kathmandu. I learned that world-class work can be done anywhere. It is clearly the choice of the individual to excel with whatever limited resource is available within the limitations of the context provided by the place.

* I would like to thank Ramadhar Singh and Arvind K. Sinha for their generous help in writing this chapter. Indian words are written using Harvard-Kyoto Protocol for devanagari script without capitalizing the first letter.

In 1987, I went to the East-West Center to study with Richard W. Brislin who spoke equally highly of J.B.P. Sinha. In Hawaii, Peter Dorfman introduced me to J.B.P. Sinha's research on the nurturant task leader. It was a joy to learn the work of an Indian scholar in the USA, about whom I had heard in my childhood. Narsingh Narayan Singh was right in referring to Sinha as a world-renowned professor.

In 1992, I went to the University of Illinois at Urbana-Champaign to do my PhD with Harry C. Triandis. Triandis had invited J.B.P. Sinha to write the review article on Indian organizational psychology for the second edition of the *Handbook of Industrial Organizational Psychology* that he was editing (Triandis, Dunnette, & Hough, 1994). I learned a lot about Indian organizational psychology from Sinha's (1994) chapter, which remains a required reading in my doctoral seminar on cross-cultural psychology even today. I recommend this article to all young researchers for it provides not only a 'thick description' (Geertz, 1973) of the field of Indian organizational psychology, but also a template for writing a review article for other indigenous psychologies.

I also had the honour of jointly working on a paper with him (Triandis, Chan, Bhawuk, Awao, & Sinha, 1995). Later there was another opportunity to co-author a book chapter with him on individualism and collectivism. After going through the first draft of our chapter and finding it to be complete in itself without his inputs (Triandis & Bhawuk, 1997), he declined to be an author. So, the editors invited him to write a paper (Sinha, 1997) that complemented and extended the ideas we had presented in our chapter. This was a new professional experience in my academic journey: academic collaboration must be meaningful to all contributors. My mentor Triandis always practiced it, and so did J.B.P. Sinha. I learnt that Indian scholars need not be a tag onto Western scholars to show an international publication! J.B.P. Sinha's contribution to the research on individualism and collectivism lies in developing a unique method of measuring the constructs, which Triandis refers to as the Sinha IndCol Scale (Triandis, 1995; Triandis, Chan, Bhawuk, Awao, & Sinha, 1995).

I met J.B.P. Sinha in person at the IACCP conference in Montreal, Canada, in 1996. I enjoyed listening to his research presentation and introduced myself to him. He was kindness personified, and responded to me as if he had always known me! He apologized for missing the 4th Asian Regional Congress of International Association for Cross-Cultural Psychology in Kathmandu that I had organized in 1992. He became a part of my active academic life since the Montreal meeting. We share our writings and seek critical comments, not mere appreciation. I have only heard J.B.P. Sinha praise other researchers including his former students. Nurturing and respecting junior colleagues is a part of his persona.

I was delighted when J.B.P. Sinha accepted my request to write a paper for the special issue of *Psychology and Developing Societies* on the theme, 'Indian Psychology: Theory, Method, and Content', which I co-edited with E.S. Srinivas. I enjoyed reading his paper, and he was generous in accepting our comments to revise the paper. I recommend Sinha's (2010) paper to all Indian psychologists, for it provides a glimpse of what Indian psychologists ought to go through to carve their space on the global stage of psychology.

## J.B.P. Sinha: The Person

J.B.P. Sinha was born in a *zamindar* family in the village of Gangeya, Muzaffarpur, Bihar. His late father, Shri Shukdeo Prasad Sinha, and late grandfather, Shri Gopal Prasad Sinha, had both significant impacts on his personal life. Both of them encouraged him to study and sheltered him from the responsibilities of managing family assets, primarily a huge land holding. His mother was a down-to-earth woman who loved him, her only son, dearly, and this love became the foundation of the emotional strength that permeates the persona of J.B.P. Sinha. His actual date of birth is 28 March 1935. However, since the family *munsi* (or accountant) who took him to school for admission did not remember the actual date of birth, so he made up his date of birth as 1 June 1936. The *munsi* thought it was convenient for accounting purposes.

Following the tradition, his marriage was arranged by his grandfather with Gita Sinha on 22 April 1954, when he was only 19 years old, studying for a BA (honours) degree. However, such as early marriage did not distract him from his studies, and he graduated top of his class, first class first, both in BA (honours) and MA from Bihar University. Mrs Sinha deserves a lot of credit for his success since she has always sheltered him from social responsibilities so that he could direct his energy on academic research. His academic success led him to go to the Ohio State University, USA, to pursue PhD, which he completed in 1965. His pregnant wife stayed back in India (their daughter was born in 1962 while he was studying in the USA) to take care of their 14-month-old son. His parents passed away when he was in his 50s, so he was blessed to have the support of his family in the critical years of his academic career.

J.B.P. Sinha started teaching at B.S. College (1958–1959), Danapur, Bihar, after completing his master's degree, and then moved to Ranchi University (1959–1962) before going to the USA for his PhD. He continued there upon his return (1965–1966). He was at the A.N.S. Institute of Social Studies, for 30 years (1966–1996), where most of his significant academic research was carried out. A.N.S. Institute of Social Studies provided him with the necessary facilities and the freedom to pursue whatever excited him most. He taught two graduate psychology courses at Patna University by a courtesy-appointment. He felt that the ancient city of Patna and the state of Bihar provided him the best place to conduct social science research in India, since here the major societal problems were magnified many times. The issues were staring researchers in their eyes if they could get away from the perspectives and methods of Western psychology, and not chase their condescending approval. During this period he frequently visited the USA and taught at Hunter College, City University of New York (1971–1973; Summer of 1974, 1976, 1977, 1979, 1981), and Wake Forest University, Winston-Salem, USA (Summer of 1994). He was also a visiting professor at McGill University, Montreal, Canada (1995–1996), and Copenhagen School of Business, Denmark (September–October, 2004). As a teacher, he has shaped the life of students all over the world, and is appreciated by students and colleagues everywhere.

J.B.P. Sinha enjoys little things in life like a cheeseburger and Coke, kebabs, a glass of milk any time, and two to three drinks of whisky a few times a week. He enjoys both Indian and Western food, vegetarian and non-vegetarian. He has a sweet tooth and mango is his favourite fruit. He is disciplined and goes for morning walks for about 40 minutes every day and also does yogic exercises for 75 minutes. For a man so widely travelled, he dislikes to travel because of the anxiety involved in traveling.

Though born in a zamindar family, he grew up living in scarcity with 14 cousins (eight brothers and six sisters). Consistent with social science research, those who experience scarcity or have less resource at their disposal are inclined to be significantly more generous, demonstrate prosocial behaviour, and want to give back to the society (Bowen & Bok, 1998; Piff et al., 2010); his upbringing in a large family and experienced scarcity became an inspiration for him to return to India after PhD. Much like the minorities in the USA studying at prestigious universities (i.e., Ivy League schools), who are inclined to give back to the society compared to their white alumni who focus more on maximizing their own careers, Sinha returned to India to serve his community and nation, knowing very well that he would have less resources for his research and living.

Sinha believes that he acquired the habit of structuring time, tasks, and relationships from his grandfather. He considers his grandfather a living example and the source of his model of nurturant task-leader in which leaders love subordinates if they perform to the level expected. He inherited idealism from his father who is viewed by him as an exemplar of the idea of *lokasaGgraha* (well-being of all) propounded in the Bhagavad Gita. His father inspired him never to compromise on ethics and to work for the common good of people and the society. Besides being the only son not wanting to live far away from his parents, the idealism of *lokasaGgraha* was the key reason that he came back to India from the USA.

Early on in his academic career, he was disenchanted by the lack of sensitivity of his foreign friends, colleagues, and collaborators to the social reality of India. He tried to build bridges, but finding it an uphill battle, he spent his energy in what he does best—research on Indian issues using novel methodology. He does not like to put his energy in playing politics in international professional organizations or in performing administrative duties in academic institutions. He loves to do research as can be seen in his long productive career.

## J.B.P. Sinha's Work

J.B.P. Sinha has contributed to the discipline of global psychology by providing a deep understanding of Indian social and organizational psychology by working with many contributors over five decades. He is a champion of the multi-method research approach. He has successfully synthesized the wisdom of Indian philosophy into Indian psychology. And with his most recent research, he has provided us a new understanding of the Indian mindset that has carved a special space for Indian psychology in the global psychology literature.

In his five-decade long career, J.B.P. Sinha has developed many psychological constructs like *dependency proneness* (*DP*; Chattopadhyay, 1975; Pareek, 1968; Sinha, 1970, 1973), which is 'a disposition to seek attention, guidance, support, and help in making decisions and taking actions in situations where individuals are capable of and justified to make up their own mind and act on their own'. He noted that this idea simply jumped out of his cultural experience (Sinha, 2010). Through a dozen of studies done with many collaborators, he successfully defined the construct and measured its antecedents and consequents to build a reasonable theory of *DP*. In doing so, his objective was to learn about *DP* to hopefully modify organizational practices that were still operating from the Western psychological perspectives of negative phenomena, which are often referred to as the deficit model of psychology. What is commendable about this line of work is that it shifted the negative view on *DP* to a positive orientation of providing emotional support in a collective decision-making and nurturing style of leadership.

Out of his work on *DP* emerged the theory of *nurturant task (NT) leader* (Sinha, 1980a), when he noticed an anomalous finding that high *DP* people took greater risk if the supervisor expected them to do so, showing him a way to address *DP*. He was inspired by the *nitizloka* that parents should shower love on the children up to the age of five, discipline them for the next 10 years, and treat them like friends when they turn 16. He also observed the cultural pattern of *aram* or the proneness not to work too hard. This observation became one of the basic assumptions for the theory of *NT leader*. The second assumption for his leadership theory was another observation that unconditional support or nurturance turned the subordinates into unproductive sycophants. He also shared with me that Durganand Sinha brought to his attention how every decision is discussed informally in the community in an Indian village, be it selection of seed for a crop or a bridegroom for one's daughter. This led him to appreciate the dialogical culture of India, which permeates the organizational life of managers.

J.B.P. Sinha spent a decade developing this theory, and showed that effective leaders in India were not autocratic or participative as recommended by Western scholars, but *NT leaders*. These leaders were found to be more effective for the subordinates who were dependence prone, status conscious, and *aram*-seeking or not so work-oriented. Such a leader was able to engage the subordinate in participation, but retained a moral superiority that was recognized by the subordinates rather than being imposed by the leader. Thus, starting with his experience, observation of people around him, and the wisdom of the *nitizloka*, he was able to field an Indian theory of leadership that is well accepted nationally and internationally.

J.B.P. Sinha was able to further extend the *NT leader* model to theories of organizational cultures (Sinha, 1980b, 1990, 1995, 2000, 2004, 2008). He found that high *NT leaders* create synergistic organizational culture. On the other hand, weak *NT leaders* create a soft organizational culture, which is less productive and more prone to external manipulations by government, union, and other stakeholders, often deviating from organizational mission and objectives. And this line of research led to a new finding that there are four aspects of the *Indian mindset—materialistic, dependence prone, collectivist*, and *holistic* (Sinha, 2014). He found much regional variation in the Indian mindset, which suggests that Indian psychology is varied and multicultural.

Thus, J.B.P. Sinha has crafted a body of knowledge that clearly marks the boundary of Indian psychology in the social psychological area. His work shows that one does not need to start with the Vedas or the Upanishads to derive Indian psychological constructs, as he has successfully used his observations of the culture to identify constructs and name them, when appropriate, using Indian terminology (*aram* culture, *apaney-paraye* (ingroup-outgroup), *sneha-zraddha* (affection-reverence), etc.). When a natural Indian term did not exist, he used English terms such as *DP*, *NT leader*, and so forth. His voluminous research work has provided a solid foundation for future researchers to craft indigenous psychological theories pertaining to Indian social psychology, which can lead to the emergence of an Indian social psychology. It should also be noted that his regard for the wisdom of the Upanishads is unconditional, and so he is encouraging young scholars to start with constructs in the classical texts, if they can use it meaningfully.

A review of his life work shows that in the first 15 years of his academic career, J.B.P. Sinha outgrew the Western framework by conducting research that addressed socio-cultural issues that were pertinent in the Indian context, and it led him to develop a methodology that was appropriate to the Indian population and organizations. In the next 15 years, he enjoyed being India's academic ambassador in the world of international psychology as an Indian cultural psychologist. This came to him with a little bit of sadness in that he realized that despite doing scientific psychological research following his graduate training at the Ohio State University, he remained an Indian cultural psychologist, whereas his Western colleagues were referred to simply as psychologists or cross-cultural psychologist, and never as American or British cultural psychologists. Inspired by this learning, akin to the wisdom from T.S. Ellio—We shall not cease from exploration, and the end of all our exploring will be to arrive where we started and know the place for the first time—in the third phase of his academic life, he focused on organizational behaviour that is rooted in the ancient Indian philosophical thoughts.

## Impact of J.B.P. Sinha's Work

In listing 250 milestones in psychology, Pickren (2014) included J.B.P. Sinha's NT leadership model. Earlier, Pickren and Rutherford (2010) had included Durganand Sinha and J.B.P. Sinha as

Indian contributors to modern psychology in their book, *A History of Modern Psychology in Context*. Indeed, J.B.P. Sinha's book on Indian mindset (Sinha, 2014) is a celebration of half a century of his academic contributions to global psychology.

I would like to end the paper with the words of Harry C. Triandis written in praise of J.B.P. Sinha in January 2014, which clearly puts him as a *cUDAmaNi* or crown jewel of scholars.

> I know him very well. I met him many times at international meetings and he spent several months with me at the University of Illinois. I found him unusually insightful about the way culture interacts with leadership styles.
>
> When I edited the International volume of the *Handbook of Industrial and Organizational Psychology* I was especially pleased to include Sinha's contribution.
>
> He is internationally known for his Nurturant-Task Leader (1980). It is one of the two most important indigenous models of leadership, the other one being the model of Misumi. When teaching about leadership I always included these two models in my presentations.
>
> Sinha has made many other contributions, such as his discussion of several models of national development and an original formulation of the meaning of 'mindset'. He has written 10 books, and has published a long list of articles. He has collaborated with eminent scholars, such as Dave McClelland, J. Misumi, and Bernhard Wilpert. I feel sure that he belongs in the set of world-class scholars. (Personal communication with Professor Harry C. Triandis, Emeritus Professor, University of Illinois at Urbana-Champaign).

# References

Bowen, W.G., & Bok D. (1998). *The shape of the river: Long-term consequences of considering race in college and university admissions*. Princeton, NJ: Princeton University Press.

Chattopadhyaya, G.P. (1975). Dependence in Indian culture: From mud huts to company board rooms. *Economic & Political Weekly*, 19(5), M30–M38.

Geertz, C. (1973). Thick description: Toward an interpretive theory of culture. In *The Interpretation of Cultures: Selected Essays* (pp. 3–30). New York, NY: Basic Books.

Pareek, U. (1968). A motivational paradigm for development. *Journal of Social Issues*, 24(2), 112–115.

Pickren, W.E. (2014). *The psychology book*. New York, NY: Sterling.

Pickren, W E., & Rutherford, A. (2010). *A history of modern psychology in context*. Hoboken, NJ: John Wiley & Sons.

Piff, P.K., Kraus, M.W. Co^te´, S., Cheng, B.H., & Keltner, D. (2010). Having less, giving more: The influence of social class on prosocial behavior. *Journal of Personality and Social Psychology*, 99(5), 771–784.

Sinha, J.B.P. (1970). *Development through behaviour modification*. Bombay: Allied Publishers.

———. (1973). *Some problems of public sector organizations*. New Delhi: National.

———. (1980a). *The nurturant task leader*. New Delhi: Concept Publishing House.

———. (1980b). *The school complex*. New Delhi: Concept Publishing House.

———. (1990). *Work culture in the Indian context*. New Delhi: SAGE Publications.

———. (1994). Cultural embededness and developmental role of industrial organizations in India. In H.C. Triandis, M.D. Dunnette, & L.M. Hough (Eds), *Handbook of industrial organizational psychology* (2nd edn, Vol. 4, pp. 727–764). Paulo Alto, CA: Consulting Psychology Press.

——. (1995). *The cultural context of leadership and power*. New Delhi: SAGE Publications.

——. (1997). A cultural perspective on organizational behaviour in India. In P.C. Earley & M. Erez (Eds), *New perspectives on international industrial/organizational psychology* (pp. 53–74). San Francisco: New Lexington Press.

———. (2000). *Patterns of work culture: Cases and strategies for culture building*. New Delhi: SAGE Publications.

———. (2004). *Multinationals in India: Managing the interface of cultures*. New Delhi: SAGE Publications.

Sinha, J.B.P. (2008). *Culture and organizational Behaviour*. New Delhi: SAGE Publications.

———. (2010). Living and doing psychology. *Psychology and Developing Societies*, *22*(1), 95–119.

———. (2014). *Psycho-social analysis of the Indian mindset*. New Delhi: Springer.

Triandis, H.C. (1995). *Individualism and collectivism*. Boulder, CO: Westview Press.

Triandis, H.C., & Bhawuk, D.P.S. (1997). Culture theory and the meaning of relatedness. In P.C. Earley & M. Erez (Eds), *New perspectives on international industrial/organizational psychology* (pp. 13–52). New York, NY: The New Lexington Free Press.

Triandis, H.C., Chan, D., Bhawuk, D.P.S., Iwao, S., & Sinha, J.B.P. (1995). Multi-method probes of allocentrism and idiocentrism. *International Journal of Psychology*, *30*(4), 461–480.

Triandis, H.C., Dunnette, M.D., & Hough, L.M. (Eds) (1994). *Handbook of industrial organizational psychology* (2nd ed. Vol. 4). Paulo Alto, CA: Consulting Psychology Press.

# 42

# Muneer Ahamed Faroqi

(1935–2017)

## P.A. Baby Shari and P. Sethu Madhavan

*Muneer Ahamed Faroqi*

Muneer Ahamed Faroqi, usually abbreviated as M.A. Faroqi, was born in Mysore on 23 November 1935. Faroqi is well-known for his tremendous contributions to psychology in India. He contributed to the profession and discipline not only through his research and publications but also through other significant activities such as establishing the department of psychology in the University of Calicut, elevating the journal *Psychological Studies* as one of the best professional journals in India, and supporting professional bodies and journals actively. This chapter attempts to articulate the contributions of Faroqi to psychology in India, based on various available sources of data as well as the personal experiences of the authors who were students of Faroqi. The first author of this chapter met him in Bangalore, specifically for collecting the information required for this chapter, on 26 July 2015, which coincided with his 50th wedding anniversary celebrations. During the visit, P.A. Baby Shari collected information required for preparing this chapter and collated his views about psychology in India and his contributions. P. Sethu Madhavan also had an opportunity to work under his supervision for his dissertation submitted for his masters course.

# Education

Faroqi completed his BA (hons) from the University of Mysore in psychology in 1955. The department has an inspiring history, high academic standards, and a rich record of accomplishments in research. M.V. Gopalaswamy, B. Kuppuswamy and B. Krishnan of this department are known for their work in the field of social psychology and Indian psychology, respectively. The fact that Faroqi was able to complete his BA (hons) from such a reputed department with first class and first rank proves his academic excellence. Moreover, Faroqi was the first person to get the vice-cancellor's HVN gold medal. He received also the Bhaba Memorial gold medal for his splendid success in BA (hons).

After completing his BA (hons) at the University of Mysore, Faroqi continued his masters at the University of Mysore under the guidance of B. Kuppuswamy and B. Krishnan (University of Mysore, 2015). Faroqi proved his academic excellence once again, by completing his master's degree with first class and first rank in 1957. During his masters, he submitted a dissertation, based on his study of the relationship between structure of group and co-operative behaviour. He used an experimental design involving school children as subjects for his study. It seems that his research work during his masters inducted and attracted him to the interesting field of social psychology and inspired him to do his doctoral research in the same field.

# Early Professional Life

After completing his masters, Faroqi joined the department of psychology in the University of Madras as a lecturer in 1957. He continued his interest in social psychology by pursuing his PhD at the University of Madras during the same time under the supervision of G.D. Boaz. His thesis was entitled 'Cooperation and Competition in Groups' and he was awarded a PhD in 1962 by the University of Madras. Faroqi continued to work in the University of Madras and was promoted as a Reader in psychology in 1966. In 1976, he left the University of Madras to join the University of Calicut as the founding head of its newly established psychology department.

# Effective Institution Builder

Faroqi has proved his effectiveness as an institution builder by establishing the department of psychology from scratch and developing it as a well-known department in the country. When the University of Calicut in Kerala started a Department of Psychology for postgraduate teaching and research, the university authorities wanted to bring an excellent academician as the founding head of the department. The search for the head of the department ended, when Faroqi agreed to take the role in 1976. Faroqi continued to work in the department until he retired from service in 1995. He played a leading and seminal role in establishing the department as one of the best departments in the country.

Though the Department of Psychology was started in the year 1976, the first postgraduate batch in psychology was started in 1977 under the faculty of humanities. While joining the Department of Psychology, P.N.O. Tharakan and Kunhikrishnan were his colleagues. Later Anita Pillai and C.B. Asha also joined him. Faroqi dreamt about collective research by the faculty members focusing on one specialized area. According to Faroqi, his wish was to streamline all the research activities to areas related to industrial psychology. However, his colleagues had diverse research interests and some of them preferred to focus on clinical psychology. Moreover, his colleagues preferred empirical studies whereas he was more interested in theoretical contributions. However, his wisdom to support the team members and their diverse interests perhaps led to the evolution of the department as an esteemed institution with a history of more than three decades of excellence and multiple specializations such as clinical psychology, industrial/organizational psychology, educational psychology, research methodology, counselling and consulting psychology, criminology and forensic psychology, health and paediatric psychology, psychoanalysis, and developmental psychology.

Contributions of Faroqi as a founding professor and head of the department are highly valuable not only for the department but also for the field of psychology. About 600 students have passed out from the department with postgraduate degrees over the years and they are spread across the world. The department also had awarded around 50 MPhil and PhD degrees so far. The quality of the laboratory and the library of this department symbolize the careful and painstaking efforts of Faroqi in building the department. The hard work and dedication of M.A. Faroqi had a major role in developing the department laboratory and library to one of the best in South India. The department was moved from humanities to faculty of science in 2003.

Faroqi had successfully guided a few PhD works and MPhil dissertation. He guided work on locus of control, achievement motivation, academic achievement and self-concept among student leaders, study and problem-solving habits of college students, and managerial effectiveness respectively.

## Participation in Professional Associations and Forums

Faroqi actively participated and supported various professional bodies and forums during his tenure. He contributed to many professional bodies and forums in various roles. He was an executive committee member of the Indian Psychology Association from 1978 to 1985, sectional president of the Indian Academy of Applied Psychology in 1984, secretary and treasurer of Madras Psychology Society between 1958 and 1974, and president of Kerala *Manasasthra Parishath* from 1979 to 1980. He had also served as a sectional president of psychology in the Indian Academy of Social Sciences.

Faroqi also contributed to the profession by playing formal roles in many academic bodies such as board of studies and doctoral committees of various universities. He served as a subject expert of University Grants Commission (UGC) from 1986 to 1987. He was dean of faculty of humanities in the University of Calicut from 1981 to 1985. He was a member of UGC panel of experts in psychology from 1983 to 1985 and the Indian Council of Social Science Research in Psychology from 1975 to 1982. He was also a member of the advisory committee on production of technical literature (Urdu) in the Ministry of Education, Government of India (1981–1984). He was also engaged in periodic assignments with state and Union Public Service Commission.

# Successful Teacher, Trainer and Consultant

Faroqi also took active interest in teaching and training using innovative methods. He took interest in various courses such as organization behaviour, education, social science, and criminology. He was associated with an application-oriented programme for industrial executives at Madras Productivity Council. In the University of Calicut, he had been trying to spearhead innovative models in teaching. Faroqi also put his effort to contribute to the profession by organizing and taking part in various training programmes and workshop for the psychologists. In 1977 and 1979, he directed two workshops on experimental psychology and organizational behaviour which were sponsored by the UGC.

In 1981, he conducted a training programme on research methodology at Sree Venkateswara University at Tirupathi. It is remembered as one of the best professional learning experience by many psychologists in South India. Faroqi also organized teacher's refresher programme, with sponsorship from UGC at the University of Calicut in 1988. The programme provided psychology teachers from Kerala, Tamil Nadu, and Karnataka to come together, share their experiences, and get trained in advanced teaching methods. He was included in the testing and selection of many industries and banks. He was a consultant for many industries. He was a course director for personnel and industrial relations programme conducted by Madras Productivity Council, Madras. He worked on quality of life concept in education and organizational contexts.

Faroqi was a good speaker and had a unique, but convincing way of sharing his views. As a speaker, he used to share his knowledge related to areas of his expertise, while humbly admitting his lack of knowledge in other areas. When quizzed about his speeches by P.A. Baby Shari, Faroqi recalled his speech during a seminar on Sigmund Freud, organized jointly by the Department of Psychology at the University of Madras and Max Mueller Bhavan. Though he was not an expert on psychoanalysis, he was invited by T.E. Shanmugan to summarize the seminar proceedings. Faroqi recalled that he started his speech by admitting that he is not a psychoanalyst by training or a Freudian by inclination. Further, he stated that he will summarize the proceedings as a layperson. However, he surprised the audience by presenting the summary of the proceedings in a highly professional manner using simple words and effective interpretations and extrapolations.

# Contributions to Professional Journals

Faroqi had a special interest in supporting and promoting professional journals in psychology. His contribution in establishing *Psychological Studies* is widely known. The journal was established in 1956 and first published by the University of Mysore, with B. Kuppuswamy as its editor. Faroqi took the responsibility of editing the journal in July 1978, and since then it was published from the University of Calicut till 2003. Misra (2009) notes that *Psychological Studies* has steadily progressed over the last six decades. Dalal (1990), in a UNESCO publication, described *Psychological Studies* as important among Indian psychology journals published by university departments. Among the journals operated by Indian psychologists to publish their research, *Psychological Studies* was noted by some authors as the most important among the journals published by Indian psychologists (Singh, 1991; Dalal, 2002). In 2000, the National Academy of Psychology (NAOP) adopted the journal as its official journal. Starting in 2009, *Psychological Studies* is published by Springer India under an arrangement with NAOP.

Apart from *Psychological Studies*, Faroqi contributed to many other professional journals and publications. He was consulting editor and member of the editorial board of different journals in Psychology such as *Journal of Psychological Research* (Madras), *Indian Journal of Applied Psychology* (Madras), *Indian Journal of Psychology* (Delhi), *Journal of Institute of Educational Research* (Madras), *Perspectives in Psychological Research* (Azamgarh) and *Journal of Military Psychology* (Allahabad).

## International Assignments

Faroqi had made significant contributions to the discipline outside India as well during his assignments abroad. During 1962–1964, he went to the University of Manchester, UK, with a commonwealth fellowship to continue his postdoctoral research. He worked under J. Cohen on 'Application of Information Theory to Visual Perception' during his stay in the UK. He also worked in Mauritius from 1989 to 1991 as an expert under the 'Indo-Mauritius Technical and Economic Co-operation' programme of the Indian High Commission. During this period, he engaged in research on various aspects of examination administration. There he also contributed as an expert in psychology to various other bodies such as the Mauritius Examination Syndicate and the Department of Administration and Social Sciences in the University of Mauritius.

## Research Studies and Publications

With a background of both traditional and innovative teaching and research departments, Faroqi had contributed to interdisciplinary research in psychology. His research experience and publications cover experimental, social, organizational, and educational psychology. He had keen interest in educational psychology and also had published a book, *Manual of Experiments in Educational Psychology*, in which he describes 17 different experiments in educational psychology (Faroqi, 1974a). He has contributed more than thirty articles in national and international journals. He had also contributed chapters to five different books.

Faroqi's doctoral research was about 'Cooperation and Competition in Groups'. In the 1950s and 1960s, social psychologists Leon Festinger and G.W. Allport had pointed out the influence of situational factors on behaviour. It was later incorporated into the theories of Roheen and Muzafir Sherief. Lewin had pointed out that situational factors affect the perception of time. Faroqi also tried to develop his research on this background. For his work on co-operation and group structure Faroqi (1958) selected adolescent students from schools to participate in the study. As per the design of the study, different briefings provided to the two groups created the experimental conditions or variations as required. The first group got the instructions that they were about to take part in an athletic meet where they will be competing with students of another class. On the other hand, the second group got the instruction that were about to take part in an athletic meet where they will be co-operating with students of another class. During his recent meeting with P.A. Baby Shari, Faroqi recalled that he had trained and used native Kannada speakers to brief the students in a standardized manner without any variations or bias. There were no actual competing situations and the design of the study involved only manipulation of the independent variables by using different briefings. The findings revealed that the participants of the 'competitive group' exhibited higher immediate motivational levels compared to the participants of the 'co-operative group'. The study focused only on the effect of briefing on the immediate motivation of the participants and did not cover the long lasting effects.

His research proved that stimulus factors influence perception of time and relationship in groups. Perception of time was quite accurate for those who engage in competition groups compared to cooperation groups. The situational influences were contributing to the perception of time in groups of adolescents who were ready to co-operate one another and compete one another. The study indicated that during friendship, or cooperation, we perceive time as a longer duration and therefore we do not feel motivated to utilize the time. During competition, time perception is as shorter and therefore we feel motivated to use the time with self-engaged, goal-oriented behaviour. During competition, time perception is as shorter and it's easy to motivate them. They use the time with self-engaged, goal-oriented behaviour.

A very interesting article of Faroqi (1970) discussed the social psychology of industrial negotiations. The changing scenario of industrial background compared to the 1930s have been discussed in the article in three distinct phases—the beginning of negotiation, the process, and the effectiveness. The article concludes that a true negotiation takes place in democratic atmosphere and also reminds that organization should guard against pseudo-democratic orientation. He points out that democratic behaviour and process must be distinguished from the submissive or defensive forms of authoritarianism. This article was also presented in the Golden Jubilee Conference on 'Psychology and the Problems of Labour', organized by the Madras Psychology Society and the Indian Academy of Applied Psychology in 1969.

Faroqi contributed a long chapter on communication and influence process in the ICSSR survey of researches in psychology edited by Udai Pareek (Faroqi, 1982). Broadly following the syntactic, semantic, and pragmatic analysis of communication, he presented a review of psychological research in communication. He also presented studies on individual and group change that could be brought through communication. One important variable that he stressed in the article is the native language of the teacher and the student. Faroqi argued, with supporting studies, that if the teacher and student use common native language, then learning becomes more effective. He noted the issue of language has wider theoretical and educational implications and called for systematic investigation with adequate controls. He observed that communication affected subject's proficiency, attitudes, motivation, and achievements. He commented on future trends of research on communication. Faroqi reviewed many books and publications by other psychologists also.

In an article about conflict and control, Faroqi analyzed the concepts of social conflict and the underlying motivations and intentions related to social conflict (Faroqi, 1974b). He tried to elaborate the nature and dynamics of conflicts and discussed different types of solutions. Faroqi also focused on positive effects of external conflict on internal structure as well as on the attempts to pacify conflicts through positive effort. He considered prosocial aggression as a survival mechanism of groups and the conflicts as protective and defensive mechanisms of the society. Faroqi stated that psychologists should focus on identifying the different sources of conflict rather than focusing on the intra- or inter-group hostility in order to plan any individual, organizational, or social interventions.

In another significant study, Faroqi analyzed the effect of group task in determining the relative efficiency of co-operative and competitive groups using an experimental design. The tendency of co-operative group to arrive at consensus had a favourable effect on problem solving only in the case of some types of problems, and not in all cases. Faroqi had also studied the effect of co-operation and competition in a group structure by employing a sociometric test and inducing the experimental 'atmosphere'. A co-operative group expressed more emotional expansiveness, showing greater amount of overlap in the 'life spaces'. The structure of a competitive group was marked by cleavage and semi-closed sub-groups (Faroqi, 1958).

Faroqi had made significant contributions to social psychological and industrial psychology. Examples of his contribution in these area include studies on origins of sociometrical rejection (Faroqi, 1960a), time perception and decision-making (Faroqi, 1965a), group structure in relation to productivity (Faroqi, 1965b) and group task and work motivation (Faroqi, 1966). He had also reported method of ranking in scaling and validation of sociometric scale (Faroqi, 1961). One of his studies was referred in a symposium on Industrial Psychology in Madras University as a significant contribution (Faroqi, 1962). Many other studies by Faroqi are also frequently cited by authors (for example, Faroqi, 1973, 1974).

Faroqi had also studied and contributed to other areas such as locus of control (Faroqi & Tharakan, 1978), intelligence (Faroqi, 1960a), study habits (Faroqi & Vyas, 1968), and so forth. Faroqi studied the common errors made by children while taking the Progressive Matrices Test (Faroqi, 1970a). He had also made a shorter version of the Progressive Matrices Test, which could be used to make an estimate of children's intelligence level. This version of the test takes only half the time compared to the original test (Faroqi, 1970b). Faroqi and S.K. Vyas developed a study habit inventory for college students (Faroqi, 1958).

Faroqi also used to publish socially relevant articles in newspapers and periodicals. For example, he published an article in *The Hindu* in 1973, about 'New Concepts in Urban Transportation'. The article presented professional views derived from social psychology, environment psychology, and urban transportation. Faroqi had foreseen the impact of population growth in the article and elaborated on changes needed in urban areas such as need for metro services, increased frequency of public transport etc. He suggested that while there should be more public transport in cities, no transport zones like areas near schools also should be marked. He suggested banning certain types of traffic in certain areas of cities. He called for involving social psychologists in planning and policy-making.

Faroqi had also conducted studies and published papers related to industrial psychology. He had published a very innovative work on industrial negotiations where he foresaw the changing scenario and predicted that the win-lose and lose-lose games played by employees and management will give way to more co-operative win-win approaches in the future. He believed that corporate will stop exploiting staff in future and will start respecting the contributions and role of employees (Faroqi, 1970c).

The brief review of the contributions of Faroqi reveals the immense impact of his work on psychology in India. His contribution to the profession and discipline ranges from research and publications, institution building, professional journals, and professional bodies to teaching, training, and consulting. He passed away on 2 February 2017 at Mysore.

# References

Dalal, A.K. (1990). India. In G. Shouksmith, & E.A. Shouksmith, *Psychology in Asia and the Pacific: Status reports on teaching and research in eleven countries.* (pp. 87–138). Bangkok: UNESCO Principal Regional Office for Asia and the Pacific.

———. (2002). Psychology in India: A historical introduction. In G. Misra, & A.K. Mohanty (Eds), *Perspectives on indigenous psychology* (pp. 79–108). New Delhi: Concept Publishing Company.

Faroqi, M.A. (1958). Cooperation and group structure. *Journal of Psychological Researches*, 2, 60–70.

———. (1960a). A note on Madras intelligence test. *Journal of Psychological Researches*, 4, 41–42.

———. (1960b). Origins of sociometric rejection. *Journal of Psychological Researches*, 4, 14–21.

———. (1961). The method of ranks in sociometric sealing. *Journal of Psychological Researches*, 6, 48–52.

Faroqi, M.A. (1962). Human motivation and industrial incentives. In C. Boaz (Ed.), *Papers in industrial psychology: A symposium* (pp. 30–46). Madras Psychological Society, Department of Psychology, University of Madras.

———. (1965a). Decision time in relation to personality. *Journal of Psychological Researches, 6,* 78–80.

———. (1965b). Group structure and productivity. *Indian Journal of Applied Psychology, 2,* 68–71.

———. (1966). Factors in group tasks motivation. *Journal of Psychological Researches, 10,* 143–147.

———. (1970a). Analysis of errors in Raven's progressive matrices test. *Journal of Educational Research and Extension, 3,* 65–83.

———. (1970b). Shorter version of Raven's progressive matrices test. *Indian Journal of Applied Psychology,* 7(1), 37–40.

———. (1970c). Social psychology of industrial negotiation. *Journal of Psychological Researches, 14,* 73–77.

———. (1973). Motivation and morale in a cooperative group. In T. Shanmugam (Ed.), *Personality and social problems* (pp. 231–256). Madras: University of Madras.

———. (1974a). *A manual of experiments in educational psychology.* Madras: M/s View Wood.

———. (1974b). Conflict and control: A psychological appraisal. *Indian Philosophical Annual, 9,* 1–8.

———. (1974c). Some studies on Raven's progressive matrices. In B. Krishnan (Ed.), *Studies in psychology* (pp. 6–18). Mysore: University of Mysore.

———. (1982). Communication and interaction. In U. Pareek (Ed.), *A survey of research in psychology* (pp. 375–414). New Delhi: Indian Council of Social Science Research.

———. (1984). Are Indians external oriented? *Psychological Studies, 29,* 101–106.

Faroqi, M.A. & Kunhikrishnan, K. (1986). Indian Personality and Character: A selected Bibliography. *Psychological Studies,* 31 (2), 215–222.

Faroqi, M.A., & Parameswaran, E. (1966). Effect of the interval between signals on temporal judgment. *20*(1), 12–17.

Faroqi, M.A., & Tharakan, P. (1978). Study habits of post graduate students and locus of control. *Perspective in Psychological Researches, 1,* 115–118.

Faroqi, M.A., & Venkatesan, V. (1973). Individual and group administration of Raven's progressive matrices test. *Madras University Journal,* (40), 80–82.

Faroqi, M.A., & Vyas, S. (1968). A study habits inventory for college students. *Indian Journal of Applied Psychology, 5,* 48–51.

Misra, G. (2009). Towards an inclusive psychology. *Psychological Studies,* 54(1), 1–2.

Singh, A.K. (1991). *The comprehensive history of psychology.* Delhi: Motilal Banarsidass Publishers.

University of Mysore. (2015, August 8). *Brief history of department.* Retrieved 21 April 2017, from University of Mysore-Psychology: http://www.uni-mysore.ac.in/psychology

# 43

# Madanlal Narsingdas Palsane

(1935)

## Bhaskar Rambhau Shejwal

*Madanlal Narsingdas Palsane*

M.N. Palsane, one of the most well-known psychologists, was born in 1935. He completed his BA from Nagpur University (1956), MA from Jabalpur University (1958), and PhD from M.S. University, Baroda (1966). He has been a Fellow of the National Academy. He retired as professor and head, Department of Psychology, University of Pune (now Savitribai Phule Pune University). Palsane started his career as a university teacher from M.S. University Baroda. After three years of teaching at Baroda, he moved to Sardar Patel University, and after serving there for seven years, he moved to the University of Pune as Reader in the Department of Psychology.

Palsane headed the department for more than 20 years. He had a long and fruitful career as a teacher, which started from the M.S. University at Baroda and continued till his retirement from the University of Pune. He taught different courses such as experimental psychology, statistics, psychometry and psychological testing, social psychology, educational psychology, and guidance and counselling. Palsane was known as a highly reputed and senior professor in the country, particularly in the field of psychometry and educational psychology. He achieved this reputation because of his specialization in the field of psychometry, which was very unique to him during his period, not only in Maharashtra but also in the country.

## Teacher-administrator and Administrator-leader

As professor and head, he developed the department and added psychometric orientation in teaching and research. The department was established on the beautiful campus of the university in 1950 under the headship of V.K. Kothurkar, who was trained at Cambridge in the experimental tradition. Palsane joined the department under the headship of Kothurkar. After Palsane's addition as a faculty, along with the experimental tradition, the department also gained the reputation for its psychometric orientation. Due to this emphasis, a psychological testing laboratory was added to the department along with the experimental laboratory, and now it possesses a collection of more than 1,000 tests. Surely, it would not have been possible without the initiative of Palsane.

Like other universities, the University of Pune also had a traditional annual system of examination. Palsane contributed in the revision of the examination and in reforms in the evaluation system in the university. He played an active role in the revision of syllabus according to the semester system, providing optional papers at the masters level. His insight in the field of educational psychology helped in enriching the syllabus not only of the MA psychology programme but also of the other programmes of the mental, moral and social science faculty of the university. During this long tenure, he worked as the director of continuing education, director of postgraduate studies, and coordinator of the centre for the interdisciplinary programme of the University of Pune. As a director of the then continuing education, he started several skill-based professional courses for children and grown-up adults who could not go for higher education for one or the other reason. Today we talk about skill-based education to the youth of the country, which Palsane had implemented in the university around 40 years ago.

Immediately after his retirement from the department, he was appointed as the director of the Board of College and University Development, a position next to the vice-chancellor of the university in the hierarchy and power structure of the university. This position was created by the Maharashtra University's Act, 1991, in all the state universities in the state. He was invited to shoulder this responsibility by the vice-chancellor of the university. Thus, he was the first director of the board of the college and university development of the University of Pune. He initiated several practices and policies, which were supported by the academic council of the university to improve the teaching, research, and evaluation in the affiliated colleges and in the university departments.

## Contribution to National-level Institutions

Palsane's contribution to national-level institutions in strengthening the functioning of these institutes is well appreciated by his colleagues. He has worked as a panel member, consultant, expert, and reviewer for the organizations such as University Grants Commission (UGC); Indian Council of Social Sciences Research (ICSSR), New Delhi; National Council of Educational Research and Training (NCERT); Union Public Service Commission (UPSC); United States Educational Foundation in India (USEFI), etc.

# Research Interest and Contribution in the Field

He has developed three psychometric tests in Marathi, namely, adjustment inventory, interest inventory, and study habits inventory, which are still widely used in Maharashtra. All these inventories are proven to be extremely useful tools in understanding the problems of adjustment of school- and college-going students, in understanding their study habits, and in providing career guidance to students. Many research studies have been conducted by using these tools.

He has published more than 40 empirical papers in national and international journals, and presented more than 25 research papers in seminars and conferences. The major concepts that he addressed in his research include psychological stress, stress and coping, daily hassles and stress, psychological well-being, crowding, stress and health in children, type A personality, driving behaviour and health, self-incongruent behaviour and health, etc. His contribution in the field of psychological stress and environmental psychology was not only significant from the Indian perspective but it also fetched an honour and recognition to him from international psychologists. During his tenure in the department, Fullbright scholars Gary Evans and Steve Lepore, both well-known environmental psychologists from the USA, opted for the Department of Psychology as a research place and developed collaborative research projects. Today the term stress is very popular and is used to describe every unpleasant experience, right from a common man's life to critical experiences in every professional's life. In the 1980s, Palsane was considered as one of the few Indian psychologists working in this field. He tried to give an Indian perspective of this concept based on our traditional and philosophical literature.

# Research Contribution

He conducted several projects, hence a reference to few is essential here to understand his academic and research orientation in the field. One of his projects was on 'Holocaust in Marathwada' with Damle, a reputed sociologist of the country. Damle was the ex-head of the sociology department of the university. The project was supported by the ICSSR to study the riots involving scheduled casts and others in the Marathwada region of Maharashtra due to re-naming of the 'Marathwada University' as 'Dr Babasaheb Ambedkar Marathwada University' by the Government of Maharashtra. This was a collaborative project involving other social scientists from sociology, anthropology, and political science under the leadership of Damle. Palsane believed in the interdisciplinary perspective in teaching and research, and there are a few more such examples substantiating this belief.

He undertook a project on the concept of stress and the techniques of dealing with it in the Indian tradition. He did a review of 'stress, theory and practice in Indian philosophy, religion, and tradition'. For this, he scanned through the traditional literature and interviewed knowledgeable people from the field and also analyzed the traditional practices people follow in their daily life. The analysis and interpretation was presented from a cross-cultural perspective. This is a fundamental source of information to the researchers working in this field. There was one more collaborative project undertaken with American psychologists on Type A behaviour pattern, driving behaviour, stress, and health in the state transport bus drivers. This study was conducted on the bus drivers, who drive buses on state and national highways, by observing them for one and a half hours while driving. The study also used multiple methods of observations such as physiological measures and observations by trained medical students, along with self-report measures. A similar study was done on American bus drivers and a cross-cultural comparison was made. A report of this study was presented in the

APA's conference and the paper was published in the *Journal of Personality and Social Psychology*. Another collaborative study was done to see the effect of '*savasana*-meditation' on essential hypertension. A consulting physician, a medical postgraduate student and a yoga expert collaborated in the study which demonstrated the possibility of control of drug intake as well as blood pressure levels through the novel technique of 'savasana-meditation' developed by the yoga expert. Another collaborative project on 'crowding, noise and children' was designed to study the effects of crowding at home on the developmental aspects of children, including their physical well-being, motivation, perception of social support, stress, adaptation, and social withdrawal, if any. This study was done on school children against the crowding and noise background in school environment. All these studies showed Palsane's interdisciplinary orientation, cross-cultural perspective, and inclination to indigenization of psychology.

He guided more than 13 PhD students. He has contributed to the *First Survey of Research in Education*, a major reference volume published by the Centre of Advanced Study in education. He also has contributed as an associate editor of its second volume, and was a contributor to the third volume which was published by NCERT. His contribution to the *Fourth Survey of Research on Psychology* by the ICSSR was a significant one and was well received.

## Model Video Course Materials

When UGC decided to make video lectures following the national policy on education, it selected 15 major subjects taught at the UG level in India. Psychology was one of the subjects where video lectures were supposed to be made with the help and guidance of national-level experts. Based on the experience, expertise, and his approach to the subject, Palsane was chosen as the coordinator for psychology. He was entrusted with the responsibility of planning, writing the scripts, inviting and appointing the expert psychologists, and producing the video lectures. He produced 300 model video lectures in psychology with the help of the other experts from the field. These video lectures were considered a major production in multimedia and were telecasted by DD2 regularly. This is yet another example of use of his expertise in completing the herculean task in a stipulated period. This speaks for Palsane's approach, competence, and commitment to the field.

After retirement, he developed an interest in poetry and has published some of his poems in Hindi and Marathi which reflect his sensitivity to human life, experiences, and existence of human beings, a subject which he tried to teach and share with his students, colleagues, and community at large.

# 44

# Rabindra Nath Kanungo

Manuel Mendonca

*Rabindra Nath Kanungo*

Rabindra Nath Kanungo joined McGill University Faculty of Management in 1969 and currently he is Professor Emeritus at McGill. He taught courses in social psychology, cross-cultural management, organizational behaviour, consumer behaviour, and human resource management. He also conducted training seminars for various management groups. Before joining McGill, he was a professor at Dalhousie University, Halifax, IIM Kolkata, and IIT Bombay, in India. In his 31 years at McGill University, he has been deeply committed to the university's mission as an institution for the advancement of learning—a commitment manifested in his outstanding contributions to scholarship, to teaching, and to the university community. His work experience as a university professor, researcher, and consultant spans both East (India) and West (Canada and the USA).

## Affiliations

Kanungo gave generously of his time and wise counsel to the innumerable faculty/university assignments and committees. He regarded this service as a natural consequence of his membership in the university community. This sense of social responsibility is also manifested in his involvement in the community at large with his efforts to promote inter-cultural and inter-ethnic understanding.

Kanungo viewed research and teaching as mutually enriching activities that created McGill's vibrant intellectual life and reputation, and diligently sought to instil in his graduate and undergraduate students the values and virtues underlying these activities. In the Indian tradition of the guru–disciple relationship, he makes rigorous demands and sets high expectations for his students, but also empowers them to cope with challenges like the gardener who prunes and nurtures young saplings into fruit-bearing trees. At the doctoral and postdoctoral level, he has supervised and guided many students and helped them launch their academic careers by directly involving them in his research. For example, one of his former students has been appointed the co-editor of the new *International Journal of Cross Cultural Management*.

At the undergraduate level, an example of empowerment is the 'peer teaching' programme— a pedagogical innovation of Kanungo in the undergraduate 'Introduction to Organizational Behaviour' course. In this programme, a pair of senior undergraduates, who first complete an intensive preparatory programme with individualized coaching by the faculty, teach the undergraduate students. This unique pedagogical approach greatly enhanced the learning of organizational behaviour of the faculty's 400-plus students each year. The senior undergraduates who teach the course also find it immensely invaluable, as evidenced by the following statement in one of the many unsolicited testimonials. 'I am now involved with the training and development program for entry to middle-level managers in technology-based firms…I got the job, to a large extent, because of my experience with the Organizational Behavior Program'.

## Awards and Recognitions

Kanungo's scholarly work has resulted in more than 100 refereed publications in professional and academic journals, such as *Experimental Psychology, Journal of Applied Psychology, Journal of Personal and Social Psychology, Academy of Management Review, California Management Review, and Psychological Bulletin,* and 20 books in the basic and applied areas of psychology and management which are frequently cited by other academics and professionals. Indeed, scholars have acclaimed that his research has significantly advanced the body of knowledge in the area of work motivation and alienation, and organizational leadership in both developed and developing countries. His latest book is *Organizations and Management in Cross Cultural Context* (2014, SAGE, with Z. Aycan and M. Mendonca). For his contributions to psychology and management, he was elected a Fellow of the Canadian Psychological Association, awarded the faculty of management chair in organizational behaviour, and invited to serve as guest editor and editorial consultant to several professional journals in Canada, India, the USA, and the UK. He received numerous awards including Commonwealth Scholar, Seagram Senior Faculty Fellowships, the Award of Excellence from the Administrative Sciences Association of Canada, and several research grants.

## Contribution to the Field of Psychology

Kanungo's scholarly work in the area of work alienation and involvement, entrepreneurship and innovation, and organizational leadership are worth mentioning.

## Work Alienation and Involvement (Kanungo, 1982)

Social scientists and management practitioners are keenly aware of the necessity of having a clear grasp of the phenomena of work alienation and involvement, which play a central role in determining the social and economic climates of contemporary post-industrial societies. Kanungo's study of work alienation and involvement grew out of his disagreement and discontent with the existing conventional wisdom regarding the phenomena of work alienation and involvement, more specifically, from the conceptualization and measurement of the phenomena.

Realizing the importance of the phenomena for the workers and organizations, psychologists and sociologists have empirically studied the phenomena for several decades, but their studies resulted in piecemeal and culturally biased theories, and contradictory findings with questionable cross-cultural generalizability. The increasing numbers of studies on work alienation had introduced increasing amounts of confusion and vagueness, rather than clarity, to our understanding. Very often, the conceptual bases of these studies are of questionable validity and limited generalizability. The results of these studies have often perpetuated many myths, rather than facts.

Kanungo dispelled these myths with a cross-culturally valid, integrative-conceptual framework and the development of appropriate measurement techniques for use in future research. He adopted a motivational framework to study work alienation and involvement for two basic reasons. First, theories of human motivation at work are generally advanced to explain all work behaviour including alienation or involvement at work. Second, the existing motivational constructs can adequately and parsimoniously explain work alienation and involvement. In addition to the use of motivational language, his approach is characterized by an emphasis on the following considerations:

1. The analysis of the behavioural phenomena is at the individual level.
2. It distinguishes the state of work alienation from its causes and its effects.
3. Work involvement is viewed as a generalized cognitive (or belief) state of psychological identification with work, in so far as work is perceived to have the potentiality to satisfy one's salient needs and expectations. Likewise, work alienation is viewed as a generalized cognitive (or belief) state of psychological separation from work, in so far as work is perceived to lack the potentiality for satisfying one's salient needs and expectations.
4. The phenomenon is caused by two sets of events—historical and contemporaneous.

His integrative-conceptual approach with appropriate measurement techniques provide a clearer and more systematic understanding of the phenomenon of work alienation across different cultures.

It also puts to rest many culturally biased and faulty conceptions regarding the nature of work ethics and job involvement, and their impact on individuals and organizations.

# Entrepreneurship and Innovation (Kanungo, 1998)

The book presents the conceptual groundwork for entrepreneurship and innovation which facilitate the development of comprehensive research-based models of entrepreneurship in the context of development. Many developing countries are in a state of transition, striving to move from a subsistence-oriented, tightly integrated, inward-looking local economy to a surplus-seeking, market-led, and outward-looking economy. Such a move is possible only with the emergence of a multitude of small-scale and rural enterprises in all walks of life. This requires the building up of a wider base of population capable of entrepreneurial behaviour.

For example, in India, the initial build-up of entrepreneurial activity took place in urban centres followed over time by a trickle-down effect in rural communities. Today, the development strategy seeks a more proactive and immediate change. While much of the policy-making in this regard treats enterprise creation as a function of appropriate economic conditions (made possible through institutional and economic interventions), others have emphasized training and attitudinal change as vital elements in the process. However, these interventions are not based on the systematic observation and research into the process through which entrepreneurship emerges and sustains itself. Hence, there is a need to develop comprehensive, research-based models of entrepreneurship in the context of development for enhancing our understanding and for practical guidance. Towards this end, based on systematic observations of a number of social scientists working in this area, the book discusses several models and related issues, briefly described below:

- Conceptual models that provide multidisciplinary perspectives on entrepreneurship and innovation. The discussion of the conceptual frameworks includes an explanation of the entrepreneurship phenomenon; a typology for theory development; the relationships among the various elements that describe the entrepreneurship process; and the critical roles of both cultural and business environment.
- A focus on the entrepreneur as a person: in particular, the role of entrepreneurial intentions and motivations in enterprise creation and growth; the problems and prospects of women entrepreneurs in the context of socio-economic development; and, the neglected issue of entrepreneurs' ethical conduct and its impact on business and society.
- A focus on small-scale and rural enterprises exhibiting entrepreneurial and innovative processes critical for their competitiveness which include critical analyses of the nature of a group of enterprises called the third-sector organizations, such as co-operatives; structure and problems; strategic and managerial dimensions that are vital for socio-economic development; and the processes of innovation in the institutional context of developing countries.
- Management skills needed for starting and sustaining the small business: in particular, bank financing and improving banking services to benefit small business entrepreneurs; small business marketing and skills needed to improve marketing operations; and the development of appropriate entrepreneurial characteristics, managerial processes, and effective support systems for enterprise sustenance and growth.

# Leadership (Kanungo & Conger, 1998; Kanungo & Mendonca, 2007)

Leadership is a ubiquitous phenomenon, and the exciting, adventurous, and romantic exploits of leaders together with their foibles and ruthlessness have been the subject of much folklore, myth, and literature. In order to understand scientifically the phenomenon of charismatic leadership, the book develops a theoretical framework based on the essential leader roles in large organizations, which are to formulate goals and to move organizational members from an existing present state towards a desired future state.

## The Charismatic Model

The model incorporates these roles in a unified conceptual framework of behavioural dimensions in three stages, described below: empirical studies in different organizational contexts and conducted in three different countries, Canada, India, the USA, have established the validity of the model.

*Stage 1—Evaluation of the Status Quo*: Before planning courses of action, charismatic leaders critically evaluate the status quo by a realistic assessment of (a) environmental constraints and resources in order to identify the deficiencies in the status quo and the poorly exploited opportunities, and (b) the needs and aspirations of the followers.

*Stage 2—Formulation and Articulation of the Future Vision*: After assessing the environment, charismatic leaders formulate an idealized vision which is discrepant from the status quo; embodies a perspective shared by the followers; and promises to meet the followers' hopes and aspirations. Charismatic leaders then articulate the vision with expressive modes of action that manifest their conviction, self-confidence, and dedication to the vision.

The more the future goal is idealized, the more discrepant it becomes in relation to the status quo. The more idealized and discrepant the goal is, the more likely is the followers' attribution that it is not just an ordinary goal and that the leader has extraordinary vision. Such a goal also provides followers a sense of challenge, a force for change.

Followers attribute charisma to the leader when the vision represents an embodiment of a perspective shared by followers; such a vision also motivates the followers to place the interests of the organization over their own interests—even at personal cost.

*Stage 3—Achieving the Vision*: In the final stage of the leadership process, effective leaders engage in behaviours which build in followers a trust in the leader's vision, more specifically, in the leader's abilities to achieve the organization's goals necessary to realize the vision.

Generally, leaders are perceived as trustworthy when they advocate their position in a disinterested and selfless manner, demonstrate a concern for followers' needs rather than their own self-interest, and also when they are seen to be knowledgeable and experts in their areas of influence.

# The Dark Side of Charisma

Charismatic leaders are remarkable change agents, able to reinvent entire organizations and societies. They are also superb examples of master communicators and motivators. Throughout history, certain charismatic leaders have been master manipulators and purveyors of evil and have produced disastrous outcomes for both followers and organizations due to factors such as flawed vision, dysfunctional relations with followers, and succession challenges.

Underlying the shadow side of charisma raises the important issue of the ethical standards of a 'good' leader. Along with the professional competence and abilities necessary to the task, A good leader must have a well formed character, that is, the moral conscience, in order to act honestly. A good leader creates a vision that other people can believe in and build together, always putting the needs of others before his own.

This strong altruistic value and orientation manifests itself on three dimensions: the leader's motives; the leader's influence strategies; and the leader's character formation. Hence, the leadership behaviours in the three-stage Charismatic model will be effective only to the extent that leaders perform these behaviours with an altruistic intent—to serve and benefit the organization and its members.

# References

Kanungo, R.N. (1982). Work alienation: an integrative approach. New York, NY: Praeger.

———. (Ed.) (1998). Entrepreneurship and innovation: models for development. Thousand Oaks, CA: SAGE Publications.

Kanungo, R.N., & Conger, J.A. (1998). Charismatic leadership in organizations. Thousand Oaks, CA: SAGE Publications.

Kanungo, R.N., & Mendonca, M. (2007). Ethical leadership. Berkshire: Open University Press.

# 45

# Anand Chintaman Paranjpe

(1936)

## Rama Charan Tripathi

Anand Chintaman Paranjpe

Anand Chintaman Paranjpe was born on 13 March 1936 in Chiplun, a small coastal town in Maharashtra. He had his primary education in Karnataka in Kannada medium, followed by schooling in Marathi medium at various places in Maharashtra. His undergraduate training in psychology was at Fergusson College in Pune, followed by an MA in experimental psychology at the

University of Pune, which he completed in 1961. He completed his PhD in social psychology in 1967 at the University of Pune under the guidance of V.K. Kothurkar. In 1966, he was awarded the Smith-Mundt and Fulbright Fellowship to study at Harvard. At Harvard, he took courses but mainly spent time dialoguing with his advisor, Erik H. Erikson. He joined as an assistant professor at Simon Fraser University in Vancouver, Canada, in 1967. He taught at Simon Fraser till 2001, where he continues as emeritus professor of psychology and humanities. As an undergraduate student, Anand Paranjpe studied philosophy with experimental psychology as a subsidiary subject. He was struck by the totally Western emphasis in his philosophy courses, and was surprised at being allowed to graduate in philosophy without a single course in Indian philosophy. Much later, reading William James's *Varieties of Religious Experience* that led him to explore the Indian counterparts of religious experience. In that context, he also came across R.D. Ranade's book *Mysticism in Maharashtra*, which turned him to reading the poetry of the seventeenth-century Marathi saint-poet Tukaram. This reading evoked a deep interest in him, which has not abated.

Anand Paranjpe's interest in experimental psychology was noticed by his teacher at the University of Pune, V.K. Kothurkar, who asked him to work as a demonstrator in the Department of Psychology. He tried to be a 'rat runner' in that capacity, but without much success. While working as a demonstrator, he was offered a position as research associate in a longitudinal study of college students at the Deccan College in Pune by Y.B. Damle, a sociologist, for three years. This led him to develop research interests in two areas—the social psychology of inter-caste relations in Maharashtra and the process of identity formation. He pursued his first interest on inter-caste relations for a doctorate under the direction of V.K. Kothurkar and studied the process of identity formation while working with Y.B. Damle. These dual interests exposed him to the seminal works of two famous psychology professors at Harvard—Gordon W. Allport's work on prejudice, and Erik Erikson's work on ego-identity. In a chance encounter, he met Erikson at Pune, who was then in India working on his book *Gandhi's Truth*. The Fulbright Fellowship in 1966–1967 happened partly due to his desire to learn from these two sources of inspiration. At Harvard, Anand focused mainly on reading up on Erikson's work on identity and having extended discussions with him on the subject. He also sat in courses offered by Stanley Milgram, Tom Pettigrew, David McClelland, and others. It was Stanley Milgram who encouraged Anand Paranjpe to focus on psychology in the Indian tradition. While at Harvard, Anand also came in close contact with another professor, the well-known anthropologist Cora DuBois, who, along with G.W. Allport and Erik Erikson, Anand considers as his mentors. It was Allport's advice and recommendation that landed him a job at Simon Fraser.

## Initial Years of Teaching

Although hired by Simon Fraser University to teach mainly social psychology, Anand developed teaching interests in theories of personality, and history and systems of psychology, both of which were areas in which he had interest but no training. His first book, *Caste, Prejudice and the Individual*, which was based on his doctoral dissertation, came out in 1970 (Paranjpe, 1970). His second book, *In Search of Identity*, was published by McMillan India and was also adopted by Wiley Interscience for worldwide circulation (Paranjpe, 1975). The book applied Erikson's theory of identity development to understand the formation of identity of the Indian youth. The book came to be widely known in academic circles from the UK to Japan and South Africa. A textbook of social and personality development by William Damon devoted several pages to this work.

It was after five years of teaching at Simon Fraser that Anand got invited to a position at IIM. Calcutta. He was attracted to it because it gave him a chance to consider returning to India. He tried it for a year, but the organizational setting with its demands for consultancy did not excite him much. So he returned to Simon Fraser in 1973. There were some other events that induced him to return to Canada. In a national conference of psychologists in January 1973, he presented a paper with two related themes—first, that psychology, particularly social psychology, should be taught with reference to Indian (and not only American) social context in mind, and second, that psychologists in India need not turn their backs on the country's rich intellectual legacy. The response to this presentation by Indian psychologists was a deafening silence. Upon presenting the same paper to colleagues at IIM, one of the colleagues said that what he was teaching was Indian psychology, which is nonsense. For, he was told, psychology is a science, and there can be no regional variations, even as there cannot be Russian physics or German chemistry.

The year in India was not all a waste. Anand was invited by Durganand Sinha for a lecture at a UGC-sponsored workshop at the University of Allahabad, and he found a new mentor who was to support him for years to come.

## Middle Phase of Career and Later

Although strongly castigated for his interest in Indian psychology, Anand thought that it was time to give it a chance. He started reading *Patanjali's* Yoga aphorisms, first in English translations, and then slowly moving on to Sanskrit text and its major commentaries. Side by side, he started reading in the area of consciousness, which was re-emerging as a topic of interest in North American psychology. He also started reading classical sources of Western psychology starting with Plato and Aristotle, using the teaching of the history of psychology as an excuse to do so. This gave him a philosophical foundation essential for work in theoretical psychology. Slowly, a comparative theoretical perspective with a focus on ontological and epistemological foundations of Western and Indian psychology started to emerge. This led to the formulation of the theme of his third book, *Theoretical Psychology: The Meeting of East and West*, which was published by Springer-Science in the PATH series in 1984. In this book, he examined several prominent approaches to consciousness in Indian and Western psychology (Paranjpe, 1984). Professorship at Simon Fraser followed soon after the publication of this book.

Throughout this phase, Anand Paranjpe developed some international connections, particularly through participation in conferences in the International Association of Cross-Cultural Psychology. Durganand Sinha's encouragement and the presence of a large Indian contingent in the annual conferences of the IACCP helped him in significant ways. The repeated invitations from Durganand Sinha and his colleagues at the University of Allahabad were also significant as they supported his commitment to carry forward his studies and work on Indian psychology. His series of visits to Allahabad allowed him to keep close touch with ongoing developments in psychology in India. During this period, while Allahabad provided him an intellectual home, Paranjpe found a counterpart in Canada with a small but dedicated group of psychologists in western Canada interested in theoretical psychology. He contributed chapters to a series of edited books that this group published.

Toward the completion of the last phase of his work on the book *Theoretical Psychology*, Anand recognized a close parallel between the Western and Indian views of personhood— in the ideas of John Locke as cognition, emotion, and volition as three pillars of personhood on the Western side, and the Vedantic notion of the person (*jīva*) as a knower, enjoyer/sufferer, and agent on the Indian side. He used this parallel as a most plausible bridge for the integration of Indian and Western perspectives in psychology. He developed this in his magnum opus *Self and Identity in Modern Psychology and Indian Thought* (Paranjpe, 1998). In this book he, compared Indian and Western views of cognition, emotion, and volition, and pointed out the contrast between the two traditions—continuing changes in the process of 'becoming a person' on the Western side, and the search of firm foundations of self-sameness on the Indian side. The experience of pure consciousness attained through the systematic transformation of cognition, emotion, and volition through the practice of *jñānā, bhakti,* and *karma-yoga*s is viewed as the key to self-realization, the ideal of personal development in Indian thought.

## Post-retirement

In a quite unexpected way, a new phase began in Anand's work when he received an invitation from Matthijs Cornelissen to give a keynote address at a conference organized by Sri Aurobindo Ashram in Pondicherry just after his retirement from Simon Fraser University. There he met a large number of like-minded scholars who shared a keen interest in interpreting and advancing psychological insights and techniques of the Indian tradition. At this conference, K. Ramakrishna Rao drafted, and helped proclaim, the Pondicherry Manifesto of Indian Psychology. This was the beginning of a movement for the revival of the long-neglected tradition of psychology in India.

Soon after the historic conference in Pondicherry, Rao initiated an idea for working toward three volumes to help promote Indian psychology—a textbook, a handbook, and a source-book of Indian psychology. Anand Paranjpe became involved in this enterprise, which saw a slow and partial completion over the following decade. With him as a co-editor along with K. Ramakrishna Rao and Ajit Dalal, the *Handbook of Indian Psychology* was published in 2008 by Cambridge University Press, New Delhi (Rao, Paranjpe & Dalal, 2008). The close collaboration between Anand Paranjpe and K. Ramakrishna Rao led to another joint volume titled *Psychology in the Indian Tradition* (Rao & Paranjpe, 2016). Anand Paranjpe's interest in the concept of *bhakti,* which arose during his undergraduate days, has stayed with him. He is presently engaged in the psychological interpretation of bhakti as evident in the poetry of various Maharashtrian saints, but more specifically of Saint Tukaram. His most recent paper on the idea of god in the poetry of Saint Tukaram testifies to this.

## References

Paranjpe, A.C. (1970). *Caste, prejudice and the individual.* Bombay: Lalvani Publishing House.

————. (1975). *In search of identity.* New York, NY: John Wiley.

————. (1984). *Theoretical psychology: The meeting of East and West.* New York, NY: Springer-Science.

————. (1998). *Self and identity in modern psychology and Indian thought.* New York, NY: Springer.

Rao, K.R., & Paranjpe, A.C. (2016). *Psychology in the Indian tradition.* New Delhi: Springer.

Rao, K.R., Paranjpe, A.C., & Dalal, A.K. (Eds). (2008). *Handbook of Indian psychology.* New Delhi: Cambridge University Press.

# 46

# Chandrashekhar Gangadhar Deshpande

(1936)

Satishchandra Kumar, Anjali Majumdar, Tejal Dhulla, Heena Kamble, and Aarti Ramaswami

*Chandrashekhar Gangadhar Deshpande*

Chandrashekhar Gangadhar Deshpande, or C.G. Deshpande or 'C.G.' as he is popularly called, was born on 23 December 1936 in Mahal area of Nagpur. He grew up near Badkas Chowk, Nagpur, in his humble middle class family along with five brothers and two sisters. His primary education was in a corporation school, which was just two furlongs away from his home, the nearness of the school being a major criterion. After completing his primary education, he was enrolled in C.P. and Berar High school, a well-known educational institution in Mahal area. G.S. Gokhale was the superintendent of this school. Deshpande passed his 11th standard matriculation examination in 1954. By this time, his father had shifted to his own house located on Tilak Road, just opposite to renowned Hislop College. With a well-known missionary college right across the road, he joined it for first year in the science stream. He was unsuccessful in the inter-science examination in the first attempt. However, after passing this examination, he joined a BA course and obtained his degree in 1959.

Subsequently, at the behest of his father, he joined the Nagpur University Law College, where he received an educational scholarship. He successfully cleared his LLB degree in 1961. He had been fascinated with psychology since his college days. His favourite teacher was Shesh, whom he fondly remembers. In those days, the University of Nagpur did not offer MA in psychology, so he decided to join the University of Pune, where MA in experimental psychology was available. V.K. Kothurkar, renowned experimental psychologist, was the professor and head of this department. C.G. Deshpande was selected for 'King Edward Memorial Scholarship' for his MA education and received ₹200 per month for 2 years. Besides, he was exempted from paying fees for the MA degree because of the prevailing rule of the University of Pune that student scoring 50 per cent or above in the examination was exempted from paying any fees. He was one such student. He stayed in Pune with his elder brother for the first year and then shifted to the University of Pune hostel. He described his hostel life in the University of Pune as very joyful and unforgettable. He received his MA degree in June 1963.

Deshpande is one of the known faces of psychology in rural Maharashtra. He practiced psychology at the grassroots level and is a link between urban and rural psychologists of Maharashtra. He narrated the events that led to his appointment as a lecturer in the reputed S.P. College of Pune. He read an advertisement in local newspaper of Pune about the post of a lecturer in psychology in S.P. College. He applied for the post, though the MA results had not yet been declared. Even on the day of interview, results were pending. Malegaonkar, the principal of the college, enquired about the MA marksheet. Deshpande told him that results had not been declared. However, he said confidently that he would score above 55 per cent, which surprised the principal. He was appointed as a lecturer with a condition that he would not join the college if he would get less than 55 per cent. Fortunately, he got his marksheet with 58 per cent and he joined S.P. College, Pune, as a lecturer in psychology in June 1963. Kaole was the head of the department, which included both philosophy and psychology.

A year later, Phatak, the principal of Chalisgaon College, approached him and asked him to join his college at Chalisgaon as head of the Department of Psychology, when the college decided to start psychology special courses. However, Deshpande declined the offer, as he was more interested in completing his PhD. He requested V.K. Kothurkar, who, as he told, always helped him in his career, to accept him as a PhD student. Kothurkar readily conceded to his request and Deshpande enrolled himself in the University of Pune in around 1965. He submitted his PhD thesis in 1968 titled 'A Comparative Study of Caste and Inter-caste Marriages in Maharashtra, with Special Reference to Personal, Familial and Societal Adjustments'.

In 1968 he had applied for the post of a lecturer in the Department of Psychology, University of Poona. He worked hard and had submitted his thesis before the interview was held. Shri Pataskar, former Governor of Madhya Pradesh, was the then vice-chancellor of the University of Poona. Deshpande was selected for the post of lecturer and he joined the Department of Psychology, University of Pune, in September 1969. He has wilfully stated that his career really started under the rich academic experience of his mentor V.K. Kothurkar after joining the Department of Psychology, University of Poona. He has always expressed his indebtedness to him. He continued on this post till 1989.

He was the director of the Distance Education Center, University of Pune, from 1985 to 1989. Along with that, he was the chairman of the Institute of Open Education, Pune, in 1987. He was also the director of the MBA Entrance Examination, University of Pune, in 1987. He held the position of Director at Population Education, University of Pune in 1987–1988. He was also the director for Adult and Continuing Education, University of Pune, 1987–1988. In 1988, he was the director of the Educational Media Research Center at University of Pune. In 1989, he was offered the post of professor and the director of Student Services Division at Yashvantrao Chavan Maharashtra Open University, Nashik, by the vice-chancellor of the institute. He accepted the offer and stayed at this position till 1991.

He joined the Department of Communication Studies, University of Pune, in 1991 as professor and head of the department. He remained in that position till 1993, after which he joined the Department of Applied Psychology and the Counselling Center, University of Mumbai, as professor and head of the department in July 1994. Although the idea of the University of Mumbai's counselling centre was proposed under the headship of Bhagwatwar, it was under the headship of Deshpande that the counselling centre was officially attached to the Department of Applied Psychology, as aided by UGC, in October 1995. He became the first director of the counselling centre. The centre was inaugurated by the renowned psychologist H.S. Asthana, and the event was presided over by Snehlata Deshmukh, the then vice-chancellor of the University of Mumbai (Annual Report, 1995–1996). He remained the head of UDAP till 31 December 1996 and worked tirelessly towards strengthening the effectiveness of the counselling centre during his tenure.

During his esteemed long career, Deshpande has also been a contributory teacher at various institutions. He was a contributory teacher at the Department of Psychiatry, B.J. Medical College, Pune, from 1968 to 1980. He was also a contributory faculty for management teaching at the Institute of Management Studies and Research, Lonavala, from 1978 to 1984. In 1985, he became a contributory teacher at the Department of Psychiatry, Armed Forces Medical College, Pune. He remained there for a year. In 1997, he was the director of the International Center at the University of Pune. In the session of 2005–2006, he was a contributory faculty for management teaching at the Institute of Management Studies, Symbiosis, in Pune. In 2008, he was appointed by the department of AYUSH as a visiting professor for Morarji Desai National Institute of Yoga in New Delhi, Ministry of Health and Family Welfare, Government of India, New Delhi. He continued this work till 2010. He guided three MPhil students and seven PhD students.

## Honours and Awards

Deshpande held many honorary positions and received several scholarships and awards. In 1982, he received the Research Associate Scholar by UGC, New Delhi. He also became the honorary president of the Pune branch of Indian Psychiatric Association in 1982 (Deshpande, 2001). Between 1978 and 1985, he worked as the chief test administrator (CTA) for about 30 different bank examinations conducted by the Institute of Banking Personnel Selection (IBPS), Mumbai. He held the position of chairman of the Board of Studies in Psychology in the University of Pune from 1983 to 1985 and in the University of Mumbai from 1994 to 1996. He was the chairman of the All India Psychological Council from 1995 to 1996 (Annual Report, 1994–1995). He received the 'Swami Pranavanand Eastern Psychology Award' at the Indian Science Congress held at Patiala in 1995 (Annual Report, 1996–1997). He was the president of the Indian Psychological Association in 1996.

Deshpande also worked as a guest editor of the *Indian Psychological Review* for its special Millennium Issue on 'Mental Health and Peace' in December 2000. He is the founder director of the Human Education Society, Pune. He started this academic organization in 2001 and ran a professional course entitled 'Diploma in Professional Skills in Psychology'. Thirty-five students in five batches completed this diploma course.

Deshpande was president of the Indian Association of Mental Health (IAMH) for two terms, from 2006 to 2011 and from 2011 to 2015. He has also been the chairman of the Indian Association of Human Behaviour (IAHB) since 2008. Through his associations with IAHB and IAMH, he gave a platform to psychologists from rural Maharashtra to express their ideas and opinions and develop their skills. He organized conferences in rural Maharashtra, and also in Pune and Mumbai. He also conducted workshops for the development of rural students, and teachers. To increase connectivity among rural and urban psychologists, Deshpande also provided a directory of psychologists who are the members of IAHB (Deshpande & Shejwal, 2014).

At present, he is a member of the academic council and general body of Morarji Desai National Institute of Yoga (MDNIY), New Delhi. He contributes as a psychologist both in terms of academic curriculum and the National Yoga Week which every year MDNIY conducts in New Delhi. C.G. Deshpande gave 15 talks at the All India Radio (AIR) and participated in 10 discussions on AIR. He also delivered 25 keynote addresses in various conferences.

## Research Contribution

Over the years, Deshpande has worked on many research projects and has published about 40 research articles in both national and international journals. He has also published a few research-based books. *On Inter-caste Marriage* was funded and published in 1972 by a grant given by the Indian Council of Social Science Research (ICSSR), New Delhi. He published a Marathi book on 'Abnormal Psychology; in 1974. It was funded by Maharashtra Universities Book Production Board and published by Continental Prakashan, Pune. He published another Marathi book in 1975 on 'Mental Health'. It was published by the University of Pune. In 1975, he worked as a chief investigator for a project entitled 'Acceptability of Chemical Fertilizers by Farmers in Hoshangabad district' conducted by the Rural Development Center, Pune, and funded by Dharamsi Morarji Fertilizers. He authored another research-based book in 1978 titled *Suicide and Attempted Suicide*. It was funded and published by UGC, New Delhi. He also co-authored Marathi books on social psychology and general psychology between 1978 and 1979. In 1980, his paper 'A Documentary Note on Suicide in Ancient Indian Literature' was published in the *Indian Philosophical Quarterly* (Deshpande, 1980).

In 1982 he did another project on 'Psychosocial Aspects of Post Graduate Students' funded by Vidyarti Sahayak Samiti in Pune. Another one of his projects in 1984, 'Personality Development' was implemented in 21 colleges funded by the University of Pune. He did a project on 'Impact of Media' in 1987 which was funded by UGC. He also wrote eight books on 'Personality Development' which were published by Yashwantrao Chavan Maharashtra Open University, Nashik. Deshpande also co-authored a book titled *An Introduction to Psychology* in 1992, published by Pratima Prakashan.

In 1995 he worked on a research project in collaboration with Schoemacher, New Castle, Australia, titled 'Eating Disorders Among Adolescents'. His project 'Indian Norms of Raven's Progressive Matrices Tests' in 1998 was funded by British Research Foundation, UK.

He also published this project as a research-based book in 2000. He conducted a study on 'Norms for Stressful Life Events; in Maharashtra which was funded by Manasayan. It was published in the the *Indian Psychological Review* in 2001. The British Research Foundation funded another of his projects, 'Tribal Norms of Raven's Progressive Matrices Test'. He published a paper for this project titled 'Raven Standard Progressive Matrices Norms for Indian Tribal Areas' along with Vanita Patwardhan (Deshpande & Patwardhan, 2006). This project was published in a book titled *Uses and Abuses of Intelligence*, edited by John and Jean Raven (2008). In 2010, he conducted another study titled 'Religious Profile of Indian Youth' which was funded by the Human Education Society, Pune. In 2013, Deshpande also wrote a report for the Human Education Society titled 'Retrospect: 2001 to 2012'. He also worked on the report for the Indian Association for Human Behaviour, which was titled 'Looking Back: 1992 to 2014'. 'Treatment Resistant Schizophrenia' was one of his major research projects funded by the UGC. This was published in 2015.

Deshpande wrote about 200 popular articles in newspapers, magazines, and periodicals. He wrote an article every week for the daily *Prabhat* (Pune) for 3 years on various subjects related to psychology such as family, personality development, interpersonal relations, and social problems. He also developed psychological tests, six of which have been published. These include Marriage Adjustment Inventory, Personal Adjustment Inventory, and Conflictive Thoughts Analysis Inventory. These three tests are available with manuals with Psychomatrix, Neelkanth House.

# References

Deshpande, C.G. (1980). A documentary note on suicide in ancient Indian literature. *Indian Philosophical Quarterly, VIII* (1), 59–64.

———. (2001). *Human relationship monograph*. Pune: Indian Association of Human Behaviour.

Deshpande, C.G., & Patwardhan, V. (2006). Raven standard progressive matrices norms for Indian tribal areas. *WebPsychEmpiricist*. Retrieved 4 September 2006, from http://wpe.info/papers_table.html

Deshpande, C.G., & Shejwal, B.R. (2014). *Indian association of human behaviour (Looking Back: 1992 to 2014)*. Pune: Sawkar Art Service.

Raven J.C., & Raven, J. (2008). *Uses and abuses of intelligence*. New York: Royal Fireworks Press.

University of Bombay. (1994, 1 April–1995, 31 March). *Annual report for the year 1994–1995* (pp. 30–31). Bombay: Author.

———. (1995, 1 April–1996, 31 March). *Annual report for the year 1995–1996* (pp. 22–23). Bombay: Author.

———. (1996, 1 April–1997, 31 March). *Annual report for the year 1996–1997* (pp. 24–25). Bombay: Author.

# 47

## Kishor Moreshwar Phadke

(1936)

Anjali Joshi and Satishchandra Kumar

*Kishor Moreshwar Phadke*

It was an early Sunday morning in Ahmedabad during 1966. Usually people lie comfortably in their bed at this time. But for Phadke, Sunday was no different from any other weekday. He was a senior scientific officer in the Ahmedabad Textile Industries' Research Association, ATIRA. His daily routine used to start at 5 AM in the morning. After completing his morning chores, at around 8 AM he headed towards Gujarat University. Sunday was his favourite day as he could sit and read in the library as long as he wished.

As usual, he went to the pile of psychology books which had been stacked in the corner of the reading room. Ah! One title was very attractive. *Experiments in Behaviour Therapy*, a book edited by

H.J. Eysenck (1964). He started reading it and was soon utterly absorbed in it. It had one section on 'rational psychotherapy' (now popularly known as rational emotive behaviour therapy or REBT) by eminent psychologist Albert Ellis, the founder of REBT. This was unheard of. Being a voracious reader, he did not take much time to read it.

The following year, he came across another book by Ellis, *Reason and Emotion in Psychotherapy* (1962). As he was reading the book, he was convinced by many of the principles and practices. He began inquiring if universities or other institutions of higher education in India could possibly offer him a systematic course in REBT, but that was in vain. People were not aware of this therapy. As he wanted to study the subject in depth, he followed the path that scores of scholars in different fields had travelled before him, the sovereign path of self-help. Alas! Even that path was strewn with several difficulties. The foremost among those difficulties was the non-availability of REBT literature in India.

Finally, he decided to import a copy of the book *A Guide to Rational Living* by Ellis and Harper (1961). For this, he approached a well-known bookseller in Mumbai. That time, there were stringent restrictions on remittance of US dollars. International shipping services used to take months for delivery. It took almost a year to receive it. Instead of quenching his passion for REBT, it augmented it so much so that soon he started toying with the idea of initiating a dialogue with Albert Ellis himself. Finally, emboldened by the experience of using REBT in his own life, he ventured to write his first letter to Ellis on 29 April 1968. Fortunately, Ellis was kind enough to reply promptly. Ellis not only replied to him once, but for several years he replied tirelessly to the series of his letters. To be precise, this most unusual correspondence course in the world lasted for 36 years.

In the true sense, it was a scholarly debate between the ascended master and his stalwart disciple. It was an exchange of thoughts between two great minds. It consisted of Phadke's innumerable queries and scientific enquiries about REBT and meticulous answers given by Ellis. Over the years, Phadke had been questioning, challenging, and attacking almost every aspect of theory and practice of REBT and in return had received not only a stream of books and articles as gifts, but also a highly individualized coaching and mentoring from the world's best authority on the subject. This correspondence is the most valuable resource for REBT scholars. It is bound in four volumes and consists of 1,351 pages. In 1987, Windy Dryden, a renowned professor of psychotherapeutic studies at Goldsmith's College, University of London, expressed his wish to see this correspondence. After studying these volumes, with great admiration, he wrote to Phadke saying that he (Phadke) really had an insatiable desire for knowledge and his attention to detail was worthy of an academic (1999). After Ellis' death, these volumes are preserved and cited in the Archives of Columbia University.

When Phadke wrote his first letter to Ellis, he had no idea that this move would cause a notable difference in his life. Spread of REBT had become his goal. Ellis applauds his contribution in apt words.

> Of all the followers, I have had, Kishore has surely been one of the most persistent and the very best. I could see from the start that he not only understood my teachings better than any other person in Asia, but was able to think about them and brilliantly add to them on his own and to present them beautifully to both professionals and members of the public. Kishore is indeed one of the most remarkable individuals I have ever met. (1999)

No wonder, Phadke is the first and the only Indian psychologist who enjoys the unique distinction of being a Fellow and supervisor of the Albert Ellis Institute for REBT, New York.

## Background and Education

Kishore hailed from a very respectable Maharashtrian family, the origins of which can be traced to the renowned nobleman, Haripant Phadke, lieutenant general in the *darbar* of Peshwas. Kishore was born on 20 February 1936. His father was a well-known general practitioner with an MBBS degree who practiced in Pune. His mother was a housewife who had studied till Standard VI. He has one younger and two elder brothers. His uncle was an illustrious communist leader and served many years in prison for the freedom movement. His family espoused a climate conducive to independent thoughts, intellectual pursuit, passion, and dedication. As a child, Kishore was a voracious reader, gobbling up any book he could get his hands on. This made him indulge in a great deal of soul-searching in his early years. This must have provoked him to join a special degree course in philosophy and masters course in psychology from the University of Pune in 1959.

## Professional Career

Turned from amateur to professional, Kishore was ready to take up his first leap in the professional world. In 1959, he began his career in the Department of Psychology, Ruparel College, Mumbai, in an ascending order of first as a demonstrator, then lecturer, and finally officiating professor and head of the department. He came to be known as an excellent and one of the most beloved professors. Soon college politics left him high and dry. In 1965, after serving for 5 years in Ruparel College, he moved to ATIRA, Ahmedabad, as a junior scientific officer in human resource (HR). Gradually, he became the senior scientific officer. Here, he got the opportunity to conduct various industry research projects. But his aspiration for teaching was not keeping him at ease. He started applying for teaching posts in universities and got selected as a demonstrator in 1969 in the University Department of Applied Psychology, University of Mumbai.

He left the university in four years and joined as faculty member at Sir Sorabji Pochkanawala Bankers Training College of Central Bank of India, Mumbai, in 1973. He trained thousands of bank officers across the country. He received numerous invitations from reputed institutes as guest speaker. But he was longing to fulfil his mission of spreading the philosophy of REBT in India. He wanted to devote himself wholeheartedly to his mission. Therefore, he needed complete freedom to design and plan the mission according to his vision. It was difficult to achieve it by staying in the comfort zone of his job. The promise of freedom was enticing and empowering.

Ellis' inspiring words rhymed within his heart:

> Keep asking yourself what you really desire in life. Keep experimenting and taking some reasonable risks to see what you think you want and you really do. But don't fool yourself that anything or everything you want, from yourself or others, absolutely must, should or ought to exist. (1981)

Finally in 1981, he resigned his teaching post at Bankers College and established his own training institute named 'Phadke Centre' with the intention of delivering education for life. It offered a variety of individual and group programmes founded on the principles and techniques of REBT. The most distinguishing feature of the centre was that it was the first citadel of learning in REBT to psychologists, psychiatrists, physicians, nurses, and professional social workers. He created his own training modules of primary and advanced workshops; each consisting of seven days which were meant only for professionals. He also devised two-day workshops for non-professionals. Thousands of trainees have attended these programmes. More than 200 organizations situated throughout the length and breadth of India, ranging from various sectors such as banking, manufacturing, medical, educational, and IT, organized his training programmes for their employees. He has trained over 10,000 executives from lower, middle, and top level of management.

That was the time when transactional analysis was popular in the corporate world. Training in REBT was unknown in the industrial world. Being a pioneer, Phadke encountered much resistance and opposition from the start, but using REBT's philosophy he has persisted, persisted, and persisted. Because of his intelligence, scholarship, and unusual energy and passion, he has built the REBT empire in India. His assiduous efforts blessed him with mastery over REBT. It was so distinguished that Indian scholars refer to his therapy as Ellis-Phadke Therapy (Joshi, 2011). Inspired by the zeal of spreading the message of rational living among his fellowmen and women, he has authored nine books in Marathi besides writing several popular articles and papers. He has also co-authored five books in English. His countless talks and sessions in various business, industrial, educational, research, and training organizations, workshops in industrial world, and courses in supervision for several future trainers have made REBT unusually influential in the Eastern world.

## REBT: The Life Goal

Phadke's first contact with REBT was in the library of Gujarat University. This library was a treasure trove of books. Every day, he studied there for hours. There was nothing he liked more than sitting in a corner and reading through a pile of books. He had started devouring two or three books a week on a broad range of subjects such as psychology, philosophy, literature, language, political science, teaching method, cultural anthropology, sociology, and many more. Not only was he an avid reader, he loved to ponder over what he read. These books availed him an opportunity to reflect on and deeply engage with issues and concerns of human behaviour. His seemingly endless curiosity helped him maintain a spirit of lifelong learning. This was the time when he first corresponded with Ellis. His deep interest in REBT evoked Ellis to send him his books and articles. Many a times, the postal delivery of this material got delayed or misplaced. But with great tolerance, he waited patiently. Today he has a collection of Ellis' well over 70 books and 500 articles and research papers. He not only read all this materials but has reviewed, analyzed, and researched them painstakingly. He devised his own methods for studying this material. He used to read the writing first, then underline important sentences and paragraphs, ruminate over them, read the paragraphs again and again, note down the meaning of difficult words in the margin, prepare brief notes, and jot down important stuff in his diary. In this way, each and every writing of Ellis was read and pondered over by him at least thrice. Eventually, it was understood so deeply that the contents were known to him by heart. Today any reference to REBT, no matter how old, is ready on his lips without opening a single book.

If a word had different meanings in different cultures, he used to invest his time and energy in searching for the authentic flavour of the word and the correct context. Because of the correct usage of words, his own diction is flawless and is marked by clarity, brevity, and precision. This is clearly displayed in his writing. In none of his books or articles can one find long sentences or rambling thoughts. The content of each of his book is well-knit, has logical order, and carries crystal clear message for readers. Being a sceptic, he used to examine Ellis writings from a scientific point of view. This investigation leads to many questions lingering in his mind. Only Ellis could answer these questions. Noting down his questions, arranging then in a logical and consistent order, retaining absolute essential points, and preparing a draft was indeed a herculean task. Each of his writing went through three drafts; two rough drafts with pencil and a final draft with ink. He had to get each letter typed and there was just one typist in the outskirts of his town. It was only after several years that he bought his own typewriter.

One may find it surprising that Phadke neither travelled abroad nor got the opportunity to observe Ellis' practice but still achieved mastery in REBT practice. The answer lies in one of his attributes: adherence. He created his unique method to learn REBT practice too. Many of Ellis' books and articles contain verbatim records of the cases he handled. Phadke started reading clients' dialogue without seeing Ellis' intervention. He used to predict what Ellis would have said in that place and then would cross check on uncovering. He used to introspect for any flaw, omission, or different interpretation from his end and improve the next time. In this way, he studied numerous cases. Now there was no need for him to cover Ellis' intervention. He could predict word for word how Ellis would have responded to any of his clients. Later on, he procured Ellis' audiotapes and, finally, he could see how Ellis conducted his sessions when he visited Mumbai.

His sedulous efforts bore fruit in 1977. The Institute for Advanced Study in Rational Psychotherapy, (currently known as Albert Ellis Institute, New York) bestowed upon him the status of 'Fellow' and later, in 1989, he was awarded the coveted honour of 'supervisor'. According to the regulations of the institute at that time, the status of Fellow was given to only those aspirants who had a postdoctorate in psychology and had completed 2 years intensive training programme of the institute. Phadke had neither a doctorate nor had he visited the institute. Extended discussions were held on this issue among the training committee members as he was not fulfilling the above criteria. Ellis stood beside Phadke and recommended him strongly. He was able to convince the committee about the significance of his work in India. Phadke was made an exception to the criteria and was awarded the unique honour. The status of supervisor enabled him to conduct training programmes for professionals. This boosted his morale and he continued to promulgate the work of REBT with fortified zeal and inspiration. His cherished dream to meet Ellis in person was fulfilled in July 1980 when Ellis visited India for three days at his cordial invitation.

## Major Contributions to REBT

In the initial stages of his correspondence, Phadke often thought that the thousands of miles of physical distance between himself and his mentor was a great handicap. Later, he discovered, it had saving grace also. As he did not have the benefit of direct supervision on his work, he was forced to rely on his own resources and to create his own techniques of practicing REBT with individuals and groups. The natural result of this experimentation was that he kept up the practice of writing about his difficulties to Ellis and seeking further clarification and guidance from him. This exciting method of learning the theory and practice of REBT compelled him to be so innovative in his approach that Ellis unhesitatingly judged him a real and valuable contributor to the therapy. 'I still feel you are the only person in Asia that I consider to be extremely well qualified to practice and preach REBT' (1981).

He has made original contributions to the theory and practice of REBT, which were greatly acknowledged by Ellis (1982, 1985). Some of his contributions to the theory of REBT are described as follows.

### 1. Denotation of 'D' Letter
In the classical form, the letter 'D' in the A-B-C-D-E theory stands for the therapeutic technique of disputing the client's irrational beliefs. Phadke expanded the letter 'D' and created modified

threefold denotation: (a) detect, (b) debate, and (c) discriminate. Ellis (1977) has incorporated this denotation in A-B-C structure of REBT (by appreciating his contribution in following words:

> Kishor Phadke, a brilliant associate of mine in Bombay, gave some special thought to point D, or Disputing, and decided to break it down into three main components:
>
> Detection
>
> Discriminating
>
> Debating
>
> I find his distinctions useful, since Disputing does largely consist of detecting your main irrational Beliefs, discriminating them clearly from your rational Beliefs and then debating these irrational Beliefs actively and vigorously. (p. 56)

## 2. Enlargement of 'B' Letter

Phadke demonstrated to Ellis that it is incorrect to classify desires, preferences, demands, and commands as beliefs—rational or irrational. In order to incorporate the human motives in the A-B-C theory, he coined the more comprehensive term for B—bedrock of biosocial forces. In the later years, he reinterpreted the letter 'B' more accurately as bipartite belief system. It includes the detection of binary message which the client signals to himself as well as the bipartite belief system, implied in that message.

## 3. Redefinition of 'C' Letter

Phadke gave a special thought to letter 'C' which was earlier described merely as consequences. He precisely named it as 'choice-blocking consequences'. In later years, he further elaborated it by making a distinction between choice-opening consequences leading to healthy emotions and choice-blocking consequences leading to unhealthy emotions.

## 4. Extension of 'E' Letter

One of the REBT proponents, Garcia (1977) suggested the letter 'E' could stand for (a) empathy, (b) emotion, and (c) experience. Phadke added yet another meaning to the letter E, namely, enthusiasm.

## 5. Modification of the Approval Principles

After closely observing the behaviour of hundreds of people, Phadke arrived at the conclusion that the principle of approval in REBT has to be supplemented by the principle of disapproval which he stated as 'No one should dislike or disapprove of me for whatever I do'. Ellis graciously accepted his suggestion and it was incorporated in his subsequent presentation of musturbatory ideologies (1979). Phadke went further and suggested a twofold classification of musturbatory ideologies instead of three—(a) what I should get, feel, and do, and (b) what I should not have to get, feel and do. This classification made the work of detecting the irrational beliefs easy.

## 6. A Review of Rationality

Phadke pointed out that the five criteria of rational behaviour proposed in REBT were not sufficiently comprehensive. They seemed to omit a vital aspect of human behaviour toward others. In order to cover that aspect, he suggested an additional criterion—rational behaviour does no needless, definite, and deliberate harm to others.

## 7. Emotive Rational Therapy

Phadke proposed that the distinction between rational emotive therapy (RET) and emotive rational therapy (ERT) can generate at least verifiable hypotheses. He further elaborated that the clients' irrational beliefs about himself may be disputed by using ERT, whereas the clients' irrational beliefs about others and the world may be disputed effectively by using RET. RET is more effective in disputing the client's inferences, whereas ERT is more effective in disputing the client's evaluations.

## 8. New Format of Teaching REBT

Phadke devised an 8A format of presenting the basic principles of REBT. A1 to A4 are used for detection of psychopathology and A5 to A8 are used for the treatment. A brief outline of this format is as follows:

A1-Assumption
A2-Appraisal
A3-Agony
A4-Astray
A5-Articulate
A6-Attack
A7-Attune
A8-Adjust

## 9. Theory of Surplus Values

This term was added by Phadke to his intervention strategies to suit the client's background. The use of this term makes easy for the practitioner to make the clients understand the surplus value they are attaching to some events in their life.

Phadke invented many innovative practices of REBT which are as follows—

1. Effective way of teaching the meaning of awful, horrible or terrible
2. The devil's advocate: An exercise in rational thinking
3. The involvement debate
4. Refinement of rational–emotive–imagery
5. Empathic role play
6. Role reversal
7. A second-order cognitive therapeutic technique
8. Emotive technique of controlling one's emotions and behaviour

Some of these techniques were used effectively for improvement of the practice of REBT. This was clearly revealed when two psychologists from California (2006) acknowledged that the technique of role reversal devised by Phadke was an effective assessment technique to increase awareness of faulty perceptions of reality.

# Work! Work! Practice!

This rational insight of REBT has had supreme importance in Phadke's life. He has worked incessantly for almost 50 years. He is a man of integrity and throughout his life he has practiced what he has preached. He has valued simplicity and peace all his life. As a bachelor, he has kept his needs to a minimum. At the age of 71, he closed down the Phadke Centre and retired from all his professional activities. Today he is 81 years old but his work has not yet stopped. With relentless efforts of 10 years, he has written his new book *Albert Ellis: A Rebellious Psychologist*. It is a comprehensive book on REBT. It is an encyclopaedia for REBT scholars which will guide them in using REBT principles efficiently in practice. It is yet to be published. He has an immense quest to learn. He is interested in knowing the developments of other psychotherapies too. He gets tremendous delight in studying these therapies. He keeps himself engaged in reading, cogitating, and unforgettable speculating over thoughts of great minds. And yes, he is still enlightening the lives of others. His doors are open to knowledge-seekers. His year's of practice in imparting knowledge and expertise to his students is not stopped yet.

One of the most unforgettable moments in his life is that Ellis held his contribution in high regard in his recently published autobiography, *All Out!* Ellis mentions that he is the only Indian psychologist whose influence on his (Ellis) life has been quite significant. Ellis says

> One of the most unusual influences on me and my work has been that of the psychologist Kishore M. Phadke, of Mumbai, India.... I would never have figured out some of the finer points of REBT without his detailed questioning, and I want to thank him for that.... He has certainly been one of my finest friends and supporters since 1968. (2010)

When asked the secret of his ceaseless vigour, Phadke replies,

> Pursuit of knowledge is a never ending process. I don't believe in instant knowledge. It requires disciplined and dedicated practice, *Sadhana*. One should have the burning desire to learn, unlearn and relearn. I craved only for knowledge and did not leave any stone unturned to acquire it.

Phadke's above words are a source of pride and inspiration to all.

## Acknowledgement

We gratefully acknowledge Rita Khear who reviewed the manuscript and made some valuable suggestions. She also made available to us a reference of Phadke's cited work very promptly.

## References

Ellis, A. (1962). Reason and emotion in psychotherapy. New York, NY: Lyle Stuart.
———. (1977). *How to live with and without anger*. Readers Digest Press, New York p. 56.
———. (1979). *The intelligent woman's guide to dating and mating*. Secaucus, NJ: Lyle Stuart. p. 200.
———. (2010). *All out*. (1st edn). New York: Prometheus Books, pp. 479, 485–486.
Ellis, A., & Harper, R.A. (1961). *A guide to rational living*. Englewood Cliffs, NJ: Prentice-Hall.
Eysenck, H.J. (1964). *Experiments in behaviour therapy* (1st edition). New York: Macmillan.
Garcia, E.J. (1977). Working on the E in RET. In J.L. Wolfe, and E. Brand (Eds), *Twenty years of rational therapy*. New York: Institute for Rational Living.
Gordon, R., & Gordon, M. (2006). The turned-off-child: Learned helplessness and school failure. (1st edn). USA: Millennial Mind Publishing.

Joshi, A. (2011, February 19) Viveknishtha Maharshee, *Loksatta*, Mumbai, p. 8. Retrieved from: http://epaper. loksatta.com/m/1254/indian-express/19-02-2011#issue/8/1

Phadke, K.M. (1981a). *A booklet*. Mumbai: Phadke Centre, p. 5.

———. (1981b). *My obsession*. Unpublished correspondence of K.M. Phadke & Dr. Albert Ellis 1968–2004 (Vol. II), p. 414.

———. (1982, 1985). *My obsession*, Unpublished correspondence of K.M. Phadke & Dr. Albert Ellis, 1968–2004 (Vol. II), pp. 476, 556, 682.

Phadke, K.M. (1999). *Adhunik sanjivani* (2nd edn). Mumbai: Tridal Prakashan, p. 8.

Phadke, K.M. & Chulani, V. (1999). *Conquering laziness* (1st edn), Mumbai: Excel Books, p. xv–xvi.

# 48

# Ashis Nandy

(1937)

## Honey Oberoi Vahali

*Ashis Nandy giving interview at Rhodes Forum in Greece, 2014*

Ashis Nandy was born in 1937 in Bhagalpur (now in Bihar) to well-to-do Bengali Christian parents. He is the eldest of three sons of Satish Chandra Nandy and Prafulla Nalini Nandy, and is the brother of Pritish Nandy and Manish Nandy. His family later moved to Calcutta (now Kolkata), where his mother taught at the La Martiniere School and subsequently became the school's first Indian vice principal. When he was 10 years old, the partition of India into India and Pakistan took place. As a child, he witnessed those trying times of conflict and the atrocities that followed. They left a deep impact on him, and much later in his adult life, he returned to study the impact of the partition on both of the affected sides. Ashis Nandy is married to Uma Nandy who is also a psychologist.

After completing his schooling at Calcutta, he went to pursue his college- and university-level education at Nagpur and Gujarat. A distinctive feature that marked his intellectual journey right from his early adult life was a searching spirit that questioned the given normative social structures. His curious and inquisitive mind led him to explore different disciplines of thought—sociology, political theory, empirical philosophy, and clinical psychology. At Nagpur, when he was pursuing his masters in sociology, Wilkinson, a Christian sociologist hailing from (the now designated) Uttarakhand region, influenced him considerably. Wilkinson was an open-minded sociologist who encouraged Ashis Nandy to experiment with his ideas and thoughts. Thinking of him as his first mentor, Nandy fondly recalls Wilkinson as being a social scientist who studied society from a qualitative angle and who was not satisfied with the analysis of social phenomenon solely from a statistical, mathematical edge. Under the guidance of Wilkinson, Ashis Nandy began to think about human formations and the ways in which life was organized by communities and groups. It is important to mention here that, even prior to his encounter with Wilkinson, Ashis Nandy had already read Sigmund Freud and had been drawn to certain psychoanalytic ideas and thoughts. In this way, since early adulthood Nandy was eager to pursue a possible dialogue between psychoanalysis and other social sciences.

After attaining a master's degree in sociology, Ashis Nandy went on to attain his doctorate in clinical psychology from the then famous, B.M. Institute at Ahmedabad. As is well known, the major theoretical perspective on offer at the B.M. Institute was psychoanalysis. It was here that with the well-known psychoanalyst Shiv Mitra, the then director of the B.M. Institute, Ashis Nandy deepened his acquaintance with psychoanalysis. Shiv Mitra had been trained under the first Indian psychoanalyst, Girindrasekhar Bose, at the Indian Psychoanalytical Society at Calcutta. Many aspects of psychoanalysis, particularly its capacity to look at all experiential phenomena as having layers of complexity, have stayed with Ashis Nandy. In his own words,

> at the B.M. Institute, I learned to look at things long enough and with empathy. The training in empathy was very deep. Psychoanalysis taught me not to demonize anyone…. It made me question our propensity to create binaries and to look at the world through simplistic frames—like good and evil, victim and victimizer, self and other…psychoanalytic training in empathy requires one to take the position of the hated one and to imagine the world from that angle too…. When I was writing about Gandhi, I offered a most empathic reading of Gandhi's killers…. My clinical training had helped me to identify equally with Gandhi as also his killers…. This does not mean that one loses ones perspective or politics. It only implies that one refuses to give in to the propensity to demonize others. (Personal communication, 9 September 2014)

Another influence of Shiv Mitra and of the clinical training at the B.M. Institute on Nandy was a regard for subjectivity and the value of understanding each and every human life in context. His teacher and mentor Shiv Mitra was an expert in the Rorschach Ink Blot Test. Under his mentorship, Ashis Nandy learnt important projective techniques, particularly the use of the Rorschach Ink Blot Test and Thematic Appreciation Test as well as the Draw a Person Test. He was impressed with the projective techniques and experimented with them for a long time. Also, it was under the influence of Shiv Mitra that, for Nandy, the unconscious, non-rational, and non-obvious aspects of human behaviour became salient as he started to think about a method to study psycho-biographical and subjective phenomenon. This early training and regard for the subjective has continued in his lifelong work of exploring communities, societies, and collective behaviour.

After receiving a doctorate in clinical psychology, by which time Ashis Nandy was already married to Uma Nandy, he came to Delhi in search of a job. His first appointment as a researcher was at the Sri Ram Institute of Industrial Relations. He was adept in non-parametric statistics and his job required him to analyze social phenomena through this orientation. However, his increasing thirst for knowledge left him somewhat dissatisfied with his job at the institute and so, soon enough, he applied for a position at the Centre for the Study of Developing Societies (CSDS), Delhi. It was here that the most memorable years of his professional life began. His interview at CSDS with the then Director of the Centre Rajni Kothari and his team, itself opened the value of listening, receiving, and dialoguing for Nandy. In an atmosphere which was much appreciative of his thoughts and aspirations, Nandy began to thrive and grow as one of India's best known intellectuals. Even today as he recounts his early years at CSDS, he remembers with a softening expression and with much gratitude, the influence of Rajni Kothari on his growth:

> The spell of the first two mentors was broken as I came to CSDS. Both of them were serious thinkers and had much to offer but in some sense they were still bound by their disciplines. With Rajni Kothari I was freed of disciplinary boundaries. I learnt to ask radical questions and to think out of the box. It was a truly liberating experience.

Other colleagues at CSDS, such as D.L. Sheth, also contributed to his growth in that extremely significant phase of his early professional life. In fact, the entire atmosphere at CSDS was such that freedom of thought, critical thinking, a questioning spirit, and a qualitative engagement with social concerns was encouraged.

It was at CSDS that Nandy started experimenting seriously with his ideas and evolved a methodology for political psychology that took into account the complexity of human behaviour, collective social processes, and unconscious dynamics. His method has remained one in which the relational dyad of the researcher and the researched is considered central. In his search for psychology as a human science, he began to emphasize relational dynamics and the centrality of ethics and stress on the subjective as well as the life historical dimension of individuals and collectives. Many colleagues and well-known thinkers, including Ivan Illich, notably contributed to his youthful and middle-aged intellectual pursuits by their encouragement. A coming together of social, political, and philosophical quests made him revisit concerns plaguing the southern part of the world with an eye which was both critical and empathic at once. It is indeed difficult to summarize his research interests; however, if one were to list the most salient ones, they would be political psychology, mass violence, cultures and politics of knowledge, utopias, and visions.

From 1992 to 1997, he was the director of CSDS and did much to help the institute flourish and bloom. As time passed, he himself became a mentor to innumerable researchers and thinkers younger to him. Many of them remember being touched by his democratic spirit, ever-alive curiosity, and friendly nature. His indomitable spirit of questioning power in all forms has led him to be recognized as one of the significant South Asian thinkers of the twentieth century. While he does not easily identify himself with any single discipline, he considers his work to be that of 'a political psychologist or a psychoanalytic sociologist' (Personal communication, 9 September 2014). His affiliation with depth psychology is of an enduring nature. In his own words:

> Amongst all the disciplines that I have dabbled with I feel closest to psychoanalysis and empirical philosophy. My language is psychoanalytical.... I would be most uncomfortable if psychoanalysis was taken away from me.... This is because, psychoanalysis is the only theory which has a conception of the whole person.... All other theories in psychology and the social sciences have a conception of 'parts' of a person. Psychoanalysis, or let us say, depth psychology has an imagination of the whole person.... I realized the value of the relational dyad and the place of dialogue long back, when I was trained in clinical psychology

at the B.M. Institute.... One of the deepest learning which has stayed with me from clinical psychoanalysis is the capacity to stay with ambiguity and complexity and not to give in to any form of intellectual reductionism or one sidedness in conceptual thinking. (Personal communication, 9 September 2014)

## Affiliations

Ashis Nandy's longest and most significant association has been with the CSDS, Delhi. Starting his career here as a Fellow, he served as the centre's director from 1992 to 1997. During his long affiliation with the centre, he has done much to consolidate the centre's growth and contribute to its intellectual energy, insist on a qualitative standard of research, and nurture younger Fellows in their research pursuits. He has also been a Distinguished Fellow, Institute of Postcolonial Studies, Melbourne; Chairperson, Executive Board, Centre for Environment and Food Security (2010); Member, Global Scientific Committee on Higher Education (UNESCO); Chairperson, Committee for Cultural Choices and Global Futures, Delhi; Member, Advisory Board, Nehru Memorial Museum and Library (1998–2005); Member, Toda Institute of Global Peace and Policy Research (2003 onwards); Member, International Advisory Board of the World Public Forum, Dialogue of Civilisations (Moscow) (2005); and Member, Advisory Body, Indian Council of World Affairs (2006 onwards).

He was Woodrow Wilson Fellow at the Woodrow Wilson International Center, Washington (1988); Member, Executive Council, World Future Studies Federation (1988–1997); Charles Wallace Fellow, Department of Politics, The University of Hull, Hull (1990); Fellow, Institute for Advanced Studies in Humanities, The University of Edinburgh (1991); UNESCO Professor, Centre for European Studies, University of Trier, Germany (Summer, 1994); Regents' Fellow, University of California, Los Angeles (1997); Member, Executive Board, Commonwealth Human Rights Initiative (1993–2004); Fellow, South Asian Alternatives (1993–2001); Member, Raja Rammohun Roy Library Foundation (1996–2000); Fellow, Wissenschaftskolleg, Institute for Advanced Study, Berlin (2004 and 2006); Visiting Fellow, Institute of Advanced Study, Nantes (2008); and ICSSR National Fellow (2007–2009).

Ashis Nandy has contributed to innumerable research bodies. The more important ones being: the International Network for Cultural Alternatives to Development, Living Economy Network, Ecology of Knowledge Network, Life-Member of People's Union for Civil Liberties, Indian Psychological Association, and Founder-Member of International Institute of Political Psychology. He has also been on the advisory boards of the Transnational Foundation for Peace and Future Research; Research Center for African-American Studies, University of California (1997–2000); Transparency International Council on Governance; Institute for Post-Colonial Studies, Melbourne; and Global Reconciliation Network.

He has been the member of Mission, SAARC-NGO Observers of Parliamentary Elections in Bangladesh, Pakistan, and India at different times (1993–1996), the member of the Jury, Asia-Pacific Public Hearing on Crimes Against Women Related to the Violence of Development, organized by Asian Women's Human Rights Council and Vimochana, Bangalore, 28 January 1995, the member of the Jury (with U.R. Anantha Murthy, H. Mehta, Justice Tiwatia, and others), Public Hearing on the Sardar Sarovar (Narmada) Project, organized by the Indian People's Tribunal on Environment and Human Rights, 4 November 2000, Delhi, and the member of the Jury, World Court of Women Against Racism, World Conference on Racism, Racial Discrimination, Xenophobia, and Related Intolerance, organized by El Taller and Asian Women's Human Rights Council, Durban, 30 August 2001.

## Member, Editorial Boards or Editorial Advisory Boards

With his vast research expertise, he has been on the editorial boards of the following journals: *Alternatives, Psychoanalytic Review, Futures, Journal of Future Studies, Manushi, Public Culture, Postcolonial Studies, Afro-Asian Dialogue, International Relations of the Asia Pacific, Inter-Asia Cultural Studies, Granthya Parikrama, Identity, Culture and Politics, Cultural Values, Deep Focus, Interculture, Periodica Islamica, Theoretical Perspectives, Global Media and Communication, The Journal of Applied Behavioral Science, South Asian Refugee Watch, The American Behavioural Scientist, Politics and the Individual, Review of International Political Economy, Inter-Asian Cultural Studies, Emergences: Journal for the Study of Media and Composite Cultures, International Journal of Indian Studies, Passages, Series on Philosophy and the Global Context, Cultural Values, Anthropology and Medicine* (formerly *British Medical Anthropology Review*), *South Asian Refugee Watch, South Asian Popular Culture, Evam, Psychological Studies, Journal of Material Culture, Journal of Cultural Research, Peace and Policy,* and *Ecumene.*

## Awards and Honours

Nandy has been honoured with the Dr Khurshid Ahmed Khan Award, given by the Pakistan Futuristic Foundation and Institute, 1997, the Anbar Electronic Intelligence Citation of Excellence, 1997. The Global Development Distinguished Senior Scholar Panel in honour of Ashis Nandy was organized with Mustapha Kamal Pasha (chair), Craig Calhoun, Fred Dallmayr, Craig Murphy, Ali Mazrui, Ahmed Samatar, and R.B.J. Walker at the International Studies Association, 42nd Annual Convention, 20–24 February 2001, Chicago. He has also been awarded the grand prize of the Fukuoka Asian Culture Prizes 2007 and was awarded an honorary doctorate from the University of South Australia, Adelaide, 2011.

## Contributions to Psychology

Ashis Nandy has written over 20 books. Some of the most widely read being: *Alternative Sciences: Creativity and Authenticity in Two Indian Scientists* (1980 [1995]); *At the Edge of Psychology: Essays on Politics and Culture* (1980); *The Intimate Enemy: Loss and Recovery of Self Under Colonialism* (1983 [1988, 2009]); *Traditions, Tyranny and Utopias: Essays in the Politics of Awareness* (1987 [1992]); *The Tao of Cricket: On Games of Destiny and the Destiny of Games* (1989 [2000]); *The Illegitimacy of Nationalism: Rabindranath Tagore and the Politics of Self* (1994); *The Savage Freud and Other Essays in Possible and Retrievable Selves* (1995); *A Very Popular Exile* (2007); *An Ambiguous Journey to the City: The Village and Other Odd Ruins of the Self in the Indian Imagination* (2001); *Time Warps: The Insistent Politics of Silent and Evasive Pasts* (2002); *The Romance of the State and the Fate of Dissent in the Tropics* (2003); *Bonfire of Creeds: The Essential Ashis Nandy* (2004); *Time Treks: The Future of Old and New Despotisms* (2007), *Ashis Nandy Reader* (2010); *Regimes of Narcissism, Regimes of Despair* (2013). He has also co-authored and edited several books including the well-known *Creating a Nationality: The Ramjanmabhumi Movement and Fear of the Self* (Nandy, Trivedi, Yagnik, & Mayaram, 1995). Amongst his several edited volumes, it is worthwhile to recount *The Multiverse of Democracy: Essays in Honour of Rajni Kothari* (Sheth & Nandy, 1996), *The Secret Politics of our Desires: Innocence, Culpability and Popular Cinema* (1998), and *The Future of Knowledge and*

*Culture; A Twenty-First Century Dictionary* (Nandy & Lal, 2005). Nandy has also written several crucial human rights reports and has been a member of significant human rights bodies. Many of his books and articles have been translated into several Indian and foreign languages, including Hindi, Telegu, Kananda, Gujarati, French, Italian, German, Turkish, Chinese, and Korean.

Considering the vast range and salience of his lifetime contributions, it is difficult, if not impossible, to summarize his efforts in carving the contours of a philosophically and methodologically rich discipline of psychology. Within his works, we can trace the foundations of psychology as an ethical pursuit—one which is humane, engaged, relational, and immersed in exploring issues of historical and contemporary value to life. While carrying a universal appeal, his writings have been of special value to South Asian cultures and societies. They present a forceful corpus of thoughtful reflections on almost all-important socio-political and cultural events in India's recent (and also not so recent) past. Encapsulated within his thought is an entire body of subversive wisdom that can be largely grouped into a few major categories:

1.  His efforts offer a powerful critique of modernity and its pertinent symbols—medicine, science, hegemony, the global market, and the modern city and its 'pseudo-elite' middle classes.
2.  Within the South Asian intellectual domain, Nandy emerges as a strong voice, questioning the politics and the very formation of the nation state and the rhetoric that goes into the making of exclusivist and violently predisposed nations and nationalities (1994). Impelled by his questioning spirit, the discipline of psychology becomes both a tool of exploration and a site where protest and critique can be registered, examined, and worked through.
3.  In his view, the psychosocial perspective should include a thorough study of differences without reducing them to hierarchies, a study of cultures and not civilizations alone, of myths and epics and not only officially sanctioned historical reconstructions, feelings and memories and not simply statistical configurations, dialogue and conversations and not a narration of human affairs through unchanging and immortalized facts (2007).
4.  Nandy is eager for psychology to include a perspective on death and otherness. Like the psychoanalyst Robert Jay Lifton, he urges psychologists and social scientists to reflect and enrich their writings by including insights that can emerge by including an awareness (howsoever partial) of our imminent death and dying. He reminds us to tread on the difficult journey of respecting the 'otherness of the other' and not simply reaffirming the self by 'making the other' into a 'mirror image' of the former.
5.  He views creativity as a lifelong process in one who is able to move beyond being exclusively 'man' or 'woman'—an androgynously inclined human being in search of meaning beyond polarities and binaries—and one who values the capacity for self-doubt and self-questioning.
6.  His works have chronicled an account of several crucial twentieth century events. He chooses not to exclusively emphasise on stories of violence and destruction, but equally so on those of resistance and compassion. By believing that our future is shaped by how we remember the past, Nandy suggests that, as social scientists, it is our task to recover versions of love and struggles and not simply those of hatred and negativity between communities (2001). This is best highlighted in his work related to the partition of India into India and Pakistan in 1947.
7.  He questions all naturalistic and essentialist perspectives and believes that social scientists can never reach 'the truth' but can help in the recovery of people's truths which are multidimensional and plural. His regard for the wisdom of the unconscious and its capacity to surprise and thus interrupt the cohesive social reading of complex phenomenon makes Nandy's work proximal to lived actualities and people's on-going struggles.

# The Question of Psychology: Its Relationship with Social and Historical Reconstruction

In the Indian context, Nandy remains a unique voice who bridges the immutable gap between psychology and sociology. Opening the space of a creative dialogue, his books bridge the divide which has hitherto made sociologists resistant to include insights from psychology and vice versa of psychologists to seriously engage with social and political phenomena. In this regard, one of the major concerns that Nandy brings up is that the teaching and training of psychology has to be inclusive of a critical, questioning eye as well as an appreciation of its relational, empathic potential. So long as psychologists remain unaware of the 'politics of psychology', there will not be a possibility to study the 'psychology of political and historical and/or cultural processes'. The a-contextual, apolitical training of psychology has prevented it from initiating a serious dialogue with societal concerns. In his work *Time Treks* (2007), as he lays the cornerstones of the ethical in psychology, he differentiates between the imperatives of natural sciences and social sciences. He reminds us that the unique responsibility which social scientists carry is to be self-reflexive and self-critical in their engagements. He also asserts that the value of social sciences lies in the capacity of the thinker to be open to relational influences and counter-transferential feelings. The perceiver and previewed are mutually liable to be transformed through their encounter which sets in place the dialogical processes.

Nandy is keen that psychology moves beyond the heavy influence of positivism where naturalizing theories, including 'evolutionary essentialism' is stressed upon. In his reading of collective processes, he emphasises on the distortion inherent in all power-driven intellectual perspectives that are quick to reduce differences to hierarchies. He says, 'As European and American standards have gained appreciation and acceptance, all non-European and Southern cultures of the World have attained the status of becoming "savage," "strange," "tribal," "childish" and thus to be "reformed and refined" by the colonial powers' (Personal communication, 9 September 2014). Nandy's effort in this arena is to move beyond polarized understandings of the victim and the victimizer and, instead, study those cultural spaces and processes through which colonization works. In his best known work, *The Intimate Enemy*, he advocates an alternative manner of understanding the relationship between the colonized and the colonizer. He suggests that the dynamics of inner and cultural change in the colonized not only enable him or her to move ahead but also help 'liberate' the colonizer ultimately (1983). It is here that he rediscovers Gandhi for himself as well as for the community of Indian intellectuals.

Nandy views the enterprise of historical reconstruction as a state-sponsored exercise providing a certain narrative structure to the past by prioritizing some memories over others. Often constructed as a linear and progressive story of success and development, in Nandy's view, the task of writing any nation's history is never an innocent exercise. Rather, the purpose of prioritizing some memories and feeling states over and above others, serves the interests of the powerful, more articulate, and dominant social classes, political parties, or cultural groups. Therefore, a 'history of sorts', that not only neglects and distorts the actual experiences of the people but also subtly (and at times, even blatantly) imposes on them a mode of cultural existence comes to define their future, even as it paints their past in some 'selectively chosen' hues and colours. In his view, and correctly so, the linear narratives of techno-science, progress, and modernity, including that of the Indian nation state, remain politically maneuvered and selectively constructed. This leads him to search for alternatives that a psychodynamically inclined researcher may seek as he/she attempts at historical reconstruction (Vahali, 2011).

Nandy is in favour of a perspective that stresses on the lives of the 'a-historical'—those who stand outside the ambit of the official historical enterprise. Here, Nandy's use of the psychoanalytic method and the psycho-biographical orientation are significantly innovative indeed. In a culture, as affirmed by Nandy, where experiences are largely symbolized through the epic and mythic modes, the possibility of revisiting one's cultural past, so as to incorporate changing emotional forces and contents, always remains an open one. By defying the very idea of historical reconstruction, his endeavour is to reconnect the myth to its moral universe and thereby confront the dominant narrative with its forgotten lives and cultures. In Nandy's view, history 'lies' not by misrepresenting reality, but by exiling emotions. Memories and the emotions that enshrine them stand witness by refusing to discard human subjectivity. Myths are not people's history or alternative history; their job is to resist history and resist the objectification of suffering and sufferers in the name of objectivity (Vahali, 2011). And so, in desiring to remain close to the sufferer's reality, he works to recreate a living saga of people's experiences by interpreting and re-interpreting different versions of myths, various forms of popular literature, and folk understandings. As he does so, for him, the psychological narrative becomes an aperture—open to potentially new and further interpretations. Here the question he sets for the discipline of psychology may be stated as: Where, in essence, lie the methodological and cultural apertures that a researcher hopes to explore, as he/she attempts to reach those subtle and deeper spaces where protest, reform and cultural change, remain intricately connected to inner transformations in the personal biography of the protester (Vahali, 2011)?

In conclusion, we may say that by questioning mechanical and rationalistic trends in the teaching of social sciences, particularly psychology, Nandy stresses that psychology is not only a discipline about humans but must remain 'humane' in its exploratory methods and diverse pursuits. He also remains concerned about the pharmaceutical taking over the relational. As he says, 'it will always take a human being to understand the pain of another in distress'. His imagination of communities and living cultures is worth pausing by: '[P]eople are repositories of knowledge and repositories of experiences'. Our task is to listen deeply to their stories of self and not to theorize over and above them. 'So long as life continues, they will themselves find a way of articulating their histories and struggles'. (Personal communication, 9 September 2014).

# References

Nandy, A. (1980). *At the edge of psychology: Essays on politics and culture.* New Delhi: Oxford University Press.

———. (1980 [1995]). *Alternative sciences: Creativity and authenticity in two Indian scientists.* New Delhi: Oxford University Press.

———. (1983). *The intimate enemy: Loss and recovery of self under colonialism.* New Delhi: Oxford University Press. (Reprinted in 1988 and with a new postscript in 2009 [2nd ed.]).

———. (1987 [1992]). *Traditions, tyranny and utopias: Essays in the politics of awareness.* New Delhi: Oxford University Press.

———. (1989 [2000]). *The Tao of cricket: On games of destiny and the destiny of games.* (2nd ed) New Delhi: Viking/Penguin, Oxford University Press.

———. (1994). *The illegitimacy of nationalism: Rabindranath Tagore and the politics of self.* New Delhi: Oxford University Press.

———. (1995). *The savage Freud and other essays in possible and retrievable selves.* New Delhi: Oxford University Press.

———. (1998). The *secret politics of our desires: Innocence, culpability and popular cinema.* London, New Delhi, New York, NY: Zed Books, Oxford University Press, St. Martin's Press.

Nandy, A. (2001). *An ambiguous journey to the city: The village and other odd ruins of the Self in the Indian imagination*. New Delhi: Oxford University Press.

———. (2002). *Time warps: The insistent politics of silent and evasive pasts*. New Delhi, London, New York, NY: Permanent Black, C. Hurst and Co., Rutgers University Press.

———. (2003). *The romance of the state and the fate of dissent in the tropics*. New Delhi: Oxford University Press.

———. (2004). *Bonfire of creeds: The essential Ashis Nandy*. New Delhi: Oxford University Press.

———. (2007). *A very popular exile*. New Delhi: Oxford University Press.

———. (2007). *Time treks: The future of old and new despotisms,* Delhi, London: Permanent Black, Seagull.

———. (2010). *Ashis Nandy reader*. Shanghai: West Heavens Project, Nanfang Daily Press.

———. (2013). *Regimes of narcissism, regimes of despair*. New Delhi: Oxford University Press.

Nandy, A., & Lal, V. (2005). *The future of knowledge and culture: A twenty-first century dictionary*. New Delhi: Penguin.

Nandy, A., Trivedi, S., Mayaram, S., & Yagnik, A. (1995). *Creating a nationality: The Ramjanmabhumi movement and fear of the self*. New Delhi, Tokyo: Oxford University Press, United Nations University.

Sheth, D. L., & Nandy, A. (1996). *The multiverse of democracy: Essays in honour of Rajni Kothari*. New Delhi: SAGE Publications.

Vahali, H.O. (2011). Landscaping a perspective: India and the psychoanalytic vista. In Grishwar Misra (Ed.), *Fifth ICSSR review of psychology* (pp. 1–99). New Delhi: Pearson Publishers.

# 49

## Sudhir Kakar

(1938)

Manasi Kumar, Anurag Mishra, Amrita Narayanan, and Ashok Nagpal

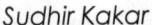

Sudhir Kakar

To write about the psychoanalyst and thinker Sudhir Kakar is to engage with a body of work that includes 22 books, a profusion of academic articles and magazine op-eds, and numerous lectures and talks; in short, a wealth of material is not easily condensed into a biography. To comment upon this prolific body of work, we have chosen, therefore, not an exhaustive summary—which would be impossible in this space constraint—attempting instead an ode, an intellectually and emotionally charged tribute that reflects each of our engagements with Kakar's work.

Now 78, Kakar lives in Goa, but has counted 25 years as a psychoanalyst in New Delhi, in addition to visiting academic appointments at INSEAD France and at Harvard University among others. Initially trained as an engineer and an economist before becoming a psychoanalyst, Kakar's work reflects his inter-disciplinary background. He has been widely regarded for extending debates and meta-theories of culture, self, and human values within the psychoanalytic arena, and his contributions have stimulated and invigorated the discipline and practice of psychoanalysis in India as well as making a mark on cultural critique and literary studies worldwide. Rarely do we encounter a stalwart whose mind reaches out to nuances of cultural-historical exploration of the myths, the fabric of social life as well as to understanding the depths of human mind and emotions. Kakar's writing does all these, flawlessly using the forms of fiction and non-fiction towards his creative purposes which have ranged from plumbing Indian cultural practices (Kakar, 2001, 2012; Intimate Relations, 1996[2008]) to both loving and interrogating Indian historical figures, those well-known (Gandhi, 1996[2008], 2001, 2004; Krishna, 1986, 2001; Tagore, 2013) and forgotten (Gandhi's Mira in Mira and the Mahatma [Kakar, 2006]; Dara Shikoh in The Crimson Throne [Kakar, 2010]).

Following his sojourn to Germany, where he received training in Freudian psychoanalysis, Kakar returned to India where he choose to be removed from institutional affiliations, while he tried to redefine the field of Indian psychology and psychoanalysis through aesthetic, philosophical and systematic, thinking and writing. To professionals influenced by his work, his example exhorts us to keep working on our own projects with diligence to the psychoanalytic method, and to keep sharing our work in the public discourse. His steady output of work and exemplary research methodology[1] offers a striking catalogue of how the social field is refined and in what depths life stories can be narrated.

In the exercise of illuminating Kakar's contributions, we would like to briefly share our own encounters with his work. Ashok Nagpal, a professor and former dean at Ambedkar University, New Delhi, and previously at the University of Delhi, followed Kakar in his journey to unravelling stories of madness and healing in Balaji (Kakar, 1982; Nagpal, 2000). In Nagpal's four decades of academic teaching and clinical work, he has carefully pursued and taught Kakar's deconstruction of India and psychoanalysis. Chief of psychology at Fortis, New Delhi, Anurag Mishra has been engaging with the clinical import of Kakar's writings, juxtaposing them with mainstream psychoanalytic ideas to extend clinical work on the ground and to develop a regular forum of exchange of ideas around clinical psychoanalysis (Mishra, 2012; Kumar, Dhar and Mishra, 2017). Amrita Narayanan, has a private practice in psychoanalytic psychotherapy and is currently working on a book of essays on women, sexuality, and cultural identity under a Homi Bhabha Fellowship. Her engagement with Kakar's work comes from her interest in women's sexuality and the geographies of psychoanalysis, in which Kakar has made a substantial contribution. She has written widely—in academic journals as well as in the popular press—on the subjects of geography and women's sexuality and their relevance during the practice of psychotherapy as well as when making cultural commentary (see, for example, Narayanan, 2013, 2015a, 2015b, 2016). Manasi Kumar has been engaging with Kakar's writing as a way to interrogate mainstream psychological and psychoanalytic thinking and to retrieve an appreciation for culturally nuanced, historically annotated, and psychologically astute writing. We make this introduction to ourselves, as the rest of this essay is a reflection of each of our involvements with Kakar, meaning that each of us has selected aspects of his work to comment upon, the subjectivity of our choices being the most meaningful way to approach a writing and thinking career that has had over 45 years of fruitful output and still counting.

---

[1] See, for example, *Intimate Relations* (1990) and *Colors of Violence* (1996).

Perhaps the most important development on Freud's work that Kakar has come to symbolize internationally is the valorization of geography in psychoanalysis. In Indian psychoanalysis, we have adopted the term 'terroir' to further precise upon the aspects of geography that makes psychoanalysis what it is. Of French etymology, borrowed from the world of wine-making, the term terroir refers to the specific place where a wine is grown. The terroir of psychology is much like the terroir of grapes, but it is the terroir of human beings: historical, geographic, cultural, social, political, religious, and spiritual.

Writing in his book *Liquid Memory*, the acclaimed film-maker and former sommelier John Nossiter says:

> [A] true expression of terroir…is very precisely means to share the beauty of a specific identity, a specific culture, with the rest of the world. It is using the local not to exclude, but to include any one of us in the mystery and distinctive beauty of an 'other'. (Nossiter, 2009, p.11)

In an era of psychological universalism, Sudhir Kakar has produced a fine psychoanalytical wine from the Indian terroir (Mishra, 2012). Resisting the impulse to Westernize, plumbing historical sources for a definition of 'Indian' that was also modern, Kakar arrived at

> [A] traditional Indian view of the person: a person who was open, porous and connected to all of existence, to the intangible human heritage that needs to be preserved and defended against those adherents of the modern model who would not brook the existence of a competing model of the person. (Kakar, 2011)

Despite these noteworthy accomplishments, however, Kakar is often overlooked by Indian psychologists. Much to our chagrin, the best intentioned beings—including bright minds with ambitions of being psychoanalysts, psychologists with cultural and social sensitivities, and eminent psychoanalysts who have visited India from across the continents—have not gone beyond an initial wave of admiration for Kakar. In other words, Kakar has not always been well understood. The roots of the indulgent admiration that Kakar has earned—that has often stopped short of a deeper engagement with the work—may lie partly in the psychic dessert in creative output that lies between Girindrasekar Bose, the first president of the Indian Psychoanalytic Association, and Kakar.

Between Bose's last publication in the 1940s, and Kakar's first in the 1970s there are only a few scattered writings that speak for Indian psychology and psychoanalysis, a fact that is perhaps related to the climate of indulgent politeness that evolved afterwards towards the lone-ranger Kakar. In an interview with the Iranian philosopher Jehanbegloo (2001), Kakar shared a speculative wish—not without a mild lament—that he be reborn as a rich poet. We wonder if Kakar's wish for the next lifetime relates also to his reception in this one: not enough questions were asked of his subtle narration, his works treated in India as the superb poems that they also are, but not enough as thoughts that could be engaged with.

Of the areas in which he been most misunderstood, Kakar's writings on the erotic stand out. Kakar's engagement with the theme of the erotic, and especially with women's voices in the erotic, has been continuous, traversing the modes of fiction and non-fiction and incorporating the most marginal of voices. Reading Kakar with an eye on women unveils the subtle political message and wish for young women's freedom in his writings. The impact of this message was perhaps most keenly felt at the 2013 New Delhi psychoanalytic conference where, though the broad topic was 'Psychoanalysis, Culture and Religion', the theme of women emerged clearly and unabashedly as one paper after another drew from Kakar to focus on retrieving marginalized voices of the Indian girl child, unpacking the enigma of female sexuality, and understanding the multidimensional identities of women in India.

Kakar's fiction writing, which increasingly overlaps of roles of sexuality, power, desire, and spirituality, is particularly potent in understanding the hope he invests in the Indian woman. In his most recent novel, *The Devil Take Love* (2015), the older poet's vulnerability towards his younger female apprentice can be read as a manifestation of a psychosocial wish that Kakar developed elsewhere: the wish of the Indian man to be female (Kakar, 2001, 2012). Such a reading is imbued with the envy of women, reflected also in ancient texts, for example, *Anushana Parva* (12. 11:53), in which during a discussion between Indra and Bishma, the duo conclude that women obtain the maximum sexual pleasure (Haksar, 2014). The leitmotif of the maternal feminine—and the implicit wish of men to be female—appears also in Kakar's lecture on Tagore's paintings of women, a lecture that mirrors Freud's (1910[1989]) deconstruction of da Vinci's maternal longings. Here Kakar (2013) plays a Winnicotian mother, a mother who searches, and uses the shape of the women's eyes to demonstrate his point that these women's life-struggles are etched in their appearance, that these women are reminiscent of Tagore's beloved sister-in-law, Kadambari, and eventually his mother, therefore, reflective of Tagore's—and Kakar's—empathy to women.

Another area in which Kakar's influence has been underestimated is in the psychotherapy consulting room. Kakar's emphasis on compassionate knowing and being is not only of meta-psychological interest but is also relevant for the praxis of psychotherapy where it becomes apparent that love, connectedness, and knowledge cannot be separated if a cure is to happen. Visualizing the unconscious as an engine that runs on parallel tracks of desire and the divine Kakar has written, 'Empathy, and the meditative state that underlies it, may well be the sluice through which the spiritual enters the consulting room, where the art and science of psychoanalysis flow together in the practice of psychotherapy'.

Love-connectedness-knowledge form the *sat-chit-anand* (truth-consciousness-bliss) of the psychotherapeutic venture means that transformative knowledge is not possible without empathy, and transformative empathy is not possible without compassion. Compassion as the prerequisite for transformative empathy and knowledge brings the spiritual also onto centre stage in the practice of psychotherapy, and adds another paradigm to consciousness, the spiritual conscious.

The spiritual in psychotherapy practice has been largely scotomized, leading to an impoverishment in psychotherapy, but Kakar's work uncovers the essentially spiritual nature of the psychotherapeutic venture and brings it centre stage. He extends the Eriksonian praxis of interrogating the psyche through an empathic engagement with historical personalities who have become almost physiognomic features of the cultures where they developed. In this venture, he extends empathy not only to the living but through an empathic use of imagination to compassionately understanding and deconstructing cultural icons who are part of the brick and mortar of the cultures which formed them. This deeply empathic understanding started with his work on Frederick Taylor (1970) the first management guru to an examination of self-proclaimed gurus and god men in India to historical personalities such as Mahatma Gandhi (Gandhi, 1996, 2001, 2004), Rabindranath Tagore (2013), Vatsyayna (2009) and Bhartihari (2015) or the psychological contours of the struggle for succession during the embers of Shahjahan's reign between the two brothers Dara Shikoh and Aurangzeb (Kakar, 2010).

Yet another of the significant accomplishments of Kakar has been his application of the Eriksonian clinical method—of which he is the foremost practitioner—and it's extension to an analysis of current events in Indian society. Of his many efforts in this regard, his study of riots and communal violence in India is one of the best examples. In *The Colors of Violence (1996)*, Kakar hails the current anti-essentialist trend and declares himself a 'primordialist' (p. 149). His extended case study of the Hindu-Muslim violence of 1990 in the southern Indian city of Hyderabad seeks to understand what enables ordinary people to engage willingly and enthusiastically in horrific acts of violence and degradation.

Kakar's primordialism emerges in his assertion that religious identity in India constitutes *the* most important basis of self-definition, one which far outweighs the salience of other axes such as caste, class, ethnicity, or language. Religious identities, says Kakar, assert themselves during times of extreme stress or perceived threat. It perceives itself 'to be threatened or under actual attack' (Kakar, 1996, p. 17). Kakar contends that violence between Hindus and Muslims in India is of a more fundamental order than violence between groups constituted along other lines. Referring to intra-religious, or sectarian violence between Vaishnavite and Shaivite Hindus, for example, Kakar suggests that it is characterized by a 'ritualized, gamelike quality which combines passion with restraint', whereas 'Hindu-Muslim conflicts: have no such play-like quality, pervaded as they are by deathly intent, with the burning down of houses, demolition of temples, mosques and shrines' (Kakar, 1996, p. 20).

Kakar argues that during periods of social tension, and following a precipitating event(s), there arises a sense of group 'fusion' in which stereotypical images of self and other come into play. When group salience becomes high, an individual thinks and behaves in conformity with the stereotypical characteristics of the group category rather than according to 'individual personality dispositions' (Kakar, 1996, p. 42). The individual acts stereotypically, 'according to the behaviour "expected" of an anti-Hindu or anti-Muslim mob' (Kakar, 1996, p. 46). The threat that precipitates these event, is often the consequence of modernization. When old, ritualized, village-based, predictable patterns of inter-communal relations are lost, the disappearance of old 'ecological niches' turns people into strangers, while the atrophy of traditional roles and identities induces loss of self-esteem. In reaction, new 'Hindu' and 'Muslim' identities are forged (their newness being crucial) where everything good is allocated to the 'self'-category, and 'the bad, the dirty, and the impure to another group' (Kakar, 1996, p. 160).

The revival of faith- and caste-based politics in recent times and the lack of political visibility of Indian leadership on issues such as women's rights, climate change, and rights of minoritized groups remind us of Kakar's work. At these times, we can value the deeper political message of Kakar's legacy: the valorization of a journey from inside to outside and the importance of valuing culture, ideas, and knowledge in the promulgation of a freer spirit.

The desert between Bose's work and Kakar's alluded to earlier, throws open several challenges to future generations in expanding the cultural imagination. Kakar has complained about the absence of the cultural idiom in case histories presented in Indian psychological writings, as exemplified by the paucity of patients' utilization of Indian mythology. This malaise, he writes, is 'not only due to a presumed increase in mythological illiteracy as a consequence of the modernizing process. It may well also be due to the patient's sensing the analyst's disinterest in such material because of his commitment to "deeper" universalistic models' (Kakar, 1992, p. 433).

Not only is Kakar's work wine in terms of its taste and quality, it also bears the feature of wine as an invitation: to be intoxicated and inspired. Inspired by Kakar, a Delhi *gharana* (school) of psychoanalysis has evolved, which continues to be guided by his work in its engagement with the peripheries and margins of society who often don't make it through the privileged doors of the psychoanalytical clinic. The invitation to drink this wine has been well met also by the work of early career researchers and postgraduate students in Delhi/Ambedkar University. The curriculum includes a focus on retrieving cultural idioms, and metaphors of suffering have become areas of interest (Kumar, Dhar, Mishra, 2017). Kakar's legacy is reflected in the work of masters and doctoral levels students and institutional efforts have been made to continue his work, for example, the revival of the Freud lecture series and the institution of the Sudhir Kakar prize for young writers in the annual psychoanalytic conference in Delhi (one of our authors, Amrita Narayanan, was its first recipient). Kakar's work has also been instrumental in inspiring the current revival of an active debate on 'what is cultural' about psychoanalysis and how the culture has changed the mainstream conceptualization of psychology and psychoanalysis in India. As the global economy escalates the already rapid pace of modernization and technological advancement, psychoanalysis and psycho-therapy is becoming very important even to traditional societies, which struggle to survive amidst a fast pace of change. In these times of great need, we feel fortunate to harvest the psychoanalytical wine that has arisen in our terroir: the work of Sudhir Kakar.

## Acknowledgement

The authors would like to thank Dr Rachna Johri for editorial assistance.

## Bibliography

Freud, S. (1989[1910]). *Leonardo da Vinci and a memory of his childhood* (Repr. ed.). (J. Stachey, Ed.; Alan Tyson, Trans,; biographical introduction by Peter Gay) New York, NY: Norton.

Haksar, A.N.D. (2014). *Man or woman? In the seduction of Shiva: Tales of life and love.* New Delhi: Penguin Books.

Kakar, S. (1982). *Shamans, mystics, and doctors: A psychological inquiry into India and its healing traditions.* New York: A. Knopf.

————. (1992). *The analyst and the mystic.* Chicago: University of Chicago Press.

————. (1996[2008]). *Culture and psyche: Selected essays.* Delhi: Oxford University Press.

————. (2001). *The essential writings of Sudhir Kakar.* Delhi: Oxford University Press.

————(2006). *Mira and the Mahatma.* New Delhi: Penguin Books.

————. (2009). *The ascetic of desire.* New Delhi: Penguin Books.

————. (2010). *The crimson throne.* New Delhi: Penguin Books.

————. (2011). *A book of memory.* New Delhi: Penguin Books.

————. (2012). *The essential writings of Sudhir Kakar.* New Delhi: Oxford University Press.

————. (2013). *Young Tagore: The makings of a genius.* Delhi: Viking-Penguin.

————. (2016). *The devil take love.* New Delhi: Penguin India.

Kakar, S., & Ross, J. (1986[2011]). *Tales of love, sex and danger* (2nd ed.). New Delhi: Oxford University Press.

Kumar, M. (2005). In a bid to restate the culture-psyche problematic: Revisiting Kakar's 'The essential writings of Sudhir Kakar'. *Psychoanalytic Quarterly, LXXIV,* 561–587.

Kumar, M. (2009). Recasting the primal scene of seduction: Envisioning a potential encounter of otherness in Jean Laplanche and Sudhir Kakar', *Psychoanalytic Review, 96*(3): 485–513.

————. (2011). Introduction. *Essential writings of Sudhir Kakar.* New Delhi: Oxford University Press.

Kumar, M., Dhar, A., & Mishra, A. (2017). Psychoanalysis from the Indian terrior. Lexington Press.

Mishra, A. (2012). *Round table on Kakar's contributions to psychoanalysis and Indian cultural discourse.* Cape Town, SA: International Congress of Psychology, 2012.

Nagpal, A. (2000). Cultural continuity and change in Kakar's works: Some reflections. *International Journal of Group Tensions, 29*(3/4), 285–321.

Narayanan, A. (2014). Ambivalent subjects: Psychoanalysis, women's sexuality in India and the writings of Sudhir Kakar. *Psychodynamic Practice, 20*(3), 213–217.

———. (2015a, March). *A review of psychoanalysis in Asia: China, India, Japan, South Korea and Taiwan, psychodynamic practice: Individuals, groups and organisations.* UK: Taylor and Francis.

———. (2015b). Inaccessible masturbation, impossible mourning, collective melancholia and the prohibition on female sexual subjects in India. In Akhtar, S. (Ed.*), Psychoanalytic review special edition: 'Psychoanalysis and India'.* New York, NY.

———. (2016). *Soul murder, wolf mother. Re-reading The Jungle Book in contemporary psychoanalytic perspective psychodynamic practice: Individuals, groups and organisations.* UK: Taylor and Francis.

———. (2017). Can the enthralled mother dream? Reflections on women and misogyny via the cultural and clinical. In M. Kumar, A. Mishra, and A. and Dhar (Eds.). *Psychoanalysis in the Indian terroir.* Lexington Press.

Noisseter, J. (2009). *Liquid memory: Why wine matters.* New York, NY: Fahrar Strauss and Giroux.

Winnicott, D.W. (1971). *Playing and reality.* London: Tavistock.

# 50

## Afzal Kureshi

(1939–1996)

### Akbar Husain

Afzal Kureshi

Afzal Kureshi was born in October 1939. After obtaining an MA degree in psychology with first division and attaining first position in Aligarh Muslim University in 1960, he did his PhD from the same university in 1966. His contribution to psychology is distinctly visible in the projective techniques. His early work from the 1960s to 1980 engages in reinterpreting and refining the field of personality assessment. He authored two books—*Adolescent Fantasy: A Study of Youth Motivation*

and *Dimensions of Interpersonal Attraction*. The insightful conceptualization of motivation and personality contained in his books and articles and his method of studying motivation through projective techniques opened new frontiers and influenced the works of personality psychologists. Synthesizing ideas from the personality theories of McClleland, Atkinson, Veroff, and Winter, he constructed projective tests, namely, AAPAS Motive Test, Power Motive Test, Fear of Failure Test, and Alienation Scale.

He received the Commonwealth Exchange Fellowship for visiting UK. In 1990, he became the regional president of the Indian Academy of Applied Psychology. He was a thorough gentleman who was highly sensitive to the feelings of others. He could easily develop an empathetic relationship with anybody who came in his contact. Perhaps his greatest contribution was to the development and growth of personality and social psychology. By 1995, he had supervised 11 PhD theses and 12 MPhil dissertations. He passed away on 10 February 1996.

# 51

# Dinyar M. Pestonjee

(1939)

## Akbar Husain

Dinyar M. Pestonjee

The discipline of psychology underwent a remarkable transformation during the twentieth century, a transformation that included a shift away from the European-influenced philosophical psychology of the late nineteenth century to the empirical, research-based American-dominated psychology in parallel with Indian dawn of psychological principles and philosophy. Without question, the eminent psychologists of India have contributed scientifically in bringing a new horizon of leadership and development across the globe. In this line, Dinyar M. Pestonjee occupies a prominent place whose contribution to Indian psychology and the society at large is commendable. Highly influential as a learning theorist, stress-management guru, social science statesman, educator, and, above all, consummate organisational behaviourist, he has over five decades of teaching experience and has successfully supervised 30 PhD candidates. He is author/co-author of 12 books and over 100 research articles.

D.M. Pestonjee was born in Aligarh on 18 April 1939 and being the youngest of five siblings of his parents, often stood to be most curious and inquisitive in nature. He was a gifted child and an avid reader who gave his father credit for surreptitiously guiding his education by bringing home books and articles and promoted him to understand the nature and science of humankind. He is a scion of the Bhamgara family from Surat whose ancestors moved to the northern part of India about two centuries ago as successful business family. His extended family members were among the most respected and noted medical practitioners in Navsari and Bombay Presidency. His wife, Mrs Roshni Pestonjee, was a graduate in philosophy and obtained double master's degree in philosophy: one from Gujarat University and the other from University of Delaware, USA. She was a senior lecturer at Sardar Patel University, Anand, Gujarat.

Providing a glimpse of academic accolades of any successful person often proves to be a window into the brilliant stature of human mind. Starting from his early school and university years, Pestonjee's academic career has been a mirror of hard work, excellence, and merit. He completed his undergraduate studies from Aligarh Muslim University (AMU) in 1959. He was a university rank holder by securing second rank in the university examinations with subjects of psychology and English and Hindi literature. He topped the university in both the literatures. Subsequently, in the year 1961, Pestonjee completed his master's degree from the same university, securing first position, as university rank holder, and was awarded the university medal for MA/MSc in psychology. After graduating, he joined Shri Varshney PG College, Aligarh, as a lecturer in psychology (1961–1962) and very soon he succeeded in qualifying the coveted UGC-JRF Fellowship in 1962. In between, while at AMU, he took advanced organisational psychology/industrial psychology as an area of interest and higher research. He also embraced organisational structure as an imperative area of research and innovation and decided to pursue his doctoral studies in the same area. Pestonjee was awarded the doctoral degree from AMU in the year 1967. Thereafter, he joined the Department of Psychology, Banaras Hindu University, as a lecturer and continued serving the department for next 15 years (1964–1979). During his stay as a faculty in the Department of Psychology, Banaras Hindu University, he initiated the 'Integration Through Interaction' inter-university football trophy between Banaras Hindu University and AMU with the help from Sultan Akhtar at AMU.

Pestonjee's basic nature of humbleness and his in-depth analysis of problems at various levels often outshined other contributors to the field of organizational/industrial psychology. Subsequently, in 1979, he made a great leap moving ahead with his skills, experience and vision to the coveted Indian Institute of Management (IIM), Ahmedabad where he was recruited for professorship in organisational behaviour and continued his academic endeavour in a different but vivid and more enthusiastic milieu till he retired in 2001. Later, Pestonjee was elevated to the L&T Group as chair professor in organisational behaviour for a period of 7 years (1992–1999). He also headed the AES Institute of Business Management, Ahmedabad (2002–2004), as director of the institute. Moreover, Pestonjee also served an adjunct professor (2004–2008) and chairman of the Doctoral Program Committee (2005–2006) at CEPT University, Ahmedabad; as chair professor, Ganpat University (2005–2008); and as dean, Faculty of Technology Management, CEPT University (2008–2013). The stature that Pestonjee has developed from all these years of service and research endeavours still continues as a cause of envy for the new generation and this has been best exemplified by his continuous service after retirement to Pandit Deendayal Petroleum University (PDPU), Gandhinagar, as the coveted GSPC chair professor. Currently, he is supervising doctoral dissertations and actively involved not merely in policy-making but also in making the new faculties and students orient toward hard work, diligence, and service to the scientific quest of human mind.

Pestonjee was awarded the Academic Exchange Fellowship of the Commonwealth Foundation to visit British universities and management schools in 1994. His vivid and enthusiastic approach towards the field of psychology and management was again recognized when he received the Mazda Foundation Award for Excellence in Science & Education in 1990. He received the Lifetime Achievement Award for Academic Excellence from AMU in 2001. In April 2003, Banaras Hindu University conferred the DLitt (Honoris Causa) degree on him. Subsequently, next year, he brought great laurel to the field of Indian psychology by receiving the Albert Schweitzer Medal for Science and Peace in April 2004. The coveted medal was introduced to honour academic excellence on the 50th anniversary of the Nobel Peace Prize.

Pestonjee's first seminal contribution towards the growing field of organisational studies was in the form of a series of books which he prepared and published during his stay at Aligarh and Varanasi. He published the series *Handbook of Psychological and Social Instruments* (1988–1991), which many researchers considered the need of hour. He soon realised that management education in India needed the boost to unravel the growing challenges of the society. Therefore, to provide orientation in such challenging field his book *Management Education in India* (1992) offered pragmatic and scientific studies on organisational structure and stress management from the educational psychological perspective. He extensively collaborated with other eminent scientists of his time such as Pramod Verma, S. Srinivas Rao, Udai Pareek, and T.V. Rao, and this subsequently culminated into a series of books and monographs, which till date stands to be landmark in the field of management studies. Anecdotally, his contribution along with Udai Pareek in the area of stress management has been a milestone in the history of Indian psychology. As evidence of the new wealth of possibilities offered by his research publications in India and abroad and also the novelty of the phenomenon he unravelled often attracts the interest of even a layperson and, thereby, provides the elegance of scientific tempo that a man of his stature could eschew in his lifetime. His immense contribution has led the international community of social science studies scholars to a better understanding of the Indian approach towards stress management and organisation behaviour. Among his better known works are *Organization Structure and Job Attitudes* (1973), *Behavioral Processes in Organization* (1981), *Second Handbook of Psychological and Social Instruments* (1988), *Third Handbook of Psychological and Social Instruments* (1997), *Studies in Organizational Roles and Stress and Coping* (1997), *Studies in Stress and Its Management* (1999), and *Stress and Work* (2013).

Pestonjee was not merely a prolific writer, but he also contributed to policy-making in the form of monographs publications such as *National Adult Education Programme in Rajasthan: Second Appraisal* (1980), *Motivation of Health Professionals*-PSG Research Report (1987) etc. Moreover, his scientific contributions not only influenced the Indian panorama, but he immensely contributed towards global efforts. For instance, he was part of the team of the Consultation of Health Manpower Management at WHO, Geneva (1985), delegate to the Extraordinary General Assembly of the International Social Science Council of UNESCO, Paris (1985), and member of the standing committee of the ISSC of UNESCO, Paris, besides many others. Additionally, his consultancy services towards industry and academia is also noteworthy which is exemplified in his Emergency Management and Research Institute (EMRI) 108 consultancy contributions on HR issues for 2,400 cases across the country in the area of job satisfaction. Moreover, he has provided many invited and memorial lectures within India in different parts of the country. Notably, Professor S. Sultan Akhtar Memorial Lecture in the 49th National and 18th International Conference of the Indian Academy of Applied Psychology at GLS in 2014 and on stress and crime on Forensic Psychology Day celebrations at Gujarat Forensic Sciences University in 2014 are praiseworthy.

At the scientific level, he emerged as an interlocutor of colleagues in many research fields in and around the globe, including policy-makers and social scientists platforms. Further, he has been part of many national governing and funding bodies in various capacities. Pestonjee was a member of the Indian Council of Social Science Research (ICSSR; 1981–1983) and was also instrumental in establishing Academy of Human Resource Development, Ahmedabad (AHRD) by the Government of India in the year 1990. He served several committees in the capacity of a member. This include the UGC Advisory Committee on Amendment of BHU Act (1987–1988), the Task Force on 'Status of Management Education in India', UGC (1989–1990), the Expert Panel on Management, UGC (1988–1991), and the Task Force on Management, All India Council for Technical Education (AICTE), New Delhi (1993–1999) among others. He was also a member, of the board of studies of various universities.

Pestonjee has contributed to various academic programmes on stress and management in his career of more than 50 years in various formats. His approach emphasises problem-specific action models and is more concerned with the systematic comparison of different action models than the general organisational structures. The persons who display characteristics to the highest degree often become eminent as a direct consequence. A necessary part of this development must be an increased fascination with those individuals who occupy the upper end of the distribution of various positive traits, such as creativity, charisma, talent, morality, spirituality, or wisdom. Pestonjee's contribution towards psychological principles and scientific methods, overwhelmingly supporting the academic fraternity to develop scientific vigour, service to the community, and, last but not the least, engraving human values in the new generation is irrevocably a historically invaluable effort.

# 52

# Sagar Sharma

(1939)

## Braj Bhushan

*Sagar Sharma*

Sagar Sharma was born in April 1939 in Rajpur village of Kangra district in Himachal Pradesh. He did his MA (psychology) in 1964 from Panjab University where he received gold medal for his excellent academic performance. Thereafter, he received his PhD from Panjab University in 1967 for his thesis entitled 'Relationship of Self-concept with Anxiety and School Achievement of Adolescents'. He was initially trained and mentored in comparative and physiological psychology by S.D. Singh, who was also the founder of Primates Lab at Meerut University.

Sagar Sharma was actively involved in cross-cultural research spanning over four decades that was carried out with the active collaboration of Charles D. Spielberger, a distinguished research professor of psychology at University of South Florida, Tampa (USA). An outcome of this research was the development and validation of Hindi adaptations of Spielberger's State-Trait Anxiety Inventory (STAI), Test Anxiety Inventory (TAI), and State-Trait Anger Expression Inventory (STAXI). In addition to the standardization of Self-Concept Inventory (SCI), a 60–item Failure Outcome

Expectancy (FOE) Inventory was devised to study self-related cognitions and evaluative concerns in failure outcome expectancies.

He worked at the Government College of Education, Chandigarh, from 1964 to 1970 and, thereafter, joined the psychology department of Panjab University, Chandigarh, where he worked till 1973. In 1973, he joined the psychology department of Himachal Pradesh University, Shimla. He worked there till 1999 and headed the department from 1973 to 1999. He also served as dean, Faculty of Arts and Faculty of Social Sciences of Himachal Pradesh University. He became University Grants Commission (UGC) national professor in 1991. He was UGC emeritus professor in psychology at Panjab University, Chandigarh, from 2000 to 2002. Besides his regular engagement at Shimla, he was visiting professor at the University of South Florida, Tampa, in 1976. In 1977 he went to Honolulu as programme associate/ Fulbright Scholar to CLI, East-West Centre, and worked on 'the cross-cultural research for behavioural and social scientists' project'. He also went as guest professor of psychology to the State University of New York, USA, in 1997 and University of Bergen Department of Psychometrics, Norway, in 1990.

His primary research focuses on stress, emotions, health, and well-being within educational, clinical, organizational, and cross-cultural perspectives. His work addresses domain-specific stresses from a holistic and interactional perspective. It encompasses examination stress, organizational stress, and life events stress vis-à-vis their association with negative and positive markers of health and well-being. Several of his work attempts to identify the personal and situational moderators or mediators of the stress-health/well-being connection.

He was president of the National Academy of Psychology–India (NAOP–India) in 2002. In 2008, NAOP conferred NAOP Fellowship to him. He was the national representative from India to the International Society of Stress and Anxiety Research (STAR) for 10 years from 1982 to 1992. He was also member of the Indian Council of Medical Research (ICMR)–Indian Council of Social Science Research (ICSSR) joint panel on health for 6 years from 1993 to 1999.

Before 1970, Sagar Sharma standardized the 'self-concept inventory' and authored two books—*Educational Psychology* and *Guidance and Counselling*. He also published around 20 conceptual papers on various aspects of psychological foundations of education. The collaboration with Spielberger made him choose anxiety as a research area. During 1970–1984, his research focused on self and anxiety. His studies revealed that self-concept (positive–negative dimensions) and self-ideal discrepancy ratings by the same high school boys and girls were not only highly correlated with each other but also had identical curvilinear relationships with their academic achievement. Thus, self-ideal discrepancies were not seen as unique correlates of anxiety and academic well-being beyond the ratings of self-concept (positive-negative dimension) alone. This implied that the amount of self ideal discrepancy is more a function of perceived self than the variation in ideal self.

He adapted the STAI in Hindi. This adaptation was facilitated by the fact that state-trait distinction is intrinsic in various language systems including Hindi and Spanish. For instance, the Hindi verb '*raha hun*' and '*rahta hun*' correspond respectively to concept of transitory state and a relatively stable characteristic or personality trait. The actual task of scale/tool adaptation turns out to be more difficult than most people realize. Languages differ enormously in the size of their affective lexicons, and the words/expressions used to describe emotional states can have a wide range of connotations. In a series of studies over years, the cross-language (English–Hindi), psychometric, and construct equivalences of the STAI have been amply demonstrated. It was seen that the Hindi STAI too has sound theoretical underpinnings and excellent psychometric quality. A book chapter on 'Cross-Cultural Measurement of Anxiety', co-authored with Spielberger (1976) outlined various strategies that were later adopted for the genuine adaptations of the STAI across more than 60 cultures/languages and dialects. A series of experimental and field studies with Hindi STAI cross-validated Spielberger's extension of drive theory that incorporates individual differences in intelligence. Simultaneously, his other studies addressed the levels/patterns of anxiety and related methodological issues across cultures and the relationships of organizational (role) stress with markers of health and well-being including trait anxiety and job satisfaction.

Between 1985 and 1999, his research focused on stress, emotions, health, and well-being. The stress-induced vital psychological signs such as anxiety, anger, and depression lead to the occurrence of a range of dysfunctional consequences for health and well-being. Sagar Sharma's work focused at the domain-specific stresses such as examination stress, test (evaluation) anxiety, and organizational stress. For assessing examination stress he adapted Spielberger's Test Anxiety Inventory in Hindi. Besides finding out the detrimental effect of test anxiety on school achievement nested in the upper ranges of intelligence, his work also established the conceptual difference between worry (*W*, a cognitive concern about the consequences of failure) and emotionality (*E*, a self-perceived autonomic arousal). He argued that test (evaluation) anxiety develops in students as a result of a parent's unrealistic expectations of a child's performance level, sustained negative feedback, punitive behaviour towards the child, particularly in performance evaluation situations, and emotionally insipid, overly strict upbringing practices. Along with Knut A. Hagtvet, University of Bergen, Norway, he developed FOE Inventory in 1995 in Norwegian as well as Hindi. This 60-item inventory measures two facets—self-related cognitions and evaluative concerns. Over a period of time, FOE Inventory has been administered in different ethnic groups spreading to six countries, namely, India, Norway, Hungary, Czech Republic, China, and the USA. It has provided consistent support for the distinction between self-referenced and other-referenced worry cognitions. It makes a difference whether blaming as a consequence of poor grades in an important examination is perceived to be 'expected from self', 'expected from significant others' such as parents, siblings, teachers, and classmates, or 'both'.

His work on organizational stress addresses the issue of the relationship of organizational stress with health and well-being in diverse groups such as medicos, bureaucrats, technocrats, managers, and teachers. He has examined the moderating role of dispositions such as type A behaviour and coping styles as well as situational variables such as social and organizational support. The appropriateness of a kind of support was seen as dependent upon the match between the type of support and the nature of the problem encountered at a given point in a life, and also who provides that support. Since 2000, he has been advocating interactional and transdisciplinary research orientations.

## Psychology in India: Reflections

Reflecting on the growth and development of psychology in India, especially research issues that continue to bother him, he says,

> Most of the so-called cross-cultural research, in fact, continues to be 'centricultural' since the goal by and large, seems to vindicate the conceptual models 'centred' in the West and North America. There are few scholars who follow *indigenization from within approach* that uses local (and not classical) languages and cultures as sources for theory, method and praxis. Mainstream Psychology in India continues to focus on finding 'differences' in psychological domains pitched at individual and group levels and negate the 'commonalities' in human functioning. Cannot we find ways to study both the differences and commonalities in psychological domains by using research designs in which both variation (differences) and invariance

(sameness) are explicitly taken into account? The significance of an interactional perspective (individual-intrapsychic and situation-extrapsychic) on research needs to be understood. We need to embrace not only cultural but also social-economic contexts in which psychological process are embedded. Cross-disciplinary, multi-level approaches are required to study and respond to pressing global issues and challenges that have both psychological and social dimensions. (Personal communication, 2014)

The ever-smiling and cheerful academician continues his journey. He has 114 journal papers to his credit. He also published two books, besides contributing 24 book chapters. He remains a source of inspiration for many.

# 53

## Vinod K. Kool

(1943)

Rita Agrawal

Vinod K. Kool

Vinod K. Kool has significantly contributed to the field of psychology in India. Born in a small town near Lucknow, young Vinod completed his undergraduate studies from Christ Church College, Kanpur and joined the University of Gorakhpur to earn a master's degree in psychology. Enjoying three scholarships at a time for his extraordinary merit, Kool obtained his master's degree with flying colours and was offered a job at his alma mater itself. Barely 19 years of age, he started his teaching career at the Department of Psychology, University of Gorakhpur, in 1962, but left it within a year on being offered the position of a lecturer at the Department of Psychology, Sagar University, Madhya Pradesh (formally known as Dr Harisingh Gour University). After working at Sagar University for barely a year, he joined the Department of Psychology at Banaras Hindu University, Varanasi, as a lecturer in 1964, where he worked till 1974, after which he moved to IIT Mumbai as assistant professor (equivalent to Reader) in the School of Humanities and Social Sciences, and it was at this premier institute that the young and determined scholar progressed in the truest sense, never to turn back again. After teaching at various universities in India for almost 22 years, he migrated to the USA and is now a faculty at the State University of New York (SUNYIT, now known as State University of New York Polytechnic Institute), Institute of Technology, New York, USA.

## Awards and Recognition

Vinod Kool's work on the motor memory of blind people was internationally acknowledged and he was the first Indian psychologist invited to present his work at the *VIII Conference on Attention and Performance* at Princeton, USA. He was also invited by the University of Swansea, Wales, to present his work at the conference on *Practical Aspects of Memory*.

While he was winning such international accolades, he was soon identified by the bureaucratic circles of India as a person worthy of undertaking immense responsibility. Therefore, recognizing his administrative acumen, zeal and commitment, profound insight into the psychology of people who are differently abled, and, above all, conviction regarding his values and his ideals, the Government of India appointed him director of the premier National Institute for the Visually Handicapped, Dehradun, in 1982. Following this, he became a consultant to several ministries of the Government of India.

Vinod Kool was also the first person to develop a comprehensive three-dimensional model for understanding the complexities of the phenomenon of non-violence. The importance of the model can be gauged by the fact that he was invited by the Peace Division of the American Psychological Association (APA) to present it at their annual meeting in 1991.

His academic brilliance has brought many laurels to Vinod K. Kool. He has been twice recipient of the prestigious Fulbright Award, and is now a Fulbright specialist in the area of peace and non-violence. His efforts in research and teaching have been acknowledged by SUNYIT, and he has been awarded with the prestigious SUNYIT's Goodell Award for Research and Creativity—the highest research award the college grants to its faculty. In addition to this, he has been asked to present his work at various institutes and universities and scientific symposia both in India and abroad. Kool has presented his work at the APA conventions at Boston, San Francisco, and Washington, DC, as well as symposia at Princeton in NJ, Columbia University in NY, and the University of Wales in UK. More recently, he addressed a colloquium on non-violence at the prestigious Einstein Potsdam Forum at Berlin, and the Hacetepe University, Turkey, invited him as visiting faculty for their ongoing programme on peace and conflict.

On January 2013, Kool came to India on an invitation from the University of Mysore as a Fulbright specialist in the area of peace and non-violence. During this trip, he not only lectured at the host university but was invited by various other universities and institutes around India, where he met a variety of students, ranging from clinical psychologists and psychiatrists in the Mysore–Bengaluru region in South India to students of the Forensic Science Institute and even the Police University in Ahmedabad in western India and the management and technology students in eastern and north-eastern India.

# Contribution

Vinod Kool has been a pioneer in more than one way. Among the first psychologists to work in the area of human information processing in India, he was also one of the few to work in the extremely challenging area of motor memory of blind people. Undeterred by the lack of sophisticated electronic apparatus and unperturbed by the meagre computing facilities available in the early 1970s, he trained a handful of students in the extremely challenging but interesting area of human information processing. His ingeniously designed experiments coupled with stringent experimental controls optimized by appropriate statistical control provided him data and insights that psychologists in the Western world were amazed with.

While working at IIT Mumbai, his research on the motor memory of blind people enabled him to get a huge grant from the Ministry of Social Welfare, Government of India, giving him an opportunity to conduct research in a highly specialized field, wherein probably there were only two other well-known faces: Roberta Klatzky of the University of California in the USA and Susan Miller in the UK.

Kool's work on the motor memory of blind people was highly acclaimed, and the lecture on the topic that he had delivered at the *VIII Conference on Attention and Performance* at Princeton, USA, was included as a chapter in the volume *Attention and Performance VIII* published by the internationally known publisher, Erlbaum.

While at IIT Mumbai, Kool embarked on another academic journey. Intrigued not by the large number of people who readily administered shocks to fellow human beings but by that miniscule percentage that refused to administer shocks in the famous Milgram experiments on obedience to authority, Kool decided to focus his research efforts on gaining further insights into the psychology of such persons. This was the starting point for his voyage into the psychology of non-violence, and Stanley Milgram himself took the initiative to contact Kool realizing the significance of the neglected minority who refused to deliver shocks in his experiments.

Realizing the need for a reliable and valid test to measure the personality differences, Kool set out on constructing a measure that has since then received worldwide recognition. This test, which has been used effectively across cultures, is called the NVT (the non-violence test). In fact, the NVT has recently been used to measure and reduce violent tendencies among prisoners in Maryland, USA.

After migrating to the USA, Kool finally joined SUNYIT in 1990. He soon realized that the psychology of non-violence will remain obsolete unless and until it is discussed and analyzed at appropriate forums. With this aim, he single-handedly organized two conferences on the psychology of non-violence. His consistent efforts to comprehend the psychology of non-violence continued unabated, and based on sound empirical findings, he gave psychology the first comprehensive three-dimensional model for decoding the complexities of the phenomenon of non-violence. In doing so, he is one of the few psychologists worldwide who has attempted to introduce a scientific temper to the study of psychology of nonviolence.

In his quest for knowledge, Kool leaves no stone untouched. On a visit to India as senior Fulbright scholar, he happened to learn of Malana, a small nondescript town in the remote Himalayas. Despite being extremely difficult to access, he took this opportunity and visited the only known non-violent community remotely surviving from the times of Alexander the Great. The culmination of such efforts is his recent book, *Psychology of Nonviolence and Aggression*, published by Macmillan-Palgrave in 2008. Evidence of his scholastic interest in the area of non-violence is seen from the fact that out of the several books Kool has authored, three are devoted to the psychology of non-violence.

One is awed by his ability to extrapolate from areas as diverse as cognition, social and developmental psychology, positive psychology, evolutionary psychology, and neuropsychology and apply them to the understanding of not only non-violence, peace, and conflict resolution in a cross-cultural context but also to various other facets of psychology, a point that is brought to the fore at every lecture he delivers.

His textbook *Applied Social Psychology: A Global Perspective* is global in the truest sense of the term, with each chapter focusing on cross-cultural perspectives of specific problems encountered and their possible resolutions through the application of social psychology principles and theories. Apart from writing such books, he has also contributed chapters to books edited by highly renowned scientists and published by leading international publishers such as Wiley, Erlbaum, Springer-Verlag, and Macmillan-Palgrave. He has further published dozens of research papers in leading peer-reviewed journals of international repute. His research papers and books have been extensively cited, and scholars continue to draw inspiration from his works. He has been on the editorial board for the APA's journal, *Peace and Conflict: Journal of Peace Psychology* and has been asked to review a large number of APA publications.

Kool is among the first few psychologists invited to become a founder member of the research committee on non-killing psychology, an initiative of none other than Glenn Paige of the Center for Global Nonkilling, Hawaii, and was invited to contribute chapters to two books on non-killing psychology.

At the age of 70 plus, when most professors would be sitting back and relaxing, Kool is still quite active and has readily accepted the invitation to act as guest editor for the peer-reviewed journal *Gandhi Marg* for a special issue devoted to the psychology of non-violence. He is currently also involved in another project under which he is finalizing a book on the psychology of technology, which is scheduled for publication soon and will be a valuable addition to his existing research output (now published, Springer International, 2016).

One can only conclude that Vinod Kool, a prolific researcher, a knowledgeable teacher, a psychologist with depth and vision, will have his name engraved in the annals of psychology forever, for not only, his contribution towards the understanding of the psychology of non-violence, but also for his work in many other important areas of psychology.

# 54

# B. Krishnan

## Mewa Singh

B. Krishnan was a great teacher, researcher, and organizer. He started his career as a lecturer in psychology (1942–1950) and became an assistant professor (1950–1958), a Reader (1958–1962) and finally a professor (1962–1977). He was a teacher of psychology for almost 35 years. As a Fulbright scholar, he went to the USA and studied at the University of Minnesota during the early 1950s. He published several research articles. He organized number of seminars and conferences during the years he headed the department in the University of Mysore.

His main research interests included personality, counselling, and Indian psychology. He developed questionnaires to study habits and introversion-extroversion. He founded and edited the journal *Psychological Studies,* ran it successfully till his retirement, and handed it over to M.A. Faroqui of the University of Calicut. It is now the best-known psychology journal from India run by the National Academy of Psychology India and published by Springer. He presided over the section of psychology of the Indian Science Congress in 1972 held at Chandigarh. He was also the president of the conferences of Indian Academy of Applied Psychology held at Madras (1968) and Mysore (1959).

He was largely instrumental in shaping the nature of psychology curriculum in Indian universities, as he was closely associated with the boards of studies in various Indian universities for almost a quarter of a century.

# 55

# Fr James Filella

Satishchandra Kumar and Anjali Majumdar

Fr James Filella

Fr James Filella was amongst the first few academicians in Mumbai who contributed in making psychology a separate discipline from philosophy. A separate board of studies in psychology was constituted at Bombay University (now the University of Mumbai) in 1957, thus, creating psychology as a separate discipline from philosophy (D'Souza & Kale, 1978). However, there were earlier attempts of establishing psychology as a separate faculty.

The first department of psychology started at St. Xavier's College, Mumbai, in 1914 under the leadership of Fr Lankes, a disciple of Spearman.[1] However, due to his untimely death, the department was closed soon after it opened (Ghorpade, 1984). The same department was reopened in

---

[1]  See http://xaviers.edu/main/index.php/psychology

1925 by Fr Molitor, but as he had to leave for Australia, it closed again in 1927 (Ghorpade, 1984). In 1939, Rev. Fr Solagran reopened the department of psychology at St. Xavier's College, but within a few years, it was renamed as St. Xavier's Institute of Education and became a separate educational institute on its own (Ghorpade, 1984). Another milestone in the setting-up of the discipline of psychology in India came in 1945, with the establishment of the Bombay Psychological Association (BPA). The BPA came into existence at the initiative of A.A. Khatri and his friend R.J. Shah. The two of them served as the first secretaries of BPA with K.A. Lalkaka as the first president (Ghorpade, 1984). In February 1948, the BPA organized its first two-day conference of psychologists in Mumbai. The first national conference of applied psychology was held at the Tata Institute of Social Sciences (TISS) under the auspices of TISS, BPA, Gujarat Research Society, and the Indian Council of Mental Health (Ghorpade, 1984). In 1954, Bombay University granted recognition to psychology as a separate discipline. The university introduced BA (special) and BA (general) degree in psychology for the first time (Ghorpade, 1984). In 1956, Smt Nathibai Damodar Thackersey (SNDT) Women's University offered a complete course in psychology (Ghorpade, 1984). Finally, in 1957, the rector of the University of Mumbai agreed to start a department of applied psychology in Mumbai at the suggestion of A.K. Jaindani (Jai Hind College), P.H. Prabhu (TISS), and G.D. Pareikh (Ghorpade, 1984). In the same year, the psychology department at St. Xavier's College was reopened under the headship of Fr Filella. Fr Fuster took over the position of head of the department soon after that, as Fr Filella had to leave for a study tour. Fr Filella held many esteemed positions at St. Xavier's College including the head of the department in 1975–1976 (St. Xavier's college magazine, 1976).[2]

## Academic Work

Father James Filella was a critical thinker. He often expressed his interpretations of the works of famous psychologists. In September 1978, he was invited to take a session as a part of the series 'Images of the Unconscious' organized by Knopf at the Max Muller Bhavan, Bombay. An abridged text of the talk titled *Jung: At the Service of the Psyche* was published in *Bombay Psychologist* (Filella, 1978). Fr Filella spoke about how Jung was never a conventional psychologist. Even when Jung followed the methods of psychoanalysis 'his conclusions were so much at variance with those of orthodox Freudian thinking that there was no other alternative for Jung but to part ways with Freud' (Filella, 1978). Fr Filella even mentions that Jung was hardly considered a scientist, rather, his contributions attained the tag of 'philosophical', 'esoteric' and 'mystical' (Filella, 1978).

Fr Filella went on to explain how one had to try to place oneself in Jung's shoes in order to understand Jung's thoughts. Jung lived in 'an age of discovery and rational enlightenment' (Filella, 1978). It was an era when scientists were discovering that even though the present existence of all things is highly differentiated, they all originated from undifferentiated entities. This led Jung to his basic query: 'How can a man be fully socialized and assimilated within a culture and retain his inner sense of personality identity?' (Filella, 1978)

Fr Filella presented Jung's basic ideas regarding the psyche and the mandala symbolism as an index of psychic maturity and divided it into four sections:

I. Directed versus non-directed thinking
II. The unconscious as a collective force

---

[2] See http://www.xaviers.edu/magazine/Alumni%20%20Section.pdf

III. The process of individualism
IV. The mandala as a symbol of the individuated self

In the directed versus non-directed thinking section of his presentation, he explained Jung's concepts, suggesting that directed thinking is 'thinking for the purpose of expressing and communicating the results of one's experience. This search for precision and accuracy leads to more and more exact forms of expression in order to reduce ambiguity in content and to ensure clarity in communication' (Filella, 1978). Since the purpose of scientific thinking is precision, reliable and valid knowledge, and unequivocal communication, it is considered as the highest form of directed thinking. However, when starting from experience and moving inward in search of self-understanding, rather than trying to communicate the experience, it is called non-directive thinking. 'As one moves from the level of experience into the inner recesses of the unconscious, one gradually discovers greater generality in the meaning of images and symbols, richer meaning contained and conveyed by them, and a stronger interplay of energy' (Filella, 1978).

While discussing the unconscious as a collective force, Fr Filella described how the deep psychological crisis that Jung went through after his feud with Freud in 1911 led to his journey of self-discovery—'the confrontation with his unconscious'. The analysis of his emotions and images allowed Jung to draw quite a few significant conclusions about the nature of the unconscious. Fr Filella also discussed Jung's idea that man is a combination of three circles of existence—the biological, the social, and the psychological.

While speaking on the process of individualization, Fr Filella explained that individuation is 'a process of growth and transformation by which an individual consciously exposes himself to all the influences of the unconscious and consistently seeks to give expression to as much of the psychic totality that surges within himself as is humanly possible' (Filella, 1978). Jung described individuation as a continuous process, a confrontation of opposites, a forging, and an integration of highly differentiated parts. The process of psychic growth is described in several steps. The first step is the unveiling of the 'persona', when an individual sheds his overdependence on the roles society has thrust on him. During the second step, the individual must come to terms with his 'shadow'. In the third stage, the individual familiarizes himself with the potential of his total sexuality. He must face himself as 'androgynous'. The development of the self is the final stage in psychological growth.

On the topic of the Mandala symbolism and expression of selfhood, Fr Filella explained that *mandals*, in Hindu tradition, are 'geometrical figures in the form of circles which contain a magic power' (Filella, 1978). He explained that Jung considered this 'magic circle' to be an expression of the psyche. In conclusion to this talk, Fr Filella mentioned the difficulty of the process of psychological growth. He elaborated that Jung learnt about these difficulties through experience. 'Jung was a man at the service of the psyche because like Freud, he did not hesitate to come to grips with his own 'psyche' whatever the consequences' (Filella, 1978).

Fr Filella was also associated with the Indian Society for Applied Behavioral Science (ISABS) for a long time. ISABS engaged in applying the knowledge of psychology to the well-being of people and organizations (Sinha, 2004). It was registered in 1972 as a professional body under the Societies Registration Act of 1860. It was involved in many T-group training and laboratory education programmes since its inception. In June 1971, Fr Filella, along with Fr Don Bielby of Holy Cross Fathers, conducted several labs for student leaders in Western India (Sinha, 2004). ISABS also followed the development of various professional resources during the first active decade of laboratory education in India. Around 1963–1968, several distinguished behavioural scientists from the USA, including Douglas McGregor, Warren Bennis, Howard Baumgartel, Fred Massarik, John Thomas, and Herman Gadon, came to India. Once laboratory education was more or less established in

India, Indian-applied behavioural scientists started going for overseas training. Udai Pareek was the first Indian scholar who received professional training at NTL in 1961 (Sinha, 2004). Fr Filella attended a programme for specialists in Organizational Development (OD) at Bethel in 1966, along with K.K. Anand, Raja Deolalikar, Paul Sirmoni, Abad Ahmed, Prayag Mehta, Manohar Nadkarni, James Fuster, and Purnima Sinha (Sinha, 2004).

The two day conference on 'Developments in Experience Based Learning' on 4–5 December 1971 organized by Francis Menezes at Poona was attended by 19 professional colleagues including Fred Massarik, Udai Pareek, Iswar Dayal, Nitish De, Pulin Garg, and Abad Ahmed. The decision to form ISABS was taken during this conference. Fr Filella was elected on the board of ISABS along with Nitish De, Udai Pareek, Ishwar Dayal, Fred Massarik, Francis Menezes, Dharni Sinha, K.J. Christopher, K.K. Anand, Pulin Garg, and Donald Bielby. Fr Filella was also elected on the executive committee. The first annual conference of ISABS was held in Poona on 6–7 August 1972. This was attended by 34 professional members, associates, and guests of the society.

In 1982, the International Council of Psychologists chose Fr Filella to represent western India in the 1982–1983 conference among several psychologists from other parts of India, including S.C. Sharma (southern India), Ramnath Kundu (eastern India), Edwin Harper (northern India), and K.P. Kulshrestha (Ghorpade, 1983). Summarizing his experiences he said, 'I realized that ICP is not just a professional association but a group of potential friends' (D'Souza & Kale, 1980). As director of Xavier Institute of Management and the head of the Department of Psychology at St. Xavier's College, Bombay, Fr Filella served as a fiscal agent of the International Council of Psychologist since 1979 and was elected as the area chairperson for the journal for India in 1984 (Ghorpade, 1983).

Fr Filella was also very interested in the psycho-social dimensions of various facets of the society. In St. Xavier's magazine, he published an article titled 'The College Climate: Sedative or challenge?' (Filella, 1979). In his paper titled 'Psycho-social Dimensions of College Climates: A Factorial Study', Volume 2 of *The Bombay Psychologist* (Filella, 1980), he portrayed the college students of Bombay in four distinct areas—home–student relationship, student–student relationship, student–professor relationship, and student–college relationship. He used this study as a preliminary step towards a better understanding of the type of educational environment existing in the colleges of Bombay.

With the help of staff members of the psychology and sociology departments of St. Xavier's College, he devised the College Environment Questionnaire.

In another paper 'The Climate in Human Institutions: A Psycho-social Matrix Model', he proposed

> a model of human climates which on the one hand safe-guards the balance between the psychological and the social elements of human situations and, on the other hand, provides a common framework in terms of which climate variables can be explicitly integrated in relation to both dimensions, psychological as well as social. (Filella, 1984)

The psychological dimensions of the matrix model are based on Maslow's approach to the study of human behaviour. Fr Filella described Maslow's work as an explanation of the dual nature of human behaviour, 'namely, the need for security and the need for self-expression as a condition for growth' (Filella, 1984). The psychological dimension in the matrix model of human climate includes vitality in the role of a third balancing anchor between security and freedom. The first anchor, security, includes the need for certainty and control. In an attempt to avoid the unknown, the cause of fear, one often sacrifices the sense of wonder and mystery. On the other hand, freedom is the 'need to be oneself with the possibility of manifesting all one's potentialities' (Filella, 1984). It is the need for growth rather than the need to impose oneself on others with impulsivity. As the balancing anchor, vitality stands between security and freedom. Vitality is a sign of being alive. 'At times, vitality expresses itself through seeking safety and certainty, and at other times, reaching out to new forms of living' (Filella, 1984).

The social dimensions of the matrix model deals with group dynamics as the locus of personal growth. Filella wrote about four major areas as the anchoring points— goal orientation, orderliness, personal attraction, and stimulus to growth. Goal orientation refers to a vision that is shared by the members of the group and gives a sense of direction. The manner in which the resources of the group are utilized is the orderliness of the group. The factor of personal interactions refers to the network of relationships which occur when people are together. The matrix model becomes a $3 \times 4$ model with the three psychological dimensions and four social dimensions that 'provides a conceptual framework that binds together the psychological and the social dimensions of human situations' (Filella, 1984).

During his tenure at St. Xavier's College, he wrote various articles. His article titled 'Centenary Programme of Renewal: An Appraisal', reflecting his opinions about the St. Xavier's Programme for Self-Renewal, was published in St. Xavier's College Magazine in 1968 (Filella, 1968). In his article 'Teaching as a Relationship' published in St. Xavier's magazine (Filella, 1971), he expressed his views regarding the attitudes and behaviour of professors in universities and how the situation needed improvement (Filella, 1971).

Fr Filella was associated with the Xavier Institute of Management and Research. The institute was established in 1963 as St. Xavier Institute of Industry 'to provide the industry with competent human resources'.[3] In 1971, Fr Filella shifted the focus on development of supervisory and managerial skills and the institute was renamed as Xavier Institute of Management (XIM), focusing on working executives and offering postgraduate diplomas to hone their managerial skills.[4] Xavier Institute of Management and Research (XIMR) was established in 2006 as a successor to the erstwhile XIM to provide managers with a global perspective in line with the requirements of a fast changing business environment.

During his association with Xavier Institute of Management, he wrote an article 'Employees: Committed workers or smooth operators?' (Filella, 1985) in *Bombay Psychologist* where he argued that the root cause of corruption was people's attitudes towards their jobs. He discussed that there are majorly two types of attitudes that people may have about their job. Many people may look at their job merely as an economic opportunity. 'They do not really want to work; they want to be employed' (Filella, 1985). For others, more than an economic contract, 'it is an opportunity for them to express their talents by means of the proper performance of the tasks assigned to them' (Filella, 1985). Fr Filella hypothesized that people who see work only as an economic contract are more vulnerable to bribery and corrupt practices. In this article, he also described Cummings and Srivastava's classification of work situations. They divided work situations into four categories— described work, contractual work, emergent work, and discretionary work. In described work, the supervisor decides a person's work and how it should be done; the person merely does what is required to be done. In the case of contractual work, both the supervisor as well as the worker consent to the work. Emergent work relies on the economic conditions of the environment or the availability of work opportunities, whereas discretionary work depends on the worker's expertise, that is, the worker decides which tasks to accept. Fr Filella argued that 'not all four types of work are equally conducive to situations where corrupt practices may occur' (Filella, 1985).

---

[3] See http://www.ximr.ac.in/htmls/about_cv.html, Retrieved on 21 April 2017.

[4] See http://www.mubs.ac.ug/index.php?option=com_content&view=article&id=1313&Itemid=641, Retrieved on 21 April 2017.

Fr Filella also analyzed the type of job contract on the basis of two components—importance of money and importance of self-expression. Furthermore, he wrote that two circumstances act as aggravators to corruption inducing work situations; 'the nature of prescribed work, and the way collective agreements about financial rewards and fringe benefits are made' (Filella, 1985). When senior clerks have to take prescribed work from inexperienced officers, they may feel unsatisfied with the compensation they get and may start looking for other sources of income. To make things more complicated, collective agreements about economic exchange between employers and workers just becomes a way of enforcing prescribed work on workers. Fr Filella pointed out that the only way to overcome corruption and malpractices at workplace is to leave them behind. He argued that as long as people approach work merely as employment or as an economic contract, there will be chances of corruption and malpractice. He also wrote that the society is already making progress towards work as a place of self-expression as well as a platform for economic stability. The set-up of high involvement of organizations introduced flat and lean organizational structures, individually enriched job designs and self-managed teams, and open and inclusive information systems with goals participatively set. He concluded the article by emphasizing that 'however rampant bribery and corruption may unfortunately be, it is a sign that there is still a spirit of individuality worth identifying and responding to' (Filella, 1985). It is necessary to get in touch with the vitality and creative dynamism which lies beyond bureaucratic organizations.

Fr Filella is fondly remembered by his students. In the book *You Moved My Life: A Tribute to Teachers* edited by Mr Viney Kirpal, a chapter titled 'A Legacy Unforgotten' is dedicated to him. This chapter has been penned by one of his students, Rehana Ghadially, who was a professor of psychology in the Department of Humanities and Social Sciences at the Indian Institute of Technology, Bombay. She describes him as a young, thin, tall Jesuit priest from Spain with 'sparkling eyes behind plain black-rimmed glasses' who 'exuded confidence and struck an authoritative yet benign pose' (Ghadially, 2004). Ghadially mentions that after retirement, Fr Filella moved to Spain. They kept in touch for some time which turned into silence with the passage of time.

# References

D'Souza, T.A., & Kale, S.V. (1978). Psychological news bulletin. *Bombay Psychologist: A Journal of the Bombay Psychological Association, 1*(1), 86.

———. (1980). Psychological news bulletin. *Bombay Psychologist: A Journal of the Bombay Psychological Association, 3*(1), 43–47.

Filella, J. (1968). Centenary programme of renewal: An appraisal. *St. Xavier's College Magazine, 1966–67,* 22–25.

———. (1971). Teaching as a relationship. *St. Xavier's College Magazine, 1970–71,* 38–44.

———. (1978). Jung- At the service of the psyche. *Bombay Psychologist: A Journal of the Bombay Psychological Association, 1*(1), 63–69.

———. (1979). The college climate: Sedative or challenge? *St. Xavier's College Magazine, 1979–80,* 22–29.

———. (1980). Psycho-social dimensions of college climates: A factorial study. *Bombay Psychologist, 2(1),* 10–17.

———. (1984). The climate in human institutions: A psycho-social matrix model. *Bombay Psychologist. A Journal of Bombay Psychological Association, 5*(2), 6(1), 65–69.

———. (1985). Employees: Committed workers or smooth operators? *Bombay Psychologist. A Journal of Bombay Psychological Association, 7*(1–2), 23–31.

Ghadially, R. (2004). A legacy unforgotten. In V. Kirpal (Ed.), *You moved my life: A tribute to teachers* (pp. 93–95). India: Sterling Publishers.

Ghorpade, M.B. (1983). Psychological news bulletin. *Bombay Psychologist: A Journal of Bombay Psychological Association, 5*(1), 59–63.

———. (1984). A chronicle of psychology in Bombay 1914–1984. *Bombay Psychologist. A Journal of Bombay Psychological Association, 6*(1), 9–17.

Sinha, D.P. (2004). *T-group team building & organisation development.* Published for Indian Society for Applied Behavioural Science. New Delhi: Raj Press.

# 56

# Nirod Mukerji

## Satishchandra Kumar and Anjali Majumdar

As the first professor and head, Nirod Mukerji, MSc (Calcutta), PhD (London), took the reins for the growth and development of the Department of Applied Psychology when it was established at the University of Bombay on 26 July 1959 (Kale, 1984). He was assisted by S.V. Kale and T.R. Kulkarni as Readers, and Jog as a lecturer (Ghorpade, 1984). While the teaching work was carried out with the additional help of four recognized postgraduate teachers, guidance in psychology laboratory practice was given by the departmental teachers (University of Bombay: Annual Report, 1959–60). The department continued to grow with the support of Mukerji. Along with MA students, PhD aspirants were also accepted in the department.

The main thrust of the department was envisaged to cater to the special needs of the complex urban human environment of an industrial maritime commercial city like Bombay (now Mumbai), which was also the financial capital of the nation, the ceaselessly throbbing heart, brain, and brawn of the country. The department was to develop the fields of 'applied' (or applicable) knowledge of psychology, especially in clinical, educational, and industrial spheres (Kale, 1984). Some innovative experiments were tried out in the initial years of the department, like orientation lectures in basic science subjects for its students who essentially came from the arts streams. There were also seminars in the fourth term of the two-year MA course; only the first three terms were for teaching (Kale, 1984).

The department started its research work comparatively early for a new department, such as the measurement of ethnic, social and linguistic prejudices among students, the personality of businessmen and executives, study of examination system and reforms, talent research, delinquency, and facial vision. Around 1964–1965, the department acquired and turned a $3 \times 5$ storeroom into a dark room and laboratory. The research students started registering right from its inception. The first to obtain a PhD was Mehroo Bengalee, who later became professor and head of the education department, University of Mumbai between 1984 to 1986, and later the first female vice-chancellor of the University of Mumbai from 1986 to 1992 (Singh, 2014). Soon a lot of other students followed and completed their PhD degrees.

Apart from the recommended syllabus, arrangements were also made for the students to visit various factories under the guidance of departmental teachers in order to gain acquaintance with the working conditions in industrial establishments. Mukerji expected this arrangement to be expanded in future to cover other institutions besides factories. Other institutional visits were organized to places such as N.M. Mental Hospital, Messrs. Hindustan Lever Ltd., Dumex (Private) Ltd.,

Taraporevala Aquarium, Tata Mills, and T.N. Medical College. The students also visited the Indian Institute of Technology, Powai, to supplement the lectures on industrial psychology (University of Bombay: Annual Report, 1962–63). By way of participating in extra-curricular activities, students also visited the anatomy department of the Seth G.S. Medical College and attended educational films arranged by the British Information Services (University of Bombay: Annual Report, 1963–64).

These visits were planned ahead and treated at par with the psychology laboratory work of the students (University of Bombay: Annual Report, 1960–61). As the department head, Mukerji also provided opportunities to the students to take full advantage of the sessions of the Indian Science Congress. He continued organizing various seminars for the department over the course of his tenure. In 1965, through the courtesy of Messrs. Sandoz (India) Ltd., a film on schizophrenia was screened in the premises of the department (University of Bombay: Annual Report, 1965–66). A tape-recorded report on Mesealin was played before two groups of invitees mainly comprising of the teachers of medicine and psychiatry (University of Bombay: Annual Report, 1965–66). Students of the Bombay Labour Institute visited the laboratory of the department to be acquainted with certain psychological tests (University of Bombay: Annual Report, 1965–66).

With Mukerji as the head of the department in the academic session 1964–1965, the National Council of Educational Research and Training agreed to finance the research project on talent search submitted by the department (University of Bombay: Annual Report, 1964–65). Mukerji was the director of the project on talent search. The major objective of this project was to undertake a follow-up study of intellectually superior children for the age group 12+ to 14 residing in Greater Bombay, and to investigate into the pattern of their assimilation in the social fabric (University of Bombay: Annual Report, 1964–65). R.N. Jog was the project officer in charge of the day-to-day progress on the project. Mukerji was also in charge of the project on delinquency. Under this project, a socio-psychological study of delinquency was intended to be made through an intensive investigation of a limited sample (University of Bombay: Annual Report, 1964–65). T.R. Kulkarni was the research officer responsible for its progress.

Under the headship of Mukerji, the Department of Applied Psychology welcomed many distinguished visitors. Prominent members of our society addressed the students as well the teachers of the department. In the academic session 1961–1962, the department was visited by the chairman of the Public Service Commission, Nigeria. The department was also visited by the Director of Anthropology, Government of India, who addressed the teachers and students of the department and delivered an interesting lecture on the problems of integration of the tribal people in India. During the academic session of 1962–1963, the department welcomed A. Orgel as a visiting professor. He delivered a lecture on modern trends in psychoanalytical theories (University of Bombay: Annual Report, 1962–63). K.J. Shone of the International Labour Organization, who also became an advisor to the Government of India, gave a talk to the teachers and students on 'What Productivity Engineers Have Borrowed from Psychology'.

During the academic session 1963–1964, under the continued headship of Mukerji, the department received Givens L. Thornton, Department of Psychology, Grinnell College, Iowa, who gave a lecture on 'Some Observations on the Present State of Psychology as a Profession in the U.S.A'. (University of Bombay: Annual Report, 1963–64). In the following academic session, the department was visited by Robert D. Meade, Fulbright visiting professor from Trinity College, Hartford, USA. He delivered a lecture on 'Motivation–Theoretical, Experimental, and Applied' (University of Bombay: Annual Report, 1964–65). Other distinguished visitors to the department include S. del Campo of Montevideo University, Uruguay, and W. Emmett, emeritus professor of the University of Edinburgh (University of Bombay: Annual Report, 1962–63). Shin-Ichi Takezawa, Rikkyo University, Tokyo, Japan (Annual Report, 1961–62); Arthur M. Whitehall, University of Hawaii (University of Bombay: Annual Report, 1961–62); D.W. McElwain, University of Queensland, Australia; W. Sutton, University of Melbourne, Australia (University of Bombay: Annual Report, 1961–62); and Ronald M. Berndt and Mrs Catherine Berndt of the Department of Anthropology, University of Western Australia, were the other prominent visitors. L. Weiskrantz of the psychological laboratory, the University of Cambridge, was invited to deliver a lecture on perceptual capacity and the organization of the visual nervous system (University of Bombay: Annual Report, 1965–66). W.R. Dixon of the Faculty of Education, University of Michigan, took several seminars on educational psychology and psychometrics along with an exchange-professor attached to the Department of Applied Psychology, University of Bombay. Dixon also delivered a talk on 'Improving Reading Performance' (University of Bombay: Annual Report, 1964–65).

Kale (1984), while writing an article titled 'A Brief Historical Note on the Development of the Department of Applied Psychology and a Look Into Future' in the special issue commemorating the silver jubilee year of the Department of Applied Psychology of the University of Bombay, applauded Nirod Mukerji, who was the first and founder head of the Department of Applied Psychology, for his vision and foresight, along with the other psychologists who managed to persuade the University of Bombay library to subscribe to some journals, such as the *Journal of Applied Psychology* or *Psychological Bulletin*, in the field of psychology right from the first year of their publication. This bold step, taken so early, makes the University of Bombay library section of psychology journals and periodicals one of the most frequently visited by the outside scholars even today.

## Academic Work

During the span of his long career, Mukerji authored many articles which were published by well-recognized journals. While participating in the Indian Science Congress, January 1960, he presented his paper titled 'Concepts of Normality–Reviewed'. It was published in the proceedings of the 47th session of the Indian Science Congress, Part III (1960). During the latter half of 1960, he wrote an article, 'Cybernetics, a New Facet of Psychology', which was published in the *Indian Journal of Psychology* (Mukerji, 1960). He also wrote an article for *The Bombay Civic Journal* in 1960 titled 'The Receding Star of Unity'.

In 1961, he attended the sessions of the Indian Science Congress held at Roorkee and presided over the section of psychology (University of Bombay: Annual Report, 1960–61). He also spoke on the topic 'Progress of Psychology in India', which was then published in the *Proceedings of the Indian Science Congress Association*, Pt. II (1961). His article 'Similarities Between Man and Machine' was published in the national newspaper *Times of India* on the 10 April 1961. Mukerji also published an article to bring focus on the prospective research aspects of psychology in India in 1961. This article was titled 'Research Needs in Some Fundamental Aspects of Psychology in India', and was Chapter XVII in *Recent Trends in Psychology*. Later, in 1961, he wrote the book *Psychopharmacology*, published by Probe in December 1961.

In 1962, he independently completed the book *Standing at the Crossroads*, which was an attempt at an analytical approach to the basic problems of psychosocial integration in India (University of Bombay: Annual Report, 1962–63). This book was published by Allied Publishers in 1963 (University of Bombay: Annual Report, 1963–64). He also wrote the article 'Frontiers of Psychopharmacology' (Mukerji, 1962), which was published in the *Indian Medical Gazette*. Another article authored by him was 'A Hundred Years Ago', which was published in *Hindustan Standard*. He also wrote 'Motivation' in 1965, published in *Bombay Textile Research Association*.

In 1965, he presented a paper, 'An Experimental Investigation into the Phenomenon of 'Proto-Vision' in the 53rd Indian Science Congress. This paper was then published in the *Proceedings of 53rd Indian Science Congress*, Part III. Another article penned by Mukerji (1966a), 'Psychology and History', was published in *The Quarterly Review of Historical Studies*. In 1965, he wrote an article titled 'Modern Science and Technology and their Impact on the Indian Spiritual Values and Traditions' (Mukerji, 1966b).

On 18 March 1968, Nirod Mukerji resigned from his post of professor and head of the department, and S.V. Kale was appointed as officiating professor and head of the department.

# References

Ghorpade, M.B. (1984). A chronicle of psychology in Bombay. *Bombay Psychologist: A Journal of the Bombay Psychological Association, 6*, 9–17.

Kale, S.V. (1984). A brief historical note on the development of the department of applied psychology and a look into future. *Bombay Psychologist: A Journal of the Bombay Psychological Association, 6*, 5–8.

Mukerji, N. (1960). Cybernetics, a new facet of psychology. *Indian Journal of Psychology, XXXV*, 1.

———. (1962). Frontiers of psychopharmacology. *Indian Medical Gazette, XCIV*(2), 44–49.

———. (1966a). Psychology and history. *The Quarterly Review of Historical Studies, V*(3), 11-14.

———. (1966b). Modern science and technology and their impact on the Indian spiritual values and traditions. *Science and Culture, 31*(2).

Singh, D. (2014). Mumbai University's first woman V-C dies. *The Indian Express*, 22 May 2014, Mumbai.

University of Bombay. (1959, 1 April–1960, 31 March). *Annual report for the year 1959–60* (pp. 55–56). Bombay: Author.

———. (1960, 1 April–1961, 31 March). *Annual report for the year 1960–61* (pp. 59–61). Bombay: Author.

———. (1961, 1 April–1962, 31 March). *Annual report for the year 1961–62* (pp. 63–65). Bombay: Author.

———. (1962, 1 April–1963, 31 March), *Annual report for the year 1962–63* (pp. LIX–LX) Bombay: Author.

———. (1963, 1 April–1964, 31 March). *Annual report for the year 1963–64* (pp. 55–57). Bombay: Author.

———. (1964, 1 April–1965, 31 March). *Annual report for the year 1964–65* (pp. 43–45). Bombay: Author.

———. (1965, 1 April–1966, 31 March). *Annual report for the year 1965–66*. Bombay: Author.

# 57

# S.P. Adinarayan

Suresh Vijayaraghavan

*S.P. Adhinarayan*

S.P. Adinarayan is a tall, fair, immaculately dressed, soft-spoken person wearing a smile that draws anyone happened to meet him. He is one of the pillars of psychology who has played a pivotal role in establishing psychological studies in India. Hence, it is appropriate in remembering him at this juncture.

Adinarayan had his schooling in Madras Christian College School and higher education in philosophy in Madras Christian College, Madras. Then he went on to University College, London, for further studies. It was here that he completed his master's degree in psychology with distinction. Thus, he became a full-fledged psychologist. He was fortunate to study and do research under the distinguished psychologist J.C. Flugel. He also studied under Zanguil at Oxford. While at the University of London, he did his dissertation on 'Colour Prejudice in England', a significant social problem that is pertinent even today. Subsequently, Adinarayan returned to India as an academically qualified psychologist. His interest in studying colour prejudice continued which resulted in a PhD thesis at the University of Madras entitled 'Colour Prejudice in India and England: A Comparative Study'. This reflects his concern with applying knowledge in psychology to understanding and solving social issues. He has the distinction of being the first Indian to take up a psychological investigation on colour prejudice in England as well as in India. His work remains a pioneer for research on colour prejudice even today.

Adinarayan is a teacher par excellence. He was loved and respected by his students. The remark of one of his students who later taught in the department at Madras Christian College is a testimony to this. He states 'Adinarayan's classes were pleasant and unrestrained and his students were content to doodle their way through his lectures. Philosophy without tears was what he aimed at and achieved. Psychology and logic were even lachrymal'. His teaching career started at St. John's College, Agra, as a lecturer. Then he joined the Madras Christian College in 1943 and continued till 1957. Between 1950 and 1957, he was the chairman of the department as well as the bursar of the college. In 1957, he joined Annamalai University as a professor of philosophy and psychology. He was instrumental in starting the Department of Psychology at Annamalai University and continued as a professor till 1969. During this period, he developed the department as a full-fledged one with a laboratory having the latest instruments and psychological questionnaires necessary to teach the subject properly to UG and PG students as well as for research.

Adinarayan's thirst to disseminate knowledge did not get satisfied with classroom lectures alone. He expanded his service by writing too. He was also a forceful writer. He has written several articles in national as well as international journals. In addition, he has written many books on the subject. The first one is *Human Mind* published by Hutchinsons University Library, London, in 1950. The first Indian edition was brought out in 1956 and the second edition in 1962. This was later translated into Tamil and Spanish proving its international standard. His other contributions are *Case for Colour*, *Social Psychology* and *Principles of Psychology*. *Social Psychology* was published by Allied Publishers in 1964. *Case for Colour* was published by Asia Publishing House. *Principles of Psychology* was brought out by Blackie and Sons Publishers Pvt. Ltd in 1986. While writing books, he kept in mind the need and expectation of the reader. Hence, he saw to it that his presentation was simple and readable without compromising the standard. In doing so, he also tried to give it an Indian orientation. His books were widely used as textbooks in many of the colleges and universities. In this context, it is appropriate to mention that psychology as a separate academic discipline had its origin in the West. Even today, psychology to a large extent is West oriented. Naturally, it was believed that psychology is more appropriate for the Western culture and irrelevant to India. But Adinarayan was convinced that psychology can equally be useful in solving problems of people in India as well. He realized that both students as well as the general public should have a proper knowledge in psychology. Hence, while writing textbooks, he had in mind the undergraduate students as well as the general public rather than advanced learners. In order to add credibility to the contents, he not only explained the important concepts and topics but also backed them with experimental studies on individual behaviour and social issues. In addition, he also tried to give them an Indian orientation so that the reader could relate the subject with her/his day to day life. This is a testimony to his commitment to the welfare of others. While giving an Indian orientation to the contents, he also saw to it could be of interest to the readers of foreign countries, that is, giving the book an international standard. Further he believed that research should cater to the requirements. Thus, one of his PhD scholars developed tests for the Indian context—Radicalism-Conservatism Scale and Religious Attitude Scale—making the research really Indian.

One should also remember that when he was writing books in those days, there were no facilities like computers, the Internet, etc. One can imagine both the physical as well as intellectual effort that he would have put in. Today, if a large number of people in India show interest in studying psychology, it is only because they see its relevance to the Indian context. Certainly, Adinarayan is one among the few who has laid the foundation for the growth of the discipline in India.

Adinarayan's writing skill was not confined to the field of psychology alone. Amidst his busy academic schedule, he found time for short stories too. Many of his short stories have been published in dailies and weeklies. Many of these short stories are published in a book entitled *A Day at the Races* published by Higginbothams. His novel *The Hilt and the Sword* was published by Christian Literature Society of Madras.

Many academic bodies chose to utilize the expertise of Adinarayan in the board of studies, selection committees, etc. He was the second president of the Indian Academy of Applied Psychology between 1964 and 1966. Nathan Marsh Pusey, the then president of Harvard University, invited Adinarayan as a visiting professor of psychology to Lawrence College, Appleton, Wisconsin, USA. He was also a visiting faculty at Davidson College, Davidson. Later, California State College, Los Angeles, invited him as a visiting professor.

He proved himself not only as an academician but also as an able administrator. At Madras Christian College, in addition to being a professor, Adinarayan served as a bursar for 7 years. In a way, his administrative experience started here. He joined Annamalai University in 1957 as a professor of philosophy and psychology. In 1963, an independent department of psychology was established and Adinarayan headed it till 1969. Thus, in addition to teaching, he proved his efficiency in administration too. The university administration decided to utilize his administrative capability for the welfare of the whole university rather than confining it to just one department. Hence, he was made the dean of the faculty of arts and also the member of the syndicate. This broadened his administrative experience. Empowered with such vast experience, he became the vice-chancellor of the university in 1969 and served for seven years.

As a vice-chancellor, he was instrumental in starting new courses and welfare measures for the staff and students. He introduced many welfare measures to the teaching as well as the non-teaching staff such as leave travel grants, dearness allowance, separate quarters to the bachelor teachers, etc. Annamalai University was started in a rural, educationally backward locality, so most of the students were from rural, educationally backward families. They had their school education in Tamil medium and the medium of education in the university was English. Hence, the students encountered many adjustment problems. The psychologist in Adinarayan woke up to reality and the humanist in him came out to give a helping hand to those young ones. This resulted in the establishment of a students' counselling centre to help students to effectively cope with their adjustment and academic difficulties. He did not stop with just the establishment of the counselling centre. He arranged to send a staff of the Department of Psychology to the USA for short-term training in counselling. This reveals the real concern for the welfare of the students' community. He tirelessly worked for the welfare of everyone. A road in Annamalai University campus is named 'Adinarayan Road' which is a proof to the significance of his contribution to the growth of the university.

The life history of Adinarayan shows his multifaceted nature, such as a great teacher, a prolific writer, a brilliant orator who combined substance with humour, as well as an able administrator. He was a man of humility who was not shy of accepting his weakness. In the preface to his book *Social Psychology*, he thanked the Allied Publishers for their patience with his 'laziness'. In short, Adinarayan was an embodiment of work, wisdom, humility, and humanism. He will always be remembered in the field of psychology.

# 58

# Shyam Swaroop Jalota

(1904–1982)

## Ram R. Tripathi

Shyam Swaroop Jalota received his basic training in experimental psychology at the University of Calcutta where he obtained MSc and PhD degrees. He joined the Department of Psychology and Philosophy, Banaras Hindu University, in 1950. His advent gave a new orientation to the discipline of psychology in the university where he got the psychology laboratory equipped with basic instruments and apparatuses suitable for postgraduate teaching. He streamlined the experimental work in the laboratory, especially on psychophysical methods, learning, and motivation. He also developed an apparatus for experiments on peripheral grouping. One of his significant contributions was the publication of two laboratory guides which had practical examples of 49 experiments that were actually conducted in the laboratory. Such a lucid presentation of the data of each of these experiments along with statistical treatment was indeed unique and helped understanding the inferences drawn in the final report of each experiment. These laboratory guides were the first ones published by any psychologist in India and were comparable to any global standards.

In addition to this, his contribution to scaling methods was also pioneering in nature. His own test of intelligence was original without any item borrowed from other tests in the USA or the UK. He also supervised the development of ability scales in Hindi, English, Punjabi, and Nepali languages by his research students. The development of an achievement scale in science was also supervised by him. Two tests of personality measurement were developed under his supervision. This was perhaps the largest volume of research in the measurement in India contributed by a single department under the supervision of one man. In 1939, he published *Introduction to Psychology* which went into several editions. The landmark in publication was his *Textbook of Psychology* in 1952. It was in 1944 that he started writing it. The manuscript was reviewed by S.K. Bose of the University of Calcutta. It was again reviewed by Mrs B.L. Iyer of Banaras Hindu University in 1951–1952. This book contained the authentic background of the historical development of psychology which was not to be found in any other book. It contained succinct account of Descartes, Spinoza, Leibnitz, and British empiricists down to the update theorists. It also contained exhaustive depictions of the nervous system, endocrinology, and conduction of nerves impulses with suitable maps and illustrations. It also had a chapter on parapsychology with experimental data of his own work on extrasensory perception after reviewing Rhine's work of Duke University. It was really very hard work that he had put in the publication of that book.

In recognition of his contribution towards the growth of psychology in India, he was honoured by being elected as the president of the section of psychology and education of the Indian Science Congress in 1959. He left Banaras Hindu University in 1959. For some time, he remained the founder head of the Department of Psychology, University of Gorakhpur, from where he went to Chandigarh and settled there. He was there as head of the department for some time but left the department owing to some controversy.

He died in 1982.

# 59

# Sohan Lal

## Soumi Awasthy and Gurpreet Kaur

*Sohan Lal*

The selection process of the armed forces in India was shaped by some of the eminent psychologists who laid down the foundation stones of one of the most robust selection system across the globe. One such eminent figure was Sohan Lal who was the chief psychologist and the first director of the erstwhile Psychological Research Wing (now Defence Institute of Psychological Research, DIPR). He assumed the role of director on 21 July 1949 and served for more than eight years till 24 October 1957. From there onwards, the institute has traversed a long way carrying out research in military psychology, and he was the guiding force for all the researches that was being carried out during this period. Under his directorship, seeds of the selection system of Indian armed forces were sowed.

The selection system for the Indian armed forces was developed under the supervision and leadership of Sohan Lal. He initiated distinct and varied researches pertaining to selection system, techniques of assessment, qualities of an average military leader, training modules for armed forces, training academies, and follow-up of candidates at the academies to make the selection system one of the most robust and comprehensive ones.

The system of selecting officers was adapted from the UK. Subsequently, the system was modified and customized as per the requirements of the Indian armed forces. Testing techniques were modified to suit Indian conditions and the tests were re-standardized on Indian samples. The developed selection system comprised three techniques, that is, 'psych', 'group testing officer (GTO)', and 'interviewing officer (IO)' referring to the psychological test, group test, and interview respectively. In other words, these three different dimensions of the assessment system assess the optimal functioning of the mind and body of personnel before they can enter into the services.

The foundation of the selection system for officers of the Indian armed forces was also laid down by a team of officers working under the leadership and guidance of Sohan Lal. Officer selection takes place through two boards, namely, service selection boards (SSBs) and air force selection boards (AFSBs). The candidates undergo a series of tests divided into two groups. First, the intelligence test is conducted in order to measure the basic intelligence of the candidates. Generally, two kinds of tests are used. One of these is a non-verbal paper and pencil test, while the other is a verbal test. Candidates who apply for technical arms such as the Royal Indian Engineers, Indian Electrical and Mechanical Engineers, and Indian Signals etc. had to take an additional test requiring basic knowledge of science subjects.

The second stage in the testing procedure was the testing of personality by the psychological department. The candidate is assessed on officer-like qualities through various projective techniques. The candidates are then passed on to the group-testing officer (GTO). He is then responsible for administering a series of outdoor tests to the candidates.

Sohan Lal was the architect of GTO technique, which is one of the pillars of Indian armed forces selection system. GTO technique consists of a series of outdoor tests which include group discussion, group planning, progressive group task, half group task, command task, individual obstacles, and final group task. With minor modification, the GTO technique is being used till date in selection centres across all SSBs and AFSBs.

Lal published the first edition of *GTO Manual* in 1956. The manual discusses the background and theory on which the system of group testing is based. The manual proved useful to the trained GTO as a reference book to be referred to when faced with difficult cases. The compilation of the GTO manual took two years. The information in the manual incorporates the results of all the experiments that had been conducted under Lal's leadership. It also includes sociometric tests, the familiarity factor in GTO tests, and the assessment of re-interview cases. The manual has undergone few revisions till date but the basic frame remains the same.

Standardization of the GTO technique was also done in 1952 under the guidance of Lal. He initiated this to empirically find out the extent of standardization of GTO's assessment. Efforts were made to achieve as much objectivity as possible in this particular field of assessment by the introduction of rating scales, centralized training, following a standardized technique, and using standard tests. The objective was to find out the exact degree of reliability and comparability of markings that has been achieved in the GTO field and express them quantitatively. For this, he started and guided in planning an experiment at two SSBs at Meerut and Bangalore. It revealed high order of reliability between the assessments of different GTOs, especially when the case of assessment by actual marks is considered. For each GTO, a high degree of similarity was also observed between his assessments by actual marks and the rating scale marks in the final series.

In order to give a more accurate exposition of the very vague and nebulous concept of 'officer qualities', one of the projects undertaken by Lal was the arduous task of compiling and defining various qualities that are to be assessed in the candidates facing the selection boards. It included thorough job analysis and guided in collecting pen pictures of 'average officer' from more than 400 officers of the Indian armed forces. Further, after rigorous analysis, officer-like qualities, commonly known as OLQs, were attained, which are applicable till date. The training to run this selection system in a standardized, objective, and effective manner was imparted to officers under the leadership of Lal. The theoretical training was conducted at DIPR and the practical training was done at the selection boards. Lal formulated a whole lot of training courses for IO, GTO, and technical officers (TO). The first batch of trainee officers and staff passed out in 1949 under the guidance of Sohan Lal.

Follow up, a very important part of the whole procedure of selection system, took shape under the supervision of Lal. Follow up was a complicated and lengthy procedure. Carefully planned follow-up projects were designed and, in the light of the results obtained, tests and selection procedure were suitably altered from time to time. The validity of the system was decided by tracking the progress of the candidates at various training academies annually. Special research was undertaken to study the withdrawal cases, cases of relegation, and so on.

One of the major objectives of the Psychological Research Wing (PRW) was the constant standardization and continuous improvement of selection system. Therefore, studies were carried out to check if the standard of assessment at SSBs and the National Defence Academy were at par.

*First batch of trainees with officers and staff of Psychological Research Wing of Ministry of Defense with Sohan Lal on its raising in 1949 (Sohan Lal sitting third from left)*

Besides officer selection, Lal took the lead in developing the system for other ranks or jawans of the Indian Army. As far as Other Rank system was concerned, the problem confronting Lal and his team was that of testing illiterate adults who, apart from lacking a proper school education, often possessed very limited experience of handling mechanical appliances. It was a challenge for the psychologists working under Lal to find out if such individuals could be psychologically tested and develop test items which could assess the qualities desired and also be comprehended by the population at large. Non-verbal group tests were devised for such groups such as symbol association test, which is a symbol digit substitution test; Maze Test, based on the principle of the Porteous Maze Test; and block-counting test etc. Few performance tests were also developed such as block design, form board, object assembly, picture sequence, colour sticks test, nail board test, and Meccano Test.

Some of the aptitude tests that were developed by Lal and his team are clerical aptitude (these were administered only to literate recruits), mechanical aptitude, Morse code aptitude, pilot aptitude test, test for airmen, sailor aptitude test, and agility test. After induction into armed forces, recruits have to complete basic military training at various training/regimental centres, where they were required to undergo these tests, on the basis of which trades were allotted to the candidates.

It is always difficult to establish any department rather than running the established department. The vision and leadership of Lal helped to lay the strong foundation stone of the Defence Institute of Psychological Research. He established comprehensive vision and mission of the institute by defining clear goals for all the young scientists to come thereafter. Lal, through his hard work and courage of conviction, has become a role model for the military psychologists working in this field. To conclude, one could say that it is easy to judge the comprehensiveness of the psychometric selection system developed by Lal and his team by the fact that, besides minor modifications the procedures, assessment protocols and methods have remained the same till date.

# 60

# W.T.V. Adiseshiah

## Soumi Awasthy and Gurpreet Kaur

Human resource is the most valued asset of any organization and, thus, the existence of an arduous selection procedure is necessary to select the right person. The responsibility for the development of a stringent selection system for officers was bestowed upon the erstwhile Psychological Research Wing (PRW; now the Defense Institute of Psychological Research, DIPR). Under the directorship of W.T.V. Adiseshiah, the institute conducted a number of studies and research for the effective maintenance, continuous improvement, upgradation, and progress of the developed selection systems. He guided the scientists and staff of his team to work towards strengthening the selection system of Indian armed forces. Most of the researches carried under his directorship were related to the revision of psychological tests, methods of assessment, and development of additional sets of tests for the Service Selection Boards (SSBs)/Air Force Selection Boards (AFSBs). Adiseshiah and his team also worked towards the preparation of a uniform standard of assessment at the various SSBs to assure that the selection or rejection of a candidate would not depend solely on the selection board which assesses the candidate.

Besides selection, numerous follow up studies were also carried out under his leadership. Researches such as development of a method of assessment for cadets at the National Defense Academy and relegation of cases at training academies were carried out to augment the efficiency amongst the borderline cadets. Factual studies were carried out to investigate into the main causes and the different stages in which relegations are effected.

The researches that were organized by him were mostly related to intelligence testing such as studies initiated to judge the relationship between intelligence test performance and final assessment of cadets at the National Defense Academy, and the relationship between the cadets' aptitude test and achievement in flying in other training academies. There were other studies conducted to analyze how age affects the performance of cadets in intelligence tests.

Adiseshiah also encouraged his researchers to study the potential of pilots and identify flying hazards. Studies such as the development of pilot aptitude test, factors underlying aircrew fatigue, and psychological study of flying hazards in the Indian Air Force were conducted by him to ensure the safety and efficiency of the Indian Air Force. Under the able leadership of Adiseshiah, PRW was able to strengthen the foundation of the Armed Forces selection system and create a niche for aviation psychology in the country.

# SECTION 2

# Psychology in Retrospect

# 61

# Psychology in Retrospect

## Braj Bhushan

Having looked at the last 100 years of existence of psychology in India, it is important to walk down the memory lane along with those who spent four to five decades active in this discipline. For this, a total of 18 senior psychologists of the country were asked to respond to a survey. Four of them had a long experience of teaching abroad while two of them had long experience in R&D. Eleven of them responded to the survey consisting of seven questions. These questions were prepared after multiple consultations with senior psychologists with diverse background. Two questions were finally merged, making a total of six questions. The idea was to learn from their collective reflection and identify the most significant scientific contribution(s) by Indian psychologists in last 100 years, leadership provided by psychologists in India in national bodies, and view psychology in comparison to other social science disciplines as well as applied branches of sciences. Further, whether psychology succeeded making a psychologists–community bridge or not, why psychologists have not been able to find place in policy-making, what are the major hurdles that do not allow full growth of this discipline of study in India, and what can help psychology develop a distinctive position both within and outside India were also explored. This chapter summarizes the thoughts of the senior psychologists who chose to respond to the survey with almost no input from the editor. This is a purely retrospective reflection.

## Summary of Responses to Question 1: Significant Scientific Contribution(s) by Indian Psychologists in Last 100 Years

When asked to reflect upon and identify significant scientific contributions made by Indian psychologists in last hundred years, there was a mixed response. According to Girishwar Misra,

> It may be worthwhile to recall that during the last century psychology has been growing in various directions and there is no one path that can claim to capture all the significant contributions to the field of psychology. It has increasingly become multivocal and diversified. It is therefore difficult to pin point the 'most significant' contribution. There are significant contributions in different specializations of psychology.... Concomitantly, the term 'significance' focuses on the dimension of relevance, which may be identified in different ways. In doing so, new questions, new interpretations, new applications of findings, development of new techniques and procedures are at premium. In other words, it is the productive-creative

element in psychological research and practice which matters as it allow for applications in the real social world. By nature the specific empirical findings that are treated significant in psychology happen to be time bound and therefore lose significance beyond certain time periods.

While D.M. Pestonjee identified key areas where Indian psychologists have collectively made significant contributions, some others recognized individual psychologists for their seminal work. According to Pestonjee, psychology has significantly contributed to agriculture and extension motivation, measurement and psychometric evaluation, clinical psychology, forensic psychology, education, sports psychology, management, and human resource development (HRD). According to Manas Kumar Mandal,

> [t]he most significant contribution has been in theorizing the construct of 'self' and 'personality' based on Indian traditional knowledge system. The other significant contributions of Indian psychologists include in making the subject matter deliverable to social processes, mental health issues and industry, to some extent in recent times. These developments are not attributable any one Indian psychologist. Instead the community of psychologists may be given the due credit despite not getting enough recognition from national or international bodies for their silent contributions.

R.C. Tripathi identified,

> the studies carried out by Jamuna Prasad in 1935 and 1950 and his student, Durganand Sinha in 1952 on 'Psychology of rumour'. Leon Festinger acknowledges that these studies provided the basis for his theory of cognitive dissonance. Festinger's theory not only led to a spate of path breaking research on attitude change but is also seen as a precursor of cognitivism in social psychology.

V.G. Mathew mentioned 'Jadunath Sinha's work on Indian Psychology'. G.G. Prabhu identified Girindrasekhar Bose but with a caveat—

> while identifying icons and their contributions I may have unintentionally overlooked the contributions of those outside the clinical speciality. Bose indicated the need to integrate hypnosis as well as evolve a culture specific 'Guru-Shishya' paradigm wherein therapy is a didactic cognitive venture. Freud respected and accepted the alternative original model of Bose. Bose along with August Aichhorn and Freud himself were just the three who were accepted as psychoanalysts on the basis of their self-analysis.... In his paper 'Aim and scope of psychology' (Bose, 1932) he put forth his views concerning psychology essentially as a science, dismissed the view that there is a special affinity between psychology and philosophy, pointed out that what has been usurped by physiology from psychology is to be reclaimed, rejected the mechanistic behavioural approach as reductionist and OPTIMISTICALLY PREDICTED THAT IN FIFTY YEARS PSYCHOLOGY WOULD BE LOOKED UPON AS GREATEST OF SCIENCES. That would have been 1982...alas!!

J.B.P. Sinha's nurturant-task leadership model has been recognized as one of the 250 milestones in the whole history of psychology. It is based on the normative concept of *sneh-shraddha* relational mode that goes beyond the Western theorization on leadership. While reflecting upon the significant scientific contributions made by Indian psychologists he says,

> [M[ost of the contributions have been made in the last 50 years or so. There are some contributions of general nature and a few are specific ones. In general, Indian psychologists have brought into the focus the following:
>
> (a)  Ancient Indian knowledge of philosophical nature that enriches our understanding the complexities of how mind works,

(b)  Cultural perspective on human behavior that shows the limitations of Western theorization by incorporating many more factors of contemporary indigenous sources, and

(c)  Problems-orientation in psychological research that provides thick descriptions of Indian reality.

He further added that

> Indian cognitive style of adding new ideas and skills to the old ones without replacing the old ones creating an amalgam of consistent, inconsistent, and contradictory values, beliefs, and practices that Indians cleverly use according to *desh*, *kaal*, and *paatra* for serving their interests and goals. The style negates the consistency paradigm of the Western psychology.

Overall, one can see some of the seminal contributions of Indian psychologists. However, a critical view also exists. Vinod Kool considers that 'whereas there are a number of good contributors, there is no one I can think of....[whose] work [are] being quoted similar to Milgram, Skinner, Bandura or others in the books of psychology'.

# Summary of Responses to Question 2: Leadership Provided by Psychologists in India in National Bodies

While looking back at the leadership provided by psychologists in India in national bodies, most of the respondents looked at the role of University Grant Commission (UGC), National Council of Educational Research and Training (NCERT), and Indian Council of Social Science Research (ICSSR), but few looked at the Indian Council of Medical Research (ICMR), Rehabilitation Council of India (RCI), Department of Science & Technology (DST) and World Health Organization (WHO), depending on their active interaction.

M.S. Thimmappa calls it 'ineffective! They have not been able to influence policies in favor of psychology in the country'. Vinod Kool recollects,

> As a senior government officer in the early 1980s, I felt that the leadership of psychologists was poorly visible compared to those shown by other social scientists, for example, political scientists, etc. I left India in 1984 but have been visiting the country every few years. Based on whatever I know now, there is nothing extraordinary that I can report here.

V.G. Mathew mentioned that 'they do not encourage original thinking and new combinations of subject areas'.

If that seems to be the case then what could be the reason? 'I believe that the contribution of psychologists to the national bodies could have been much more because it has become a personal platform for advancement or promotion of one's own status and priority....' said Malvika Kapur. Sharing his personal experience R.C. Tripathi said,

> I have been a member of the UGC, also Chairman/convener of the Psychology panel, member of the ICSSR and of the core group of the NCERT.....While I was the Convener of the psychology subject panel of the UGC we had taken some far reaching decisions while developing the model curriculum for psychology. One such decision was to have a separate degree—BPsy and MPsy—for students who will train to become psychology professionals in various applied fields. Except for the University of Allahabad, no other University picked it up. The RCI did recognise the nomenclature of Psy.D. for a doctoral degree in

Rehabilitation Psychology. As a consequence, we still have poorly trained psychologists who are unable to deliver on the ground.

He further adds,

Psychologists haven't had a great deal of say in the ICSSR which traditionally has been dominated by the economists. Psychologists have done much better at the NCERT but have not been able to influence decisions related to educational policy which more often than not is guided by the political philosophy of the government in power. There is a view that psychologists will continue to play a marginal role unless there is a strong professional body of psychologists.

Girishwar Misra echoed similar view highlighting specific examples,

It's a relative question. As such these governmental funding agencies have been operating within a given official framework which is primarily bureaucratic in nature and have weak mechanisms to support innovative work. The people at the helms of affair are politically appointed and are required to follow the mandate given by the political thinking at the time. The institutions are often headed by economists as if they represent the entire spectrum of social sciences. Out of these central institutions, Prof. Shib K. Mitra, was a psychologist who was Director of NCERT for a term. As far as leadership role goes, psychologists have been participating on the managing boards of these institutions. Psychology is included in the activities of these institutions. The NCERT has a Department of Psychological Foundations of Education. Other departments too have links with psychology. However, it is to be noted that centrality is given to the field of education. UGC and ICSSR funds research projects, seminars and other research grants to psychology and other social science disciplines. In the scheme of various policies there is little explicit scope for growth and development of the field of psychology. The kind of inputs and requirements solicited by the policy makers are quite different and they do not give due importance to human factors. No psychologist so far has been invited to contribute to planning activities at the national level. The academic culture of psychologists focuses more on the intrinsic psychological processes that operate at individual levels, having little significance on a broader scale for society or nation at large. National Institute of Rural Development and Panchayati Raj does provide some scope for contributions by psychologists. The institutions in health, industry and education sectors employ psychologists and the awareness of the role of psychology in improving health and well-being is now increasing.

A different view also emerged. 'I find it very commendable that currently the UGC has formed an Expert Committee for the purpose of proposing a new model curriculum for psychology' said Anand Paranjpe. According to Manas Kumar Mandal,

[T]he leadership provided by psychologists has been limited to giving fund to undertake research. In the process, a huge data-base has been generated on Indian subjects, and a good number of publishable research papers have come out (though very few meta-analysis of data-base has been undertaken).

Then came a much deeper reflection. J.B.P. Sinha said,

Very weak, primarily because the strength in the leadership emanates from how strong the general body of scientific psychologists we have in the country. Our support base is very weak. Naturally, it is difficult to raise voice at the national level, claim resources, or defend the research projects submitted for sponsorship.

G.G. Prabhu was very categorical,

> [M]eaningful contribution to the programmes of the national level bodies or to the building of national level policies is possible at three levels....icon, group or ad hoc. First, if the subject has well recognised/ respected and accepted icons of national/ international repute (M.S. Swaminathan, *Verghese Kurien*, Raja Ramanna, Abdul Kalam level) the concerned policy formulating authorities on their own do contact the said persons for advice. To the best of my knowledge we did/do not have such a stalwart in the field of Psychology for long though G.S. Bose belonged to the category. I am afraid that from among the best we have in the country those who can be placed as 'top rate' (leave alone 'outstanding' or 'rare') are difficult to come by (no offence meant). So this route is closed to psychology.

## Summary of Responses to Question 3: Psychology in Comparison to Other Social Sciences and Applied Sciences

While looking at psychology with respect to other social science disciplines as well as applied branches of sciences it seems that in spite of completing 100 years psychology is yet to achieve the desired status. The senior psychologists elaborate on this. Anand Paranjpe said,

> In my view, the primary reason for the poor performance of the discipline of psychology in comparison to allied disciplines is the blind following of Anglo-American textbooks, theories and methods. During their training at BA and MA levels, the students are asked to replicate what are thought to be classical experiments in the history of Western psychology....The excessive importance given to 'methodology' prevents the study of more relevant of important topics for which a ready-made (or 'made in the USA') method cannot be found. As Kurt Danziger (1990) has pointed out, excessive importance assigned to 'methodology', which he calls 'methodolatry' (to rhyme with idolatry) is the bane of all psychology, meaning of course Western psychology, of which psychology in India is a faint replica....Although there is no doubt at all that following the natural science model has its own benefits, sticking closely to this model has its own disadvantages. The focus in this model is on the search for universal laws that putatively apply equally across time and across cultures. Leaving aside the question whether any such laws have been discovered, the problem in the assumption of the existence of universal laws is that culture-specific forms of behaviour are ignored. Indian society as such is not the focus for much of psychology as has been practiced in India. Although this idea of universal psychology has been duly criticized in the US, many psychologists in India seem to follow a behaviourist model, which promoted the pursuit of universal laws relevant at all times. The emphasis on timeless laws is to ignore the ways in which history shapes social behavior in communities. Here is a concrete example based on my own experience of how historical background of social issues is ignored...This brings me to note another problem arising from the idea of psychology fashioned after the natural sciences. By their very nature, the natural sciences aim at the study of objects and observable events in nature, whether the objects be sub-molecular particles, chemical reactions, bacteria and viruses, or planets and galaxies. Natural sciences are 'objective' in this sense, and also in the sense of being founded on observations in the 'public space' outside of the private domain of dreams, desires, and consciousness. Science, in other words, is committed to 'looking out' towards the world of objects, and not at the 'inner world' of the mind, its contents and processes. Early behaviorists who were strictly committed to the natural science model declared that mind was not accessible for public observation, and was therefore out of bounds for the science of psychology. B.F. Skinner, a radical behaviourist, took the 'outward look' of science even more seriously. In his view, psychology must exclude from its domain not only the mind but also the self. Following an expression used by Max Meyer (1922), an early behaviourist, Skinner declared that psychology must study only the 'other-one'....Such a perspective on the subject matter of psychology is ingrained in psychology as commonly practiced in India, whether knowingly or

unknowingly. There is an important implication of this implicit perspective since it militates against the incorporation of traditional Indian perspectives which focus mainly on the self and self-improvement, rather than on controlling someone else's behaviour.

Looking back at history, G.G. Prabhu recollected,

It is on the advice of Brijendranath Seal that Sir Ausutosh (VC), in 1916, approved the introduction of the postgraduate programme at the Calcutta University. Seal himself looked into the Psychology programmes in operation abroad and drew up a programme for introduction at CU. It was introduced in the Science faculty and with scientific rigour….The introduction of the subject was in the academic (University) setting but from the beginning there was emphasis on the applied and professional issues so that the subject can be of utility to the community/society. Emphasis was on clinical, industrial and ability/ personality testing. Service was provided to the community in all the three areas as the training included the imparting of soft skills. As a result some post MA specialisation diplomas also came into being….On the organisational side, the Indian Psychological Association came up as well as its journal. The Indian Psychoanalytical Society too got established and its journal 'Samiksha' came up. Psychology, along with Education got a section in the Indian Science Congress which at that time was the cardinal scientific body….So during the first 50 years of its existence psychology was a robust scientific subject coupled with professional service potential and was recognised and respected as such by the society….Thus from its inception to the fifties psychology was at its best. It was a PG subject in just 10/12 Universities but it was the golden era of recognition and respect. It is this good luck and position of psychology that brought about the bad luck and its decline.

According to J.B.P. Sinha,

Part of the reasons is the nature of psychological research that is being conducted in India. The bulk of research is still imitative of the Western research, based on alien scales that are hardly relevant to the Indian reality, and worse, poorly collected data without any analytical thinking going into it. Even those who try to break this inertia are grooved in studying person-based variables without being able to relate them to the societal needs or realities….They can neither think of doing innovative research nor do they allow their students to do so. They have created a network of similar deadwoods who together are accumulating worthless studies of practically no value….There is a more serious constraint, maybe it affects other social sciences also. Our society has not developed mechanisms to distinguish geed research from the bad ones, and reward the former and sanction the latter. Politics have polluted educational institutions to the extent that you need the patronage of a powerful politician, not only in order to get access to resources, but also to be recognized as scholars.

According to Manas Kumar Mandal,

The primary reason has been attributable to our inability to conceive large-scale program that has the components of inter-disciplinarity, complementarity, inter-institutional compatibility and deliverability. In fact, our inclination to continue with low-risk and low-gain research pushed us behind other branches of social sciences.

Girishwar Misra added,

Hundred years is too short a time to develop a discipline. Yet the presence of the field of psychology is increasingly being felt in areas like counseling, media, health, workplace, public debates and discussions. The social forces operating in the Indian context have been critical. Policy formulation has had no place in the formal discourse of psychology…. We need to remember that social sciences deal with fluid content but often maintain impermeable boundaries and maintain insular existence without effort towards interdisciplinary communication. This state of affairs is primarily owing to issues of disciplinary identity and related benefits like academic positions and research funding. In fact the departments which include courses from other departments/disciplines completely rely on their own inputs without looking at the state of know how in the interdisciplinary area dealt with. Consumerism and materialism are determining the outputs of the discipline. The shift from agricultural to industrial to information age has posed new challenges where the market forces are defining the transactions.

## Summary of Responses to Question 4: Psychology–Community Bridge

Examining whether psychology succeeded making a psychologist–community bridge in the past 100 years in the country, all the senior psychologists were very explicit. 'We have not succeeded because we have not established our relevance to the day-to-day life of our people at large', said M. S. Thimmappa. G.G. Prabhu said,

> A discipline should essentially go in for the bridge with the community if it functions as a profession and renders service to the community. The amount and the quality of service provided determines the recognition the community accords the profession…nothing new…good old Weber said that the role and function of a profession determines its status. If one looks at the status of psychology in India today, one can deduce how the community perceives it and what it thinks about it. Sad!

Sharing his thoughts Manas Kumar Mandal said,

> The subject matter has not been succeeded in making the bridge since the perceptible benefits derived out of this science has not reached to the population at large. This is because as a community, we have not tried to assess the need of the society, the risk that may be mitigated by the professionals in the field, and clearly discernible outcome that may showcase our capability as psychologists.

What could be the reasons for this? R.C. Tripathi said,

> One reason for this is that most departments of psychology in India do not address societal or community level issues either at the teaching or at research level. Allahabad University's department was the first one and, perhaps, the last one to address issues of social change and national development. Only a few departments have teaching programmes which encourage students to undertake projects in the community settings. One reason for this may be that psychology attracts a very large number of female students who may be some what reluctant to go out and work in the community settings because of their security concerns.

According to Anand Paranjpe,

> The tendency to imitate Western psychology has led to a pervasive tendency to study issues that are 'then and there', and avoid issues that are 'here and now'. In the process or training as a psychologist, the student adopts an impersonal stance, and gets uprooted not only from her personal experience in one's own life but also from her embeddedness in the community.

J.B.P. Sinha said,

[W]e still do not think in terms of community. We are happy with small size samples, verbal responses, and textbookish choice of variables that do not lead to any conclusions that might interest the community.

Elaborating the way forward, Vinod Kool said, 'Indian psychologists must first develop national/ international standards for meeting criteria/ accreditation, follow certified guidelines for ethics in research, and more to enhance their credibility'. G.G. Prabhu further elaborated,

> First, training in Psychology at postgraduate level does not stress this aspect the way social work training does. A Psychologist is hardly exposed to the NGOs and community agencies and the manner in which working with them is to be negotiated. What is not included in the training programme runs the risk of being considered as trivial by the trainee. As felt and pointed out by the NGOs newly trained psychologists tend to show arrogance in their attitude about the 'ignorance' of the NGOs and the Community agencies about the theoretical base of many of the issues.... Psychology training in India is predominantly theory-based (with Western orientation and with minimal indigenous orientation) and is weaker when it comes to training in skills, attitudes, values and ethics. This weakness came in between 1955 and 1985 when the training programmes in psychology expanded rapidly.

However, there was a different voice. V.D. Swaminathan said,

> To be realistically positive, psychology in India is currently making 'a psychologists-community bridge'. The process is slow. Therefore, the process has to be accelerated by factors which operate on macro and mega levels by which I mean policies and powerful media, especially electronic media. The main reason for this is IGNORANCE. A lot of misconceptions which are unique to each and every culture have to be cleared.

Girishwar Misra stated,

> The teaching of psychology, its research traditions and professional practices do have space for social contribution. They deal with important fields of human affairs, such as, mental health and well-being, holistic human development, behaviour in the workplace, understanding the structure and function of group dynamics, interpersonal and inter-group relationships, conflict resolution, social influence, and many more. It was, therefore, expected that a bridge will be formed. Unfortunately that orientation has been very weak. Clinical psychology and organizational psychology have done better than other areas of psychology.

All the senior psychologists felt the need for bridging this gap. Summarizing this G.G. Prabhu said, 'Undoubtedly psychology should bridge the gap but it will be a herculean effort. Massive changes in training, attitudes and the mind set are not very easy to bring about'.

## Summary of Responses to Question 5: Psychologists in Policy-making

Even after 100 years of existence, psychologists have not been able to find place in policy-making. J.B.P. Sinha clarifies,

> Policy making requires that you suggest ways that are feasible to adopt for inducing changes. Psychological variables are mostly dependent on economic, societal, and political factors. Hence, psychologists at best have been able to suggest how the impact of these causal factors can be made effective, smooth, or less harmful. They have supplementary role. Even in these matters, they have failed. For developing psychology as a policy science, you need a paradigm change. Psychologists have to assume a much direct role of defining (a) what development means, (b) how it can be steered by initiating psychological process by (c) exploring the psychological process in the construction and operation of economic, societal, political,

etc. factors. Such an exercise requires active collaboration with other social sciences without playing the second fiddle. Psychologists need multi-disciplined groundings with focus to keep psychological factors in focus.

While taking this issue further, R.C. Tripathi said,

Many policy makers still believe that Psychology is not much more than common sense which they already have in plenty. Even today, a very large number of people have no clear idea about what psychologists study and how and where they can intervene effectively. Seeing a psychologist and seeking his/her help is still not viewed in very positive terms by a large number of people, although, this perception has changed considerably over the years.

What are the reasons for this? 'We hardly have occupied positions of influence in sufficient number in the nation', said M.S. Thimmappa. Manas Kumar Mandal said,

For making policy, the subject matter (and those who profess) needs to go beyond theory building; shall undertake directed basic research so that principles of application are identified and subsequently, discovery of solutions are possible. Once these are done, translational outcomes are possible through end-user integration. With such practices in place, policy will slowly come out to benefit the population at large.

Anand Paranjpe was categorical,

If we cannot study problems that matter in one's own life, the researcher may not get fire in her belly arising from the personal need and urgency to solve it. Also, when the topic of research is borrowed from outside and not from something happening in one's neighborhood or village, how can we say anything relevant about a policy that the government should adopt? Anthropologists who study the caste system, or sociologists who study social structure in a village, naturally have something to say about social life here in India, something that is relevant for government policies regarding social and political affairs. Daniel Kahneman is an exceptional psychologist who has done experimental studies about behavior that are relevant to decision making in an economic context, and hence his findings resonate with economists. People in commerce and industry find his studies relevant.

Considering this a global phenomenon, Vinod Kool said,

This is a universal problem for psychologists. In their book, *Aggression and war*, Groebel and Hinde argued that this is due to the limitation of the subject itself. More community forums and public dialogue will help to improve the situation in addition to other efforts.

Recollecting an event during G.S. Bose's time, G.G. Prabhu said,

Concerning, Bose there is documented evidence that Col Taylor wanted to consult him for his advice on developing mental health facilities in the country. As Bose was not available 'for quite some' after the 1st January Taylor left Ranchi for Calcutta and had to miss, as he puts in writing, attending the new year midnight service for the first time in three decades....If single individuals who can change the course of history are not available, the alternative is by united efforts and action. This is what one sees in the West where psychology has become meaningful in society. (1) Psychologists function as united professional groups (association/society etc. APA is an outstanding example) at local, regional and national level (2) They are more proactive than reactive and are always on the look out for issues where Psychologists can make meaningful contributions (3) the moment any Member Psychologist identifies an issue, they communicate and build up an in-house lobby and it is reported to the nodal group which in turn....(4) calls a meeting to discuss/debate the issue. (5) If merit is seen in the suggestion, a Task Force is formed to go into the details and submit an ACTION PLAN REPORT. This becomes the official policy of the Group and the profession. More often than not this is submitted to the concerned authorities to create awareness among them about the emerging societal problem and the manner in which Psychology can make its inputs to mitigate/overcome/solve the concerns. The subject–society link up is established in an orderly and meaningful manner and not in an ad hoc fashion at an individual's level.

He further elaborated,

This is where the role of the professional bodies…come in. For the last nearly 50 years Psychology in India is without an effective national level professional body. We are supposed to have 'three or four national level bodies' which are so in the office of the Registrar of Societies rather than in reality (I am founder general secretary of one of them, Indian Association of Clinical Psychologists 1968 so no bitterness please, it is only sad musings of an 82 year old).

Malvika Kapur also echoed similar sentiments. She specifically mentioned the 'absence of a psychological council to mandate academic and professional psychology, while other professions like medicine, nursing, law and engineering have recognized this need long time ago'.

G.G. Prabhu further underscored,

Psychology in India lacked towering icons. Psychology has seen that we have assassinated professional bodies and hence destroyed the possibility of collective united action…hence our representation in the policy making bodies is notional (*naam ke vaste*), ad hoc and hence its 'voice' in policy making is feeble and is at the individual level. The representative(s) go/went in at her/his individual capacity like the 'guest appearance' made in films and had/have no continuity or a longitudinal involvement for sustainable impact making contribution(s). They did not have much of knowledge about the views of the others and later no infrastructure to back them up to put their views into action and demonstrate its worth. The presence proved to be a good ego trip and a reassurance of 'self worth' which in some instances assisted them at the most to get some research funding from the agency concerned or in some isolated instances the establishment of 'advanced' 'model' centres in the place of their work. A Statesman, it is pointed out has a vision for the nation and its future while a politician can at his best think at the most about his village, constituency or the district. Representation of psychologists, to my mind, at the most is at the the 'I, me, myself' level. It would be the happiest moment of my sun set years if I am proved wrong and anyone points out the issues concerning the subject or the profession for which they fought for (even though they might have lost the cause) in national bodies. Unless one puts forth a document for consideration there is nothing that can get approved!!!....Yet another issue which needs to be focussed on is the controlling of the 'delusion' of omnipotence in the subject/subject/area by Individual Psychologists…. Having entered the field in 1956 and specialised in clinical area by 1961, I have seen that 'my area' getting further branching out as…counselling, health, rehabilitation, clinical neuropsychology, school and forensic psychology in the last 50 years. In India this does not seem to get respected or practiced as any one with a MA/MSc in Psychology deems it fit to accept the membership of a policy forming group or participate in the mass media debate as 'specialist' irrespective of ones own experience/expertise (or rather the lack of it).

Agreeing to this limitation of the discipline, R.C. Tripathi said,

I point this out this in a book that I have done recently with Y. Sinha entitled *Psychology, Development and Social Policy*. One reason for this is that most policy makers have yet to understand the role that micro variables play in shaping the macro. They also have little knowledge of how micro variables can be manipulated and used for intervention. It is easy to do it in case of the macro. All one has to do is to issue a fiat to organizations associated with the state. The politicians as well as the bureaucrats prefer this approach because macro-level economic policies catch immediate public attention and can be cashed for political gains. Micro-level policies not only take a long time to fructify there is very little political mileage one can draw from it. Unless Psychologists are able to show how and why macro policies fail due to the non-recognition of the micro variables, they will have little say in the framing of social policy.

Girishwar Misra elucidated,

The reasons as to why psychology has been unable to make a mark in policy making are multifold. First, the field of psychology focuses upon understanding the individual within a theoretical framework and practice largely from an individual's perspective. With such a bias as the predominant ideology the lone individual remains as the frame of reference. The pervasiveness of individualistic ideology makes it rather difficult to capture the macro-level communal perspectives. Second, psychology with its emphasis on scientific method, objectivity, reductionist approach, poor data management along with disregard for macro data further adds to the overall limited perspective on application to larger environmental settings. Significantly, these aspects bring in inadequacy in developing suitable group-level interventions which impact the masses. Third, psychology as a field of study was transported from the Western world. The alien abstract model of Western conception of human processes was adopted, and researched upon, without much thought being given to the socio-cultural contexts nor the Indian modes of thinking and behaving.

He further cited the 'main reasons for psychology's non-inclusion in policy making' as follows:

a.  Individualistic bias of psychology and limited degree of social sensibility.
b.  Microscopic and reductionist approach and disregard for macro data and environmental settings.
c.  Poor data management at group-/aggregate-level and therefore inadequacy in developing suitable group-level interventions.
d.  Greater linkages with psychological world.
e.  Use of an alien abstract model of man who is rational decision maker.

## Summary of Responses to Question 6: Identifying Major Hurdles and Developing a Distinctive Position for Psychology

Identifying the major hurdles that do not allow full growth of psychology as a discipline of study in India Manas Kumar Mandal categorically stated,

(a) our mindset to remain within the discipline, (b) ignorance about the research methods of hard sciences, (c) inertia of psychologists to go beyond soft products (like tests) or processes, (d) inability to undertake mega-program that may leave impact, (e) bias for non-quantifiable research, (f) micro-planning for science and technology (S&T) or translational research, etc. In sum, the growth of this discipline is possible by having passion-driven as well as purpose-driven research and not with either alone.

'[R]ed tape,.....the personnel at the apex level in universities and colleges, poor measures of selection of faculty and its consequence in supervision and development of research' were identified as key obstacles by Vinod Kool. On the other hand, according to V.G. Mathew the 'tendency of

senior psychologists to dominate over young psychologists and not allowing them academic freedom to think independently and create their own new trends of thought and research' is the major
impediment.

Turning the search within, R.C. Tripathi suggests that

instead of looking around for external hurdles, we should be reflecting on where we have faulted and what
hurdles we face internally. I believe that we are not training our students well. There are also stereotypes
associated with psychology which we have not challenged enough. Psychologists have not been able to
make use of the media to highlight major psychological issues. We have not attempted to make psychology relevant to our socio-cultural context.

Recollecting the heritage Anand Paranjpe articulated,

we in India have inherited a long and rich tradition of psychological insights and techniques that are
embedded in the large number of schools of Indian thought. Important among such schools of thought,
such as Yoga, Vedanta and, Buddhism that have been clubbed under the label of 'philosophy' while
neglecting their psychological significance. The contributions of such schools are focused not only on
consciousness, especially the higher states of consciousness, but also on cognition, emotion and volition,
which are topics of significance for psychology.

Vinod Kool also emphasized on this reminding that

the study of self has been with us from the time the science of psychology came to existence, but its core
topic, self-control, which helps us manage our self and the society at large, was not even brought to attention by the psychologists where psychology originally grew as a science. It was brought to the forefront
by two criminologists from the backyard of psychology. And indeed it was buried in the backyard of
Indian psychology, too—the yoga, the satyagraha of Gandhi, the focus on fasting, the power of maun vrat
(silence), and a lot more. Look, we are now learning a lot more about it through fMRI and other studies….Rather than imitating and blindly following the Western approach, the Indian psychologist should
make use of what is rooted in India. Further, to make their contribution meaningful and useful, they
should avoid exotic expressions and align themselves with neurological and simulated evidences.

D.M. Pestonjee underlined the need for 'picking up appropriate indigenous ideas and constructs
and applying these to modern life and societies. Also highlighting how these can help other societies'. Highlighting similar sentiment, Anand Paranjpe said,

The study of the nature of happiness ignored ever since Freud initiated studies in pathology, and the mainstream psychology generally focused on the dark side of the human condition. However, happiness and
other 'positive' aspects of experience are becoming topics of interest in an emerging area of studies called
positive psychology. It is in this field that traditional Indian insights are relevant, and these are making an
impact on contemporary psychology. Psychologists in India will do well to build on the traditional insights,
and conduct empirical studies on the effectiveness of traditional techniques of spiritual development that
promise attainment of higher states of consciousness and high levels of happiness. This, it seems to me, is
the best way to develop a distinctive position both within and outside India.

The need to reposition psychology was felt by all. D.M. Pestonjee reiterated the need for 'making
ourselves more relevant professionally so that people see the value of the discipline in various areas
and activities'. 'To me, the data from Asian settings can confirm, modify, or challenge Western social
knowledge, and understanding of social processes such as fairness, leadership, and relationship

formation cannot be fully understood without including participants of different ages and cultures' said Ramadhar Singh. G.G. Prabhu emphasized the need to 'form a single "Psychological Council of India" to license and regulate the field of psychology as whole'.

Girishwar Misra added to this,

> The growth of discipline of psychology in India is hampered on account of interrelated factors. Post-Independence new psychology departments were established across Indian universities. These indicated the need and urge to grow as a discipline. However, the standards of teaching programmes across these departments have been highly varied. For example, this is noted in terms of syllabus framework where there is little innovation in the form of including new innovative and cutting edge areas of study, limited choice is given to students to study sub-disciplines of psychology, often the same syllabus is taught for decades, pedagogy and use of technology towards effective teaching remains restricted. Adoption of newer strategies, conduction of regular workshops and learning new concepts and alternative modes of knowledge is lacking and often met with resistance. Very few psychology departments allow and welcome change and put in the necessary efforts to grow and develop…Further, lack of academic curiosity and paucity of desire to extend the boundaries of the syllabus by incorporating other more relevant domains like religion, beliefs and cultural practices, apart from addressing social problems also poses a hurdle to growth. Psychology in the world setting is growing by leaps and bounds with new areas of study and applications coming up. Keeping up with the challenges of modern living and understanding human life in changing times along with timely research allows psychologists world over to capture the stresses and trials of the twenty-first century. Growth of any discipline must include two basic standpoints. It must allow for the possibility of any student to progress towards becoming a pure scientist committed to the growth of pure knowledge, as well as, allow another student to be more application-oriented where s/he is capable of going out into the real world, engaging with the real world challenges and help in the growth and welfare of the masses. Such an approach will not only open up newer careers but make psychology a popular discipline that leaves a positive mark on human life. Next, inadequate provision of learning concepts, explanations and theories relevant to Indian setting and based on Indian wisdom brings in another issue worth considering. Adoption of the Western model may have served some initial purpose but limited exposure to the physical, social and interpretive perspectives prevalent in the Indian society and culture continue to be noticeable. Further, restricted syllabus, limited field training, absence of methodological rigor and lack of team work often lead to one shot studies. One shot studies are conducted at a given time and absence of any follow up leads to incomplete and half-baked knowledge base. Absence of established professional bodies, leadership qualities amongst the psychologists, team spirit and work contribute towards another hurdle in making psychology a stable and consistent field of study. Fragmented efforts in varied directions characterize the discipline. The need is to integrate these efforts. Psychologists in India need to work together to make their discipline thrive and contribute towards societal development.

What is the way forward? J.B.P. Sinha said,

> Only psychologists can turn the table. Till now only a few internally motivated psychologists have been carrying the cross. It will not do. There has to be a systemic intervention. Either educational institutions have to demand quality and socially relevant research or professional organizations of psychology have to create mechanisms for promoting quality research of applied nature.

R.C. Tripathi stated,

> It also needs to break the mould it has been in for the past many decades. It needs to build on its interfaces with biological sciences, human sciences, social sciences, literature and culture in teaching and research. There is a strong need to connect with the community. I also feel that Psychologists need to

become proactive in critiquing social policies and in contributing to greater understanding of paradigms of sustainable development. They need to use their science to build a conflict free, a world that focuses on 'being' and not on 'having'.

We need to hear the voice of G.G. Prabhu 'Psychologists refused to evolve a collective voice. Self-centred interests had won. Looking at the present day political scene I wonder whether it is the Indian mind set and psyche and not just that of the psychologists'.

## Final Comments

There are many lessons that we could learn from the aforesaid material presented by the leading scholars of psychology in India. As I read their comments, I came to learn that while the growth of psychology in India has been extremely steady, it also offered a balance between the Eastern and Western approaches regarding common issues on pedagogy, practice of psychology as a profession, and its application in fields ranging from education to law, medicine, and engineering. As Arnett argued in his article in the American Psychologist (2008) that the American psychology would not have a bright future by neglecting the behaviour of the remaining 95 per cent people in the world, Indian psychologists have responded smartly by already addressing the salient issues confronting psychology in both hemispheres—the East and the West. As the reader will glance through the pages of this book, he/she will find ample evidence to attest to this conclusion.

Let's accept, think, reflect, and work towards the future.

# About the Editor and Contributors

## Editor

**Braj Bhushan,** Professor, Department of Humanities and Social Sciences, Indian Institute of Technology (IIT) Kanpur.

## Contributors

**Rita Agrawal,** Director and Professor, Faculty of Management and Technology, Harish Chandra Post Graduate College, Varanasi.

**Hari Shanker Asthana,** former Professor, Department of Psychology, and Vice-Chancellor, University of Saugor, Madhya Pradesh.

**Soumi Awasthy,** Scientist 'F', Defence Institute of Psychological Research, Delhi.

**Amitranjan Basu,** Shaheed Hospital, Chhattisgarh.

**Anuradha Bhandari,** Professor, Department of Psychology, Panjab University, Chandigarh.

**Nrisingha Kumar Bhattacharyya,** former Professor, Department of Applied Psychology, University of Calcutta, Kolkata.

**Dharm P.S. Bhawuk,** Professor of Management and Culture and Community Psychology, University of Hawaii at Manoa, Honolulu, USA.

**Nandita Chaudhary,** Associate Professor, Lady Irwin College, University of Delhi, New Delhi.

**Ira Das,** Professor and Head, Department of Psychology, Dayalbagh Educational Institute, Agra.

**Chandrashekhar Gangadhar Deshpande,** former Professor, Department of Applied Psychology, University of Mumbai.

**Tejal Dhulla,** Faculty Associate, Global Family Managed Business, S.P. Jain School of Global Management, Mumbai.

**Vishnu Vasant Gavraskar,** Professor and former Head, R&D, Institute of Banking Personnel Selection, Mumbai.

**H.S. Eswara,** former Professor, Faculty of Communication, Bangalore University Bengaluru.

**Akbar Husain,** Professor, Department of Psychology, Aligarh Muslim University.

**Anjali Joshi,** Associate Professor L.N. Welingkar Institute of Management Development and Research, Mumbai.

**Velusami Kaliappan,** former Professor, Department of Psychology, University of Madras, Chennai.

**Heena Kamble,** Research Scholar, University Department of Applied Psychology and Counselling Center, University of Mumbai.

**Gurpreet Kaur,** Scientist 'E', Defence Institute of Psychological Research, Delhi.

**Vinod K. Kool,** Professor of Psychology, State University of New York Polytechnic Institute, USA.

**Chithprabha Kudlu,** Independent researcher, affiliated to Washington University St. Louis  as a Research Associate.

**Manasi Kumar,** Senior Lecturer, Department of Psychiatry, University of Nairobi, and Honorary Research Fellow, Department of Psychology, University of Cape Town, South Africa.

**Satishchandra Kumar,** Professor, University Department of Applied Psychology and Counselling Center, University of Mumbai.

**P. Sethu Madhavan,** Advisor, Tawazun, United Arab Emirates.

**Anjali Majumdar,** UGC Junior Research Fellow, University Department of Applied Psychology and Counselling Center, University of Mumbai.

**Amal Kumar Mallick,** former Professor, Department of Sociology, Kalyani University, Kolkata.

**Sonali Bhatt Marwaha,** Research Associate, Laboratories for Fundamental Research, California (based in Visakhapatnam, India).

**Jyoti S. Madgaonkar,** Professor, Department of Psychology, University of Mysore, Mysuru.

**V. George Mathew,** former Professor, Department of Psychology, University of Kerala.

**Manuel Mendonca,** Professor, School of Continuing Studies, McGill University, Canada.

**Anurag Mishra,** Chief, Psychoanalytical Unit, Fortis Healthcare, Gurgaon.

**Ramesh Chandra Mishra,** Professor, Department of Psychology, Banaras Hindu University, Varanasi.

**Girishwar Misra,** Vice-chancellor, Mahatma Gandhi Antarrashtriya Hindi Vishwavidyalya, Wardha, Maharashtra.

**Ajit Kumar Mohanty,** former Professor and ICSSR National Fellow, Zakir Husain Centre for Educational Studies, School of Social Sciences, Jawaharlal Nehru University, New Delhi.

**Namita Mohanty,** Professor, Department of Psychology, Utkal University, Bhubaneswar.

**Divya G. Mukherjee,** Professor, Department of Psychiatry, R.G. Kar Medical College, Kolkata.

**Ashok Nagpal,** Professor of Psychology and Dean, Academic Services, Ambedkar University Delhi.

**Amrita Narayanan,** Psychoanalytic Psychotherapist, Homi Bhabha Fellow, Goa.

**Dipes Chandra Nath**, former Professor, Department of Applied Psychology, University of Calcutta, Kolkata.

**Rauno Parrila,** Director, J.P. Das Centre on Developmental & Learning Disabilities, Professor, Department of Educational Psychology, University of Alberta, Edmonton, AB Canada.

**Dinyar M. Pestonjee,** former Professor, Indian Institute of Management Ahmedabad.

**Raghubir Singh Pirta,** former Professor, Department of Psychology, Himachal Pradesh University, Shimla.

**Indira Jai Prakash,** former Professor, Department of Psychology, Bangalore University.

**Surabhi Purohit,** former Associate Professor, Department of Home Science, University of Rajasthan, Jaipur.

**Ahalya Raguram,** Professor, Department of Clinical Psychology, National Institute of Mental Health and Neurosciences (NIMHANS), Bengaluru.

**Aarti Ramaswami,** Associate Professor and Academic Director, Global MBA School, Essec Business School Asia-Pacific, Singapore.

**Mewa Singh,** Life-Long Distinguished Professor, Department of Psychology, University of Mysore.

**Ran Bijay Narayan Sinha,** Professor and Head, Department of Psychology, B. S. College, Danapur, Patna.

**Mithila B. Sharan,** former Professor, Department of Humanities and Social Sciences, IIT Kharagpur and IIT Patna.

**P.A. Baby Shari,** Associate Professor, Department of Psychology, University of Calicut, Kerala.

**Bhaskar Rambhau Shejwal,** Professor, Department of Psychology, Savitribai Phule Pune University.

**Vadakkupet Swaminathan,** Professor, Department of Psychology, University of Madras.

**Giridhar Prasad Thakur,** former Professor, Department of Psychology, Mahatma Gandhi Kashi Vidyapeeth, Varanasi.

**Rama Charan Tripathi,** former Professor, Department of Psychology, University of Allahabad.

**Ram R. Tripathi,** former Professor, Department of Psychology, Banaras Hindu University.

**Honey Oberoi Vahali,** Professor, School of Human Studies, Ambedkar University Delhi.

**Suresh Vijayaraghavan,** former Professor, Department of Psychology, Annamalai University, Tamil Nadu.

# Index